THE METHUEN
DRAMA HANDBOOK OF
INTERCULTURALISM AND
PERFORMANCE

Methuen Drama Handbooks is a series of single-volume reference works which map the parameters of a discipline or sub-discipline and present the "state-of-the-art" in terms of research. Each handbook and companion offers a systematic and structured range of specially commissioned essays reflecting on the history, methodologies, research methods, current debates, and future of a particular field of research. *Methuen Drama Handbooks* provide researchers and graduate students with both cutting-edge perspectives on perennial questions and authoritative overviews of the history of research.

The Bloomsbury Companion to Dance Studies
edited by Sherril Dodds
ISBN 978-1-3500-2446-5

The Methuen Drama Handbook of Theatre History and Historiography
edited by Claire Cochrane and Jo Robinson
ISBN 978-1-3500-3429-7

The Methuen Drama Companion to Performance Art
edited by Bertie Ferdman and Jovana Stokic
ISBN 978-1-3500-5757-9

Forthcoming
The Methuen Drama Handbook of Gender and Theatre
edited by Sean Metzger and Roberta Mock
ISBN 978-1-3501-2317-5

THE METHUEN DRAMA HANDBOOK OF INTERCULTURALISM AND PERFORMANCE

Edited by Daphne P. Lei and Charlotte McIvor

methuen | drama

LONDON • NEW YORK • OXFORD • NEW DELHI • SYDNEY

METHUEN DRAMA
Bloomsbury Publishing Plc
50 Bedford Square, London, WC1B 3DP, UK
1385 Broadway, New York, NY 10018, USA
29 Earlsfort Terrace, Dublin 2, Ireland

BLOOMSBURY, METHUEN DRAMA and the Methuen Drama logo are trademarks of
Bloomsbury Publishing Plc

First published in hardback in Great Britain 2020
This paperback edition published 2023

Cover design: Louise Dugdale
Cover image: Puppeteers rehearsing for the finale of the ASEAN (Association of Southeast
Asian Nations) Puppet Exchange (APEX). Photograph by Jennifer Goodlander

A catalogue record for this book is available from the British Library.

A catalog record for this book is available from the Library of Congress.

ISBN: HB: 978-1-3500-4047-2
       PB: 978-1-3503-3622-3
       ePDF: 978-1-3500-4048-9
       eBook: 978-1-3500-4046-5

Series: Methuen Drama Handbooks

Typeset by RefineCatch Limited, Bungay, Suffolk
Printed and bound in Great Britain

To find out more about our authors and books visit www.bloomsbury.com
and sign up for our newsletters.

To Milo, Rafe, and Theo

CONTENTS

KEYWORDS

Chapters arranged alphabetically by author surname

Roaa Ali, "Subversive Immigrant Narratives in the In/visible Margin: Performing Interculturalism on Online Stages"

Keywords: Arab Americans, civic engagement, ethnic minority, Middle-Eastern, multiculturalism, online theatre, polyculturalism, representation, South Asian and North American performance

Arnab Banerji, "What Lies beyond Hattamala? Badal Sircar and His Third Theatre as an Alternative Trajectory for Intercultural Theatre"
Keywords: Bengali theatre, group theatre, Indian People's Theatre Association, intraculturalism, postcolonialism, Badal Sircar, South Asian performance, Third Theatre

Jennifer Goodlander, "Beyond HIT: Towards Regional Interculturalism through Puppetry in Southeast Asia"
Keywords: Association of South East Asian Nations (ASEAN), collaboration, dance, Hegemonic Intercultural Theatre (HIT), puppetry, regional interculturalism, Southeast Asian performance

Lisa Jackson-Schebetta, "Interculturalidad: (How) Can Performance Analysis Decolonize?"
Keywords: contemporary art, decolonial, installation, Interculturalidad, Latin American performance, modernity/coloniality, Pedro Reyes

Ketu H. Katrak, "Mamela Nyamza and Dada Masilo: South African Black Women Dancer-Choreographers Dancing 'New Interculturalism'"
Keywords: African performance, choreography, dance, Dada Masilo, Mamela Nyamza, queer performance, sexuality, South African dance

SanSan Kwan, "Acts of Loving: Emmanuelle Huynh, Akira Kasai, and Eiko Otake in Intercultural Collaboration"
Keywords: Homi Bhabha, butoh, collaboration, contemporary, dance, duet, East Asian performance, Emmanuelle Huynh, improvisation, Akira Kasai, Emmanuel Levinas, loss, love, new interculturalism, Eiko Otake, talking, Third Space

Bi-qi Beatrice Lei, "Decentering Asian Shakespeare: Approaching Intercultural Theatre as a Living Organism"
Keywords: Anglocentrism, *bangsawan*, East Asian theatre, Golden Bough Theatre, Japan, William Shakespeare, Taiwan, Takarazuka Revue

Daphne P. Lei, "Introduction"
Keywords: East and Southeast Asian performance, majoritarian, minoritarian, mobility, New interculturalism, Silk Road, temporality, waves

Diana Looser, "Connecting the Dots: Performances, Island Worlds, and Oceanic Interculturalisms"
Keywords: indigeneity, new interculturalism, Norfolk Island, Oceanic performance, Pacific Islands, trans-indigeneity, Tuamotu Archipelago

Charlotte McIvor with Justine Nakase, "Annotated Bibliography"
Keywords: acoustic interculturalism, Asian interculturalism, cross-cultural theatre, globalization, Hegemonic Intercultural Theatre (HIT), hourglass of cultures, interculturalism-from-below, intercultural performative, internationalism, intersectional interculturalism, interweaving, intraculturalism, Modernism, multiculturalism, new interculturalism, Orientalism, performance ecology, postcolonial performance, postmodernism, pre-expressivity, primitivism, rhizomatic interculturalism, social drama, social interculturalism, taxonomic theatre, theatre anthropology, Theatre of Convention, Third Theatre, Via Negativa, waves

Charlotte McIvor, "Conclusion"
Keywords: New interculturalism, waves

Emily Sahakian, "The Intercultural Politics of Performing Revolution: Maryse Condé's Inter-Theatre with Ariane Mnouchkine"
Keywords: Caribbean performance, Maryse Condé, Ariane Mnouchkine, revolution

Marcus Cheng Chye Tan, "(Re)Sounding Universals: The Politics of Listening to Peter Brook's *Battlefield*"
Keywords: acoustemology, acoustic interculturalism, *Battlefield*, Peter Brook, intercultural theatre, *The Mahabharata*, performance soundscapes, rhythm, South Asian performance, universalism, vocality

Min Tian, "The 'Dis/De-' in the Hyphen: The Matrix and Dynamics of Displacement in Intercultural Performance"
Keywords: deconstruction, displacement, hybridity, interweaving, networking, new interculturalism

Angeline Young, "ReORIENTing Interculturalism in the Academy: An Asianist Approach to Teaching Afro-Haitian Dance"
Keywords: Afro-Haitian dance, Asianist pedagogy, Caribbean performance, dance, intercultural labor, reOrientation

LIST OF ILLUSTRATIONS

NOTES ON CONTRIBUTORS

Roaa Ali's research explores the representation of ethnic minorities and the politics of cultural production, and the ways in which artists and activists attempt to decolonize both spaces. She joined the Centre on Dynamics of Ethnicity (University of Manchester) in 2018 as a Research Associate, and is currently researching ethnic minority access to and presence and representation in the cultural industry. Ali completed her PhD at the University of Birmingham, where she focused on post-9/11 Arab American theatre, explored representations of Arabs post-9/11 and how Arab American artists are producing counter-artistic narratives. Her recent publications include "Homegrown Censored Voices and the Discursive British Muslim Representation," in *Research in Drama Education: The Journal of Applied Theatre and Performance (RiDE)*, "Digitizing Activist Art: Widening the Platform for Civic Engagement," in the *Journal of Arts and Community*, and "Outside the Comfort Zone: Intercultural Events in Suspicious Times," in *Accessibility, Inclusion, and Diversity in Critical Event Studies*. Her forthcoming publications include a monograph titled *Resistant Narratives Post 9/11: Dramatic and Digital Arab American Voices* and a collection of essays titled *Arabs, Politics and Performance*, co-edited with Samer Al-Saber and George Potter. Ali serves on the editorial board of the *IPED (Interdisciplinary Perspectives on Equality and Diversity)* journal. She is a co-founder of the ASTR's Transnational Committee and a member of ASTR, IFTR, BSA, and TaPRA.

Arnab Banerji is an assistant professor of Theatre Arts at Loyola Marymount University, Los Angeles, California. He received his BA and MA in English Literature from Jadavpur University, Kolkata, India, and his PhD in Theatre and Performance Studies from the University of Georgia in 2014 where he wrote a dissertation on the Bengali group theatre in Kolkata. Banerji spent the 2014–15 academic year as the ASIANetwork Luce Foundation Postdoctoral Teaching Fellow at Muhlenberg College where he offered introductory and advanced courses on Asian Performance. His research and reviews have appeared in *Asian Theatre Journal*, *Theatre Journal*, *TDR*, *Sanglap: Journal of Literary and Cultural Inquiry*, and the *South Eastern Review of Asian Studies*.

Jennifer Goodlander is an associate professor at Indiana University in the Department of Comparative Literature. She has published numerous articles and two books: *Women in the Shadows: Gender, Puppets, and the Power of Tradition in Bali* (2016) and *Puppets and Cities: Articulating Identities in Southeast Asia* (Methuen Drama, 2018). Goodlander performs Balinese *wayang kulit*, or shadow puppetry, locally and internationally. Her current research looks at transnational Southeast Asian identities as expressed in performance, literature, and art. She is also the current president of the Association of Asian Performance.

Lisa Jackson-Schebetta is an associate professor of theatre at Skidmore College, Saratoga Springs, New York. Her first book was *Traveler, there is no road: Theatre, the Spanish Civil War, and the Decolonial Imagination in the Americas* (2017). Her second book examines performance and peacemaking in Colombia.

Ketu H. Katrak is Professor of Drama at the University of California, Irvine (UCI). She was founding Chair of the Department of Asian American Studies (1996–2004) at UCI, and prior to that had taught at the University of Massachusetts, Amherst, and Yale University. She is the author of *Contemporary Indian Dance: New Creative Choreography in India and the Diaspora* (2011); *Wole Soyinka and Modern Tragedy: A Study of Dramatic Theory and Practice* (1986); and *Politics of the Female Body: Postcolonial Women Writers of the Third World* (2006) among other co-edited books and essays published in journals such as *Modern Fiction Studies* and the *Journal of Asian Studies*. Katrak was on the Fulbright Specialist Roster (2010–15) and was the recipient of a Fulbright Research Award to India (2005–6) and a Bunting Institute Fellowship (Harvard/Radcliffe, 1988–9), among other awards. She worked as dramaturg for the Oregon Shakespeare Festival's (OSF) production of the Ancient Sanskrit drama *The Clay Cart* (2007), and for OSF's Education Office for their production of Nigerian Nobel laureate Wole Soyinka's drama *Death and the King's Horseman* (2008).

SanSan Kwan is an associate professor in the Department of Theater, Dance, and Performance Studies at the University of California, Berkeley. Her research interests include dance studies, Asian American studies, theories of space and kinesthesia, and interculturalism. Her book *Kinesthetic City: Dance and Movement in Chinese Urban Spaces* was published in 2013. Kwan is editor, with Kenneth Speirs, of the anthology *Mixing It Up: Multiracial Subjects*. Her article on cartographies of race and the Chop Suey circuit, a group of Asian American cabaret entertainers who toured the nation during the Second World War era, is published in *TDR*. Kwan's essay on contended understandings of the term "contemporary" across dance genres and communities is published in the *Dance Research Journal*. Additional articles can be found in *Theatre Survey, Representations, Performance Research*, and other periodicals and anthologies. Her current book project is titled *Love Dances: Loss and Mourning in Intercultural Collaboration*. Kwan remains active as a professional dancer and is currently performing with Lenora Lee Dance.

Bi-qi Beatrice Lei is Founding Chair of the Asian Shakespeare Association, a scholarly organization dedicated to enhancing inter-Asian exchange and collaboration in the study and performance of Shakespeare and to promoting communication between Asia and the rest of the world. The two books she has co-edited, *Shakespeare in Culture* (2012) and *Shakespeare's Asian Journeys: Critical Encounters, Cultural Geographies, and the Politics of Travel* (2017), offer fresh perspectives on Asian Shakespeare and intercultural performances. She is also co-editing the Arden

Shakespeare series Global Shakespeare Inverted. Lei received her PhD in English from New York University, and has published on Sidney, Shakespeare, early modern culture, intercultural theatre, films, television, and popular culture. She has taught at National Tsing Hua University and National Taiwan University, and is Founding Director of the Taiwan Shakespeare Database, an open-access online performance archive hosted by NTU's Research Center for Digital Humanities. Lei serves as Trustee of the International Shakespeare Association. She is currently Assistant Director of the Shakespeare Association of America and is co-organizing, with Yong Li Lan, the 2021 World Shakespeare Congress in Singapore.

Daphne P. Lei is Professor of Drama at the University of California, Irvine. She is the author of *Operatic China: Staging Chinese Identity across the Pacific* (2006), *Alternative Chinese Opera in the Age of Globalization: Performing Zero* (2011), and *Uncrossing the Borders: Performing Chinese in Gendered (Trans)Nationalism* (2019). Lei is known for her advocacy for diversity, equity, and multiculturalism through performance. She is the founder and director of Multicultural Spring, a program that promotes multicultural performance since 2007, and the founding director of Theatre Woks, a theatre group that cultivates Asian American talent and promotes diversity (since 2015). Lei is the former president of the American Society for Theatre Research (ASTR, 2015–18).

Diana Looser is an assistant professor of Theater and Performance Studies at Stanford University, California. Her research interests include historiographic, ethnographic, and intercultural approaches to performance, Pacific Islands studies, and transpacific studies. She is the author of *Remaking Pacific Pasts: History, Memory, and Identity in Contemporary Theater from Oceania* (2014), and her essays have appeared in numerous journals and edited collections. Her current book project, *Moving Islands: Contemporary Performance and the Global Pacific*, explores the international linkages forged by Pacific Islander artists in the first two decades of the twenty-first century.

Charlotte McIvor is a senior lecturer in Drama and Theatre Studies at the National University of Ireland, Galway. She is the author of *Migration and Performance in Contemporary Ireland: Towards a New Interculturalism* (2016) and the co-editor of *Interculturalism and Performance Now: New Directions?* (with Jason King, 2019), *Devised Performance in Irish Theatre: Histories and Contemporary Practice* (with Siobhan O'Gorman, 2015) and *Staging Intercultural Ireland: Plays and Practitioner Perspectives* (with Matthew Spangler, 2014). She has published in journals including *Theatre Topics, Modern Drama, Irish University Review, Irish Studies Review* and multiple edited volumes on contemporary theatre and performance.

Justine Nakase completed her PhD at the National University of Ireland, Galway, where she was an Irish Research Council postgraduate scholar. Her dissertation, "Performing Scalar Interculturalism: Race and Identity in Contemporary Irish Performance," examined mixed race and minority ethnic Irish identities through theatre, sports, and dance. She is currently co-editing a two-volume collection on Irish women playwrights.

Emily Sahakian is Associate Professor of Theatre and French at the University of Georgia. Her first book, *Staging Creolization: Women's Theater and Performance from the French Caribbean*, was published in 2017. The book illuminates previously neglected Francophone Caribbean women writers who can be considered among the best playwrights of their generation and draws from original archival research and oral histories to document for the first time the history of their plays' international production and reception—in the Caribbean, in France, and in the US. While scholars have generally framed "creolization" as a linguistic phenomenon, Sahakian theorizes it as a performance-based practice of reinventing meaning and resisting the status quo, and thus expands our broader understanding of Caribbean theatre's aesthetic qualities and cultural composition. In addition to her publications on French Caribbean theatre, she is the author of essays on contemporary Caribbean performance, nineteenth-century French melodrama, and international French-language theatre festivals. With Andrew Daily, Sahakian is preparing a critical edition and translation of *Histoire de nègre* (Tale of Black Histories), a Martinican play created collaboratively under Édouard Glissant's direction.

Marcus Cheng Chye Tan is Assistant Professor of Drama and Higher Degrees Programme Leader at the National Institute of Education, Nanyang Technological University, Singapore. He is the author of *Acoustic Interculturalism* (2012) and has published extensively on intercultural theatre, music and sound in performance, and Asian Shakespeares in journals such as *Theatre Research International*, *Contemporary Theatre Review*, *The Drama Review* and *Performance Research*. Tan is also co-editor of *Performing Southeast Asia: Performance, Politics and the Contemporary* (2019) and is the convenor of the Music Theatre Working Group at the International Federation for Theatre Research, Associate Editor of the *Journal of Interdisciplinary Voice Studies*, and online content manager for *Theatre Research International*.

Min Tian earned his second PhD in Theatre History from the University of Illinois at Urbana-Champaign after securing his first PhD from the Central Academy of Drama in Beijing, China. He has taught as associate professor at the Central Academy of Drama and currently works at the University of Iowa. Tian is the author of *The Use of Asian Theatre for Modern Western Theatre: The Displaced Mirror* (2018), *Mei Lanfang and the Twentieth-Century International Stage: Chinese Theatre Placed and Displaced* (2012), *The Poetics of Difference and Displacement: Twentieth-Century Chinese-Western Intercultural Theatre* (2008), and *Shakespeare and Modern Drama: From Henrik Ibsen to Heiner Müller* (2006). He is also the editor of *China's Greatest Operatic Male Actor of Female Roles: Documenting the Life and Art of Mei Lanfang, 1894–1961* (2010).

Angeline Young is a dance scholar whose research combines critical dance studies, geography, and ethnography to examine how bodily movement and space produce "choreographies" of social justice. Her dance works, teaching, scholarship, and research activities have received funding and support from numerous local and national organizations including the Arizona State University (ASU) Center for the Study of Race and Democracy, the ASU Gammage Artistic Scholarship fund, the

ASU School of International Letters and Cultures Research Grant, the Hope and Robert Heimann Scholarship in Dance, the Herberger Foundation, the Nanyang Technological University in Singapore, Taiwan Ministry of Education, and the US Fulbright Student Program. Young is also the founder/artistic director of the Pan Asian Dance Performance Coalition at Arizona State University, a campus organization that promotes wellness in academia and advances social justice initiatives of diversity and inclusion via dance performance and community engagement opportunities. She is currently working on a project that examines Chinese choreographies of labor in Italy.

ACKNOWLEDGMENTS

We would like to offer sincere thanks to the staff at Methuen Drama who have supported us throughout this project from commission to completion, especially publisher Mark Dudgeon, but also Lara Bateman who has tirelessly supported us with all our queries in the final stages.

Thanks go to McIvor's National University of Ireland, Galway colleagues who directly supported the completion of this volume through their support at key stages particularly Patrick Lonergan, Marianne Ní Chinnéide, Muireann O'Cinnéide, Catherine Morris, Maura Stewart, Ian Walsh, and Miriam Haughton, with wider thanks to colleagues and students in Drama and Theatre Studies and English particularly. She also extends thanks to external colleagues including Siobhán O'Gorman, Emilie Pine, Emine Fişek, Shannon Steen, and Rustom Bharucha, who have been critical interlocutors at key points in this companion's completion.

McIvor would like to acknowledge funding from the National University of Ireland, Galway's School of Humanities Research Incentivisation Fund and the Returning Grant for Academic Carers (Vice President for Equality and Diversity), which contributed towards the completion of this volume.

Lei would like to express her greatest gratitude to Charlotte McIvor, for her invitation to embark on this amazing journey full of adventure and discovery, and for her tolerance, kindness, and friendship. Together with McIvor, their acknowledgement extends to all contributors, for their brilliant voices and endless patience as the anthology was taking shape.

The completion of this companion in its final stages would not have been possible without the copy-editing and critical feedback of Justine Nakase (who also contributed to the annotated bibliography), and we are incredibly grateful for her support of this project and her intellectual engagement.

Finally, we would like to acknowledge our family and kinship support systems who have supported us day to day in the completion of this companion in close proximity or across geographical space, but particularly our sons to whom this volume is dedicated: Milo, Rafe, and Theo.

Daphne P. Lei and Charlotte McIvor

Introduction

DAPHNE P. LEI

"What's that?" My three-year-old son pointed at the flickering fire on the TV screen, the beginning of the film version of Peter Brook's *Mahabharata*. I was preparing to teach my first PhD seminar—Intercultural Theatre—as a postdoc fellow at Stanford in the early 2000s. Though anxious, exhausted, and truly overwhelmed by life as a young academic and mother (three-year-old and an infant), I paused the video to engage his curiosity. I explained the conflicts between freedom of artistic (re)creation and (in)adequate cultural borrowing, to the extent that a little boy could understand. He immediately asserted that Brook was wrong to use *Mahabharata* this way. "Why?" I asked, surprised by his determination. "Because it is *something very precious* [to Indian people]!" Without understanding any complicated colonial history and power imbalance, politics or cultural ownership, he uttered his basic instinct as a human being. Pure and simple. This childish voice represents a type of affect *felt* by the least powerful in the process of intercultural theatre-making. This voice is often too painful to articulate, too embarrassing to acknowledge, too feeble to be heard, or often deliberately silenced when uttered. Over the years, this tiny but firm voice has remained with me when I observe, study, write, and make intercultural theatre. That voice has marked the beginning of my journey.

When Charlotte McIvor and I started planning for this anthology, we surveyed the field of intercultural performance with the intention to discover holes, or rather, vast unexplored terrains around the globe. We purposely looked for the hidden crevices and niches, neglected affect, and silenced voices. We wanted to listen to minoritarian voices and understand knowledges on the margin and from below. A quick look at the history of intercultural theatre reveals the urgency of reconceptualizing the field. Ric Knowles rightly points out at the beginning of *Theatre & Interculturalism* the "enterprise" of intercultural theatre, whose history and criticism are "firmly located in the west, where the resources and reasons to dominate exchange are concentrated." Throughout the "long twentieth century," from Vsevolod Meyerhold, William Butler Yeats, Antonin Artaud, Bertolt Brecht, Jerzy Grotowski, Eugenio Barba, Peter Brook, and Robert Wilson, to Richard Schechner, the history of intercultural performance has been largely dominated by what Knowles calls "charismatic" white men from the West, with Ariane Mnouchkine one notable (but still notorious) exception.[1] Our first step, therefore, was to deliberately seek out scholars on African, Latin American, Middle Eastern, Asian, and Oceanic performances—areas less covered in current (Western) scholarship—to connect distinctive minoritarian voices to the global intercultural narratives. We soon realized that the majoritarian–minoritarian maps go beyond the West–rest economic and geographic divide and colonial history: performance genres, methodology and pedagogy, as well as theorization and discourse of intercultural performance should also be part of the considerations as we map out the unseen/unheard/unspoken/unfelt territories.

We are at a critical juncture in human history when everything seems effortlessly and instantaneously connected because of the advance of technology; techno-globalism gives us a faulty sense of hope that we are living in a borderless world. Therefore, it is essential to revisit the capability and restriction of travel, traffic (and "trafficking"), movements, as well as the routes/roots of both local and global intercultural theatre. When travelers move through space, they have a physical and sensual contact with the environment; therefore, we want to imagine the materiality of such intercultural impact in ecological terms as well as in affective and experiential (phenomenological) aspects. It is equally important to remember that all kinds of interculturalism takes *time*, and intercultural time is always partially repetitive, cyclical, and overlapping. Temporality and mobility need to be considered *together* as we study the patterns of intercultural formation in performance, and the theoretical movements that analyze and categorize them.

Historically speaking, the Silk Road was an important route between the East and West, along which cultures took root. For centuries, Sinologists were baffled about the sudden blossoming of classical Chinese theatre (what the West calls "Chinese opera") during the twelfth–thirteenth century; its unique prosimetric style did not seem to have a clear predecessor in Chinese literary and performance history. At the beginning of the twentieth century, the missing link was finally found in the hidden caves of Dunhuang, a major trading city along the Silk Road in western China.[2] Among the great number of handwritten/painted scrolls were a number of scrolls of *bianwen* (literally transformation text), a storytelling form from India which was used to popularize Buddhism but also as secular entertainment. The text is alternated between vernacular prose and rhymed verse and between narration and impersonation, with music (recitation and singing) and visual aids. The stories are of both Chinese origin and with intercultural influences. Dated back to the Tang Dynasty (618–907) and Five Dynasties (907–960), these painted scrolls, which are full of contemporary intercultural references, filled a hole in the evolution of Chinese performance from antiquity to medieval times and rewrote the history of Chinese theatre. Other preserved non-dramatic texts—in Chinese, Sanskrit, Tibetan, Ughur languages, and even Hebrew—also reflect the hybridity and multiculturalism of the region. The revelation of the caves and their contents, not unlike the freeing of the chained prisoners from the Platonic caves, created a sort of ontological crisis for the histories of Chinese art, dance, theatre, and other areas. The root of the iconic pure *Chinese* opera was the putrid mud of pollution, hybridity, and interculturalism.[3]

The "Silk Road" is still used as a prominent symbol for interculturalism, such as through Yo-Yo Ma's "Silkroad" organization (first conceived in 1998), which is marked as "music, radical cultural collaboration, and passion-driven learning for a more hopeful world."[4] Today, myriads of silk *roads* have been woven into a silicon worldwide *web* which constitutes a cyberspace. Such space can be used for its theatrical potential for a more hopeful world, as the "counterpublics or alternative publics" of the "video plays" created by Silk Road Rising[5] to combat the post-9/11 racial discrimination against Middle Eastern and South Asian Americans. While the rising conservatism in hegemonic world powers have shut down many border crossings, there is always the Silk Road hidden from view, such as the Silk Road on the Darknet.[6] The parallel universes occasionally bend, intersecting and interculturalizing with one another and creating new intercultural borderlands, where the hopeful and radical, "safe and unsafe," as well as "the prohibited and forbidden"[7] are doomed to meet and interact. The modern Silk Road is multiple, simultaneous, and almost limitless.

Routes can be blocked, passes can be closed, but no matter how densely the routes can be interwoven, how tightly connected networks can be established, or how tangled the rhizomic or mycological underground growth can be imagined, there are still uncovered spaces between the lines. Following Knowles, we believe it is imperative to keep working towards the fundamental recognition of interculturalism and interculturalization as ecological *systems* worked out over time from below,[8] especially by minoritarian subjects. Instead of continuing to pursue collaborations that re-rehearse clearly crossed lines or charted routes, we believe that theatre and performance studies must recognize interculturalism/interculturalization as a continually unstable and turbulent *process* that has more in common with the movements of the ocean—waves, tides, currents, tsunami, disintegration and reintegration, displacement and emplacement—than the fixed intentions of (usually) Western travelers who have crossed oceanic (and other) surfaces on many kinds of artistic and/or spiritual journeys in search of renewal elsewhere inaugurating HIT (Hegemonic Intercultural Theatre)[9] as a genre unto itself, ghosted by colonial, imperial, and/or racist legacies.

The ocean covers 71 percent of the earth's surface; the ocean never ceases moving, connecting, and recycling. Ocean waves never visit the shore and return home "empty-handed"—they always leave something behind and take something away. Oceanic motions which affect all of humanity—persistent and permeable, pervasive and invasive—more closely resemble the movements of intercultural performance that we must trace today—from historical and contemporary vantage points—and the process through which subjects—whether individual or collective—may come into contact with one another. As editors, we present the anthology as modeling a new oceanic ecosystem that accounts for some of the neglected "climate change" of intercultural theatre but also points towards as yet uncharted and still shifting waters.

As Charlotte McIvor describes in the annotated bibliography at the end of the book, the history of intercultural performance theory can be seen as three waves: while the old wave needs to recede in order for the next one to rise, the water, dirt, and plankton continue to be passed on to the next wave either as waste or as nutrient. Waves simultaneously cleanse and pollute the shore: unlike the Dunhuang Caves, these crevices and caves along the shore are never watertight; they are the fertile ground to nurture intercultural organisms and generate minor currents to be included in the major waves. For example, how should one conceptualize all the decentered Asian Shakespeare performances over time? Bi-qi Beatrice Lei proposes that these should be seen as new living organisms instead of derivatives from London, a theoretical position that this companion embraces.[10] Erosion is a "temporary" loss but the disintegrated old form never vanishes; it is transformed into the new in the process of *interculturalidad* articulated by Lisa Jackson-Schebetta in her chapter. As the editors of the book, both standing on our respective shores—Charlotte McIvor in Galway, Ireland, facing the Atlantic Ocean, while I'm in Newport, California, facing the Pacific—we see this volume as an important collection of specimens floating in the Third Wave in the history of intercultural theatre. Although the planktons from the first two waves are still suspended in our waters, the new major movement patterns of the Third Wave—decentralization, connecting dots, internet performance, interculturalidad, new pedagogical and performance methodologies, trans-indigenization, and oceanic interculturalisms—present a new ecology of minoritarian-centered intercuturalisms.

An important new consciousness of the Third Wave of interculturalism is the understanding that the ongoing processes of interculturalization constitutes interculturalism ontologically and epistemologically, and that there is no "pre-interculturalism." As Leo Cabranes-Grant writes, "Distinctions between pure and impure practices are not produced by intercultural relations—they are *already* there as part of a complex chain of networking operations that flow through, against, and because of them."[11] Although interculturalization suggests an action that deliberately mixes two or more distinctive cultures, many cultures, especially those affected by colonialism and displacement, are undoubtedly "always already intercultural," such as the Bengali theatre analyzed by Arnab Banerji, or the performances in Tuamotu Archipelago (French Polynesia) and in Norfolk Island (Southwestern Pacific) discussed in Diana Looser's chapter. Even with displacement and emplacement, theorized by Min Tian, "performance ecologies"[12] of new interculturalism are still preconditioned and pre-encultured. It is with this kind of understanding that the authors featured in this companion are able to ride the Third Wave of interculturalism without taking an essentialist view from their distinctive shores. The chapters in this book deliberately amplify minoritarian voices that have been marginalized or entirely absent in the previous waves of debate, despite ongoing token gestures of inclusion/exchange (particularly through practitioner contributions) or the vanguard work of scholars like Rustom Bharucha and Min Tian (who is featured in this companion) within the first two waves of intercultural performance theory as outlined in our annotated bibliography.

As editors, we wish to suggest to readers the necessity of a networked and/or rhizomatic intercultural reading practice for this companion, following Knowles and Cabranes-Grant's recent methodological applications of these theoretical models to new (Third Wave) interculturalism; we also wish to invite readers to imagine how the chapters might "flood" over each other to generate new intercultural thoughts for the next wave. Therefore, we first present a "traditional" table of contents organized thematically—an act of classification we will flesh out here in closing this introduction. However, we also provide an alternative listing of the chapters, with each chapter accompanied by a set of keywords to guide readers across the companion. By providing an option for the reader *not* to approach the collection exclusively through our curated thematic lens (as have all major previous edited collections on interculturalism and performance—see the annotated bibliography), we hope to make available a non-hierarchical and flexible trajectory of the ideas within this companion that empowers readers to follow the currents of debate and case studies engaged by our contributors according to individual trajectories that will remix and retexture the work gathered here through their own idiosyncratic reading practices. Through inviting readers to refuse taxonomic models of intercultural performance theory and forge their own path, we communicate structurally the proliferation and cross-fertilization of anti-hierarchical theoretical and methodological approaches from below and across and between, indicative of intercultural performance theory's Third Wave.

In Part One, "HIT's (Hegemonic Intercultural Theatre) Counter-Currents," contributors revisit key intercultural figures from the First and Second Waves including Peter Brook and Ariane Mnouchkine through the lens of new intercultural approaches. These chapters prioritize minoritarian/non-Western perspectives on these artists and their works and present alternative methodologies including acoustemology and historiography to challenge these HIT artists' ripple effects in the moment or over time.

With an acoustemological approach, Marcus Cheng Chye Tan critiques Brook's *Battlefield*, a *Mahabharata* redux (Singapore, 2016) in Chapter 1, "(Re)Sounding Universals: The Politics of Listening to Peter Brook's *Battlefield*," and proposes a new way to approach intercultural theatre sonically. The seventy-minute intercultural adaptation of *Mahabharata* is Brook's renewed attempt at performing humanist universals. Tan points out that in the soundscape of *Battlefield*, every sound (vocality, accent, rhythm) produced is already resounding or referral, which indexes social, ethnic, cultural, political, and historical meanings. The erasure of ethnicity and nationality as a means of universalizing an Indian story ironically foregrounds the actors' distinctive cultural and ethnic identities. Tan proposes a politics of listening, which shifts the rhetoric on Brook's works from *mise-en-scène* to acoustics. Listening interculturally offers new interpretations which are not accessible through seeing.

In Chapter 2, "The Intercultural Politics of Performing Revolution: Maryse Condé's Inter-Theatre with Ariane Mnouchkine," Emily Sahakian discusses how Maryse Condé "borrowed" from Ariane Mnouchkine's *1789* to stage *An tan revolisyon* (In the Time of Revolution) for the bicentenary celebration of the French Revolution in Guadeloupe, a French overseas department in the Caribbean. As "inter-theatre with Mnouchkine," Condé "appropriated" Mnouchkine's *1789* but mocked the failed History and the unrealized idealism of the French Revolution (*liberté, égalité, fraternité*); the oppressed—the enslaved population during the time of the revolution as well as the people of color in the Caribbean today—were also brought to the forefront in the production. With Condé's theatrical tools—doubt, derision, and deconstruction—*In the Time of Revolution* decenters the French Revolution transatlantically; it also disrupts intercultural ideas of appropriation and postcolonial scripts of resistance.

In Chapter 3, "What Lies beyond Hattamala? Badal Sircar and his Third Theatre as an Alternative Trajectory for Intercultural Theatre," Arnab Banerji critically examines the famous Bengali actor-playwright Badal Sircar's proposed but failed "Third Theatre," which is supposed to be a synthesis and yet alternative to the First Theatre (rural, folk, traditional Indian theatre) and Second Theatre (Western proscenium theatre of the colonial legacy). However, Banerji discovers the flawed nature of such concept: the urban-based and Western influenced intercultural theatre seems like an act of regurgitating the "universal" idea of Western interculturalism. An example of such irony is that Kathakali inspired Grotowski training methods are transmitted via Schechner to Sircar to create a "Third Theatre." Banerji points out that cultural appropriation is not just a Western phenomenon; Sircar's uncritical borrowing of Western intercultural tactics to subsequently mine indigenous regional West Bengali folk forms is as problematic as that of the infamous Peter Brook.

Part Two gathers contributions which test and refine the move towards networked and/or rhizomatic understandings of intercultural performance ecologies. The chapters in "Networking New Interculturalisms" suggest following old networks (West–East) in oppositional and multi-centered pathways or considering abolishing the idea of networks altogether and instead connecting dots and mapping relationalities that yield multifaceted knowledges, whether experienced in real life or in the virtual space of the digital.

Bi-qi Beatrice Lei deconstructs the binarism in intercultural Shakespeare and decenters "Asian Shakespeare" in her chapter, "Decentering Asian Shakespeare: Approaching Intercultural Theatre as a Living Organism." In the context of intercultural theatre, Shakespeare plays are often seen as traveling in a centrifugal motion (London to Asia) and Asian languages and aesthetics as joining in Shakespearean performances in a centripetal motion (Asia to London). Lei argues that Asian Shakespeares should be seen as new living organisms and not offshoots of London, in order to rid them of racist narratives of Anglocentrism which deprives Asia of subjectivity. Two contemporary popular productions, *Shakespeare: The Sky Filled with Eternal Words* by Japan's Takarazuka Revue and *A Midsummer Night's Dream* by Taiwan's Golden Bough Theatre, are examples to illustrate that the expansion of current critical discourse is necessary. "Thinking Oceanically" (instead of Continentally), Diana Looser invites us to "connect the dots" of island indigeneity, trans-indigenization, and ocean interculturalisms. Chapter 5, "Connecting the Dots: Performances, Island Worlds, and Oceanic Interculturalisms," examines two performances: a historical, indigenous performance from the Tuamotu Archipelago in French Polynesia (*Te Reko no Tutepoganui*), and a contemporary performance from Norfolk Island in the southwestern Pacific (*The Mutiny on the Bounty Show*). Through analyzing these performances, Looser discusses the dialectic between stability and movement, land and sea, history and contemporaneity, as well as local and global. She encourages new meanings for the term "intercultural" regarding Oceanic performance as well as further dialogue about the place of Oceanic performance within world theatre.

In Chapter 6, "Subversive Immigrant Narratives in the In/visible Margin: Performing Interculturalism on Online Stages," Roaa Ali calls for interculturalism to replace multiculturalism as a theatrical and political practice, with Silk Road Rising (SRR) as her case study. The Chicago-based theatre was created as a platform for Middle Eastern and South Asian American self-representation after the 9/11 attack. SRR challenges the marginalized position of these minority groups in the political, ethnic, and religious discourse on US multiculturalism by advocating interculturalism/polyculturalism. In order to broaden its scope and go beyond the financial and physical confine, SRR creates a virtual space that tries to be "artistic, egalitarian, democratic, and visionary." The increased accessibility to both the performance and audience participation in an alternative form is what Ali calls an "intercultural counterpublic," where immigrants' expressions will not be restricted by walls, national borders, and racial stereotypes.

Part Three, "Interculturalism *as* Practice," zooms closer in on artists' processes of collaboration and exchange: in the creation of new professional work and professional artist exchanges, but also in the classroom. Yet, the authors also consider how collaborations outside of Western-directed networks still present structural hierarchies within artistic collaborations that threaten the fluid processes of interculturalization even while undertaking projects in its very name, suggesting that as scholars, we need to keep working at the micro-sites of collaboration locally and regionally as well as nationally and transnationally.

Jennifer Goodlander extends the principles of HIT in order to understand "One ASEAN," a multi-year multi-layered project of the ASEAN (Association of Southeast Asian Nations) Puppet Exchange. While the West is not present in the project, an experience similar to HIT, caused by material hierarchies, uneven resources, and many constraints outside of artistic control, is still felt by many artists from diverse artistic traditions and ten countries. Chapter 8, "Beyond HIT: Towards Regional Interculturalism through Puppetry in Southeast Asia," examines the process and superstructure of intercultural collaboration and interrogates aspects of aesthetics, language, tradition, and modernity related to One ASEAN, which Goodlander characterizes as both a success and missed opportunity.

Love as a connecting agent during the incommensurable intercultural encounter is the topic of SanSan Kwan's Chapter 8: "Acts of Loving: Emmanuelle Huynh, Akira Kasai, and Eiko Otake in Intercultural Collaboration." The two works analyzed are *Spiel*, an improvised duet between Vietnamese French choreographer Emmanuelle Huynh and Japanese butoh artist Akira Kasai, and *Talking Duet*, an improvisation between Huynh and another Japanese, butoh-inspired choreographer, Eiko Otake. Through language, imitation (playback and reperforming), kinesthetic exchange, acknowledgment of imbalances and differences, and their attempts to *speak* over the gaps, and through *love*, these performers in intercultural duet engage their audience to participate in the third space—the private duo becomes a public trio. Using love as a metaphor and guiding principle, Kwan imagines the potential of genuine exchange and mutual understanding of differences in future intercultural collaboration, despite the inevitable struggle and frustration.

Angeline Young's Chapter 9, "ReORIENTing Interculturalism in the Academy: An Asianist Approach to Teaching Afro-Haitian Dance," imagines a new paradigm for intercultural performance training in the twenty-first century. Combining "action research methodology" (which generally involves four steps: plan, act, observe, and reflect) and her specific model of "reORIENTation," Young seeks to formulate her intercultural performance pedagogy in college dance education. Her process of teaching Afro-Haitian dance from an Asianist perspective, which foregrounds practices of "explicit acknowledgment," "elastic discourse," and "multidimensionality," is an interdisciplinary intervention against hegemonic dance pedagogy in American classrooms, as well as enacting a "democratic" process and environment where micro-level exchanges happen frequently.

In Part Four, "Testing the Limits of New Interculturalism," contributors push on the potential blindspots of this currently cresting theoretical wave, whether in terms of interrogating the relationship between postcoloniality and sexuality, a still Western-tilted center of discourse within "new interculturalism," or the urgency of not doing away with decolonization as a central modality of intercultural performance and theoretical practice.

Ketu H. Katrak engages "new interculturalism" in the context of South African contemporary dance and choreography in Chapter 10, "Mamela Nyamza and Dada Masilo: South African Black Women Dancer-Choreographers Dancing 'New Interculturalism.'" Dancer-choreographers Mamela Nyamza and Dada Masilo challenge the socio-political and gender discriminations based on race, gender and sexuality, colonial and elitist definition of "high art," and state and international funding practices in South Africa, with their innovative intercultural choreography, combining ballet, traditional Zulu and Xhosa dance, and contemporary dance. The audacious and creative choreography—be it bare-chested male dancers in tutus and vigorous hip-shaking in *Swan Lake*, or a Bible lesson with the book in the dancer's crotch—present anti-colonial, anti-authoritarian, and anti-patriarchal resistance, but also explains that such resistance, even coming from below, is multi-layered, hybridized, and tainted with colonial and patriarchal legacies.

In Chapter 11, "The 'Dis/De-' in the Hyphen: The Matrix and Dynamics of Displacement in Intercultural Performance," Min Tian proposes a different, historically grounded perspective to counter various recent intercultural theorizations such as interweaving and network. He believes that any universal, syncretic, or transcendental approach to intercultural theatre is to deny the matrix and dynamics of displacement and emplacement which are historically and socio-politically grounded. Intercultural performance is a socio-politically, culturally, and aesthetically centered process of inter-displacement and re-placement of historically, culturally, and aesthetically conditioned and differentiated theatrical forces, cultures, and traditions.

In Chapter 12, "Interculturalidad: (How) Can Performance Analysis Decolonize?," Lisa Jackson-Schebetta analyzes *Palas por pistolas* (*Shovels for guns*) by the Mexican artist Pedro Reyes and asks a question: can performance analysis decolonize? To battle the problem of increasing homicide in Mexico, Reyes asked citizens to surrender their guns in exchange for household goods, and he melted the metal and turn them into shovels for planting trees. Although the gun-transformed shovel symbolizes new life regenerated from death, the gun (the material) remains: it is just reimagined and re-employed. Similarly, the US–Mexico weapon trafficking remains. Jackson-Schebetta theorizes such transformation processes as performances of *interculturalidad*, a vital nuancing of decolonial action that illuminates anew the ways in which imperialism continues to thread through intercultural performance, and coloniality is within postcoloniality.

Part Five, "Interculturalism(s): Mapping the Past, Reflecting on the Future" contains Charlotte McIvor and Justine Nakase's Chapter 13, the "Annotated Bibliography," which provides readers with a chronological mapping of the evolution of intercultural performance theory over the three waves: emergence and backlash (1970s–late 1990s), consolidation (early 2000s–2010), and the "Other" interculturalism(s) (2011–present). They also sketch modernist genealogies of experimentation and provide key terms for each section. The companion closes with

McIvor's "Conclusion," which considers further the contemporary political and ethical stakes of recommitting to interculturalism as a theoretical lens, and calls for even more radical opening of scholarly discourse in this area, particularly driven by scholars and artists located in the Global South.

Keeping our central ocean metaphor in mind, we hope these diverse minoritarian voices offer a more fluid (pun intended) way of approaching intercultural performance and methodology, horizontally or vertically, in terms of spatiality and temporality. Occasionally there are tsunami waves that completely alter the local geological and ecosystem and generate a new trend, new movement, new wave. Offshore cavities might become new intercultural tide pools frequented by ocean waves which share their content with the world. Sometimes old substances lost in the tsunami might be carried back to the shore by ocean waves and haunt the newly established organisms; a new form of interculturalism will therefore be engendered. This is how ocean waves can help us understand that time is both forward-moving and repetitive, governed by regulative rhythms but also yielding surprises. The continuous rising of the sea level as a result of global warming is a new temporal and spatial hegemony that no one should ignore, while repetitive "human errors" such as wars, forced migration, and inequality also cultivate new grounds for interculturalism that are as persistently devastating as they are potentially generative. Yet this "doomed" future owing to the flaws of humanity might also inspire openings for creative resistance. By amplifying minoritarian voices and imagining new paradigms, we offer our companion as a gesture of both resistance and hope to inspire more undercurrents to rise to the surface and carry us forward to the future.

NOTES

1. Ric Knowles, *Theatre & Interculturalism* (Houndsmill, Basingstoke, UK: Palgrave Macmillan, 2010), 2, 22.

2. The local people of Dunhuang had known about these caves for centuries, but it took the "discovery" of a British archeologist, Aurel Stein, in 1899 to get the attention of the world. In 1907, Stein began shipping the scrolls for the next few years (8,000 in total) to London. In 1954, the British Museum made all of their Dunhuang collection available to the world on microfilm.

3. Daphne P. Lei, *Operatic China: Staging Chinese Identity across the Pacific* (New York and Houndsmill, Basingstoke, UK: Palgrave Macmillan, 2006), 1–2.

4. See the organization's website, https://www.silkroad.org.

5. See the chapter by Roaa Ali. The company's website defines the company as "America's First Theatre and Media Arts Organization Dedicated to Telling Stories of East Asian, South Asian, and Middle Eastern Communities." https://www. silkroadrising.org.

6. The Silk Road is an online black market on the Darknet, which is an overlay network hidden from regular web browsing. Best known for its trading of illegal drugs, ironically this alternative Silk Road is like the underground railroad or the hidden caves of our time.

7. Gloria Anzaldúa, *Borderlands/La Frontera: The New Mestiza* (San Francisco: Aunt Lute Books, 1987), 3.

8. Ric Knowles considers intercultural spaces as "ecology" because "everything that happens in an ecosystem affects everything else within that system" and "the health of an ecosystem is best judged by the diversity of its species rather than by the competitive success of individual components or species." See Knowles, *Theatre & Interculturalism*, 59.

9. HIT is "a specific artistic genre and state of mind that combines First World capital and brainpower with Third World raw material and labor, and western classical texts with Eastern performance traditions." See Daphne P. Lei, "Interpretation, Intervention, Interculturalism: Robert Wilson's HIT Production in Taiwan," *Theatre Journal* 63, no. 4 (2011): 571–86.

10. See also Alvin Eng Hui Lim, "Routes and Routers of Interculturalism: Islands, Theatres, and Shakespeares," in Charlotte McIvor and Jason King (eds.), *Interculturalism and Performance Now: New Directions?* (London: Palgrave Macmillan, 2019), 61–87.

11. Leo Cabranas-Grant, *From Scenarios to Networks* (Evanston, IL: Northwestern University Press, 2016), 5.

12. See note 8.

PART ONE

HIT's (Hegemonic Intercultural Theatre) Counter-Currents

(Re)Sounding Universals: The Politics of Listening to Peter Brook's *Battlefield*

MARCUS CHENG CHYE TAN

RE-SOUNDING THE PAST

The opening scene of Peter Brook's recent production *Battlefield* (2015) conjures an imagined spectacle of ten million dead bodies; it is a vast "sight," "a field of endlessness,"[1] acoustically engendered by the rhythmic beatings of a solitary djembe that cyclically mark a beginning after the end of the devastating battle between the warring Pandava and Kaurava families. The deep resonance of vibrating pulses attunes one to the sense of the epic as the acoustemic breadth expands beyond the bare proscenium stage. Solemnly, Sean O'Callaghan, who plays the blind King of Hastinapur, Dhritarashtra, enters the scene of desolation and declares twice emphatically that "The war is over."[2] Shortly after, Yudhisthira, now King of the Pandava kingdom, laments at the scene of a battlefield "covered with heads, limbs, all twisted together in great heaps."[3] Played on a barren stage saturated with orange-red hues to signify a scorched earth, and accompanied by a silent soundscape broken by the monotonous lamentations of Dhritarashtra, the somber and pensive tonality of *Battlefield* is set.

Thirty years after the canonical yet highly controversial nine-hour production *The Mahabharata* (1985), co-creators Marie-Hélène Estienne and Peter Brook return to the Sanskrit epic, the Mahabharata,[4] to translate and transpose the later *parvas* (volumes) in an adaptation that explores the costs and consequences of the Kurukshetra war. Unlike Brook's 1985 theatrical epic, *Battlefield* is an abridged seventy-minute performance that focuses on death, grief, and hope. It sketches the lessons and lamentations of Yudhishthira after the war, and excavates selected excerpts from the parables of the Mahabharata's "Shanti parva" ("Book of Peace"), "Anushasana parva" ("Book of Instruction / Precepts"), and "Ashvamedhika parva" ("Book of Horse Sacrifice"). This revisited stage adaptation, written by Jean-Claude Carrière, is an attempt to (re)assert the sacred text's contemporary relevance in this age of conflict. As Estienne and Brook espouse, "In it [the Mahabharata] we find all the questions of our lives, in a way that is at once contemporary and urgent . . . and its always astonishing stories, allow us to bring to the stage this situation, which, belonging to the past, reflects at the same time the harsh conflicts of today."[5]

To speak of *Battlefield* is to necessarily invoke the past: *Battlefield* is *The Mahabharata* redux. Ontologically, appreciation of this reduced sequel can only be derived from its past—the mythical historical past of the great tale of Bharata, and Brook's own mythology carved from his most controversial and notable work. Staged as a scenographic replication of the empty space of *The Mahabharata*, *Battlefield*'s "beingness" and its relation is inextricably tied to the past of not only its notable precedent but also the epic *itihasa* (history) that is the Mahabharata. Like its former incarnation, the principles and patterns of performance are identical: the barren stage of earthy hues, the simulated *kurta*s, and a multi-ethnic, multicultural cast. Mimicking its controversial predecessor, the production makes similar claims to transcendent and transcultural universals. Encoded in Brook and Estienne's pronouncement, as cited above, is a covert claim to an underlying humanism characterized by death, suffering, war, and redemption. It is also one that collapses temporal, religious, and cultural difference as material for a "universal" theatre, with this reifying Margaret Croyden's observations of the 1985 production that Brook, in *The Mahabharata*, "synthesis[ed] all his previous theatrical inventions, did nothing less than attempt to transform Hindu myth into universalized art, accessible to any culture."[6] Such a perspective is further affirmed when Brook, in a recent interview with the *Straits Times*, readily claimed the experience of producing *The Mahabharata* as something "like the complete works of Shakespeare that India had kept possessively. Done in every part of India, but never allowed to travel. We felt it our duty to say, 'Sorry, India, this isn't only yours.'"[7]

Without revisiting Rustom Bharucha, Gautam Dasgupta,[8] and other scholars' criticisms of Brook's orientalist attitudes, appropriative affinities, and disregard for the religious and cultural contexts of the Mahabharata, this chapter seeks to examine more closely the neo-universal theology advocated in *Battlefield*. Indubitably, *Battlefield* is a renewed attempt at performing universals. As M. Taourirt, in a blog review, observes, "*Battlefield* is about universality. The script, the actors, the acting, the props and the place, all contribute."[9] An analysis of Brook's resurrected humanist endeavor could spur reconsiderations about the efficacy of spiritualist neo-universals, and while this chapter will consider the politics of seeing and its relation to cultural translation and identity performance, its focus remains primarily on the acoustemologies of *Battlefield* and in particular the politics of listening—to vocalities and rhythms—as they possibly reify or contradict a sense of "universality." Scholarly discourse on intercultural theatre has been predominantly occupied with visual acuity located in the *mise-en-scène*, yet the totality of a stage performance necessitates a listening to the soundscapes as that provides an accompanying and possibly alternative analytical framework to comprehending the interstices of cultural practice in intercultural theatre; the matter of what one listens to in the soundscapes of performance—the layered and syncretic plays of cultural sounds, musics, accents, and vocalities—become imperative, for aurality is a necessary experience in the reception of an intercultural performance. Listening "can reposition one's understanding of interculturalism and the intercultural process."[10]

OF (LISTENING TO) UNIVERSALS

In *Performance, Identity and the Neo-Political Subject*, Matthew Causey and Fintan Walsh argue that theatre and performance criticism need to move "beyond" a politics of identity based on the "primacy of identitarian sameness/difference."[11] They observe that identity-based struggles remain politically limited and neoliberal capital has consumed identitarian distinctiveness as a new commodity that then markets difference in/as sameness. Citing Badiou, Rancière, Žižek, and Jean-Luc Nancy, all of whom in their own ways have called for a "shared humanity over differentiated identity,"[12] Causey and Walsh purport that there needs to be new universalist ethics and perspectives embraced by the neo-political subject, for identity-based politics have resulted in greater division and reified difference.

There is much in Causey and Walsh's provocation that is noteworthy, particularly in their call for "other ways of doing and thinking about politics"[13] vis-à-vis theatre and performance in an age of neoliberalism. Critical discourses in intercultural performance exemplify the limiting identitarian distinctions of "them/us," "Self/Other," "foreign/local," "West/East," and have vehemently dismissed orientalism(s) in the guise of universality, with these resulting in an endgame where debates on cultural politics have become self-limiting. Identity discourse remains fundamental in postcolonial and intercultural critique, and Brook's *The Mahabharata* remains the performance par excellence of orientalist appropriation and imperialist representation of an-Other culture.

In a similar tangent but anchored in a discussion of "intercultural performance," Erika Fischer-Lichte interrogates the ontology of "interculturalism" as it is and has come to be understood. Historically, as Fischer-Lichte posits, Western and non-Western theatres have always had cultural interactions, exchanges, and relations; borrowing, adaptation, and translation not necessarily linguistic but also performative were commonplace in theatres before the twentieth century. The label "intercultural theatre" as it has evolved with contemporary performance is, as Fischer-Lichte argues, one that is deeply rooted in "power and racial politics"[14] marked by a postcolonial consciousness. Intercultural theatre thus has become entangled with issues of cultural (and national) claims to ownership and theatrical borrowing and exchange, particularly between Western and non-Western forms of theatre, and has become a "deeply political act fueled by hegemonic interests and aspirations."[15] Performances that appropriate other cultural or religious texts are done in the belief that these works contain universal truths and values, and intercultural theatre perpetuates a Western universalism (with particularism accorded to the non-West). For Fischer-Lichte, the discourse on intercultural theatre, both in its practice, criticism, and scholarly study, is based on several problematic assumptions about cultural ownership and the politics of identity that need to be interrogated. Thus, like Causey and Walsh, Fischer-Lichte calls for a (re)new(ed) understanding of theatrical exchange and interchange—an interweaving of performance cultures, an "aesthetic *Vor-Schein* . . . the anticipation in and by the arts of something that will become social reality much later, if at all."[16] Such interweavings (rather than being intercultural) go "beyond postcolonialism" and beyond identity politics so as to celebrate the move "within and between cultures," the state of "in-betweenness that will change spaces, disciplines, and the subject."[17] Interweaving performance cultures enables considerations of (performance) cultures that neither negate or homogenize differences but permanently destabilize and invalidate authoritative claims to authenticity.[18]

While there is, agreeably, a necessity to move beyond identity politics, the material and phenomenological realities of confronting cultural difference in and outside performance remain a very real condition. While one can privilege promoting a "post-identity" subject(ivity) in, as Causey and Walsh suggest, electronic environments and virtual theatres, the reception of live bodies, ethnically inscribed and phonemically charged, are not variables that can (or should) be easily dismissed. Likewise, the call for "interweaving" as an alternative label and discursive practice to intercultural theatre practice in the hopes of renegotiating universalisms, particularisms, cultural Selves/Others, and politicized identities does little to engage with the materialities of race (and culture) as received, perceived, and *heard* by spectators; the performance of identity remains distinct from the reception of such performativities. How one listens to cultural (or racial) identities remains a consideration that has not yet been sufficiently engaged in intercultural discourse, for sound permits other ways of knowing and difference is often heard, not merely seen.

Consequently, this chapter interrogates the possibility of a post-identitarian politics in performance, and *Battlefield* is an apt case study of how reinvented universalisms that purport a shared humanity and which attempt to elide the politics of race and culture, or the politics of difference, remain little more than a return to (and persistence of) the same. *Battlefield* is performed by only four actors who, while adopting primary characters, play multiple roles. In the spirit of Brook's principle of the "empty space," the Singapore program cast list identifies them as merely "actor/actress" even though Jared McNeill plays Yudhishthira, Carole Karemera plays Kunti, Ery Nzaramba performs Krishna and Bhishma, and Sean O'Callaghan is Dhritarashtra. Much can be said about the politics of race and ethnicity given that there is an Irish Caucasian, a Rwandan,[19] a Rwandan-Belgian, and an African American. Color-blind casting has now become a commonplace politically correct act(ion) to perform racial equity in Western theatre, and while spectatorship can accommodate "color-blindness" via a willing suspension of disbelief accompanied by a will to ignorance, the body is always already inscribed with race and, phenomenologically, that remains a material confrontation of an-Other. Recalling his seminal work on the phenomenology of theatre, Bert O. States reminds us that:

> we see that the I of the actor is not all the I of the character he is playing . . . the actor's first person is what appears before us as the character, the begin that has, in effect, no voice of its own but whose very presence and way of appearing constitute the act of direct speech within the indirect speech in the enacted event . . . No matter how he acts, there is always the ghost of a self in his performance.[20]

In *The Mahabharata*, the multi-ethnic cast of over twenty nationalities was Brook's attempt at performing through the body, via the liminality between the actor and character, the universality of a Hindu epic; it is, as he claims in an interview with

Jonathan Kalb, a work that "doesn't belong to India. It is a great heritage of India, but it has meaning for others . . . [T]hese works have a meaning not for Indians, or for white people, but for this being called Man. The Mahabharata belongs to mankind."[21] The parade of different ethnicities and nationalities was Brook's attempt at performing "mankind," though one could critique the narrow range of ethnic representations on his stage. Actor Sean O'Callaghan echoes this simplistic view with his belief that, "When we have Rwandan, Belgian, American, Irish actors, and a Japanese musician, that immediately makes it universal."[22] The intention of Brook's "erasure" of ethnicity and nationality as a means of universalizing is reversedly observed by one of his actors who ironically foregrounds identity differences. While one can easily question how the performance of five nationalities equate with "universal" mankind, the majority presence of dark-skinned actors (Nzaramba, Karemera, and McNeill) whose ethnicities reflect an African genealogy further prompts one to ask if Indians and Africans are (visually) "similar" and therefore substitutable. Such a performativity of race is certainly not intentional, yet it engenders important questions about performing race in intercultural forms.

The concern is less about a promotion or rejection of performance universals and universals in performance than about sense and sensitivity to how and what universals are purported, and for whom. In the context of this chapter, one asks what "universals" are listened to or, as Jean-Luc Nancy maintains, what structure of the subject and of sense is resonated between the sound object and the listening subject?[23] Hearing necessarily remains a negotiation with meaning, and "to understand at least the outline of a situation, a context if not a text, to listen is to be straining toward a possible meaning and consequently one that is not immediately accessible."[24] In advocating "universals," there are meanings that are not always immediately accessible till one listens—sound permits a way of knowing, otherwise known as acoustemology. Coined by acoustic anthropologist Steven Feld, acoustemology is the specific relation between acoustic experience and epistemology; it explores "sonic sensibilities, specifically of the ways in which sound is central to making sense, to knowing, to experiential truth."[25] In any performance, and in particular intercultural performance, there is a density of sounds in interplay. These "acoustemic stratigraphies" require attention for they involve a complexity of "peeling back and exposing layers of experiential knowing through sound, of listening as habitus,"[26] and of the poetics and politics of these sonic interjections. Experiencing *Battlefield* and comprehending the performance's politics of cultural practice require an active listening and an auditory intervention.

(RE)SOUNDING VOCALITIES: THE POLITICS OF PHONOLOGY

In *Listening*, Jean-Luc Nancy explains how "meaning (*le sens*) consists in a reference (*renvoi*). In fact it is made of a totality of referrals: from a sign to a thing, from a state of things to a quality, from a subject matter to another subject or to itself, all simultaneously."[27] Likewise, sound is "made of referrals . . . it resounds, that is, it re-emits itself while still actually 'sounding', which is already 're-sounding' since that's nothing else but referring back to itself."[28] Resounding becomes an apt metaphor to consider the intimate relationship between "meaning" and "sound," and acoustemics, in *Battlefield*, for both are comprised of a series of referrals. It is thus useful to examine the sounding voices and vocalities of resonating bodies and the associative meanings consequently resounded. Accompanying the ethnic bodies on the stage were various accents, each echoing referrals that confront the "universal" quality advanced in the performance. Like "color-blindness," vocality—one which encompasses all the voice's manifestations that range from speaking, singing, intonation, and accent to rhythm and stress—can be "ignored" yet phenomenologically it resounds with intention; vocality can refer (or index) "social meanings not wholly determined by linguistic content."[29]

What results from the sounding "loop" of meaning and reference, in the vocal-scape of *Battlefield*, interrogates the possibilities of Brook's "empty space" as a dramaturgical strategy of communicating universality. As Leslie Dunn and Nancy Jones observe, the conception of vocality is a "cultural construct,"[30] one that advances from a concern with the phenomenological roots of voice, for the "acoustic and expressive qualities of the voice are as much shaped by an individual's cultural formation as is her or his use of language."[31] In the performance, the actors' accents resound with identity markers that spur one to interrogate the ethnicities and nationalities represented on the stage. Seeing and *listening* to *Battlefield* provokes questions on the politics of cast selection in the performance of a Sanskrit epic.

In sociolinguistics, vocality and identity are intimately entwined, for accent can reveal locality, socio-economic status, ethnicity, caste, and social class. Alene Moyer, in *Foreign Accent: The Phenomenon of Non-native Speech*, notes how "accent is one of the primary means by which others judge us; it is not just interpreted as a signal of linguistic competence, but also of attributes like status, trustworthiness, reliability, etc."[32] Listening to the vocal soundscape of *Battlefield* reveals a superficial celebration of multiculturalism and multi-racialism bound by Brook's vision of universal truths found in a universal text, yet such vocalities resound with political and already politicized identities.

While all the actors possess an accent, the most audibly notable belonged to Ery Nzaramba, whose native Kinyarwanda accent[33] lingered in his delivery of lines regardless of the role he assumed. Even though he spoke in a common tongue shared by all other actors, the vocal inflection became an akoumenological trace of ethnicity and, in particular, nationality.[34] Voice and vocality are embodied experiences; they are produced by a sounding/voicing body that is then experienced by other bodies. These sounds are engaged and related through the body, and as such listening to voices, vocalizations, and vocalities is a relational process, it is "always already affective, perceived as a call appealing for a response"[35] and "every voice . . . contains uncanny traces of a company of others."[36] Likewise, the other bodies on the stage resound with a trace of their ethnic accents with some more perceptible and distinct: Carole Karemera's vocality uncovers her African roots,[37] and Sean O'Callaghan's distinct hybrid English-Irish accent reveals his "company of [ethnic] others." In performance, and in particular intercultural performance whose ontology is predicated on the (inter)play of alterities and otherness, accents matter, for an embodied listening to these vocalities resounds with a consciousness of difference. Listening is a phenomenological experience and as F. Joseph Smith posits, "a truly phenomenological attitude is one of listening,"[38] for sound provokes meaning through the bodily and the sensational. Distinctly, listening to the mélange of accents is an akoumenological experience that can lead to an indexical perception of alterity. While that otherness can be consciously ignored, it does not negate the materiality of the phenomenon—differing accents resound with dissimilarity to a listener's sonic sensibility. There is no "neutral" accent since every sonorous body resounds with one, yet "[a]n accent can mark or distinguish someone or something in relation to something else."[39]

This alterity is necessarily political, for in *Battlefield* this "someone or something else" becomes distinctly race-bound, given the history of criticism laid against Brook's neo-imperialism in the 1985 production. Race, then, in addition to its distinct visual signifiers, "is not muted but [also] has a very loud and specific sound."[40] While such a polyphony of vocalities can reify the efficacy of universal lessons extracted from the Mahabharata, since a common "voice" is found in the narrative spoken by diverse ethnicities and nationalities, the sounding body, in its resounding and referring, underscores difference; it leads an active listener to query the racialized (and nationalized) bodies on the stage.

While accents remain an important quality of vocality, another audible aspect is the vocalization of words. When listening, the phonetics of speech patterns in the performance perforate the narrative's universals with acoustemological difference. The frequent mispronunciation of Sanskrit names become sonic interruptions that further reify the various phonological identities of the actors. The sounds of words serve as an audial reminder of the phenomenological body and the akoumenological effects of words *as* sounds in performance. While one recognizes that the performing language is English and the Mahabharata is intentionally translated into the language of India's colonizer, ironic or otherwise, the names of the characters and places found in the epic remain. These Sanskrit designations and titles become phonologically appropriated in *Battlefield*. In the performance, the actors frequently "mispronounced" names such as "Yudhisthira," "Karna," "Ganga," "Dhritarashtra," and "Duryodhana." In a scathing review of *Battlefield* performed in Mumbai in 2016, Kiran Nagarkar berates Brook and the actors' lack of desire or effort to "check on the pronunciation of this [Karna] or any other name and practice the right stresses."[41] In the second scene where Kunti requests Yudhisthira to perform the funeral rights for Karna, both actors McNeill and Karemera ignore the distinctions between short and long vowels and the resulting rhythmic placements necessary in Sanskrit pronunciation, in this case the "a" of both syllables, with this resulting in a repeated mispronunciation of the name of Yudhisthira's half-brother and son of Kunti. "Yudhisthira" is uttered as four syllables, "you-dish-tee-raa," with the final vowel vocalized, but in Sanskrit pronunciation, the short vowel "a" in a final syllable accompanied by a last consonant is meant to be half-silent; it is correctly pronounced as "yudhiSHTHira," in which all vowels are short and there is a pause between "SH" and "TH," with these being cerebral or retroflex sounds (called *murdhanya* in Sanskrit).[42] "Dhritarashtra" is correctly pronounced as "dhRtarASHtra," where the second "a" is long and the "r"s rolled. In the performance, it was enunciated as a four-syllable name, "dee-te-rash-traa."[43] While the final "a" is commonly vocalized today and also possibly encouraged by contemporary Sanskrit teachers, keeping this syllable half-silent or silent is a convention that is still common in northern India when reading Sanskrit, and it is derived from the idea of preserving "prana" (or breath) inspired by the Rishis in the Hindu Vedas.

Ironically, the history of phonology can be traced to the *Ashtadhyayi*, a treatise on Sanskrit grammar by Indian grammarian Pāṇini in the sixth to fifth century BCE, written in 4,000 sutras.[44] It contains the science of phonetics and grammar of the Vedic religion and includes a mathematical model of metarules, transformations, and recursions of the Sanskrit language. In the *Ashtadhyayi*, the auxiliary text Shiva Sutras introduces a comprehensive list of phonemes and description of a phonological system of the Sanskrit language, along with a notational system that is used in the main text, with these expounding on aspects of morphology, syntax, and semantics. Additionally, Sanskrit is known as the *deva pasha*, or the language of the gods/divine language, and the vibrations of each enunciation resonates with energy. The language is still considered by many Hindus as "elevated," spiritual, and ritual,[45] and whose precise utterance and enunciation create meanings through acoustic vibrations. In Vedic, Hindu, and Buddhist mantras that still employ Sanskrit phonology, the pronunciation of the words and musicality, including the rhythm, of the utterance channel energy. It is the sound vibrations and sequential flow of sounds that also communicate and, as some believe, heal (such as in the Vedic hymns and chants). Sound, intention, and meaning are thus integrally aligned. Reading Sanskrit words with incorrect or absent diacritical marks (or "anglicizing" them as English words) results in either a different meaning and/or "energy" transmitted. Rhythm as well, as marked by the accented diacritics, is important and completely determines the meaning of the word. For example, "ananda" means unhappiness or joyless while "ānanda" means great inner happiness or bliss; "kāma" has to do with the fulfillment of desires in the world, while "karma" is the law of action and reaction.[46]

The importance of sounding and pronunciation in Sanskrit, as such, cannot be overstated and the anglicization of specific terms and names can be regarded as a form of acoustemic violence resulting from linguistic appropriation. Recognizably, *Battlefield* does not employ Sanskrit terms apart from the names, yet these still resound with meaning. The misplacement of accent points and diacritics, as well as the inattention to vowel sounds, could indicate different names. The importance of the vowel "*a*" <ɑː> is significant in the Sanskrit tradition as seen in the Bhagavad Gita which states

Of letters I am *a*. Of compounds I am the dual.
I alone am unending time, the Founder facing every side.[47]

"*a*" <ɑː> is thus believed to be the origin of all vowels and basis of all speech. In *Battlefield*, yet another mispronunciation of names is that of the river "Ganga." Throughout the performance, Ganga is continually mispronounced by McNeill as "Gang-geh" <gæŋə>, when the appropriate pronunciation is "Ganga" ("Gung-gah") <gʌŋɑː>; this is perhaps due to the influence of American sonicities in which the <ʌ> vowel is absent. The varied pronunciation of names exposes the rupture of performance and purpose. It exposes the contradiction of intention and possibility and the gap of hollow translation: universalism is always located in

Otherness—of cultures, texts, and contexts. Without an acknowledgement and address of the tensions in translations and transpositions, linguistic or acoustic, these forms of plasticized appropriation will continue to "re-sound" across contemporary intercultural performance.

ON RHYTHM AS UNIVERSAL

The acoustic element that impressed most spectators and reviewers was the consonant drumming that accompanied the storytelling all through the seventy minutes. *Battlefield* opens with the deep, thunderous timbres of the djembe played by musician and composer Toshi Tsuchitori, who also created and performed the music for *The Mahabharata*. However, unlike *The Mahabharata*, which consisted of an elaborate soundscape of various sonicities, textures, and timbres, this revival had only the rhythms of Tsuchitori's solitary West African drum. According to Akshita Nanda, the arts correspondent of Singapore's main broadsheet, the *Straits Times*, Tsuchitori's drumming is both "text and metaphor" that denotes Shiva's drumming, on the damru, of the cosmos into existence.[48] The drumming, as Nagarkar also observes, evokes the drumming "in the primeval silence at the beginning of life itself."[49] It pounds out the "circular rhythms of relentless time, inescapable destiny and the cycles of death and renewal that the characters [of *Battlefield*] must recognize and finally, accept."[50]

Such an indexical association can most certainly be made, though it remains unclear if Tsuchitori (or Brook) had such intentions (or knowledge). Still, rhythms possess potential to communicate universals affectively since beat, meter, and tempo are fundamental to all music and all human speech patterns. Ethnomusicologists have long recognized the primacy (and primalcy) of rhythm in organized sounds and music of all cultures. Theo Van Leeuwen posits that metrical tempo is inherently associated with time and provides a link between physiological time and social timing through which social activities are ordered.[51] Drumming rhythms reflect the internal beats of a person but, in listening, also regulates them in ritual and musical performance. Drums are a core instrument in all musical cultures whose function is primarily to structure musical development through tempo and also stir the deeper pulsations within listeners. Rhythms and tempo create a community of listeners with cadence. While other universal qualities in music are still debated, scientific studies have empirically proven that rhythmic structures and time-beats remain one of the characteristic statistical universals in all music.[52]

Perhaps the universal lessons in the Mahabharata Brook had hoped to communicate could be carried by the regulated, rousing rhythms of Tsuchitori's djembe, yet such a potential did not seem to have been fulfilled. The absent effects of rhythmic "universality" are evident in the unmoved Singapore audience who remained uninspired and bored.[53] Employing the basic techniques of the "bass," "tone," and "slap" (or "gun dun," "go do," "pa ta") in djembe drumming, Tsuchitori relegated the instrument to the simplistic dramaturgical functions of filling the silence between scene transitions and creating rhythmic ornamentation to the foregrounded conversations between characters. Apart from the opening and the closing moments of the performance, which heralded meaningfulness in the drumming of the cosmological cyclicality of time and of life, the rhythms became incidental, sonic fillers that did little more than underscore the tensions in selected dramatic moments or indicate a movement from the main plot to the play-within-play sequences of the parables recounted by the characters. One such functionary rhythm was employed in the second scene, when Kunti explains Karna's lineage and reveals herself to be the mother—the drumming did little more than mark the recount with a different tempo. In the performance of the parable involving the compassionate and just King Usinara, a pigeon and a hawk, taken from the Mahabharata's "Vana Parva," accented beats and rhythm merely accompanied the character's purposed gestures and so gave (sound) effect to action. Likewise, in a significantly truncated and altered adaptation of "Ashavamedhika Parva," which narrates Yudhisthira's generosity when performing a *yajna* shortly after his coronation,[54] and the lessons imparted by a cursed *Rishi* (holy man) turned mongoose, the drumming served to emphasize the dramatic actions of Yudhisthira awarding his robes to the mongoose. While the forceful drumming that opened the performance drew significant attention to the importance of rhythm, pattern, time, and temporality—recurring themes in the Mahabharata— it faded into an acoustic background as the play progressed and lost its significance as a mode of communicating deeper "truths"; Tsuchitori's improvised drumming (and drumming patterns) became incidental, random, and less purposeful.

In traditional West African contexts, dances and their accompanying dance performances are uniquely associated with specific events, and each rhythm has a purpose, time, and place. Drummers, as Eric Charry notes, "play rhythms that give people strength and courage before or during a trial and honour them when they have passed through it. Drumming is above all a communal event that demands participation from all present."[55] If Brook and Estienne's intention was to excavate the past for contemporary relevance, the drumming did little to create a sense of communality for both actors and audience, or a universal connection between past and present. And while one cannot fairly critique the performance of instruments today based on their traditional function, a salient question that arises then is one of purpose and sonic choice—why and for what purpose is the drumming? Was it simply to fill the silent void and "empty space"? If rhythms and tempo served as little more than incidental sound, it is necessary to interrogate the necessity and efficacy of the selected instrument: why a djembe, since any other rawhide drum would fulfill the same function? Tsuchitori notes in an interview, "I studied this drum before in Africa, but I don't play like an African."[56] The ambiguous statement, which belies assumptions about "who" Africans are and if a collective "they" have an identical way of playing, reifies the question of the instrument's random selection. While traditional instruments and performance methods are no longer necessarily bound to specific ritual or ceremonial functions today, the djembe remains among the more iconic instruments of West African culture, with origins attributed to the Mandinka people from as early as 1300 CE.[57] Returning to Nancy's association of meaning, sound, and reference, one is led to ask what meanings are resounded by the rhythms of the djembe in its self-referentiality. As the resonating rhythms are non-acousmatic, since Tsuchitori sits downstage left and remains visible throughout the entire performance, the djembe becomes not merely a sonic signifier of African culture but also a visual one.[58] With the majority presence of actors with African roots and an instrument that is iconic of traditional West African heritage, is the *mise-en-scène* advocating an "Africanization" of an ancient Indian epic? Or is the universality of mankind prompted with a subtle suggestion of scientific theories that hypothesize that the first modern humans (homo sapiens) shared a single origin in Africa?

THE TUNING OF THE EARS

In *The Audible Past*, Jonathan Sterne postulates that the interior experiencing of sound cannot be divested from the exteriority of conditions since the "elusive inside world of sound . . . emerges and becomes perceptible only through its exteriors,"[59] and an understanding of the history of sound is external and contextual; "sound is an artifact of the messy and political human sphere."[60] While Brook's principles of the "empty space" encourages an effacement of the phenomenological experience of listening and seeing, one that advances a color-blindness and deafness, how any intercultural work or cultural adaptation is listened to cannot be divested from its politics. More significantly, *Battlefield* compels the audience to listen to their own process(es) of listening and to ask how ears are (at)tuned to assumed universals and acoustemic appropriations sanctioned as liberal performance practices. Considered more broadly, an active listening—to vocalities, accents, rhythms, and frequencies—can become an alternative, productive methodology for experiencing and understanding the resonances and vibrations of politics and meaning, and political meanings, in intercultural works.

Revisiting the issue of universalism and the neo-political subject, Causey and Walsh advance Alan Read's belief that there exists in scholarship and practice an irrational postmodern suspicion towards universals and that more thorough consideration needs, now, to be given to the possibility of universals in cultural and political debate, one that can be located in the "generality of affect."[61] While one would agree with Read that the fear (and loss) of universals to theatre has been this loss of affect, the universals performed in *Battlefield* attempt to be, as Žižek posits, an "encompassing container of the particular content, the peaceful medium background to the conflict of particularities";[62] it "elide[s] difference."[63] As a performative act, in its seeing and listening, race, ethnicity, and class differences become underscored paradoxically because the body and its reception are erased and made invisible. As a performance event, the arbitrary selection of parables promoted an altered and truncated narrative that lacked coherence. *Battlefield* served to the audience hackneyed truisms and tropisms as anthropocentric "universal truths." Platitudes such as "No good man is entirely good; no bad man is entirely bad," "Time is indifferent to nobody," and "Every union ends in separation" became soundbites that, while possibly resounding with some measure of truth, contained no resonating effect because they were reduced and stripped from context.[64] To consider universality is to acknowledge that it must be "an arena of antagonism and contestation,"[65] not blanket truisms or affect. It encompasses an active politics of listening and a listening to how others listen.

Ears listen differently, as evidenced in Nanda's admittance of her befuddlement at the lukewarm response of the Singapore audience, given that responses at the

Bouffes du Nord were contrary—the Paris audience was, according to her, leaping to their feet demanding encores. While Nanda attributes this to poor amplification and the acoustics of the Capitol Theatre, the response at the Bouffes du Nord raises critical questions of its resounding acclamation. Was it a recognition and affirmation of the humanist universals purported by Brook and Estienne in their version of the Indian epic, or was it an ovation dedicated to the past of Peter Brook? It is not implausible to postulate that the reaction in Paris is a celebration of nostalgia, particularly for those who witnessed Brook's magnum opus thirty-years ago;[66] it is an ovation to the past but equally an approbation of the myth that is Peter Brook. As coda and swansong, Brook's "re-staging" of his most (in)famous work is a means of monumentalizing memory and a search for reputational immortality, one that would resound in the Western theatre tradition. Perhaps in that intention is a meta-performative action that is itself the true universal statement of *Battlefield*.

NOTES

1. Peter Brook, quoted in Akshita Nanda, "Death and Grief in Peter Brook's Newest Play Battlefield," *Straits Times*, November 3, 2015, http://www.straitstimes.com/lifestyle/arts/death-and-grief-in-peter-brooks-newest-play-battlefield.

2. Taken from the Singapore Repertory Theatre's (SRT) private recording of *Battlefield* at the Capitol Theatre, Singapore on 17 November 2015.

3. SRT's private recording of *Battlefield*.

4. The unitalicized form refers to the text while the italicized indicates the production.

5. *Battlefield* Programme Notes, Singapore Programme, 2015, n.p.

6. Margaret Croyden, "Peter Brook Transforms An Indian Epic for the Stage," *New York Times*, August 25, 1985, http://www.nytimes.com/1985/08/25/arts/peter-brook-transforms-an-indian-epic-for-the-stage.html.

7. Nanda, "Death and Grief," n.p.

8. See Rustom Bharucha, "A View from India," in David Williams (ed.), *Peter Brook and the Mahabharata: Critical Perspectives* (London: Routledge, 1991), 228–52 and Gautam Dasgupta, "*The Mahabharata*: Peter Brook's Orientalism," in Bonnie Marranca and Gautam Dasgaupta (eds.), *Interculturalism and Performance: Writings from PAJ* (New York: PAJ Publications, 1991), 75–82.

9. M. Taourirt, "Sean O'Callaghan Embodies the Universality of Battlefield," *Culture Xchange*, January 6, 2016, https://culturexchange1.wordpress.com/2016/01/06/sean-ocallaghan-embodies-the-universality-of-battlefield/.

10. Marcus Cheng Chye Tan, *Acoustic Interculturalism: Listening to Performance* (Houndsmills, Basingstoke, UK: Palgrave Macmillan, 2012), 22–3.

11. Matthew Causey and Fintan Walsh, "Introduction," in Matthew Causey and Fintan Walsh (eds.), *Performance, Identity and the Neo-Political Subject* (New York: Routledge, 2013), 1.

12. Causey and Walsh, "Introduction," 6.

13. Causey and Walsh, "Introduction," 3.

14. Erika Fischer-Lichte, "Introduction: Interweaving Performance Cultures—Rethinking 'Intercultural Theatre': Toward an Experience and Theory of Performance beyond Postcolonialism," in Erika Fischer-Lichte, Torsten Jost, and Saskya Iris Jain (eds.), *The Politics of Interweaving Performance Cultures: Beyond Postcolonialism* (New York: Routledge, 2014), 8.

15. Fischer-Lichte, "Introduction," 8.

16. Fischer-Lichte, "Introduction,"12.

17. Fischer-Lichte, "Introduction,"12.

18. Fischer-Lichte, "Introduction,"12.

19. Ery Nzaramba, however, has trained and lived in Belgium and the UK for some time. Despite that, he identifies as "Black/African." See http://www.castingcallpro.com/uk/actor/profile/ery-nzaramba.

20. Bert O. States, *Great Reckonings in Little Rooms: On the Phenomenology of Theater* (London: University of California Press, 1987), 124–5.

21. Peter Brook and Jonathan Kalb, "The Mahabharata Twenty-Five Years Later," *PAJ: A Journal of Performance and Art* 32, no. 3 (2010): 70.

22. See Taourirt, "Sean O'Callaghan," para 4.

23. Jean-Luc Nancy, *Listening*, trans. Charlotte Mandell (New York: Fordham University Press, 2007).

24. Nancy, *Listening*, 6.

25. Steven Feld, "Waterfalls of Song: an Acoustemology of Place Resounding in Bosavi, Papua New Guinea," in Steven Feld and Keith H. Bass (eds.), *Senses of Place* (New Mexico: School of American Research Press, 1996), 97.

26. Steven Feld, "Acoustemic Stratigraphies: Recent Work in Urban Phonography," *A Journal for Experiments in Critical Media Practice*, http://sensatejournal.com/2011/03/steven-feld-acoustemic-stratigraphies/.

27. Nancy, *Listening*, 7.

28. Nancy, *Listening*, 7–8.

29. Leslie C. Dunn and Nancy A. Jones, "Introduction," in Leslie C. Dunn and Nancy A. Jones (eds.), *Embodied Voices: Representing Female Vocality in Western Culture* (Cambridge: Cambridge University Press, 1994), 1.

30. Dunn and Jones, "Introduction," 2.

31. Dunn and Jones, "Introduction," 3.

32. Alene Moyer, *Foreign Accent: The Phenomenon of Non-native Speech* (Cambridge: Cambridge University Press, 2013), 19.

33. Interestingly, Nzaramba lists his native accent as "South African" on his profile page. See http://www.castingcallpro.com/uk/actor/profile/ery-nzaramba.

34. For a sample of this accent trace, hear the "voicereel" at http://www.castingcallpro.com/uk/actor/profile/ery-nzaramba.

35. Alice Lagay, "Towards a (Negative) Philosophy of Voice," in Lynne Kendrick and David Roesner (eds.), *Theatre Noise: The Sound of Performance* (Newcastle upon Tyne: Cambridge Scholars Publishing, 2011), 57–69, 64.

36. Lagay, "Towards a (Negative) Philosophy of Voice," 64.

37. Carole Karemera trained in Belgium but returned to her homeland, Kigali, Rwanda, in 2005. See http://www.africultures.com/php/?nav=personne&no=7110. To hear her voice (and accent), listen to the interviews on https://archive.org/details/Women_of_Rwanda_265.

38. F. Joseph Smith, *The Experiencing of Musical Sound* (New York: Gordon and Breach, 1979), 41.

39. Shilpa S. Davé, *Indian Accents: Brown Voice and Racial Performance in American Television and Film* (Baltimore: University of Illinois Press, 2013), 3.

40. Davé, *Indian Accents*, 11.

41. Kiran Nagarkar, "What Exactly did Peter Brook have in Mind when he Decided to do 'Battlefield'?" *Scroll.in*, March 13, 2016, http://scroll.in/article/805026/what-exactly-did-peter-brook-have-in-mind-when-he-decided-to-do-battlefield.

42. Sanskrit sounds can be classified into guttural, palatal, cerebral, dental, labial, semi-vowels, sibilants, and compound vowels. Cerebral (or retroflex) sounds are dental sounds in which the tongue is curled back and placed toward the roof of the mouth. These are sound qualities unique to Sanskrit-based languages, and vocalizations in English do not possess such an identical placement of the tongue.

43. I have personally consulted a Brahmin at Sree Ramar temple in Singapore regarding the Sanskrit pronunciation of terms and names in the Mahabharata.

44. See Pāṇini, *The Ashtadhyayi*, Book 6, trans. by Srisa Chandra Vasu (Benares, India: Sindhu Charan Bose, 1897).

45. See Adi Hastings, "Licked by the Mother Tongue: Imagining Everyday Sanskrit at Home and in the World," *Journal of Linguistic Anthropology* 18, no. 1 (2008): 24–45.

46. There is a useful and comprehensive website that introduces voice and aspiration in Sanskrit. See learnsanskrit.org, http://www.learnsanskrit.org/.

47. Bhagavad Gita 10:33. See *The Bhagavad Gita*, trans. Winthrop Sargeant, ed. Christopher Key Chapple (Albany: State University of New York Press, 2009), 443. Here, the translation is "Of letters I am the letter A, / And the dual of compound words; / I alone am infinite time; / I am the Establisher, facing in all directions (i.e. omniscient)."

48. Akshita Nanda, "Art of Story-telling at its Finest in Peter Brook's Battlefield," *Straits Times*, November 18, 2015, http://www.straitstimes.com/lifestyle/arts/art-of-story-telling-at-its-finest-in-peter-brooks-battlefield.

49. Nagarkar, "What Exactly," n.p.

50. Nanda, "Art of Story-telling," n.p.

51. Theo Van Leeuwen, *Speech, Music, Sound* (London: Macmillan, 1999), 6.

52. See Patrick E. Savage, Steven Brown, Emi Sakai, and Thomas E. Currie, "Statistical Universals Reveal the Structures and Functions of Human Music," *Proceedings of the National Academy of Sciences of the United States of America* 112, no. 29 (2015): 8987–92, https://www.pnas.org/content/112/29/8987.full.

53. See Isaac Tan, "Brook Makes Audience Battle Boredom," *Isaac Tan: Views on & Reviews of the Arts*, November 22, 2015, https://isaactanbr.com/.

54. This refers to a ritual of sacrifice, worship, offering, and devotion to the Gods for specific occasions.

55. Eric Charry, *Mande Music: Traditional and Modern Music of the Maninka and Mandinka of Western Africa* (Chicago: University of Chicago Press, 2000), 198.

56. Saumya Ancheri, "The Mahabharata does not Leave you: Notes from Peter Brook's Third Play about the Epic," *Scroll.in*, February 15, 2016, http://scroll.in/article/803515/the-mahabharata-does-not-leave-you-notes-from-peter-brooks-third-play-about-the-epic.

57. See Tanya Y. Price, "Rhythms of Culture: Djembe and African Memory in African-American Culture Traditions," *Black Music Research Journal* 33, no. 2 (2013): 227–47.

58. Price also notes how, in the US today, many African Americans are reconnecting with their African roots through music and musical instruments such as the djembe.

59. Jonathan Sterne, *The Audible Past: Cultural Origins of Sound Reproduction* (Durham, NC: Duke University Press, 2003), 13.

60. Sterne, *The Audible Past*, 13.

61. Alan Read, *Theatre, Intimacy and Engagement: The Last Human Venue* (Basingstoke, UK, and New York: Palgrave Macmillan, 2007), 84.

62. Slavoj Žižek, *The Parallax View* (Cambridge, MA: MIT Press, 2006), 34–5.

63. Read, *Theatre, Intimacy and Engagement*, 84.

64. See Nagarkar, "What Exactly," on why *Battlefield* lacked coherence and context.

65. Read, *Theatre, Intimacy and Engagement*, 84.

66. One such example would be recognized theatre critic Michael Billington, who writes of how memories of his experience sitting at a quarry 14km outside of Avignon, spectating the Mahabharata in 1985, came flooding back as he viewed *Battlefield*. See "Peter Brook to Rekindle the Magic of the Mahabharata," *Guardian*, January 13, 2016, http://www.theguardian.com/stage/2016/jan/13/peter-brook-battlefield-young-vic-theatre-mahabharata.

CHAPTER TWO

The Intercultural Politics of Performing Revolution: Maryse Condé's Inter-Theatre with Ariane Mnouchkine

EMILY SAHAKIAN

Through her 1989 epic play *An tan revolisyon* (In the Time of Revolution), the Caribbean writer Maryse Condé discerningly borrows from the French director Ariane Mnouchkine and her Théâtre du Soleil's theatrical practices of staging history, thereby enacting a critical homage. Spatially, textually, and in its processes of collective creation and interactive reception, *In the Time of Revolution* makes direct reference to the Soleil's landmark production *1789* (created in 1970), both to establish a theatrical influence and to sarcastically relativize the Soleil's political engagement with French history. Christiane Makward aptly characterizes Condé's play as a "transatlantic, triangular space, with Guadeloupe at the center; a lucid reading of history, whether Eurocentric, Afrocentric or Caribbean-centric; the questioning of received ideas and myths; and a deep-rooted compassion without the sugarcoating for the smaller nations of today's world without borders."[1] Condé's use of Mnouchkine's *1789* is best theorized neither as an intercultural appropriation nor a postcolonial or decolonizing revision, but rather a "creolization," that is, a performance-based reinvention,[2] of the Soleil's play that transforms its meanings and resists the status quo of how we tell histories—both of revolution and of theatrical interculturalism.

I have argued elsewhere that *In the Time of Revolution* reclaims the intercultural theatrical tradition and repossesses the concept of the universal human for a Caribbean audience: Condé uses theatre to "reorder and rearrange the opposing poles of human unity and difference and thereby reject the static or essentialist cultural and racial scripts imposed upon Caribbeans, while simultaneously affirming

Caribbean culture, history, and lived experience."[3] In this chapter, I wish to expand this research by offering a closer view into the composition and cultural implications of Condé's inter-theatre with Mnouchkine in order to carefully tease out Condé's intercultural, historiographic theatrical practice. Attention to the intricacies of Condé's critical homage to Mnouchkine additionally enables a reimaging of these two pioneering women artists, as I will suggest in the coda to this chapter.

As a paradigmatic case study from the late 1980s, *In the Time of Revolution* shifts and complicates the histories English-language scholars have told of "intercultural theatre," since it brings to the foreground an early intercultural performance that was multiple, decentered, and consciously political. The 1980s is commonly characterized as a time when European artists, particularly Mnouchkine and the Paris-based English director Peter Brook, "develop[ed] the discourses of theatrical interculturalism" by "split[ting] the world into a 'west and the rest' binary."[4] Condé defied that binary cultural logic, but she used similar techniques, appropriating Mnouchkine (who is commonly viewed as one of the prime appropriators) freely, in the spirit of "indebtedness and homage," to quote Maria Shevtsova's accurate qualification of Mnouchkine's theatrical pillaging of Eastern performance cultures.[5] Condé's inter-theatre with Mnouchkine may appear to correspond to the hourglass model proposed by Patrice Pavis, in which one culture is translated for another,[6] insofar as *1789* and Mnouchkine's method serve as raw material, filtered through Condé's own sensibilities and agenda, as well as through the staging and audience reception. But this transfer does not occur between two cultures presupposed to be homogeneous, pre-existing entities, but rather from two "interweaving performance cultures," to borrow Erica Fischer-Lichte's term. While Fischer-Lichte underlines such performances' transformative, utopian potential,[7] for Condé, the picture painted is grim, and the act of theatrical transfer exposes and subverts the underlying, uneven cultural terrain on which her theatrical work intervened: one in which Guadeloupean culture and history was presumed to be an (invisible) subset of the dominant French perspective, with the French Revolution commonly assumed to have given rise to the universal, humanitarian values of *liberté, égalité, fraternité*.

REMEMBERING REVOLUTIONS

To understand Condé's project, *In the Time of Revolution* must be placed in the context of 1989 Guadeloupe, when the island celebrated the bicentenary of the French Revolution at the risk of whitewashing Caribbean historical realities and perspectives. A little background information on Guadeloupe may be helpful here. Since 1946, Guadeloupe has been a French overseas department, that is, an administrative division of France located across the ocean. Given its status as part of France, it might appear logical that, alongside the rest of the country, Guadeloupe would celebrate the 200th anniversary of a series of events that form the overriding cultural landmark in the collective French psyche. However, remembering the French Revolution was complicated for the people of Guadeloupe, which is a former slave colony. The human rights ensuing from the French Revolution, put forth in the Declaration of the Rights of Man and of the Citizen of 1789, were not extended to the enslaved, and a man's right to "property" was reiterated by the decree. In 1794, abolition was decreed, but slavery was subsequently reinstated by Napoleon Bonaparte in 1802. Guadeloupe, in fact, remained a French slave colony until 1848, more than half a century after the onset of the French Revolution in 1789. For the bicentenary, the president of Guadeloupe's Regional Council, Félix Proto, commissioned Condé to write a play and provided a generous government subsidy of 700,000 francs for the production.[8] As Proto may have anticipated,[9] Condé's play answers the invitation by exposing its flawed logic, aiming to show that "the French Revolution means nothing for a Caribbean person."[10] While this message is polemical, true to Condé's reputation as a *provocatrice* who leads her readers to face ugly truths and thus to sharpen our critical acumen,[11] the play displays an incredibly conscientious treatment of historical complexity and refuses to embrace any kind of essentialism, idealized historical hero, or myth.

To create her play, Condé drew from Mnouchkine's theatrical practice, specifically her historical epic *1789* and, to a lesser-extent, its sequel, *1793*. Almost two decades earlier, in 1970, at a time of disillusionment following the May 1968 events in France, the Soleil had revisited the French Revolution not to retell the myth, but rather to renew its too-quickly abandoned promises. By making its audiences participants in the unfolding of history, *1789* celebrated the triumph of the French working class, while showing how the idealistic myth of *liberté, égalité, fraternité* remained unrealized: the people's revolution was hijacked by the bourgeoisie, which became the new ruling class. Mnouchkine's practice of staging history served as a supreme model for Condé to write a play that, instead of veneration and reverence for an untouchable myth, demystified the French Revolution—in her case, specifically for the people of Guadeloupe.

From a Caribbeanist vantage point, Condé deployed several of the Soleil's methods to her own ends. In addition to deconstructing the myth of the French Revolution, *In the Time of Revolution* relativizes the struggles of the French, fills in gaps in Mnouchkine's account, and puts these histories of revolution and upheaval in a transatlantic perspective. Furthermore, Condé strikes a decidedly different tone. *1789* celebrated the unrealized ideals of the French Revolution and anticipated a future revolution to come that might be a continuation of the worker and student strikes of May 1968.[12] Condé's play, in contrast, is pervaded by cynicism toward revolution and insinuates that the corruption of those in power may be inevitable. Condé's three main tools were, as she has stated, doubt, derision, and deconstruction.[13] Revolution, for Condé, is not French history, but rather a shared, transatlantic history, in which people of color in the Caribbean were continually underserved and betrayed. The Haitian Revolution represents a moment of triumph, but contemporary poverty and corruption in Haiti suggests that its promises also remain unrealized. Condé, in the manner of *1789*, calls to question the extent to which Toussaint Louverture and other revolutionary heroes ever served or even considered the average Guadeloupean. Borrowing from *1789* enabled Condé to criticize the very act of commemorating, first, the French Revolution, and then, by extension, revolutions more broadly, in Guadeloupe.

CRITICAL HOMAGE: BORROWING FROM MNOUCHKINE, DECENTERING FRANCE

Condé's inter-theatre with Mnouchkine is a kind of critical homage, which performs an artistic debt to the French director, even as it decenters France and relativizes the Soleil's project. Condé has spoken of her admiration for Mnouchkine's theatre in several places. In an interview with Alvina Ruprecht, she recounts having seen all of Mnouchkine's plays and describes the French woman as the single theatre artist who has left the most important mark on her work, particularly for her use of space and refusal of a single tone.[14] Elsewhere she states that Mnouchkine's *1789* and *1793* showed her that history can be material or fodder for theatre par excellence.[15] In her interview with Ruprecht, Condé explained that, as she created her play, she consulted a series of videos of Soleil productions, *1789* in particular.[16] In a recent personal email correspondence, she recalled having seen *1789* performed several times, and having discussed the project with her friend, Soleil female actor Myrrha Donzenac, who is from Martinique.[17]

Though Condé had previously worked collaboratively with theatre artists, notably the Guadeloupean artist José Jernidier, *In the Time of Revolution* represents her first and only attempt at Mnouchkine-ian collective creation. At the heart of the project was a partnership between Condé and her close friend Sonia Emmanuel, who directed the show; the two women even lived under the same roof, like Mnouchkine's troupe does. The play was also nourished by collaborations with Jernidier and his popular TTC + Bakanal troupe.[18] Condé relied on Jernidier's mastery of both the Creole language and farce. Like the Soleil, the actors worked with musicians. There were two orchestras: the contemporary Caribbean group Kafé and a classical orchestra that played the compositions of the Chevalier de Saint-Georges, an accomplished eighteenth-century *mulâtre* violinist and fencer. Analogous to the Soleil's inviting of distinguished historians to help them better grasp the complexities of the French Revolution, Condé consulted with and read works recommended by eminent historians; her play showcases a sophisticated, academic understanding of the complex alliances and upheaval of this moment in time.[19]

Condé's play borrows from Mnouchkine's an aesthetic, corporeal, and dramaturgic approach to staging history. One notices at first glance that Condé's use of space refers to *1789*, as the podiums used in the production of *In the Time of Revolution* recall the raised rostra of *1789*. While the Soleil used five platforms to split the focus and put the audience in the center of the action, Condé used three—to signify three geographical spaces: France, Haiti (Saint-Domingue), and Guadeloupe. This transnational stage design enables Condé to tell histories of revolution in multiplicity, following the echoes and reverberations. The pervasive use of meta-theatre, the epic historical project, the deliberate anachronisms, and the episodic structure, with quick alternating between different tones (serious and grotesque, dialogue and dance), all recall Mnouchkine's formal and aesthetic project.

Both plays use the aforementioned techniques in order to "free socially-conditioned phenomena [in this case, the myths about revolution] from the stamp of familiarity which protects them against our grasp," to borrow Bertolt Brecht's words.[20] In *1789*, the estrangement effect is accomplished primarily through the device of the actors as *bateleurs* (acrobats), who perform the events of the French Revolution as in a fairground production before the spectator's eyes, and, in some cases, with the spectator's participation. Much like a living newspaper, the actors perform, animate, spread news of, criticize, and contextualize events, as contemporaneous theatre artists did (for illiterate populations) during the time of the French Revolution. For Condé, in contrast, it is a storyteller (*conteur*) character who is the main vehicle of Brechtian estrangement and critical consciousness-raising. Zéphyr is a cynical, sardonic mediator, who poses provocative questions, makes fun of events and historical heroes, and helps the audience to see the Guadeloupean perspective. Condé's *conteur* may have been partly inspired by Mnouchkine's,[21] but he is also a reimagining of the Caribbean storyteller. The traditional Creole *conteur* tells and retells familiar stories, vitally transmits information, knowledge, and a sense of community, and engages his listeners through several call-and-response tactics (such as *Cric! Crac!*). Inherited from the plantation context, where gatherings of enslaved Africans were often surveyed by overseers, the Creole storyteller typically uses sarcasm and dissimulation to make statements about current events and criticize those in power. Condé's storyteller is an anachronistic character who seems to transcend time. He died, as he says at the play's opening, in a historic battle at Sartine Square (the site of the performance) to free Guadeloupe from the English in 1794,[22] but he also makes himself present in the spectator's current time (1989) by poking fun at their dreams of BMWs, VCRs, and vacations to Caracas. He jokes anachronistically that he grew up dreaming of becoming Victor Hugo, but Hugo was not born until 1802 (eight years after Zéphyr's reported death).[23] He is also a deliberately androgynous character: the Guadeloupean actor, director, and storytelling specialist who created the role of Zéphyr, Gilbert Laumord, recalled Condé's reminders that he should feminize his acting style.[24] According to Condé, her *conteur* dissuades spectators from identifying passively with the events and characters depicted onstage, and works, instead, to prompt them to react in a dynamic, engaged way.[25]

Like the Soleil, Condé wished to tell a people's history and to acknowledge, as Zéphyr states, "those anonymous figures whose names history does not remember."[26] In a similar manner to the Soleil, Condé creates characters to represent average Guadeloupean people and borrows from *1789* the device of silent women with candles in white to remind spectators of the presence of women, too often omitted from the history books. From a Guadeloupean perspective, Condé takes the Soleil's project to the next level, offering up, in Deborah Gaensbauer's terms, "a piece of theatre that challenges the method of even a liberal institution like the Théâtre du Soleil."[27] Wishing to draw popular audiences, the Soleil had decided to focus their play on the French Revolution because they saw it as "the only piece of popular heritage common to anyone who had passed through the French school system."[28] The French Revolution was also part of the popular heritage for the people of Guadeloupe, particularly Condé's generation, whose public-school curricula were virtually identical to French schoolchildren's.

Condé also deconstructed black and postcolonial historical myths. Largely thanks to the successes of the Négritude movement and several influential historians, the heroes of the Haitian Revolution—especially Toussaint Louverture—and the

Guadeloupean revolutionary Louis Delgrès were similarly untouchable legends in Guadeloupe. Using comic exaggeration, as the Soleil does, Condé quotes Toussaint and Delgrès, pokes fun at these anticolonial heroes, and refuses to espouse any kind of mythification. Condé's Toussaint disquietingly recalls a slave master and even the French king. When his people ask the land to be distributed to them, he responds that they "deserve the whip!"[29] He sits on a throne (mirroring the French king), and José Jernidier, who created the role of Toussaint, recalled using sharp, forbidding, royal gestures.[30] It is no surprise that Condé was criticized in Guadeloupe for having portrayed Toussaint Louverture as a dictator.[31] Furthermore, Condé's questioning of Haiti's role in the contemporary moment and of her depiction of Haitian–Guadeloupean fraternity as an unrealized promise offsets the common mythification of Haitian independence.

Revisiting scenes and moments depicted by *1789* afresh, *In the Time of Revolution* decenters France and instead shows perspectives relevant to the people of Guadeloupe. The Creole-language title, *An tan revolisyon* (In the Time of Revolution), clearly signals the play's decentering of France in order to speak about multiple, intersecting revolutions—French, Haitian, and Guadeloupean—and puts the perspectives and experiences of Caribbeans center stage. The subtitle, in French, *Elle court, elle court la liberté* (Freedom is running, running), refers to a French children's song about chasing a ferret in order to emphasize the elusiveness of freedom for enslaved peoples during this time of historical and political upheaval. The text, and particularly the first act titled "1789," contains lines, characters, and moments borrowed directly from the Soleil's production, revisited in a new light. Condé thereby leads readers and viewers familiar with Mnouchkine to see *1789* and its political project with fresh eyes.[32]

In the first act, Condé shows how distant the concerns of the French underclasses that led to the French Revolution were from the reality of enslaved Caribbeans, and how the revolution of 1789 did nothing to improve the conditions of the enslaved. The Soleil's production opens with various vignettes that vividly show French peasants struggling to no avail to feed their children, access clean water, pay their taxes, and make their voices heard. By referencing and relativizing these scenes, Condé reminds us that enslaved Caribbeans had an even more primordial need: freedom from bondage. Freedom—*la liberté*—is, as Condé writes, the play's only heroine.[33] Condé's play opens with an introduction by the storyteller, which includes a reading of separate censuses in Guadeloupe and France, which distinguishes the two geographical spaces and reminds spectators of the three-tiered, racialized caste system in the colonies: whites on top, followed by *mulâtres* or free people of color, and the majority of Guadeloupe's population, black slaves, who can be sold at their master's whim.[34] This both sets up a parallel between the three classes in France—nobility, clergy, and the common people—and troubles that parallel, by introducing the vital difference of a group of people treated as property.[35]

Throughout the play, Condé glosses over and truncates scenes borrowed from Mnouchkine's plays, makes fun of them, and transforms their messages. Condé relativizes the struggle of the French people (shown on a platform to the right) by juxtaposing it with experiences in Guadeloupe (on the left). She sets up this convention from the start. Her first vignette features two characters and several lines taken directly from a memorable early scene of *1789*. The original scene from *1789* dramatizes the problems associated with the *cahiers de doléances*, that is, a list of the people's grievances to be heard by the king. In this stylistically grotesque scene, three comically simple-minded peasants rejoice that, now the king can hear their concerns, there will be no more repressive taxes, no more floods or plagues, and no more empty bellies. Particularly zealous to tell the king of the problem of the "gabelle" (salt tax), the peasants joyfully prepare to write their grievances, but the tone changes abruptly as they realize they have no paper. They decide to use a white sheet, and happily go to write again, but a new problem: they have no ink. Gaspard tells Nestine to cut him, so she can write with his blood. She is disgusted at first, but acquiesces and poses to write. Only then do the peasants remember that they are illiterate; none of them know how to write even the first letter of gabelle. Their grievances will not be transmitted to the king.[36]

While *1789* uses the stylized techniques of commedia dell'arte to foreground the failure of the king's promise to hear his people's grievances, Condé's shows only the French peasants' moment of hope, leaving out the disappointment that ensues entirely, before turning towards Guadeloupe. Nestine and Gaspard's beginning lines are quickly called out and interrupted by Zéphyr, who sardonically instructs his Guadeloupean audience, "Leave them their moment of joy! It's not often that their eyes shed tears of joy! For us in Guadeloupe, the month of May 1789 is no different than other months. No sun, no joy!"[37] The message is clear: while the *cahiers de doléances* failed to serve French peasants as promised, no one ever even pretended to listen to the concerns of enslaved blacks, who were categorically counted as less than human. The point is driven home even more forcefully as the scene slices to a slave master verifying that his foreman has thoroughly beaten the slave Jean Louis and added pepper to his wounds as punishment for the crime of speaking of freedom. Not only are the concerns of enslaved people not heard by France, but the enslaved are punished for speaking their desires. The Caribbean, it is suggested, was in even greater need of a revolution than France.

In a similar manner, Condé reuses snippets from the most memorable scene of the Soleil's play, the storming of the Bastille, in order to relativize French historical experiences. While the Soleil actors drew audience members into small groups to hear them tell the story, inviting them to identify with the common people who stormed the Bastille, Condé holds the French perspective at a critical distance by recounting it in a cursory manner and bluntly interrupting the French peasants' lines with the Carmagnole dance and popular revolutionary song "Ca ira."[38] Furthermore, the storming of the Bastille is upstaged by the bloodier suppression of resistance in the colonies, as Condé shows a bloody massacre of slaves and free people of color, their bodies strewn across the stage floor, and subsequently cared for by women in white and honored by the Nèg Mawon (fugitive black slave).[39] Condé again juxtaposes Stages 1 (France) and 2 (Guadeloupe). On Stage 1, the people lament the replacing of the nobles by the bourgeoisie—"Only the rich have been given the right to vote!"—and we hear the iconic line from *1789*, "The revolution is over!" Yet, in Guadeloupe, the message is more harrowing: "For you there never was a revolution. For you the word means nothing! The Revolution doesn't exist!"[40] Though Guadeloupean slaves and people of color fought, and suffered a bloody defeat, their revolution was suppressed more violently than the French. In consequence, the French Revolution, with its promises of equality and freedom for all men, had no impact in the Caribbean.

Both *1789* and *In the Time of Revolution* dramatize the hypocrisy of the 1789 Declaration of the Rights of Man and of the Citizen, but while the Soleil focuses on France's contradictory treatment of enslaved blacks, Condé emphasizes the agency of the enslaved and their desire for freedom. In a scene set in Saint-Domingue, *1789* plays with stereotypical, exoticizing views of the Caribbean. Two corrupt plantation owners, a white man and a mixed-race woman, rock and sway slowly in the tropical winds, fanned and waited upon by their black slaves—white actors performing in streaks of brownface make-up (their faces are not completely brown, which estranges audiences from the convention). A man from the National Assembly enters to read the decree. As he reads the first article, the enslaved are ecstatic to learn of the law protecting equality among men. They joyously start to run down the aisles, but are called back—and return reluctantly, with their heads bowed—when he skips to the seventeenth article affirming a man's inviolable and sacred right to property.[41] The critique of the contradiction in French law is transmitted by way of the enslaved people's disappointment and the return to the status quo (the corrupt plantation owners swaying again and smilingly eerily). Condé, in contrast, shows enslaved people who, though they are too wise to expect to be helped by any French law, demand their freedom—which they know *should* be an inalienable right. To foreground that critical distance, the 1789 declaration is heard in Condé's play as an echo: "Men are born and remain free and equal in rights. Men are born and . . ."[42] The echo emanates from the French podium and reaches an empty podium for Guadeloupe, where slaves, masters, and foremen fill the stage space to listen to the mysterious voice.[43] In contrast with Mnouchkine's, Condé's slaves demand their freedom in Creole: "Libèté! Libèté!" Yet, as in *1789*, a white planter affirms that the enslaved do not count as men: "They're not talking about you. They're talking about men. Not about slaves!"[44]

The project of recentering the Soleil's production unfolds additionally as a filling in of gaps in the story that Mnouchkine tells (and, of course, gaps in the popular rendering of the French Revolution). Characters and situations from the Soleil's production are revisited from the Guadeloupean perspective. For example, while the Soleil shows Necker, the Swiss banker who had exposed the problem of the king's spending, as an advocate for revolution and someone the people "considered as our friend,"[45] Condé cites his anti-slavery plea to the national assembly.[46] While the first act of Condé's play, "1789," is very much in dialogue with Mnouchkine's, in subsequent acts, Condé offers up new historical material, which she subjects to the same process of sardonic deconstruction. In the Soleil's sequel to *1789*, *1793*, there is a discussion of slavery presented from the point of view of Louise, a woman who tells her family's experiences of slavery. She discusses the Haitian Revolution from individual everyday women's perspectives.[47] Louise was played by Myrrha Donzenac, and Condé recalls having been impressed by her performance.[48] It is significant that Condé calls her second act "1794" (the Soleil's play covers 1793 and 1794), since this one-year difference recenters the abolition of slavery in the French colonies (and France's broken promise to enslaved Caribbeans)

FIGURE 2.1: Theo Sainsily as Dessalines rouses a crowd in Maryse Condé's *In the Time of Revolution*, 1989. Photograph by Emily Sahakian and Thomas Stewart; video courtesy of José Jernidier.

and enables Condé to depict Toussaint Louverture, though certainly a political hero, as another man corrupted by power. As Zéphyr sardonically moralizes, the "worst intoxication comes from wearing a uniform."[49] The last Act of Condé's play, "1802," covers a period in history that the Soleil's production does not acknowledge: the reestablishment of slavery by Napoleon Bonaparte in Guadeloupe, the rebellion led by Guadeloupean revolutionary Louis Delgrès, and the capture and imprisoning of Toussaint Louverture.[50]

Condé's spectators learn that the defeat of the English in Guadeloupe in 1794 for Revolutionary France was largely thanks to the enslaved and free people of color who fought for their liberty, including the storyteller Zéphyr who died at the site of a historic battle at Sartine Square (the site of the performance, as noted above). The French Revolution was won (in not so small a part) thanks to the labor of black Caribbeans, who fought for their freedom and were subsequently betrayed by the reinstatement of slavery. While the Soleil's *1793* covers the Terror in France, Condé's Zéphyr slyly links the execution of white Creole royalists in Guadeloupe with the labor of plantation slavery.

> Victor Hughes [the French-born governor of Guadeloupe, who recruited soldiers of color to fight at Sartine Square][51] wastes no time in becoming the Robespierre of the tropics. On Sartine Square, now renamed Victoire Square, he installs the guillotine. And from that day on, Monsieur Anse, the executioner, a distinguished Mulatto, raised in Paris if you please, a pleasing violinist whose pockets were always full of candy for the children, was no longer out of a job. Cut heads like sugar cane. Clack, clack, clack . . . Cut heads like sugar cane. Clack, clack clack![52]

Even as he deliberately blurs borders between France and Guadeloupe, Zéphyr makes known the hypocrisy of Hughes and the naming of the square "victory square," when that victory did not ultimately benefit Guadeloupe. The mixed-race executioner, raised in Paris, is unclassifiable in binary postcolonial logic, but the irony of associating Paris with civilization is clear. And the repetition of the line "cut heads like sugar cane," followed by the sound of the guillotine, drives home the message that blacks and people of color labored—bloodily—for a revolution that has yet to serve them sufficiently. As it makes this biting critique, the scene's comedy is captivating: Zéphyr farcically mimics a royalist's gait as he repeatedly walks up to the guillotine, and then abruptly throws prop guillotined heads high into the air. A janitor (anachronistically) sweeps up the heads to throw them away in the trash.[53]

In conclusion, Condé's play takes as its premise the interconnectedness of French and Caribbean histories: it dramatizes a transatlantic historical experience of a "time of revolution" (to borrow Condé's title), that is, 1789–1802, in France, Guadeloupe, and Haiti. Through meta-theatre, rapid shifts in tone, and storytelling traditions, *In the Time of Revolution*, like *1789*, invites its spectators to actively make their own meanings from a complex, multilayered representation of history's lived experiences, untold stories, and brutal violence. In Stéphanie Bérard's words, it "aptly represents the fragmented, scattered and confused history that writers [and spectators] attempt to reconstruct."[54] However, in contrast with Mnouchkine, and against a long-standing status-quo of valuing the French Revolution over the Haitian Revolution (not to mention the nearly-forgotten revolution in Guadeloupe), Condé puts Caribbean historical realities and perspectives center stage, which were already intertwined with French ones (due to, of course, slavery and colonialism). Her play bears witness, as Leo Cabranes-Grant might say, to "the heterogeneous history" of the French-Caribbean (violent) intercultural encounter she stages, as opposed to counting interculturalism as the result of a theatrical translation, which would imply "a strategic essentialism" of the two cultures.[55] The narrative that emerges from Condé's Mnouchkine-ian treatment of these interlaced histories of political upheaval, bloodshed, and the (re)instatement of a political order evinces a shrewd critique of the complex ways in which the people of Guadeloupe and the greater Caribbean have been historically oppressed, dehumanized, and underserved. Condé's inter-theatre with Mnouchkine both enables her to tell this transatlantic history through theatrical metaphor and reveals the blind spots of Mnouchkine's more nationally-bound project.

CODA: REPOSITIONING THE ARTISTS

The deliberate ways in which Condé, during a time period associated with infamous European theatrical appropriations, borrowed from Mnouchkine's theatrical practice prompts a revisiting of both women and particularly the ways they have been classified culturally. In English-language scholarship, Mnouchkine's work has been considered a forerunner of the politically-ineffective tradition that Daphne Lei calls Hegemonic Intercultural Theatre (HIT), which "combines First World Capital and brain power with Third World raw material and labor, and Western classical texts with Eastern performance traditions [as in Mnouchkine's Shakespeare cycle]."[56] This case study reveals not only the complexity of influence, but how neither of the two women played the simplified roles assigned to them by an intercultural–postcolonial binary.

Mnouchkine, who appears as a more complex figure in French-language scholarship, has long borrowed freely from cultures outside of her own, but her work has always been politically motivated. Apparently influenced by Antonin Artaud,[57] she wished to escape the confines of European theatre's emphasis on psychological realism by turning to non-Western, mostly Asian, cultures as well as Western influences, like commedia dell'arte and the Bread and Puppet Theater from the US. She infamously stated that "theatre is oriental" (a phrase borrowed from Artaud and Jacques Copeau as well).[58] The production of *1789* is precedent for her so-called intercultural works of the 1980s, such as the *Shakespeare Cycle* or the *Indiade*. But telling stories of cultural Others—and making them relevant to French spectators—was always a preoccupation for Mnouchkine, whose family fled the Russian Revolution and experienced anti-Semitism and the deportation of Mnouchkine's grandparents under Vichy France. Françoise Quillet describes Mnouchkine's interest in "the Orient" as an ongoing driving personal interest, present from her first works.[59] Mnouchkine, who was influenced by Jean Vilar's popular theatre, has the reputation in France of an avant-garde artist who fights for the working class, refugees, and the underprivileged. At least five of the company members were saved from refugee camps.[60]

Condé's works, in contrast, are often labeled with culturally-specific, strategically essentialist language—black woman's writing, Caribbean literature, postcolonial literature. Culturally finite labels irritate Condé, who is resolutely anti-essentialist. While critics have tended to use the tenets of postcolonialism and identity politics to make sense of her writing, Condé questions and refuses the label of "Caribbean" writer and warns against "preserving erroneous categories and using definitions that no longer correspond to anything meaningful."[61] Having lived and worked in Guadeloupe, France, the United States, and several countries in Africa, Condé is a world writer. She has stated, in language that resembles Mnouchkine's, that she believes that theatre must be nourished by other theatres in order to avoid withering away.[62]

Much as Condé's play prompts its spectators to ask why we remember certain revolutions and forget others, my consideration of Condé's appropriation of Mnouchkine's theatrical practices might prompt us to ask: why is Condé's work less known than Mnouchkine's? The question might be partially resolved by considering the two plays' vastly different scales of spectatorship and diffusion. *1789*, attended by almost 300,000 spectators,[63] was one of the Soleil's most popular and influential pieces. It played for nearly three years (and could have easily gone on longer had the company so wished), and it has been captured and further circulated through a filmed version, which Mnouchkine herself created from footage of several of the final performances. In contrast, Condé's play ran for only two nights. It was sold out both nights, attended by more than 2,000 spectators, but subsequently the director and actors were not able to tour to other islands throughout the Caribbean, as they had hoped, due to the difficulty of obtaining financial resources and perhaps the provocative nature of the play. Though official Guadeloupean radio and TV had programmed the production, they failed to air it, which Condé believed, as she stated in an interview with Nick Nesbitt, to be a kind of boycotting of her message.[64] Condé's play's potential for impact, perhaps like Guadeloupe's suppressed revolution, seems to have been prematurely cut short.

Despite its restricted run, *In the Time of Revolution* suggests an alternative genealogy of intercultural theatre practice, one that would not begin with a global, commodifying avant-garde, through which European artists exerted their power and cultural capital through insensitive theatrical appropriations, but rather reveal itself as always involving multiple, decentered flows of influence. Borrowing can simultaneously involve a political critique and an artistic homage; it can entail cultural commodification and be consciously political. It is not accurate to speak of the ways Condé and Mnouchkine moved beyond the postcolonial–intercultural binary, for that binary never served to describe either woman's artistic practice.

NOTES

1. Christiane Makward, "Preface," in Maryse Condé, *An tan révolisyon* (Paris: Editions de l'Amandier, 2015), 168.

2. See Emily Sahakian, *Staging Creolization: Women's Theatre and Performance from the French Caribbean* (Charlottesville: University of Virginia Press, 2017), 11–16.

3. Sahakian, *Staging Creolization*, 54.

4. Ric Knowles, *Theatre & Interculturalism* (New York: Palgrave Macmillan, 2010), 21.

5. Maria Shevtsova, "Interculturalism, Aestheticism, Orientalism: Starting from Peter Brook's *Mahabharata*," *Theatre Research International* 22, no. 2 (1997): 102.

6. Patrice Pavis, *Theatre at the Crossroads of Culture*, trans. Loren Kruger (London: Routledge, 1992), 4–5.

7. Erika Fischer-Lichte, "Introduction," in Erika Fischer-Lichte, Torsten Jost, and Saskya Iris Jain (eds), *Politics of Interweaving Performance Cultures: Beyond Postcolonialism* (London: Routledge, 2014), 10.

8. Françoise Pfaff, *Conversations with Maryse Condé* (Lincoln: University of Nebraska Press, 1996), 87.

9. Condé speculates that Proto probably expected her to write an anti-establishment piece. Alvina Ruprecht, "Le Théâtre de Maryse Condé: Entretien de Maryse Condé avec le Pr Alvina Ruprecht," *L'Arbre à Palabres* 18 (2006): 154.

10. Ruprecht, "Le Théâtre," 154.

11. See Dawn Fulton, *Signs of Dissent: Maryse Condé and Postcolonial Criticism* (Charlottesville: University of Virginia Press, 2008), and Nicole Simek, *Eating Well, Reading Well: Maryse Condé and the Ethics of Interpretation* (Amsterdam: Rodopi, 2008). Edited volumes entitled after Condé's provocations include Noëlle Carruggi (ed.), *Maryse Condé: Rébellion et transgressions* (Paris: Karthala, 2010); Madeleine Cottenet-Hage and Lydie Moudileno (eds.), *Maryse Condé: Une nomade inconvenante* (Guadeloupe: Ibis Rouge, 2002); Nara Araújo (ed.), *L'œuvre de Maryse Condé: à propos d'une écrivaine politiquement incorrecte* (Paris: L'Harmattan, 1996).

12. *1789* reveals that behind France's official three classes—nobility, clergy, and the "third estate," that is, the common people—there was the bourgeoisie, which, though supposedly part of the popular, common class, actually held power and influence, first

over King Louis XVI before the revolution and then, more officially, as leaders of the people. The bourgeoisie found a way, as power shifted from the monarchy to the "people," to steal the revolution from the common people.

13. Maryse Condé, "Autour d'An Tan Revolisyon," *Etudes Guadeloupéennes* 1, no. 2–3 (1990): 165.

14. Ruprecht, "Le Théâtre," 157.

15. Condé, "Autour," 164.

16. Ruprecht, "Le Théâtre," 154.

17. Personal email correspondence, January 3, 2019.

18. For more on Jernidier, see Françoise Naudillon, "Le théâtre populaire de José Jernidier," *Africultures*, March 2010, http://www.africultures.com/php/?nav=article& no=9340.

19. Condé credits Max Chartol for helping her to see the possibility of a distinctly Guadeloupean reading of the Revolution, and then historian colleagues at Berkeley (and particularly Peter Koch), who, in Condé's words, were "not prisoners to a monolithic version of history." Condé, "Autour," 165; Ruprecht, "Le Théâtre," 154.

20. Bertolt Brecht, "A Short Organum," *Brecht on Theatre: The Development of an Aesthetic*, ed. and trans. John Willett (London: Methuen, 1964), 192.

21. The storyteller plays a very minor role in *1789* and is more present, though still marginal, in *1793*.

22. Maryse Condé, "In the Time of Revolution: Run, Liberty, Run," trans. Doris Y. Kadish and Jean-Pierre Piriou, in *An tan révolisyon* (Paris: Editions de l'Amandier, 2015), 169.

23. Condé, "In the Time of Revolution," 216.

24. Makward, "Preface," *An tan révolisyon*, 166.

25. Condé, "Autour," 169–70.

26. Condé, "In the Time of Revolution," 232.

27. Deborah B. Gaensbauer, "Protean Truths: History as Performance in Maryse Condé's *An Tan Revolisyon*," *French Review* 76, no. 6 (2003): 1141.

28. Adrian Kiernander, *Ariane Mnouchkine and the Théâtre du Soleil* (Cambridge: Cambridge University Press, 1993), 71.

29. Condé, "In the Time of Revolution," 206.

30. Personal interview with José Jernidier, Avignon, July 21, 2014.

31. Frank Thompson Nesbitt III, "An interview with Maryse Condé at Columbia University, April 12, 1997 regarding the play *An tan revolisyon*," in "Revolution in Discourse: Writing History in French Antillean Literature," PhD dissertation, Harvard University, 1997, 244.

32. It is certainly possible that some of Condé's spectators in Guadeloupe had seen Mnouchkine's play in Paris or in Martinique, where it was performed at the Festival de Fort-de-France in 1973 (program consulted at the Département des Arts du spectacle, Bibliothèque nationale de France, WNG 575 (1973–1999)). The play was

also widely diffused by the film the ensemble created during the last performances of its 1973 revival.

33. Condé, "Autour," 167.

34. Condé, "In the Time of Revolution," 171.

35. As Deborah Gaensbauer notes, the French census pattern "mirrors a chronology appended to the Théâtre du Soleil's published version" while including the performance of a slave auction scene as an additional introduction to the players involved and the institution that reinforces their place in a rigid three-tiered racialized caste system. Gaensbauer, "Protean Truths,"1146.

36. Théâtre du Soleil, *1789* in *1789: La revolution doit s'arrêter à la perfection du bonheure* [followed by] *1793: La cite révolutionnaire est de ce monde* (Paris: Théâtre du Soleil, 1989), 12–13. In a subsequent scene documented in the film, a cunning peasant draws a picture to communicate his grievance and need for two cows to the king. But his message never reaches the king, since it must be transmitted by someone who has access to him: each man on the chain leading up to the king has his own concerns and dismisses the grievances of those below him. *1789*, dir. Ariane Mnouchkine (Ariane Films, 1974).

37. Condé, "In the Time of Revolution," 174.

38. Condé, "In the Time of Revolution," 179. In the Soleil's *1793*, actors also dance the Carmagnole (Théâtre du Soleil, *1789*, 74).

39. Condé, "In the Time of Revolution," 179–82.

40. Condé, "In the Time of Revolution," 189.

41. Théâtre du Soleil, *1789*, 38. My description is based on viewing the film *1789*.

42. Condé, "In the Time of Revolution," 185.

43. Condé, "In the Time of Revolution," 186.

44. Condé, "In the Time of Revolution," 186.

45. Théâtre du Soleil, *1789*, 26.

46. Condé, "In the Time of Revolution," 185.

47. Théâtre du Soleil, *1789*, 71–3.

48. Ruprecht, "Le Théâtre," 155.

49. Condé, "In the Time of Revolution," 203.

50. As Ruprecht notes, these events are often ignored by French historians. Ruprecht, "Analysis of An tan révolisyon," *An tan révolisyon*, 162

51. Condé, "In the Time of Revolution," n. 2, 169.

52. Condé, "In the Time of Revolution," 203.

53. Video consulted containing the second act, "1794," and the second half of the third, "1802," José Jernidier's personal archives.

54. Stéphanie Bérard, *Theater of the French Caribbean: Traditions and Contemporary Stages*, trans. Tessa Thiery and Jonathan S. Skinner (Pompano Beach, FL: Caribbean Studies Press, 2014), 203.

55. Leo Cabranes-Grant, *From Scenarios to Networks* (Evanston, IL: Northwestern University Press, 2016), 9–10.

56. Daphne P. Lei, "Interruption, Intervention, Interculturalism: Robert Wilson's HIT Productions in Taiwan," *Theatre Journal* 63, no.4 (2011): 571.

57. As Miller points out, Mnouchkine has never claimed Artaud as a source. Judith G. Miller, *Ariane Mnouchkine* (London: Routledge, 2007), 17.

58. See Ariane Mnouchkine, "The Theatre is Oriental," in Patrice Pavis (ed.), *The Intercultural Performance Reader* (London: Routledge, 1996), 93–7.

59. Françoise Quillet, *L'Orient au Théâtre du Soleil* (Paris: L'Harmattan, 1999), 17–21.

60. Miller, *Ariane Mnouchkine*, 14.

61. Maryse Condé, "What is a Caribbean Writer?" in *Journey of a Caribbean Writer*, trans. Richard Philcox (London: Seagull, 2014), 9. See also "Instructions on How to Become a 'Caribbean' Writer," in *Journey*, 10–17.

62. Ruprecht, "Le Théâtre," 158.

63. Kiernander, *Ariane Mnouchkine*, 86.

64. Frank Thomas III Nesbitt, "Revolution in Discourse: Writing History in French Antillean Literature," PhD dissertation, Harvard University, 1997, 242.

CHAPTER THREE

What Lies beyond Hattamala? Badal Sircar and His Third Theatre as an Alternative Trajectory for Intercultural Theatre

ARNAB BANERJI

The first edition of the *Asian Theatre Journal* in 1984 included an incendiary article by Rustom Bharucha, "A Collision of Cultures: Some Western Interpretations of the Indian Theatre." Bharucha picked specific examples from the creative and critical oeuvres of prominent Western theatre critics and practitioners and critiqued their treatment of elements of Indian theatre. Bharucha stated in the piece that the exemplary attitudes that he scrutinized in his substantial essay correspond to an "attitude to the East [that is] shaped by certain constructs and images of the Orient that prevail in the West."[1] The essay provoked a rather strong back and forth between Bharucha and one of his subjects of enquiry in the article, Richard Schechner. Schechner argued in a response that was included in the second issue of the journal that Bharucha demonstrated a significant lack of understanding of not only his but also of Western approaches to Eastern art forms in general. Bharucha responded by using examples from Schechner's own body of work on intercultural performance such as the pitfalls of imagining the other as "not another but the projection of one's own ego."[2] The fierce rat-a-tat between these two scholars more than three decades ago is a testament to the anxiety surrounding intercultural performance—especially between members of a source culture with those from an appropriating culture.

I revisited this exchange to refresh my memory of how interculturalism has been construed and imagined as a process of cultural evaluation and appropriation where the agency lies with the Western observer/academic/performer. Bharucha's critique identifies Schechner as an interlocutor who not only controlled but also dominated and shaped the conversation around the use of Eastern cultural artifacts indiscriminately in his creative pursuits. Schechner in his defense quoted from a

1983 keynote address delivered at a conference in Kolkata (erstwhile Calcutta): "For in learning about the Other we also deepen our grasp of who we ourselves are: the Other is another and a mirror at the same time. We learn about our own aesthetics when we study the dance of another place and/or time."[3] Critics like David Williams while writing about Ariane Mnouchkine's Théâtre du Soleil, or Patrice Pavis's extolling of Brook's *Mahabharata* (incidentally the favorite punchbag of every intercultural discussion), have on the other hand praised the ways in which these artists have been able to summarize the Indian experience within the confines of their respective expansive stage spaces and vocabularies.[4]

At the same time, however, intercultural performance was a way for artists specializing in Pavis's "superior bowl" of source culture to exploit a global marketplace for their art form.[5] Schechner references some instances of showcasing Eastern cultural artifacts in the West under the aegis of the intercultural project.[6] He did not seem to be cognizant, at the time, of the economic forces at play facilitating such cultural exchanges. The intercultural project, albeit controversial, sometimes allowed non-Western artists to earn coveted and elusive dollars to complement the meager institutional or private support received at home. The interest of Western enthusiasts in a particular form often determined the extent and length of support that an artist or an art form received.

This chapter, however, is not an attempt to indict traditional artists or theatremakers from the 1980s and 1990s in India who responded enthusiastically to Western demands for an exotic presentation of India. Neither is it a survey of intracultural theatre that the intercultural project generated, which created a modernized and hackneyed mélange of multiple traditional art forms repackaged for the global performance market. Similar practices continue to exist and flourish in several Indian cities under the guise of innovative performance practice, "Indian theatre," often characterized as a reinvention of classics which continue to tour internationally earning misplaced praise from Western orientalists who marvel at the spectacle but seldom delve into the philosophies of the imbibed performance forms thrown hastily together in response to a neoliberal marketplace which India entered after 1991. All of the above are extremely important and relevant points of enquiry, but ones that are not the purpose of the present exercise.

This chapter is an investigation of the Bengali group theatre, a performance culture in India, and how it has drawn, and continues to draw, inspiration from Western theatre and culture to inform its core. I argue that the Bengali group theatre, centered on Kolkata in eastern India, owes its existence and sustenance to a regular influx of Western inspiration. I will demonstrate that every significant development in the history of this largely urban theatre phenomenon both before and after Indian independence in 1947 was instigated by the infusion of a foreign cultural influence which was embraced and celebrated wholeheartedly by local practitioners.

My purpose is not to challenge the premise that interculturalism as a performative phenomenon is not hegemonic. Patrice Pavis's "inferior bowl" of the target culture in his hourglass structure of cultural transmission recognizes the hegemony of the process, albeit as an excuse for the unbridled borrowing from the East by the West.[7] Pavis's structure for cultural transfer, however, discounts the socio-cultural hegemony that the West and Western artists bring to the equation during cultural exchanges. His mischaracterization of the self-effacing inferior bowl obfuscates the misuse and misappropriation of cultural artifacts that has been questioned by critiques of intercultural projects. My aspiration, however, is to nuance and substantiate the conversation on interculturalism by demonstrating that the phenomenon is a two-way street. This street is fraught with hazards on either side, especially when the appropriating culture does not understand nor try to understand the source culture adequately. The resulting conversation peels back more layers and allows a deeper insight into the intercultural phenomenon and reveals how it was always already a tool substantiating the Western claim to be not only the center of global culture but the savior of non-Western traditions from ignominy.

This chapter is a dialogue that examines intercultural theatre exchange from one of the "sources" of artifacts: India. I do not attempt the impossible of investigating the entirety of contemporary Indian theatre practice to tease out elements of intercultural theatre exchange that has informed so much of contemporary performance practice in India. Instead, I look closely at one of India's most consistent contemporary theatre cultures—the Bengali group theatre. After an initial survey of the group theatre to elucidate the frequent intercultural exchanges that informed its creation, development, and continued repertory, I attempt a deep dive into the work of one of this theatre's most well-known practitioners, the playwright-actor-manager Badal Sircar. I will demonstrate, by looking at Sircar's development as a theatre artist, his emergence as one of India's leading experimental practitioners, and the eventual failure of his form of theatre, that his oeuvre and its genesis was largely dependent on his cursory second-hand exploration of traditional Indian performance practice via his interactions with Western theatre practitioners. Sircar's approach to creating his brand of performance is in a vein that is typical of a vast array of intercultural theatre exchanges. Sircar's style, I argue, never emerges into its own as a consequence of the careless intercultural experiments which characterized his core theatrical practices. And although venerated by some contemporary practitioners as groundbreaking, his Third Theatre has failed to have a lasting impact on Indian theatre beyond token inclusion in academic studies as an experimental curiosity.

It is tempting to evaluate Sircar and his work within the discourses of postcolonialism. Postcolonial theory, however, as Erica Fischer-Lichte explains, has always been more interested in the political rather than the aesthetic experience of a cultural work.[8] The aesthetic dimension, Fischer-Lichte explains, has been evaluated under the aegis of "intercultural" performance.[9] As I hope to demonstrate in this chapter, Sircar's theatrical oeuvre was always more of an aesthetic journey to find a form that would distinguish him as a genius. His cursory understanding of traditional Indian performance and willingness to forcibly incorporate elements of traditional art forms to simply plug gaps in his own theatre is a reminder of similar creative processes in the West. Sircar's use of non-traditional performance spaces and his clarion call to the masses to join a procession are examples of a bourgeois adventurist politics bereft of the concerns of being a postcolonial subject. His concern for the aesthetic over the political and his penchant for learning and adapting what was essentially a Western take on what they imagined to be "Indian" make Sircar and his work a perfect topic for an intercultural rather than a postcolonial evaluation. While Sircar is the specific case study under scrutiny in this chapter because of the ways in which he has been identified and deified in contemporary theatre scholarship as a maverick, his lack of political investment and the tendency to regurgitate Western material can be discerned more widely in much of Bengali group theatre, making it an excellent subject to inaugurate new conversations on the state of intercultural performance in a neoliberal world.

BENGALI THEATRE'S COLONIAL ORIGINS AND REVOLUTIONARY INFLUENCES

The practices of Bengali group theatres from Kolkata, eastern India, are arguably one of the greatest drivers of India's active contemporary theatre culture. Performance companies, largely amateur in structure, calling themselves groups, produce and perform plays on shoestring budgets throughout the year in the dozen or so performance venues of Kolkata and its suburbs. Group theatre is distinct from the several indigenous performance forms that originate in the rural hinterlands of west Bengal and is essentially urban in nature. The group theatre often integrates indigenous performance vocabulary into its performative structure while retaining its urban character. Its plays embody a very particular kind of neoliberal aesthetic that celebrates the proscenium stage and a cerebral acting school of performance. The roots of the Kolkata-based group theatre culture's bias towards the formal Western structures of performance can be traced to the colonial character of the region's earliest theatre history, dating back to the late eighteenth century.

The Kolkata *nouveau riche* were inspired by the colonial entertainment of the British settlers to start experimenting with European style theatre. Arguably, the first Bengali proscenium style performance was heralded by a European, Herasim Steppanovich Lebedeff (1749–1817). A native of St. Petersburg, Russia, and a self-taught violinist, Lebedeff found his way to India with an English band. He first arrived in Chennai (erstwhile Madras). A linguist at heart, Lebedeff wanted to learn Sanskrit, a language that the conservative Brahmins from southern India wouldn't teach him. He eventually made his way to Bengal where he found the language teacher that he was looking for, who not only taught him Sanskrit, but also instructed him in Bengali.[10] The same language teacher, Babu Golak Nath Dass, inspired Lebedeff to "present [his] play publicly."[11] The plays themselves were Bengali-language translations of a Moliere and a little-known English play, *The Disguise*. At its very inception, then, "modern" Bengali theatre aimed at creating a *desi* version of a foreign original. The performative style thus inaugurated continued into the early days of the Kolkata theatre and has bled into its modern-day iterations as well.

A brief hiatus followed Lebedeff's early experiments with introducing the Bengali language to the proscenium theatre and using it as a conduit for modern dramatic thought. When Bengalis finally picked up the idea of the proscenium-style theatre, they did so by emulating some of the finest British theatres in Kolkata. Brajendranath Bandyopadhyay credits the colonial education system, which had introduced the middle class in Kolkata to British literature, as the impetus for creating a colonial style theatre for the "pleasure of all classes of society."[12] In separate studies, Bandyopadhyay, Lal, and Chaudhuri have also traced the reception of the colonial import that had the most influential impact on the Bengali theatre enthusiast during these early days of theatre—William Shakespeare.[13] With Bengali dramatic writing still in its infancy, the Bengali theatre enthusiast found a treasure trove in Shakespeare. Translations of the Bard's work, which is too broad and too well documented a phenomenon to be regurgitated here, formed a staple of the early Bengali theatre corpus. It is evident then, that in spite of being a distinctive and unique performance form in its own right, Bengali proscenium theatre owed not only its existence but also a substantial portion of its creative output to borrowed content from European originals. Bengali theatre, it can therefore be argued and substantiated, is an intercultural exercise of mixing and matching cultures—European style with a Bengali aesthetic, and Shakespearean content with an Indian delivery system.

The modernist playwright Rabindranath Tagore (1861–1941) is possibly an exception to this rule, in that his style, while embodying Western principles, went beyond those limits in fiercely exerting its own originality. Bengal's most celebrated literary icon and India's national poet, Tagore was no less a theatre enthusiast. And being the creative genius that he was, he went on to revolutionize Bengali dramatic writing with his original approach. It is unfortunate, however, that most of Tagore's theatrical creation was not widely accepted by Bengali theatre aficionados. Critics, both in the West and in India, have spent a lot of time trying to pin a Western critical trajectory onto Tagore's work but as Lal observed, Tagore's "characteristic plays come across as entirely Indian" and are undoubtedly "the exclusive product of an Indian genius."[14] I am tempted to surmise that theatremakers, during Tagore's lifetime, were unable to assess and appreciate his work because there was no available Western reference for them to evaluate the work against. This is perhaps also why critics aiming an appraisal of Tagore sought to draw parallels between Western dramatists and Tagore rather than evaluating his work simply on its own merits. More recently, some of Tagore's plays have found a home in the Bengali theatre repertoire, but his contemporary theatrical homecoming has been rife with domestic trouble and misunderstanding, a result of the lackadaisical approach to Tagore and his critical insight into theatre over time.[15]

Contemporary Bengali theatre—the kind that one can see in Kolkata today—is a twentieth-century phenomenon. This theatre stemmed from the ruins of a progressive sociocultural movement that emerged in the early twentieth century paralleling the nascent communist movement in India. The Communist Party of India (henceforth CPI) was seen as suspect by the British colonial administration, particularly in light of the CPI's initial denunciation of the Second World War as an imperialist war, and was wary that its Indian cadre might attempt to overthrow British rule in India while the government was focused on managing the European war effort. In an effort to quell any hint of insurgence, British administrators orchestrated a concerted effort to delegitimize and vilify the CPI, ultimately declaring it illegal. In spite of the ban, progressive writers continued to gather under the aegis of left-leaning organizations in order to, as Bharucha so enthusiastically puts it, "abandon those debased qualities of Indian literature that the Bengali theater exemplified so egregiously."[16] Bharucha's passion for the cause was reflected in the fact that a short time later, these same writers created the Indian Peoples' Theatre Association (henceforth IPTA), realizing the "potential of popular theater as an effective weapon in the fight for national liberation from British imperialism and fascism, and in the struggles of peasants, workers, and other oppressed classes."[17] The IPTA began functioning as the cultural wing of the CPI, although the organization was officially identified as the cultural front of a different progressive organization to avoid a crackdown by the colonial authorities.

IPTA membership was drawn from a fairly wide socioeconomic spectrum. The group's stated objective was to create a pan-India people's theatre movement that aimed at raising artists' voices against the present rulers of the country.[18] The organization aimed at revitalizing the stage by creating socially conscious theatre and promoting traditional arts. Towards this end, members of the group began a concerted effort to study and understand folk and traditional art forms from various parts of India. Irrespective of these lofty intentions, however, IPTA was an urban phenomenon and somewhat divorced from the vast Indian hinterlands. And in accordance with the purposes of the present discussion, the immediate inspiration for IPTA was not homegrown but—like its governing ideology of communism—a foreign import.

Darshan Chowdhury notes that the immediate influences on and inspiration behind the formation of the IPTA were several left-leaning sociocultural organizations from across the world. He offers a detailed analysis of the styles and methods of several of these organizations including the Peoples' Theatre from Soviet Russia, the Chinese Peoples' Theatre, and Romain Rolland's The People's Theatre.[19] Chowdhury's claims are corroborated by Khawaja Ahmad Abbas, a progressive writer during the 1940s. Abbas also adds the Little Theatre Groups from England and the WPA theatres from the United States as influences on the creation of the IPTA. Not unlike their Russian and Chinese counterparts, the Indian communists imagined the cultural front as playing a part in bringing about social change in the country. Like the Russian Peoples' Theatre, IPTA members created compact plays that were easily transportable to the remotest corners of the vast subcontinent. Like the Chinese Peoples' Theatre, the IPTA cadre took the message of communism as a friend of the poor to the general population, all the while raising awareness of the perils of foreign occupation, imperialism, and the political mainstream's ineptitude and indifference to the suffering of the masses.

But in spite of its progressive message, liberal agenda, and concerted opposition to the decadence of the Bengali commercial stage, the IPTA brand of theatre was essentially a foreign import repackaged for consumption in India. From the initial days of the progressive theatre movement, the political forces had treated its artists as peripheral to the communist cause, often questioning the artists' allegiance to and understanding of communist ideology.[20] The political problems intensified in the immediate aftermath of the Indian independence in 1947, when the federal government adopted the stance of the departed colonial administration in viewing the CPI and its sympathizers with suspicion.[21]

THE NEW THEATRE AND CONSOLIDATION OF BENGALI THEATRE AS AN INTERCULTURAL EXERCISE

The Bengal branch of the IPTA, arguably one of its most active units, disintegrated in March 1948 under the pressure of concerted attacks on the CPI by the Indian

National Congress-led federal government. A little more than a month later in May 1948, Shombhu Mitra, erstwhile senior member of the Bengal IPTA, launched an independent performance company, Bohurupee, ushering in the New Theatre movement. The New Theatre movement (which eventually would became the group theatre movement) was a hybrid blend of colonial performance aesthetics, with its characteristic decadence, and a progressive performance vocabulary that is minimalistic and message-driven. Even though both styles that individually informed and led to Bengali group theatre were revolutionary in their own right, they were nevertheless foreign. This exercise of borrowing and drawing inspiration from cultural elements that are not necessarily indigenous is an intercultural exercise. And Bengali theatre from its earliest history has embraced it wholeheartedly. The period since 1948 has witnessed Bohurupee splintering into multiple smaller groups, with these groups generating a steady output of performances in Kolkata and its suburbs. It is interesting, however, that even in the last seven decades, each period of new development in the Bengali theatre is inspired by imbibing an international style into its ever-expanding toolkit.

Shombhu Mitra's Bohurupee inaugurated the Bengali New Theatre movement by staging Tagore and Sanskrit classical plays. Mitra was decidedly more interested in the aesthetics of performance rather than its political purposes. His choice of plays in the initial days of the New Theatre movement that he was inaugurating is proof of his interest in exploring a large variety of performance styles for his creative purposes. Incidentally, both Tagore's and Sanskrit theatrical treatises do not require elaborate stage design and champion an aesthetic of minimalism. Tagore goes a step forward, as Aparna Dharwadker reminds us, and compares dramatic performance to an "uxorious husband" to the "loyal wife" of the poetry.[22] It is interesting, therefore, that Mitra would inaugurate this distinctive urban theatre journey by appropriating texts that espouse an aesthetic contradicting his. Both *Raktakarabi* and *Mrchhakatika* are remembered today by theatre folklorists in Kolkata not only for the histrionics on display but also their scenic elements. Mitra's insistence on forcing a classical system onto a contemporary theatrical language is also evident in his acceptance of the Sangeet Natak Akademi's (India's government-run performing arts academy) designation as a guru when the institution began soliciting and disbursing stipends to sustain trainee performers. Under the government's scheme, trainee artists could apply for institutional fellowships to be mentored by an expert teacher who was referred to as the guru. The guru in the traditional sense of the term is one who not only controls the intellectual pursuits of a pupil but also exerts considerable control over his/her person—an approach to performance training that is a perhaps too much at variance with modern performance culture.

Mitra's group also inaugurated the practice of bringing the best (and occasionally the random) from world theatre to the local stage through the reimagining and staging of Western classics. Their celebrated productions of Western plays included Bengali-language adaptations of Henrik Ibsen's *A Doll House* and *An Enemy of the People* and Sophocles' *Oedipus Rex*. Mitra was also at the helm of a Kolkata team that collaborated with the German director Fritz Bennewitz on a Bengali-language adaptation of Brecht's *The Life of Galileo*, including a critically acclaimed portrayal of Galileo by Mitra himself.

Following closely on the heels of Bohurupee, several groups that either splintered from Mitra's team or from a team that had already separated itself from this "parent" organization began crowding the parallel Kolkata theatre circles. Notable among them is the group Nandikar, which until recently was celebrated in the city for its fondly remembered adaptations of Luigi Pirandello, Bertolt Brecht, and Anton Chekhov. The same holds true for Chetana, another one of the old vanguard of Kolkata-based theatre. Even when the content was locally sourced, as in the case of the Anya Theatre production of *Madhab Malanchi Kainya*, the stylistic choices remained consistently foreign in inspiration. Even the most prolific and eclectic among Bengali playwrights, Mohit Chattopadhyay and Utpal Dutt, frequently drew inspiration from literary predecessors in the Euro-American traditions, as discussed by Dharwadker amongst others.

More recently, and especially in the last decade or so, more Bengali group theatres have turned to sharing and telling homegrown stories. The shift is a result perhaps of the ease with which not only foreign plays but foreign travel has become accessible to Bengali directors and actor-managers. The exposure to international theatres and the latest in theatre design, tech, and use of space has found its way into contemporary Bengali theatre, albeit at a much lower production value. Among the steady stream of foreign imports that has had a telling impact on contemporary Bengali theatre performance is avant-garde and anti-establishment theatre introduced, performed, and promoted by Badal Sircar (1925–2011).

BADAL SIRCAR AND THE SHORTCOMINGS OF BENGALI INTRA-INTERCULTURALISM

Badal Sircar was born on July 15, 1925 in Kolkata in what Anjum Katyal has called a "middle middle-class" family.[23] Sircar was a voracious reader, especially of plays, particularly comedies. Katyal calls his insatiable reading of Bengali plays and his addiction to radio plays the seeds that sowed a lifelong love for the theatre in the young Sircar. Manujendra Kundu, in his critical assessment of Sircar's work, reminds us that the studious Sircar was an introvert and suffered from an inferiority complex that also affected his participation in the theatre.[24] Sircar blames his middle-class status as well as the psychological pressure from the society around him for not pursuing theatre even during his college days.[25] Sircar and his friends grappled with political ideologies and found it hard to find one that appealed to them. Sircar, Kundu tells us, blamed himself later in life for his youthful callousness and nonchalance about both local and global events.[26] Sircar moved briefly to Maharashtra in western India to work as an apprentice engineer, where he found a refuge in the local CPI office and began to frequent it. He was in Maharashtra when India became independent in 1947. Upon his return to Kolkata, Sircar started work as a college professor and became an active member of the CPI, holding several local leadership positions. When the party was declared illegal in 1948 by the Congress government, Sircar was able to fly under the radar and continued working in minor capacities.

Sircar's disillusionment with the CPI leadership and their commitment to communist ideology continued to haunt the young engineer. He discovered the British town planner Thomas Sharpe's celebrated 1940 book *Town Planning* shortly after moving into relatively comfortable government housing in central Kolkata. This chance development was to change the course of his life, beginning with his enrollment on a two-year diploma in town planning at his alma mater, B. E. College (Bengal Engineering College, now the Indian Institute of Engineering, Science, and Technology). Sircar followed this up with another two-year course on town planning at University College London in 1957.[27] His time in London, as recorded by Sircar himself, and as discussed by Kundu, seems to have had a decisive effect on his continued but little-explored interest in theatre. Sircar used his meager resources to regularly watch the stalwarts of the British stage while in the British capital. He did not particularly care for musical comedy, but seemed to have taken a liking for American domestic realism, reporting that Eugene O'Neill's *Long Day's Journey into Night* particularly moved him.[28]

Upon his return to India in 1959, Sircar joined the Calcutta Municipal Corporation as a valuer and surveyor. The most important episode, however, during this period of transition was the advent of a group called Chakra. This was a cultural group that got together on Saturdays to discuss anything to their liking. Invariably, due to Sircar's presence, the group would present plays. *Boro Pisima* (Elder Paternal Aunt), a play that Sircar wrote in April 1959, was the first presentation from the group. Very soon they started getting invited to present Sircar's plays in a variety of venues. It was during this period of intense activity that Sircar created one of modern Indian theatre's greatest masterpieces, in 1963: the abstract, absurdist play *Ebong Indrajit* (And Indrajit). This landmark text was published with the young critic Samik Bandyopadhyay's assistance in the celebrated theatre journal *Bahurupi*, a publication of the Shambhu Mitra-led theatre group of the same name.

Sircar, however, was not one to be tied down with the name, fame, and attention that this play garnered across the nation. He took off for France in 1963 to realize a lifelong dream of visiting the country—and for a nine-month training course. Sircar's playwriting reached prolific proportions during his time in France and then later in Nigeria where he landed a job in Eunugu. In between, he visited Kolkata where he revived Chakra and held readings and staged some of his new work.

During this time, the theatre group Bohurupee signed an agreement with Sircar to exclusively stage his works. This arrangement continued until the late 1960s when he moved back to India after the Nigerian civil war broke out. Sircar, Kundu reminds us, had agreed to work with Bohurupee because he had felt that there was quite a lot to be learned from Shombhu Mitra, the patriarch of Bohurupee. And Bohurupee, for their part, although by now an acclaimed theatre group, lacked a steady resource for original material and Mitra had not failed to notice Sircar's genius in some of his early work. Kundu correctly assesses the contribution of Bohurupee and Shombhu Mitra in molding Sircar's early career by giving the young maverick playwright a steady platform to showcase his work on the national stage, even though the playwright occasionally disagreed with the dramaturgical interference of the group and its director.

Kundu notes that Sircar's own company, Satabdi, was created on August 29, 1967, although the initial iteration was short lived because Sircar closed it down due to what Kundu describes as "apathy and exasperation."[29] In spite of his national reputation as a playwright, Sircar does not appear to be settled as a performer in the years immediately preceding the establishment of Satabdi. He still seems to have been searching for a form that would be uniquely his, a form that would distinguish him as an artist. And yet he was unable to zero in on either a language or a performance idiom that was separate from the theatre that was playing around him. It was perhaps to give his search a new platform that Sircar gave up the steady performance platform that he had with Bohurupee and created Satabdi, a venture that didn't satisfy him to the extent that he might have hoped for.

At the time of Satabdi's creation, however, Sircar was already an important name in the national theatre scene thanks to *Ebong Indrajit* (And Indrajit). The exposure and fame that this work accorded him led to his being selected to participate in a government-sponsored cultural tour of the USSR and Eastern Europe. Sircar recalls that during the tour he saw "Yuri Lyubimov's productions of *The Good Person of Szechwan, Galileo, Ten Days That Shook the World,* and the rehearsals of *Mother* at the Taganka Theatre in Moscow."[30] In addition, he was also exposed to Jari's pantomime and the work of the Činoherní klub in Prague and the work and philosophy of Jerzy Grotowski. These experiences would all have a profound influence on his ultimate formulation of the Third Theatre.

Back in Kolkata, Sircar staged three of his proscenium plays with a rejuvenated Satabdi, though the productions still did not reflect his exposure to the avant-garde theatre he had witnessed abroad, except for a partial application of Grotowski's Poor Theatre. Based on Sircar's own observations on these early experiments, Kundu concludes that his use of the Grotowskian approach to theatre allowed Sircar to make his theatre vocabulary "inexpensive" and take advantage of the perpetual penury of theatre groups in Kolkata.[31] At the same time, Kundu reminds us, Sircar was celebrating himself as a herald leading theatre practice in Kolkata in a hitherto unexplored direction—towards the Third Theatre.

In her laudatory appraisal of Sircar's work, Anjum Katyal paraphrases the latter's thought processes which led to the Third Theatre: "In a nutshell, there is a dichotomy between the existing rural, folk, traditional theatre (which is the First Theatre) and the Western-influenced, proscenium stage of the city theatre (which is the Second Theatre); his attempt is to explore the possibility of a synthesis between these two—a Third Theatre."[32] It is interesting that Sircar's hope and aspiration to synthesize the folk with the urban seems strikingly similar to the Western quest for the pure or the universal, which underlies much of the intercultural project. Even though set on a direction, Sircar felt that his training was inadequate to undertake this project singlehandedly.[33] Accordingly, he responded to an invitation from Richard Schechner, whom he had met in Kolkata in 1971, to visit New York and observe the work of Schechner's company, the Performance Group. Sircar left for New York in July 1972, and over the next several weeks watched several off-Broadway and off-off-Broadway performances, attended rehearsals of the Performance Group, met with avant-garde theatre artists Judith Malina and Julian Beck of the Living Theatre, visited UC Berkeley and Vancouver as a guest of the Performance Group, and learnt the work of the group and its leader Schechner from very close quarters.[34] But even before his visit to North America, Sircar and Satabdi had attended workshops led by Anthony Serchio, director of the La Mama theatre. This workshop introduced Sircar to the "cat series" set of exercises formulated by Grotowski. The international experiences of Sircar hint at the significance of imported and borrowed ideas in his theatrical vision, and he has mused on the importance of training in the classical arts, while observing the perseverance of the Performance Group and other North American avant-gardists working on acquiring the craft. Sircar saw a connection between Bharatanatyam and sitar training and that of the avant-gardists.[35] However, he didn't connect the dots to their deliberate study of traditional Indian theatre training, the rigor and strict regimen of which were an inspiration for the Schechners and the Grotowskis in crafting their Western-located robust, reclusive, and exclusive training routines.

Schechner found Sircar's interest in his methods of performance training to be the continuation or completion, as he called it, of an "interesting circle":[36] "Badal's use of the ideas and exercises he observed that summer completed a very interesting circle, because I had learned the core of those exercises from Grotowski, who had taken them, or adapted at least of them, from *kathakali*. I taught them to Sircar, who brought them back to Calcutta."[37] Schechner was undoubtedly thrilled at being able to equip an Indian theatre practitioner with the wherewithal and vocabulary of an Indian performance form. Yet, Schechner's exposure of Sircar to this performance form and training through his own Western lens seems to ultimately have had a pedagogical rather than a practical effect on Sircar and his work. Bharucha and Srampickal both seemed to have picked up on this grey area of Sircar's work, albeit with different levels of critical insight and engagement. Bharucha, while not belittling Sircar's stance, dubbed Sircar and Satabdi's frequent rural sojourns to stage their work as exercises in "self-depreciation and romanticization of rural life."[38] Srampickal's reports from the field, after noting what he felt were natural and folk connections in Sircar's work, record the observations of a young theatre enthusiast who is only able to appreciate the playwright's work from a distance. He also records Sircar's use of "abstract techniques" in his village workshops, which failed to connect with his audience.

Theatre director Heisnam Kanhailal attended Sircar's workshop in Imphal after the playwright had returned from his North America trip, equipped with the latest techniques from the Schechner and Grotowski toolsheds, in 1972 and then again in 1973. Kanhailal reminisces that Sircar's emphasis on breaking "urban sophistication," and his use of games like "mirroring" and "blind" were learnt from foreign teachers who had in turn appropriated these techniques from other cultures.[39] These issues, Kanhailal opines, were not particularly relevant to Manipur and its theatre enthusiasts, many of whom were not plagued by urbanity and sophistication. Sircar's games were also only too familiar to the Manipuris whose indigenous cultures had always had versions of these exercises in its active social repertoire. Kundu chronicles several other episodes from Sircar's workshops in the Sunderban hinterlands as well as his work with prostitutes in Kolkata's red-light district. Such episodes, Kundu argues from anecdotal evidence, revealed Sircar's "urban sophistication," his inability to communicate with the masses, and his imposition of a top-down, largely foreign theatre training regimen.

While unabashedly acknowledging that he had spent little time learning about Indian folk and traditional performance,[40] Sircar was still ready to criticize these practices as "backward" despite occasionally borrowing material from the myriad folk theatre vocabularies for use in his own work.[41] In his treatise on the Third Theatre, Sircar recognized that what he was proposing might have appeared to be "influenced by the experimental theatre of Europe and America" and that his sole purpose was to import such practices to India,[42] but based on his personal experience he contended that Western practitioners learned much from Indian folk theatre, while city bred theatre artists in Kolkata failed to make use of what was available to them—a treasure trove of source material. The truth, as Kundu painstakingly demonstrates, is that Sircar, like his city-bred brethren in the Kolkata theatre fraternity, knew next to nothing of traditional Indian performance and that these forms therefore did not affect his thinking about the Third Theatre in any significant way, despite his protests to the contrary.

Kundu draws on a number of excerpts and anecdotal references from the works of Schechner, Grotowski, Littlewood, and Lyubimov alongside Sircar's writing to demonstrate that these theatre thinkers, directors, and practitioners were the key influences that inspired Sircar to create his synthesized form of theatre.[43] In other words, Sircar adopted and infused practices that were hardly ever indigenous to his immediate surroundings to create a hybrid form that was primarily dependent on a consciously imported technique. Sircar's focus on Western models to inform his work was not a development that began with the Third Theatre. Even his most celebrated play, *Ebong Indrajit* (And Indrajit), which was first published in 1965, may have been influenced by Sircar's reading of contemporary Western lyrical playwrights during his time in London. The "absurdness" that was ascribed to this text by the directors who encountered the play supposedly prompted Sircar to investigate this style of playwriting. However, Sircar denied that this school of writing had any influence on this particular play. Kundu argues that the bourgeois, urban middle-class sentimentality, angst, and existentialism so palpable throughout *Ebong Indrajit* in fact reflects Sircar's own middle-class roots and upbringing. Even if it was directly influenced by Western dramaturgies of the Theatre of the Absurd in vogue at the time, *Ebong Indrajit* stands on its own merits, and this and Sircar's other theatrical works captured the imagination of theatremakers across India from the 1970s onwards. The point is, however, that Sircar's theatre was neither a rote Western imitation, nor unique or specific to his socioeconomic surroundings—it was an intercultural enterprise whose influence on the international evolution of this performance genre during the period in question has yet to be fully investigated or even acknowledged.

During a freewheeling interview, the noted theatre director Probir Guha from the Kolkata suburb of Madhyamgram elaborated on how theatre practices are shaped by region, food habits, climate, and upbringing. He suggested that a practice crafted for a sausage-eating, beer-guzzling German performer would fail to work on a rice-eating, tea-sipping Bengali and vice versa. Similarly, Guha continued, a performance practice with its roots in the soil and air of Purulia or Birbhum cannot be superimposed on the urban finesse of someone born and raised in Kolkata and vice versa. He opined that in spite of these differences it would be possible to facilitate cultural exchange between distant and disparate cultures, giving the example of his own theatre group's work with traditional art forms. In this case, actors are sent to the villages of Purulia and Birbhum to train in a traditional art form through a series of intensive workshops and then return the city to be submerged once again in the regular training regime of their own urban theatre practice. It is only after a month has passed that the performers are asked to recall certain physical actions from their experience in the villages several weeks earlier. Whatever their bodies and minds remember, Guha concluded, is what the intercultural exchange can facilitate and no more. A top-down imposition of a regimented intercultural practice, like the one Sircar imported from his tryst with Western avant-gardists, institutionalizes an imbalanced cultural transformation but doesn't facilitate an exchange. Like Bharucha, I believe in the possibilities of intercultural exchange,[44] but the exchange should be such that it opens up spaces for exploration and dialogue rather than create abstract and exclusive silos for artistic practice, like the ones that Sircar's blind copying of Western practices seems to have spawned.

As this chapter argues and demonstrates, cultural appropriation is not simply a Western tactic to incorporate Eastern performance aesthetics into its performance vocabulary. It is equally about practitioners from the Global South misappropriating non-local art practices. Interrogating this parallel version of intercultural practice gives us a deeper critical insight into intercultural performance practice and aesthetics and the ways in which it guarantees Western hegemonic ideas of cultural superiority. The Kolkata-based Bengali proscenium theatre developed primarily under British influence and, in order to emulate British performance, has continued to sustain and enrich itself with creative content and critical input from a Western performance vocabulary, often only after very brief encounters with the same. This pattern of intercultural exchange replicates the cultural appropriation of the West-to-East exchanges of previous centuries. The uncritical celebration of "Occidentalism," however, and especially in this case, reinforces the status quo by accepting rather than challenging the cultural hegemony of the West.

Badal Sircar, one of Kolkata theatre's most celebrated artists, was a wholehearted votary of this form of cultural exchange and built his legacy by appropriating Western theatrical idioms and imposing them on an Indian milieu. In his experiments, Sircar's theatre never became the symbiotic Third Theatre that he envisaged—one that embodied both the rural and the Westernized urban Indian theatre. With his very urban concerns, and his very urban training both in India and abroad in both political ideology and performance practice, Sircar was never able to move beyond his urban sophistication and its reliance on Western practices as the blueprint for theatrical advancement. Consequently, his plays (which did not lack dramatic merit but were not ideologically or stylistically original) remained urban in their effect and purpose. Sircar and his group toured around Bengal extensively and were received enthusiastically by theatregoers and the masses alike, perhaps in the same vein that Bharucha believes a young boy masquerading as Rama in Brooklyn would find himself—an "alien exhibit."[45]

The failure of Sircar to include the "life of Bengal" in his theatre—which Bharucha was too soon to pronounce as its distinguishing characteristic—is perhaps the reason that his brand of theatre lost its appeal in the early 1990s.[46] Based on an astute study of Sircar's autobiography and anecdotes from erstwhile group members and Sircar's former wife, Kundu concludes that Sircar became a celebrity and a phenomenon unto himself. The institutionalization of what was supposed to be an egalitarian effort further alienated the Third Theatre and its grassroots practitioners from its fountainhead—Badal Sircar.[47] I would also like to emphasize that the style and philosophy of the Third Theatre, largely as a result of careless ideological transfer from the West, became dated and static, not unlike similar imports in the history of the Kolkata-based Bengali theatre. The Third Theatre today wears a jaded, tired, and hackneyed look, as witnessed by the author during a performance of Sircar's *Hattamelar Opare* (Beyond the Land of Hattamala) in 2012 by Satabdi. Sircar's former colleagues have remained steadfast in their adherence to the minimalism, choreography, and interactive style that became the trademarks of Sircar's theatre, but the play seemed distant and irrelevant, with its content unchanged to reflect contemporary times—a mere relic of a revered theatre form rather than a living political entity. In many ways it recalled Peter Brook's *Battlefield*, a sad reminder of what might have been a formidable theatrical intervention to facilitate purposeful cultural exchange. The issues with intercultural performance persist, no matter which way (West to East; East to West) the borrowing is carried out, except when the cultural barter is carefully nuanced and negotiated. And while Western hegemony ensures that orientalism, be it in the form of the colonial enterprise or the more liberal intercultural theatre, can be a viable career option, occidentalism, as seen in the case of Bengali theatre and specifically Badal Sircar's Third Theatre, leads to a staid phenomenon better suited to theoretical reflection rather than actual practice.

STALE OLD WINE IN A NEW BOTTLE, OR SOME CONCLUDING THOUGHTS

Royona Mitra locates the genesis of Akram Khan's choreography during the time when cultural diversity was being encouraged in British society.[48] Mitra considers Khan's evolving choreography to be part of his formative training in *kathak*, the South Asian classical dance form, and his formal training in modern dance. The resulting new interculturalism that Mitra claims for Khan's work showcases a socio-politically dynamic aesthetic that celebrates cultural similarities without discounting differences. Mitra regards Khan's choreographic aesthetic as a critical intervention that dislodges what Una Chaudhuri has called "the handful of works and artists that have occupied interculturalism's center stage."[49] Her identification of the points that set Khan's work apart from what she calls the "predominantly white, Western project of intercultural theatre" is central to understanding where Mitra places Khan, that is, both inside and yet outside the intercultural spectrum and therefore heralding a new interculaturalism.[50] Mitra cites Khan's embodied experience of being an insider-outsider to multiple cultural milieus, his personal and embodied starting points for his works (which make the works more accessible while not threatening the source culture), and the "ambivalent and ephemeral" quality of his aesthetic as the distinguishing qualities of his work.

When seen in the critical light that Mitra has shed on Khan and his role in the evolution of a new British dance aesthetic, the shortcomings of the intercultural in Sircar's work in late-twentieth-century Bengal become even more evident. Khan's choreography offers a bold new vision of what British modern dance should be like in an increasingly diverse nation. It is a new product that combines the best of several worlds and yet doesn't owe its allegiance to any one of them. Sircar, on the other hand, bought into a white, Western project of interacting with Eastern cultural artifacts. He adopted the broad based, essentialized (and therefore reductive) Western view of India into the body of his work, inaugurating in the process a theatre that was a domestic version of an occidental project. The always already intercultural environment of the Bengali theatre welcomed Sircar's intervention as an experimental innovator, but once the novelty wore off, the politically bereft cultural commodity that was his work was relegated to the sidelines since it could not evolve beyond its immediate context. Ultimately, Khan's work is political and is as unabashedly South Asian as it is British, thus exposing what Mitra sees as a multilayered version of his self as the new intercultural subject beyond the narrow definition of cultural appropriation and the constraints of the postcolonial. And it is here that Sircar in particular and Bengali group theatre in general have very often floundered—failing to distinguish themselves from the way the West wants us to imagine ourselves and to imagine something new instead.

NOTES

1. Rustom Bharucha, "A Collision of Cultures: Some Western Interpretations of the Indian Theatre," *Asian Theatre Journal* 1, no. 1 (Spring 1984): 1.

2. Rustom Bharucha, "A Reply to Richard Schechner," *Asian Theatre Journal* 1, no. 2 (Autumn 1984): 260.

3. Richard Schechner, "A Reply to Rustom Bharucha," *Asian Theatre Journal* 1, no. 2 (Autumn 1984): 252.

4. David Williams, *Collaborative Theatre: Le Théâtre du Soleil* (New York: Taylor and Francis, 1998); Patrice Pavis, *Theatre at the Crossroads of Culture* (New York: Routledge, 1992).

5. Pavis, *Theatre at the Crossroads of Culture*, 180.

6. Schechner, "A Reply to Rustom Bharucha," 251.

7. Pavis, *Theatre at the Crossroads of Culture*, 180.

8. Erika Fischer-Lichte, "Introduction: Interweaving Performance Cultures—Rethinking 'Intercultural Theatre': Toward an Experience and Theory of Performance beyond Postcolonialism," in Erika Fischer-Lichte, Torsten Jost, and Saskya Iris Jain (eds.), *The Politics of Interweaving Performance Cultures: Beyond Postcolonialism* (New York: Routledge, 2014), 15.

9. Fischer-Lichte, "Introduction: Interweaving Performance Cultures," 15.

10. Balwant Gargi, *Theatre in India* (New York: Theatre Arts Books, 1962), 108.

11. Sushil Kumar Mukherjee, *The Story of the Calcutta Theatres: 1753–1980* (Calcutta: K.P. Bagchi and Company, 1982), 8.

12. Brajendranath Bandyopadhyay, *Bangiya Natyasalar Itihas: 1795–1876* (Calcutta: Bangiya Sahitya Parishad, 1998), 7.

13. See Bandyopadhyay, *Bangiya Natyasalar Itihas*, and Ananda Lal and Sakunta Chaudhuri (eds.), *Shakespeare on the Calcutta Stage: A Checklist* (Kolkata: Papyrus, 2001).

14. Ananda Lal, *Three Plays* (New Dehli: Oxford University Press, 2001), 6.

15. I am reminded of the 2012 adaptation of Tagore's *Bisarjan* by Suman Mukhopadhyay. While the adaptation boasted some extraordinary performances and had a compelling design to complement the performance, the performance itself, I felt, became an artistic vehicle more than a political statement. The same can be said about the 2004–5 Rangroop production of Tagore's romantic comedy *Sesh Raksha*. While talking about Tagore on the contemporary Bengali stage, most commentators celebrate Bohurupee's commercially successful Tagore adaptations, particularly the 1954 staging of *Rakta Karabi*.

16. Rustom Bharucha, *Rehearsals of Revolution: The Political Theater of Bengal* (Honolulu: University of Hawaii Press, 1983), 34–5.

17. Nandi Bhatia, "Staging Resistance: The Indian People's Theatre Association," in Lisa Lowe and David Lloyd (eds.), *The Politics of Culture in the Shadow of Capital* (Durham, NC, and London: Duke University Press, 1997), 432.

18. Zohra Segal, "Theatre and Activism in the 1940s," in Geeti Sen (ed.), *Crossing Boundaries* (Hyderabad: Orient Longman, 1997), 31.

19. Darshan Chowdhury, *Gananatya Andolan* (Calcutta: Anustup, 1982).

20. Chowdhury, *Gananatya Andolan*, 290–3.

21. Chowdhury, *Gananatya Andolan*, 290.

22. Aparna Bhargava Dharwadker, *Theatres of Independence: Drama, Theory, and Urban Performance in India since 1947* (Iowa City: University of Iowa Press, 2005), 58.

23. Anjum Katyal, *Badal Sircar: Towards a Theatre of Conscience* (New Delhi: Sage Publications, 2015), 1.

24. Manujendra Kundu, *So Near, Yet So Far* (New Delhi: Oxford University Press, 2016), 63.

25. Badal Sircar, *Purano Kasundi* (Calcutta: Lekhani, 2006), 73.

26. Kundu, *So Near, Yet So Far*, 64.

27. Sircar, *Purano Kasundi*, 187.

28. Sircar, *Purano Kasundi*, 71.

29. Sircar, *Purano Kasundi*, 76.

30. Sircar, *Purano Kasundi*, 124.

31. Sircar, *Purano Kasundi*, 124.

32. Katyal, *Badal Sircar*, 130.

33. Badal Sircar, *On Theatre* (Kolkata: Seagull Books, 2009), 25.

34. Sircar, *On Theatre*, 25–9.

35. Sircar, *On Theatre*, 29.

36. Cobina Gillitt, "Richard Schechner," *Asian Theatre Journal* 30, no. 2 (Fall 2013): 282.

37. Schechner, "A Reply to Rustom Bharucha," 282.

38. Rustom Bharucha, *Theatre and the World: Performance and the Politics of Culture* (New Delhi: Manohar, 1990), 305.

39. Kundu, *So Near, Yet So Far*, 137.

40. Kundu, *So Near, Yet So Far*, 212.

41. Kundu, *So Near, Yet So Far*, 213.

42. Sircar, *On Theatre*, 17.

43. Katyal, *Badal Sircar*, 220–4.

44. Bharucha, "A Collision of Cultures," 3.

45. Bharucha, "A Reply to Richard Schechner," 258.

46. Bharucha, "A Reply to Richard Schechner," 258.

47. Kundu, *So Near, Yet So Far*, 247–59.

48. Royona Mitra, *Akram Khan: Dancing New Interculturalism* (New York: Palgrave Macmillan, 2015), 16.

49. Una Chaudhuri, "Beyond a 'Taxonomic Theater': Interculturalism after Postcolonialism and Globalization," *Theater* 32, no. 1 (Winter 2002): 34.

50. Mitra, *Akram Khan*, 23.

PART TWO

Networking New Interculturalisms

Decentering Asian Shakespeare: Approaching Intercultural Theatre as a Living Organism

BI-QI BEATRICE LEI

The general conception of Asian Shakespeare, and by extension global Shakespeare, has been predominantly Anglocentric: Shakespeare's plays travel from London to various parts of Asia in a centrifugal motion, and Asian languages, theatres, and aesthetics join Shakespearean performance in a centripetal motion. Intercultural exchange is thus perceived to be binary, between the Shakespearean origin and a target Asian theatre, both fixed cultural entities. *Kabuki Twelfth Night*, *jingju Macbeth*, and *kathakali Othello*, among others, are compared to their sources, and their transformation of Shakespeare is judged to be reducing or enhancing, embellishing or blemishing, more this or less that. Complementing this centrifugal approach to Asian productions is a centripetal gravitation, an inclination to register various theatres under the flag of Shakespeare. The revived Shakespeare's Globe aggressively promotes both agendas. The 2012 Globe to Globe Festival hosted thirty-seven productions, each Shakespearean title in a different language. To make it a round trip, on April 23, 2014, the 450th anniversary of Shakespeare's birth, Shakespeare's Globe launched a centrifugal global tour of *Hamlet* to 197 countries.

On the official website of this ambitious project, Peter Brook is cited under the subheading "Why Tour the World?":

> The six simplest words in the English language are "to be or not to be." There is hardly a corner of the planet where these words have not been translated. Even in English, those who can't speak the language will at once recognise the sound and exclaim "Shakespeare!" ... Everyone, young or old can today find an immediate identification with its characters, their pains and their interrogations.[1]

Expressed in superlatives and hyperbole, this barefaced Anglocentrism is quite typical in discourses on Asian or global Shakespeare. According to this logic, non-Western elements in an intercultural performance only serve to validate the alien but universal Bard. This explains why the discussion is often "*xiqu* Shakespeare" or "Noh Shakespeare," not "Shakespeare(an) *xiqu*" or "Shakespeare(an) Noh." From a binary and Anglocentric perspective, Asian theatre is merely a modifier, a performance style, and matter for the Platonic-Shakespearean form.

This chapter proposes to decenter Asian Shakespeare and to instead approach Asian theatres as living organisms. Many Asian theatres, especially non-elite genres, constantly update by incorporating new elements, be they thematic, formal, or technical. Even for a Shakespearean adaptation, Shakespeare's story and characters, dialogues and poetry, philosophy and sentiment, are among the many eclectic components that jointly create a whole. For theatre practitioners, anything that can make the show a success goes in, in whatever form it works best. Contrary to an Anglocentric mindset, performing Shakespeare in Asia does not necessarily suggest reverence, rivalry, or deliberate revision—Shakespeare does not always act as an authority to be obeyed or overthrown, or a center to turn to or away from. John Russell Brown started his inquiry into Shakespeare and Asian theatres with "how far shall we try to stage Shakespeare's plays as they were originally performed?"[2] This question, indeed, may never be raised.

This is not to deny the existence of canonical approaches to Shakespeare in Asia, by European colonizers and by locals, or consciously revisionary, anti-colonialist productions, but to affirm the vast variety beyond these categories. An organic hybrid Asian Shakespeare existed centuries ago, and remains vigorous today. In modern times, culture travels with unprecedented scope and speed via international festivals, films and television, and the internet. East–West binarism—visualized as Patrice Pavis's hourglass model—can hardly account for this vibrant network of cultural flow that goes in all directions.[3] In studying theatrical interculturalism, each community, each performance group, and each production must be treated as the subject, the center, so the full picture can be revealed.

This chapter does not propose to describe or theorize what Asian Shakespeare was, is, or should be. Instead, the goal is to falsify the predominant description and theorization, and to prove the impossibility of such an attempt. I will examine two contemporary examples—*Shakespeare: The Sky Filled with Eternal Words* by Japan's Takarazuka Revue and *A Midsummer Night's Dream* by Taiwan's Golden Bough Theatre—to illustrate decentered interculturalism in practice. Rather than a center of gravity, Shakespeare is one of the many nutrients that feed these organic performances—along with traditional operas, revues, Broadway-style musicals, pop songs, films, television, and circus, as well as mythology, history, folklore, *manga* and *anime*, and video games.

THE CENTRIFUGAL FALLACY

That Shakespeare came to Asia with Anglo-American colonization and imperialism is a fallacy, or at least an incomplete story. Above all, a unified Asia has never existed. On the one hand, the borders separating Asia from Europe, Africa, and Oceania are arbitrary and controversial. On the other hand, Asia encompasses an immensely different East Asia, Southeast Asia, South Asia, North Asia, Arabia, Central Asia, and West Asia. Over the past few centuries, different parts of Asia underwent varied colonial and imperial experiences. In addition to the British and the American, the non-Anglophone Dutch, Spanish, French, Portuguese, Russian, German, Italian, Austro-Hungarian, and Belgian powers each established colonies, trading posts, or concessions. Apparently, Shakespeare was not on their agendas. Shakespeare formally entered the curricula in areas directly or indirectly governed by the British and the American—the subcontinent, Malaya, Burma, Hong Kong, and the Philippines. But colonial indoctrination hardly extended past these locations. After all, the British East India Company's goal was primarily economic. When the doors to the vast Chinese market were forced open in the mid-nineteenth century, the company was plainly more interested in imposing opium upon the Chinese than Shakespeare.

In Southeast Asia, Shakespeare first arrived in Indonesia with Dutch merchants in 1619, and vernacular translation and performance in Malaya and the Philippines at the dawn of the twentieth century preceded Shakespeare's official appearance in colonial education.[4] Parallel to the canonical Shakespeare studied and performed in school, liberal adaptations in *bangsawan* theatre, a young operatic genre derived from India's Parsi theatre, were popular in Malaya. Heavily improvised and tailored to local tastes, *bangsawan* freely borrowed stories of European, Indian, Chinese, Arab, and Malay origins, and featured melodrama, hybrid music, elaborate costumes and sets, spectacles, and topical allusions. Comedy and slapstick were the highlights of a performance, and the plot was secondary. Not only did *bangsawan* adopt stories from multiple origins, but the actors, musicians, and performance styles were also transnational and transcultural. When *bangsawan* troupes traveled from British Malaya to British Burma, Dutch-controlled Indonesia, the American Philippines, and independent Siam, they again mixed in local actors, styles, and audience preferences. A "mestizo form," *bangsawan* embodied cultural flow on all levels and in all directions.[5] Contrary to the Anglocentric assumptions, Shakespeare's text "was really of little consequence."[6]

A different scene emerged in the Far East. Western powers did not control Japan, China, and Korea directly, but starting in the late nineteenth century some intellectuals eagerly sought Western thought in the hope of strengthening their nations, peoples, and cultures.[7] Shakespeare—along with Jean-Jacques Rousseau, Charles de Montesquieu, John Stuart Mill, Charles Darwin, and Thomas Henry Huxley, among others—was foremost a thinker, figuring in historical, social, economic, legal, and political discussion. Few could read him in English, and vernacular translation existed only in fragments, such as Polonius's proverbial wisdom, Hamlet's "to be or not to be" soliloquy, and Brutus's forum speech in *Julius Caesar*. It was through the vernacular translation of Charles and Mary Lamb's *Tales from Shakespeare* that Shakespeare's stories and characters became widely known. Many early productions were based on vernacular versions of the *Tales*, not on Shakespeare's originals. However, these are translations broadly defined. Lin Shu, Shakespeare's Chinese popularizer, did not know English. He relied on an interpreter and rendered the stories into classical Chinese. His liberal rewriting departs immensely from the Lambs', and farther still from Shakespeare's originals. Lin's Hamlet and Ophelia, for example, are a married couple.[8] Japan initiated the canonical Shakespeare in East Asia: translating Shakespeare in full (by Tsubouchi

Shōyō, completed in 1927) and performing him in realist theatre, as opposed to traditional operatic theatres. Established in 1928, the Tsubouchi Memorial Theatre Museum of Waseda University was modeled on the Fortune Placehouse, with *Totus Mundus Agit Histrionem* ("All the World's a Stage" in Latin) inscribed on the front of the stage. Along with Japan's imperialist aggression, Bard fever spread to Korea and Taiwan. The first performances in Taiwan (1904) and Korea (1909) were both in Japanese, and the first Korean translation of Shakespeare (1922) was based on a Japanese translation.[9] Significantly, Japan did not just act like a British satellite or a transfer point for a centrifugal trip. Japan's Shakespearean export was both in Japanese and Japanized. *Osero*, an adaptation of *Othello* premiered in Tokyo in 1903 and staged in Taiwan the next year, depicts the title character from an outcast Japanese class who is appointed as Taiwan's colonial governor. More than linguistic, geographic, and historical transformation, the play also employs Japanese theatre's stock characters and topical allusions.[10] Set as the background for dramatic action, Taiwan was not merely the cultural receiver but also contributed to the play's design, music, and dance. Thus, instead of being shipped centrifugally from the London origin to an Asian destination in a carefully bubble-wrapped crate, Shakespeare has traversed through multiple, even circular routes. Shakespeare operates more like a cargo: along the journey some goods are sold, others bought, so he arrives at every port in a somewhat different shape.

THE CENTRIPETAL FALLACY

Asia's Shakespearean productions have frequented international arts festivals in recent decades. Productions using elements from Asia's performance traditions are particularly popular, such as Ninagawa Yukio's *Macbeth* at the Edinburgh International Festival, Wu Hsing-kuo's *The Kingdom of Desire* at the Avignon Festival and *King Lear* at the Sibiu International Theatre Festival, Ong Keng Sen's *Desdemona* at the Adelaide Festival, and Yang Jung-Ung's *A Midsummer Night's Dream* at the Globe to Globe Festival; all four Asian directors have also brought their works to London. While these productions differ from one another significantly, together they give the impression that Asian Shakespeare, and by extension Asian theatre, is largely high-profile, in period dress, with music and spectacles, and carrying serious cultural and intercultural agendas.

Festival productions, however, are only a small sampling of Asia's Shakespeare, and a very selective one at that. The majority of Asian performances, Shakespearean and otherwise, are targeted at local markets, of which only a fraction is occupied by traditional theatres. Across Asia, Shakespeare is performed in all styles, including realist Shakespeare in modern dress with no music, teen Shakespeare in rock and roll musicals, and avant-garde Shakespeare in experimental little theatres. The narrowly defined Asian Shakespeare has been largely shaped by the West: international festivals commission productions, which hew to the tastes of Western audiences, or invite those productions that meet Western expectations. Despite their outstanding quality, the best-known works of Asian Shakespeare can hardly do justice to the overall scene. Shakespeare has often served as a catalyst for theatrical interculturalism, but not necessarily between East and West. Ong Keng Sen's pan-Asian, multilingual productions are the most notable examples. In 2012, the National Theatre Company of China and the National Drama Company of Korea collaborated on a production of *Romeo and Juliet*, with a Chinese director Tian Qinxin and Korean actors, set during the Chinese Cultural Revolution. Most recently, in 2016, Taiwan's Our Theatre also collaborated with Ryuzanji Show, a Japanese director, on *Macbeth: Paint It Black!* Beyond the stage, Asia's Shakespeare spin-offs travel fluidly across Asia as popular music, films, television, graphic novels, and animation. An example is the Japanese *Civilization Blaster*, derived from *Hamlet* and *The Tempest*: the ten-volume *manga* version was translated into Chinese and published in Taiwan and Hong Kong, and the *anime* version was dubbed in Mandarin and aired in Taiwan. In addition to East–West cultural traffic, inter-Asian exchange also contributes enormously to intercultural Shakespeare.

THE TAKARAZUKA REVUE'S SHAKESPEAREAN EXTRAVAGANZA

The Takarazuka Revue has generated keen critical interest, but its productions are rarely discussed in the context of Asian Shakespeare in spite of its extensive Shakespearean adaptations and Shakespeare-inspired productions: *Twelfth Night*, *The Tempest*, *Romeo and Juliet*, *Julius Caesar*, *A Midsummer Night's Dream*, *Much Ado About Nothing*, *Antony and Cleopatra*, *The Winter's Tale*, *Hamlet*, *The Two Gentlemen of Verona*, *The Two Noble Kinsmen*, *West Side Story*, *Kiss Me Kate*, and *Roméo et Juliette: de la Haine à l'Amour*.[11] Takarazuka's Shakespeare presents a rich case for studying interculturalism in practice. A living organism feeding on, digesting, absorbing, and transforming nutrients from all sources to serve its various needs, as well as constantly adapting itself to its environment, Takarazuka developed its unique style and culture over the past century. With a live orchestra, elaborate and fast-changing sets, and dramatic lighting, attractive young girls dressed in stunningly flamboyant costumes enact melodrama and romance with songs and dance. Dramatic performance is paired with a revue, culminating in a finale against the background of an illuminated, stage-wide staircase. What Takarazuka offers is a fantastical dreamland, a sensational entertainment that is neither Eastern nor Western but exists solely on stage. Takarazuka writes original stories and also adapts existing plays, novels, films, operas, musicals, and comics. The source can be *Gone with the Wind*, *War and Peace*, or *Farewell, My Concubine*, yet the result is always a distinctly Takarazukan show, and that is precisely what Takarazuka's devoted fans seek. The most common questions asked when discussing Asian Shakespeare—about fidelity, language, (post)colonialism, Oriental aesthetics and Orientalism, and so on—simply seem out of place here.

Takarazuka is above all a commercial theatre, and its birth was closely tied to Japan's political, social, economic, technological, and cultural changes. After isolating itself from the world for two and a half centuries, Japan opened the door and underwent wholesale Westernization in all areas during the Meiji period (1868–1912). Founded in 1913, Takarazuka was a creative invention by Kobayashi Ichizô, an ingenious businessman riding the wave of the new era. It embodied a revolutionary, multidimensional business model in a changing economy. Founder of the Hankyu

Railway, Kobayashi built his empire in electrified railways and residential development. In his scheme to develop and modernize the small spa town of Takarazuka, now the terminus station of a new railroad line, he opened a resort with tourist charms to attract passengers—a botanical garden, a zoo, an amusement park, and an indoor swimming pool. The swimming pool, however, proved a costly business mistake upon a ban on the mixed swimming of men and women. To cover his loss, Kobayashi decided to turn the closed pool into a performance venue featuring live theatre.

This was the time when new theatre forms modeled upon Western performances were being developed.[12] Kobayashi combined three novel elements—Western music, Western dance, and girl performers—into a success formula. Japan's classical theatres only employed male actors; *geisha* (female entertainers) bordered on servitude and prostitution, at least in popular imagination. Actresses in modern theatre were rare and of dubious status. Probably with the swimming pool failure in mind, Kobayashi ensured that the performances followed the moral code of the time. He employed an all-female cast, and emphatically one of "good girls," so romancing on stage would be perceived to be purely fictional and physical contact would be acceptable. His vision was to offer "wholesome entertainment for the entire family, a theatre that would be financially and culturally within reach of ordinary people."[13] Kobayashi's business continued to grow—including department stores, movies, and a baseball team—and so did the Takarazuka project. Within a decade he had built grand theatres accommodating 3,000 people and with the latest technology, and in 1924 founded a music school to train his young actresses in strict discipline. Their motto is "modesty, fairness, and grace" and they cannot marry before "graduating," that is, retiring from the troupe, to be good wives and wise mothers. Although Takarazuka's performances borrowed generously from Western shows with blatant eroticism, such as Moulin Rouge and the Ziegfeld Follies, their costumes remained modest and their eroticism subtle—Kobayashi took pains to ensure that Takarazuka did not degenerate into a striptease revue. Performers wear a high neckline showing no cleavage, and kisses are visibly fake. Kobayashi's vision of mass entertainment has succeeded: Takarazuka's five troupes now produce 1,500 performances and serve 2.6 million spectators annually.[14]

To commemorate the 400th anniversary of Shakespeare's death, Takarazuka presented *Shakespeare: The Sky Filled with Eternal Words*, a fictional account of the Bard's life, paired with the revue *Hot Eyes!!*[15] The poster, which took up walls in subway stations and ad spaces on trains, provides some hint about how Takarazuka approaches Shakespeare. Against a dark red background with a scattered, flying alphabet, most of the space is taken up by the image of the characters William Shakespeare and Anne Hathaway. The main title "Shakespeare" is in hard-to-read cursive, with a small Japanese *katakana* transliteration and a small subtitle in Japanese under it. By contrast, "Hot Eyes" is in glossy red and all capitals, followed by two exclamation points. Apparently, the beautiful stars—especially the *otokoyaku*, the male role—and their "hot eyes" appeal to the predominantly female audience more than Shakespeare's name or his text.

The script by Ikuta Hirokazu recounts Shakespeare's life from an eighteen-year-old boy in a humble Stratford household to a successful London playwright beloved by Queen Elizabeth, mixing facts, fiction, and excerpts from his works. In the first half, the protagonist William resembles Romeo, reciting sonnets and enacting the balcony scene with Anne Hathaway, who has been arranged to marry a rich man named Paris. Exiled from Stratford, William takes Anne to London to start his playwriting career. Like Othello, he explodes with ungrounded jealousy, and Anne leaves with their son Hemnet, who falls ill on the journey and dies. Meanwhile, the aristocrats enact political intrigues drawn from *Hamlet*, *Macbeth*, *Richard III*, and *Julius Caesar*. Accused of treason, William is made to create and enact a new play to appease the Queen. Breaking off his role as Leontes in *The Winter's Tale*, William is shocked to find the statue of Hermione come to life—impersonated by Anne. In front of the Queen, the couple reconcile, and William wins the Queen's pardon as well as the coat of arms that his father has long sought.

Historians and Shakespearean scholars can easily point out the anachronism and inaccuracy. *The Winter's Tale*, for example, is generally thought to be written years after Queen Elizabeth's death. Some plot twists are also less than convincing. But Takarazuka never meant to represent history. This is certainly an idealized and romanticized version of Shakespeare, beautifully impersonated by Asaka Manato, the top *otokoyaku* of Takarazuka's Cosmos Troupe. She wears long wavy hair, tied in a ponytail in the back with long loose bangs hanging on the sides, and there is not the least suggestion of realism, especially when compared to the familiar image of Shakespeare with a high forehead, beard, and mustache. To support the historical theme, there is plenty of "Shakespeareness." In addition to *Romeo and Juliet*, *Othello*, *Macbeth*, and *The Winter's Tale*, whose plots and characters are blended into the plotline, a few well-known scenes and characters also flash on stage: Oberon, Titania, Puck, the witches from *Macbeth*, Hamlet, Gertrude, Polonius, Caesar, Brutus, and the Dark Lady, among others. A number of recognizable lines are recited nearly verbatim: Sonnet 18, Jaques's "All the world's a stage" speech from *As You Like It*, Macbeth's "Tomorrow, tomorrow" soliloquy, part of the balcony scene from *Romeo and Juliet*, and Queen Elizabeth's 1559 speech to Parliament, in which she said she was married to England and had her people as her children. Visually, we see early modern streets lined with timber-framed Tudor houses, the Globe Theatre, yellowed quarto pages as backdrop, a maypole, and the iconic Queen.

Takarazuka's creative use of Shakespearean materials cannot withstand scholarly examination, but this does not affect its popularity or profitability. Emphasizing Takarazuka's appeal as fan-driven, Lorie Brau claims that "Indeed, the drama of Takarazuka performances does not reside in the plot, but in this anticipation of the star's revelation."[16] This is perhaps true for the diehard fans, if not everyone in the audience, but it is nonetheless important to support the star's lovability, not only with her make-up and costumes, voice and movement, but also with consistent suggestions in the plot to support fan fantasy. I argue that the intended fantasy in this play is happy marriage. In the mock balcony scene, after Anne (speaking Juliet's lines) asks how William comes and he replies (in Romeo's lines) with "love's light wings" and protests that he is not afraid of any danger, he immediately asks her to marry him. Shakespeare's Romeo only complains about being "unsatisfied"; it is Juliet who broaches the subject of marriage. This may seem a minor change, but it contributes significantly to the protagonist's lovability. William's dramatic career gets in the way of conjugal happiness, but it also eventually enables their reunion. Somewhat awkwardly, the Virgin Queen demands a play with the theme "the love between husband and wife" because as someone who never married, she would like to know what marital love truly means. This request seems out of character for the historical Queen Elizabeth, yet it enables the miraculous "resurrection" of the dead (lost) wife Hermione (Anne), and a happy grand reunion. It also reinforces William's image as a loving, devoted husband. Obviously, Takarazuka's Shakespeare is not authentic and canonical; nor can it be said to embody Eastern philosophy or aesthetics. While the Bard's name may invoke reverence and submission, Takarazuka treats Shakespeare's texts like it would treat its other sources: it freely selects, modifies, and invents to suit its purposes, taking no pains for fidelity or historical accuracy. As part of Asia's Shakespeare, Takarazuka's Shakespeare can only be decoded by centering the study on the theatre company, its background, performers, and fans, and not on Shakespeare.

THE GOLDEN BOUGH THEATRE'S "ANYTHING GOES" SHAKESPEARE

Based in Taiwan, the Golden Bough Theatre provides a complementary case. Both Takarazuka and Golden Bough feature music, ostentatious costumes, and melodramatic excess, and both are entertainment-oriented instead of cerebral. Both offer a fantasy land, a hyperreal experience. Yet, in many ways they are in polar opposition. Takarazuka is grand, uptown, professional, disciplined, feminine, graceful, modest, and safe, while Golden Bough is small, grassroots, amateurish, nonchalant, masculine, erotic, and even vulgar and provocative. If Takarazuka's modesty is hypocritical, Golden Bough's blatant eroticism is profane. If Takarazuka exemplifies kitsch highly professionalized and refined, what Golden Bough presents is crude, juvenile, and almost passive-aggressive. Most of Golden Bough's productions are original, but it has also adapted *Romeo and Juliet* (twice), *A Midsummer Night's Dream*, and *Hamlet*, among which the outdoor performance of *A Midsummer Night's Dream* offers a most illuminating case study.[17]

Wang Rong-yu, founder of Golden Bough, grew up in a family practicing *gezaixi*, also known as Taiwanese opera, with his mother specializing in male roles.[18] As a boy, Wang felt ashamed of his mother's career, and with good reason. After the Chinese Civil War, the defeated Chinese Nationalist government retreated to Taiwan in 1949 but continued a Sinocentric cultural policy for decades; by safeguarding cultural orthodoxy, the government hoped to win the world's recognition of its political orthodoxy.[19] Mandarin Chinese, originally the dialect of Beijing, was the official language, and the only language taught and allowed at school before English was introduced at seventh grade. *Jingju*, the court entertainment of imperial China, was honored as the national opera and promoted along with the Confucian canon and calligraphy as the gems of Chinese culture. By contrast, local culture was suppressed. Although Minnan (also known as Holo and Taiwanese Hokkien), a dialect originating in the southern Fujian (Hokkien) province of China, was the native language for most locals, it was associated with illiteracy and backwardness. *Gezaixi*, an operatic theatre in Minnan, also suffered discrimination.[20] Unlike the more classical, elite, or literary *xiqu* genres such as *jingju* and *kunqu*, with centuries-old traditions and fixed scripts, *gezaixi* was a new, hybrid genre relying largely on improvisation, mostly performed outdoors on temple grounds or at folk festivals, and labeled as a lower-class entertainment lacking artistic merit.

Taiwan's nativist movements emerged in the mid-1970s, after the government lost its United Nations seat and official relations with most countries. In 1988, the first Taiwan-born president was inaugurated. Under the rising "Taiwan consciousness," *gezaixi* and other local cultural practices gained momentum, being sponsored, studied, revived, and renovated. In the same year, Wang began his theatre training in Jerzy Grotowski's acting techniques. More importantly, he started to explore the local culture he once despised from fresh perspectives—meditation, temple rituals, religious pilgrimage on foot, indigenous tribal rituals, Tai Chi, *qigong*, and martial arts. He also reconnected with *gezaixi* with the help of his mother. When he started Golden Bough in 1993, he was ready to employ all these resources to create a new theatre. His belief is that "The most touching is the culture springing from native land."[21] There is no consensus, however, on what precisely native culture is. Strictly speaking, only Austronesian aboriginal culture truly originated in Taiwan. The majority of the population are of Han Chinese descent, though their ancestors may have arrived 400 years ago or seventy. Taiwan culture has also been influenced by its colonizers (primarily Japan, but also Spain and the Netherlands) and the USA, and most recently by Korea as well. Last but not least, new immigrants by marriage, most of them from China and Southeast Asia, also enrich local culture.

Wang's interpretation of native culture is an eclectic hybrid, as manifested in Golden Bough's signature "opera drama" (also known as *opeila* and *hupiexi*), a subgenre of *gezaixi*. The Japanese pronunciation of "opera" puns on "nonsense" in Minnan, so "opera drama" denotes both "operatic drama" and "nonsense drama" or "anything goes drama," and free synthesis and wild anachronism are a given.[22] The birth of "opera drama" was the result of historical contingency. Developed in Taiwan under Japanese colonization, early *gezaixi* was no more than a regional branch of *xiqu*, largely sharing the same repertoire, musical instruments, movement, costumes, and make-up with other national and regional *xiqu* subgenres—the only defining features were the Minnan dialect and *gezai* tunes. Masters from other *xiqu* genres were often hired from China to train local practitioners. In 1936, right before the Second Sino-Japanese War erupted, the Japanese colonizers forced assimilation and banned all Chinese elements in performances. *Gezaixi* practitioners had to adopt Western or Japanese instruments and tunes, wear *kimonos* or modern dress, and perform plays based on a variety of non-Chinese sources for eight years. With Japan's defeat in the Second World War the ban was lifted, but severe competition in the postwar era stimulated the troupes to be creative by adding new elements such as acrobatics, bawdy jokes, and even striptease. As opposed to traditional *gezaixi*, the term "opera drama" suggests a mash-up of music, costumes, styles, languages, and even characters and stories.

While the first "opera drama" was a necessary compromise, Golden Bough's version pushes the style to an extreme and expresses deliberate defiance against probability, propriety, elegance, decency, and professionalism. Excessiveness is exhibited in the melodramatic and strenuous acting, comedy and slapstick, lingering kisses and erotic poses, verbal profanity, as well as the visuals. Actors shout their lines at the top of their voices, move in exaggerated slow motion, and dress like Christmas trees. As if amateurish quality attests to authenticity, unrestrained energy, and sincerity, the singing and dancing are unabashedly unpolished. Mash-up is manifested in every aspect. Actors freely switch between Mandarin and Minnan, and also speak some simple English and Japanese. Music, live or prerecorded, mixes original songs, popular songs in Mandarin, Minnan, and English, and well-known themes from classical music.

It is in this unique "opera drama" aesthetics that *A Midsummer Night's Dream* unfolds. The play focuses on A-Nan, derived from Hermia, whose psychological journey in love, dream, and reality comprises the plot. As in Shakespeare, she is caught in a four-person love complex, and young love is further complicated by a family feud reminiscent of *Romeo and Juliet*. Devastated at the discovery that her mother and her lover's mother are erotic rivals and deadly enemies, A-Nan falls into a trance and wanders to Dreamland, an alternative space that looks like a flashy TV game show and is ruled/hosted by Empress Desire. Unless A-Nan wins the game, namely breaking the spell of Love Oil, she will be stuck in Dreamland, unable to return to reality. As part of this game, both young men loved and hated by A-Nan get anointed and turn to pursue her friend instead. She manages to reanoint her lover and turn him around, but then realizes that he is no longer the same person. He is now merely a slave of love, loving her uncritically and unconditionally, with no feeling or thought of his own. The only way to break the spell and to free his soul is to tell him she does not love him. A-Nan makes the heartbreaking decision, and by doing so wins the game and is sent back to reality. She wakes up and realizes that what has happened to her in Dreamland is just a dream, and she is still caught in the original situation. While she is happy to see her lover unchanged, the unrequited suitor shows up with a gun. Enraged by A-Nan's rejection, he shoots her dead. This, however, turns out to be another dream. In reality, nothing has happened.

Golden Bough does not provide resolution or reconciliation. Instead, it offers music, dance, spectacles, comedy, and a display of intense emotion and sexual desire. A-Nan's mother is conveniently portrayed as the director of a traveling "opera drama" troupe, where A-Nan is the lead. Performed outdoor in the dark, the play starts with the troupe's rehearsal of a show, a mysterious fire dance against ethnic music using a flute and percussion, climaxing with A-Nan's stunning fire swallowing and fire breathing. Taking full advantage of the outdoor environment and the Dreamland setting, actors emerge from a tree, or from the side or back of the audience, creating surprising effects. A-Gui, the Puck figure acted by the play's playwright-director Shi Dong-lin, nimbly performs magic tricks, fire twirling, tumbling, and break dance.

Comedy and slapstick, not plot-pertinent, abound. The making of markedly low-tech spectacles is made into an amusing spectacle itself. Instead of using automatic stage machinery such as a revolving stage, a dropping device, or laser projections, actors turn the wheeled center stage by hand and run around with a basket of flower petals, which they drop on the lovers, and use hand-held sparklers, bubble guns, and

FIGURE. 4.1: Shi Dong-lin (left) as A-Gui, the Puck figure, in *A Midsummer Night's Dream*. Photography by Chuang Kung-ju. Courtesy of the Golden Bough Theatre.

glow-in-the-dark products to enhance dramatic effects. The metatheatricality brings the actors closer to the spectators, breaking the fourth wall and turning the performance into a party, a game-playing act that is shared by the actors and the knowing audience alike.

This intimacy is characteristic of Golden Bough. The audience for Taiwan's modern theatre comprises mostly college students and young professionals living in the metropolitan areas, mostly female, and almost all performance venues are located in urban areas. Golden Bough is based in rural Tamsui and Bali outside metropolitan Taipei, and the troupe has created a local audience by appearing regularly at community centers and schools, as well as ingeniously turning local historical sites into outdoor theatres. *A Midsummer Night's Dream* premiered in the yard of the historical Tamsui Customs Officer's Residence, a colonial building nicknamed the "Little White House." Dedicated to performing for "the people," Golden Bough is emphatically low-profile and grassroots. Imitating the practice of earlier *gezaixi* traveling troupes, it brings shows to parks, schools, temple grounds, and night markets in villages and small towns all over Taiwan, some of them performed on a truck.[23] Over the years the troupe has reached many who would not consider dressing up and watching a performance at a grand theatre—laborers, the elderly, and children—people who would probably not, contrary to Peter Brook's statement, care for Shakespeare at all.

CONCLUSION

Both Takarazuka and Golden Bough depart markedly from the stereotype of Asian theatre, and their Shakespeare is largely excluded from the narratives of Asian Shakespeare, even though both groups come from Asia and their Shakespeare is enormously popular among their local audiences. Asian theatres can be ancient or modern, elite or grassroots, serious or recreational, philosophical or physical, and grand or small. There is a wide spectrum and the list can go on. The two examples presented here illustrate that the current critical discourse must be expanded and revised. Asian Shakespeare needs to be approached with an open mind, to be liberated from the racist narratives of hegemonic Anglocentrism, which deprives Asia of subjectivity.

Each theatre is a living organism, which feeds according to its unique needs and absorbs what it wants, adapts itself to the environment, grows, and even mutates. East–West binarism—with the concepts and tropes of parent/child, mentor/mentee, tyrant/rebel, colonizer/colonized, spirit/flesh, sense/sensibility, or rivalry or marriage—fails to account for intercultural theatre in practice. To have an insightful and in-depth discussion of any Shakespearean production or adaptation, the theatre being discussed must be treated as a subject, as the center and not an offshoot of London. As subjects, Takarazuka and Golden Bough are no doubt omnivorous. For Kobayashi and Wang, the answer to "Why Shakespeare?" may just simply be "Why not?" To answer Brown's question on how far a contemporary adaptation should be from Shakespeare's early modern theatre, both may say "As far as it takes to make the show a hit."

NOTES

1. Official website of the Globe to Globe *Hamlet*, Shakespeare's Globe, http://globetoglobe.shakespearesglobe.com/hamlet/about-the-project.

2. John Russell Brown, *New Sites for Shakespeare: Theatre, the Audience and Asia* (London: Routledge, 1999), 190.

3. Patrice Pavis, *Theatre at the Crossroads of Culture* (New York: Routledge, 1992). Pavis's dichotomy has been challenged, most notably by Rustom Bharucha, *Theatre and the World* (London: Routledge, 1992), and Jacqueline Lo and Helen Gilbert, "Toward a Topography of Cross-Cultural Theatre Praxis," *Drama Review* 46, no. 3 (2002): 31–53. More recent calls for revision of intercultural theories include Ric Knowles, *Theatre & Interculturalism* (Basingstoke: Palgrave MacMillan, 2010); Jonathan Pitches and Li Ruru, "The End of the Hour-Glass: Alternative Conceptions of Intercultural Exchange between European and Chinese Operatic Forms," *Studies in Theatre and Performance* 32, no. 2 (2012): 121–37; Marcus Cheng Chye Tan, *Acoustic Interculturalism: Listening to Performance* (Basingstoke: Palgrave Macmillan, 2012); Daphne P. Lei, "Interruption, Intervention, Interculturalism: Robert Wilson's HIT Productions in Taiwan," *Theatre Journal* 63, no. 4 (2011): 571–86; Phillip Zarrilli, T. Sasitharan, and Anuradha Kapur (eds.), "Special Issue on 'Intercultural' Acting and Actor/Performer Training," *Theatre, Dance and Performance Training* 7, no. 3 (2016).

4. My account of early Shakespearean footprints in Southeast Asia outside colonial classrooms is based on excellent research: Judy Celine Ick, "Shakespeare, (Southeast) Asia, and the Question of Origins," in Bi-qi Beatrice Lei and Perng Ching-Hsi (eds.), *Shakespeare in Culture* (Taipei: National Taiwan University Press, 2012), 214–25; Judy Celine Ick, "The Augmentation of the Indies: An Archipelagic Approach to Asian and Global Shakespeare," in Bi-qi Beatrice Lei, Judy Celine Ick, and Poonam Trivedi (eds.), *Shakespeare's Asian Journeys: Critical Encounters, Cultural Geographies, and the Politics of Travel* (New York: Routledge, 2017), 19–36; Evan Darwin Winer, "Spectres of *Hamlet* in Colonial and Postcolonial Indonesia," in Alexa Huang and Charles Ross (eds.), *Shakespeare in Hollywood, Asia, and Cyberspace* (West Lafayette, IN: Purdue University Press, 2009), 172–82; Nurul Farhana Low Bt. Abdullah, "Bangsawan Shakespeare in Colonial Malaya," in Alexa Huang and Charles Ross (eds.), *Shakespeare in Hollywood, Asia, and Cyberspace* (West Lafayette, IN: Purdue University Press, 2009), 139–51.

5. Ick, "Augmentation of the Indies," 23.

6. Low, "Bangsawan Shakespeare in Colonial Malaya," 149.

7. Early Shakespeare in Japan, China, and Korea has been well documented. For more extensive accounts, see Kawachi Yoshiko, "Shakespeare's Long Journey to Japan: His Contribution to Her Modernization and Cultural Exchange," in Bi-qi Beatrice Lei, Judy Celine Ick, and Poonam Trivedi (eds.), *Shakespeare's Asian Journeys: Critical Encounters, Cultural Geographies, and the Politics of Travel* (New York: Routledge, 2017), 38–44; Sano Akiko, "Shakespeare Translation in Japan: 1868–1998," *Ilha do Desterro* 36 (2008): 337–48; Zhang Xiao Yang, *Shakespeare in China: A Comparative Study of Two Traditions and Cultures* (Newark: University of Delaware Press, 1996), 97–113; Lee Jongsook, "Colonial Shakespeares: Shakespeare in Korea, 1906–1945," *Shakespeare Review* 32 (1997): 115–41.

8. For a list of Lin's alterations, see Perng Ching-Hsi, "Chinese *Hamlets*: A Centenary Review," *Multicultural Shakespeare: Translation, Appropriation and Performance* 2 (2005): 52–5.

9. Kim Kang, "Political Shakespeare in Korea: *Hamlet* as a Subversive Cultural Text in the 1980s," in Bi-qi Beatrice Lei, Judy Celine Ick, and Poonam Trivedi (eds.), *Shakespeare's Asian Journeys: Critical Encounters, Cultural Geographies, and the Politics of Travel* (New York: Routledge, 2017), 124.

10. For a full account of *Osero*, see Robert Tierney, "*Othello* in Tokyo: Performing Race and Empire in 1903 Japan," *Shakespeare Quarterly* 62 (2011): 514–40.

11. The Takarazuka Revue is most often studied in the context of gender, sexuality, and pop culture; see Jennifer Robertson, *Takarazuka: Sexual Politics and Popular Culture in Modern Japan* (Berkeley: University of California Press, 1998) and Leonie Rae Stickland, *Gender Gymnastics: Performing and Consuming Japan's Takarazuka Revue* (Melbourne: Trans Pacific Press, 2008). For Takarazuka's history and development, see Zeke Berlin, "Takarazuka: A History and Descriptive Analysis of the All-Female Japanese Performance Company," PhD dissertation, New York University, 1987, and Yamanashi Makiko, *A History of the Takarazuka Revue Since 1914: Modernity, Girls' Culture, Japan Pop* (Leiden: Global Oriental, 2012). Takarazuka's Shakespearean

productions are discussed in the context of popular culture by Yoshihara Yukari, "Popular Shakespeare in Japan," *Shakespeare Survey* 60 (2007): 130–40, in which the author provides a brief annotated list of Takarazuka's Shakespearean productions before discussing its *Julius Caesar* in detail, and Minami Ryuta, who discussed Takarazuka's *Twelfth Night*, "Shakespeare for Japanese Popular Culture: *Shojo Manga*, Takarazuka and *Twelfth Night*," in Dennis Kennedy and Yong Li Lan (eds.), *Shakespeare in Asia: Contemporary Performance* (Cambridge: Cambridge University Press, 2010), 109–31.

12. For concise accounts of the birth and early development of Japan's modern theatres, see Brian Powell, "Birth of Modern Theatre: Shimpa and Shigeki," and Nakano Masaaki, "Interlude: Modern Comedies and Early Musicals," in Jonah Salz (ed.), *A History of Japanese Theatre* (Cambridge: Cambridge University Press, 2016), 200–25, 226–9.

13. Lorie Brau, "The Women's Theatre of Takarazuka," *Drama Review* 34, no. 4 (1990): 84.

14. "How the Inimitable Takarazuka Revue Comes to Life," the official website of the Takarazuka Revue, http://kageki.hankyu.co.jp/english/about/about2.html.

15. *Shakespeare: The Sky Filled with Eternal Words*, written and directed by Ikuta Hirokazu and produced by the Cosmos Troupe of the Takarazuka Revue, was premiered with *Hot Eyes!!* at Takarazuka Grand Theater on January 1, 2016. The DVD containing both shows is commercially available.

16. Brau, "The Women's Theatre of Takarazuka," 84.

17. *A Midsummer Night's Dream*, written and directed by Shih Dong-lin, produced by the Golden Bough Theatre, was premiered at the Tamsui Customs Officer's Residence on September 7, 2007 and has been restaged several times. A full performance video of the first edition is available online with English subtitles at the Taiwan Shakespeare Database, http://www.shakespeare.tw. I have written elsewhere on Golden Bough's *Yumei and Tianlai*, an adaptation of *Romeo and Juliet*: Bi-qi Beatrice Lei, "'O Heavy Lightness, O Serious Vanity': Camping *Romeo and Juliet* in Postcolonial Taiwan," in Poonam Trivedi and Minami Ryuta (eds.), *Re-playing Shakespeare in Asia* (New York: Routledge, 2010), 314–20.

18. Official website of the Golden Bough Theatre, http://www.goldenbough.com.tw/director.htm.

19. I have written elsewhere on the politics of languages and theatres in Taiwan: Bi-qi Beatrice Lei, "'Thou Orphans' Father Art': Shakespeare in Taiwanese and Yue Operas," in Douglas A. Brooks and Yang Lingui (eds.), *Shakespeare and Asia* (*Shakespeare Yearbook* 17) (Lewiston, NY: Edwin Mellen Press, 2010), 199–232.

20. For a full account of *gezaixi* politics, see Huei-Yuan Belinda Chang, "A Theatre of Taiwanese: Politics, Ideologies, and Gezaixi," *Drama Review* 41, no. 2 (1997): 111–29.

21. The official website of the Golden Bough Theatre, http://www.goldenbough.com.tw/2006/en/profile.htm.

22. The original term is *opera* (*opeila*), the Taiwanese pronunciation of the Japanese transliteration of the English word "opera," with the accent falling on the second syllable. The Mandarin pronunciation of its Chinese written form is *hupiexi* (*hupie* drama, namely nonsense drama). The genre has been studied extensively by Teri J. Silvio, including an article on works by Golden Bough: Teri J. Silvio, "Tai/Kuso/Camp: 'New Opeila' and the Structure of Sensibility," *Inter-Asia Cultural Studies* 10, no. 3 (2009): 341–60.

23. Liu Yongfeng, "Bringing Theater to the People: Golden Bough Theatre," trans. Geof Aberhart, *Taiwan Panorama,* August 2015, https://www.taiwan-panorama.com/Articles/Details?Guid=6295a947-9d25-42f6-9a0e-210de9378628&CatId=2.

CHAPTER FIVE

Connecting the Dots: Performances, Island Worlds, and Oceanic Interculturalisms

DIANA LOOSER

How do we consider the relationships between performance and interculturalism in an area as vast and heterogeneous as Oceania? Comprising over 25,000 islands spread over one quarter of the earth's surface and grouped into twenty-six countries and territories, the region formally spans the Pacific Ocean from Rapa Nui (Easter Island) in the east to Palau in the west, and from Hawai'i in the north to Aotearoa (New Zealand) in the south. Organized in the early nineteenth century into the imposed geocultural categories of Polynesia, Melanesia, and Micronesia, this expansive oceanic world has always exhibited an uncontainability that flows across and beyond these and other boundaries, disclosing a diverse and densely networked region that both reveals and resists its multiple colonial overlays and variegated structures of state governance. Due to its geography, the Pacific has long been a space of crossings and connections. In contrast to military and old-school anthropological views of the hermetic, microcosmic island laboratory, many indigenous Pacific cultures trace linked histories and contemporary trajectories of movement and exchange, where roots lead back to routes and forward into routes again. Whereas many Pacific sites are remotely situated and have peripheral access to the world's resources, they are also variously implicated in a deep palimpsest of exploratory, migratory, religious, commercial, military, and administrative itineraries that have crafted Oceania's (sub)regional, national, and diasporic contours. Epeli Hau'ofa's foundational vision of Oceania as a "sea of islands" has turned on these circumstances, refuting Western neoliberal dismissals of small-scale and dependent Pacific Island states by foregrounding the ocean as a fecund arena of mobility, reciprocity, and interdependence that represents "the essence of the global system."[1] This emphasis on connections is not to deny the deep specificity of place or the legitimacy of claims to ancestral home ground, but to acknowledge, as Katerina Teaiwa does, that human identification and activity across the Pacific are marked by the rooted/stable and the traveling/dynamic working together in shaping identity and sustaining social life;[2] as she observes, "history and culture are only ever contingent and always happening between people and place, bodies and lands, and the vast oceanic spaces that hold, connect and transform them."[3]

These circumstances have given rise to a panoply of performance styles and frameworks that confound any single definition or application of interculturalism in performance. This chapter does not set out to survey this wide-ranging and variable output but rather attempts to capture a small part of this complexity by juxtaposing two performances that serve as methodological case studies. These are a historical, indigenous performance from the Tuamotu Archipelago in French Polynesia that entwines pan-Polynesian sources as well as various trans-indigenous and imported influences stimulated by the international trade routes of the pearling industry, and a contemporary performance about the blended British/Tahitian genealogy of the Norfolk Island community in the southwestern Pacific, read in the context of the islanders' contested relationship with Australia. While these ostensibly disparate works may seem—on the surface—to have little to do with one another, on their own and together they teach us about some of the surprisingly extensive intercultural linkages that frequently characterize small island communities. Both performances exhibit the dialectic between stability and movement, land and sea, that centers the ocean as a medium of exchange, pushing against territorial designations while suturing the island Pacific to multiple sites beyond the region. There is also a historiographic focus in each case study that traces legacies of movement and interrelation, a preoccupation with tracking multi-stepped and multilayered genealogies that reinforce and rescript linked communities in the present. The two examples gesture to how the indigenous and non-indigenous pass into and through each other, producing new formations that are then subject to further travel and transculturation. In this regard, the performances demonstrate, as Leo Cabranes-Grant usefully reminds us, that cultures are not rigid or stable but are always mixing, moving, and revisiting; thus, hybridity is a source of the intercultural encounter, not only its effect.[4] As he puts it, "Distinctions between pure and impure practices are not produced by intercultural relations—they are already *there* as part of a complex chain of networking operations that flow through, against, because of them."[5]

This acknowledgment is important for performance from Oceania because, too often in theatre and performance studies, the Pacific Islands are conceived of as isolated, insignificant dots in a wide and empty ocean, whose cultural production is largely invisible in academic conceptions of world performance that still privilege continental terrestriality. Consequently, I have decided not to choose case studies from larger, well-resourced regional sites like Aotearoa New Zealand, Fiji, or Hawai'i, although they are intense nodes of interaction and there is much of import to be said about that work in this critical context. Instead, I look deliberately at work from places often deemed remote, tiny, and secluded, expressly to show how they are not. The interculturalisms embedded in the embodied and material performances from the Tuamotus and from Norfolk attach their communities to significant processes of world-making and modernity, reaching out across space and time in webs of active association and interchange. Oceania is certainly not a homogenous and harmonious space—defined by schisms and dissension as well as by affiliations—

yet its islands are not alone and its sea is not a vacancy, and any approach to Pacific performance must reckon with this vital fact. In mapping a selective intercultural topography of Oceania in what follows, I hope that "connecting the dots" will reveal a partial yet salutary picture of this still largely uncharted scholarly and creative terrain and its contributions to world performance.

TE REKO NO TUTEPOGANUI, TUAMOTU ARCHIPELAGO

In his definition of a "new interculturalism," Ric Knowles is largely correct to locate these rhizomatic, processual, "performance-from-below" collaborations within the contemporary milieu of the global, diasporic city.[6] Yet his focus also opens room for thinking about other ways in which indigenous communities have worked performatively to forge connections and solidarities with each other, especially over time. How can we talk about works from the historical past that are also multi-sited and horizontal in their approach, that incorporate the trans-indigenous traffic of people, ideas, and materials in/through performance in ways that stitch together larger intercultural communities already inflected with previous and ongoing processes of exchange, and that weave together divergent theatrical traditions while troubling the common assumption that theatrical forms and conventions per se are foreign constructs that mediate all staged indigenous performance?[7] Although the policies, situations, and strategies that Knowles discusses are distinctive and arise from present-day conditions, some of the intercultural dynamics he champions might be understood to own a longer history, foregrounding persistent sets of preoccupations and techniques that bespeak a continuity of indigenous intellectual and artistic practices.

The intractable challenge, however, is that documentary evidence of such performance practices—customarily transmitted in oral and embodied mediums in the Pacific—is almost always enfolded within European textual records and therefore becomes an intercultural performance of another sort: one that emerges from historical attempts at cross-cultural understanding, but an encounter that takes place, performatively, within larger performances of colonial expansion and the ethnographic activities that supported them. The contemporary (in my case, Pākehā)[8] scholar's encounter with the performance document constitutes yet another intercultural performance in its attempt at a hermeneutic rapprochement—one that involves parsing accretions of remediation and linguistic and cultural dissonance. Rather than attempt to capture the "original" performance beneath it all (although one can of course say something about it), we might do better to treat the work—like all performances—as bound inextricably and continually with its circumstances of production, reception, and recording. If we accept Cabranes-Grant's own archivally-situated argument that intercultural performances are "less about mediatory encounters between *authentic* cultural expressions than about the enactment of specific networks of collaboration and adjustment,"[9] then the focus shifts to reconstructing those "relational webs of labor and maintenance" that sustained intercultural occasions and that are ongoing, unfolding, and morphing, "producing new relational entanglements along the course of their processual elaborations."[10]

I want to draw attention to a particularly layered intercultural performance documented in the early twentieth century: *Te Reko no Tutepoganui, te Ariki ko te Moana* (The Recitation/Drama of Tūtepo[n]ganui, Lord of the Ocean)[11] from the Tuamotu Archipelago, a chain of seventy-six islands and atolls in eastern Oceania covering an area about the size of Western Europe that currently comprises an administrative division of French Polynesia, a *pays d'outre mer* (overseas country) of France. *Te Reko no Tutepoganui* offers an example of how an indigenous play of this period demonstrated existing relations of autochthonous trade and exchange that provided the circumstances for the performance to take place, informed its ritual, mythic, and narrative constructs, and aided the creation of its material objects. Additionally, the play augments pre-contact vernacular forms and production contexts with materials and methods gleaned from foreign visitors and new or renewed contact with other Pacific Islanders facilitated by the motilities of colonial enterprise. In this regard, the performance is revelatory of how local, trans-indigenous labor networks intersected with those of what Stewart Firth terms the Pacific's "first globalization,"[12] lasting from the 1850s until 1914, "when Pacific Island economies began to be integrated into the global economy" with the arrival of planters, miners, labor recruiters, and traders keen to capitalize on Oceania's raw materials (here, pearls and mother-of-pearl shell).[13] In line with the emphasis on how intercultural relations are translocalized, rerouted, and remade, I also look at how the performance continues to push into our present in the form of a contemporary artisanal encounter that leads to new intercultural transformations that privilege indigenous becoming.

Te Reko no Tutepoganui was first recorded in writing in 1912 by Parisian traveler, anthropologist, and symphonic/opera composer August-Charles Eugène Caillot, who produced a full script in Tuamotuan with a parallel French translation.[14] The *reko*, which Caillot renders as a "Parler (Drame)" (a spoken enactment or presentation),[15] was reportedly an old form that possibly survived more intact because of the remote situation of the Tuamotus (meaning "islands out in the ocean"),[16] although by the early 1900s, traders, missionaries, and visiting French officials had wrought major changes to the islanders' language, lifestyle, and village structures.[17] Caillot writes, "One cannot fail to be surprised to find among Polynesians, so degenerated since their conversion to Christianity, a genuine piece of theatre; but will the astonishment be any less when one learns that this play is not their work, but that of their cannibal ancestors? Yet this is what the natives declare unanimously in the islands where this play is still performed today."[18] While we do not know the actual age of the play, numerous earlier records from central Polynesia indicate that pre-colonial dramatic enactments of this sort were common, representing a broad range of professional and amateur enterprises that pointed to theatre as a coherent social institution, and which incorporated and adapted new foreign elements into its pre-existing structures.[19]

The *reko* was performed by pearl fishermen, and was repeated each season at the Tuamotuan atoll officially opened for pearl diving, including the adjacent islands of Hikueru, Takume, Raroia, Taenga, and Nihiru.[20] The performance that Caillot witnessed occurred on Hikueru (comprising three square miles of land encircling a central lagoon) and was directed by Te Iho-o-te-pongi, a man from Raroia renowned for his scholarly and historical knowledge.[21] It took place at night, illuminated with torches, in a public area near the center of the village in front of the assembly house. The audience stood or sat around the edge of the playing space, and the performance's temporal frame was demarcated by the beating of a large wood and sharkskin drum.[22] The *reko* consisted of sustained dramatic dialogue between multiple characters, with solo and ensemble action, and included detailed oral "stage directions" regarding the characters' blocking, gestures, and feelings, which were explained to first-time viewers by those who had already seen the show. Caillot says little about costuming, but the actor portraying the sea deity Tutepoganui (literally, "on which stand a great number of shells") was a very tall man who wore a large, ornate, full-head mask carved from a coconut log to represent a monstrous human head, lavishly adorned with marine vegetation and fixed, wooden, shell-shaped decorations to depict the clams, oysters, and other pearl shells that formed part of Tutepoganui's person and entourage in

FIGURE 5.1: August-Charles Eugène Caillot's sketch of the mask of Tutepoganui, created by Mangarevan craftspeople and worn by Tuamotuan performers on Hikueru in 1912. The image is taken from August-Charles Eugène Caillot, *Mythes, Légendes et Traditions des Polynésiens* (Paris: Ernest Leroux, 1914), 95.

legend and in the play. The mask was finished with paint and a voluminous moustache and beard (possibly of horsehair, a European adaptation), and was created by craftspeople from Mangareva (one of the Gambier Islands, located at the southeastern terminus of the Tuamotu Archipelago, but which has a distinct language and culture).[23]

Set in legendary times, the play begins in a canoe on the water. Rogomatane, a fisherman from the island of Vavau (the old name for the region of atolls where the play was performed), offers a fish in tribute to Tohoropuga, the sea chief (*ragatira*) in charge of marine products. To Rogomatane's surprise, Tohoropuga appears, evinces curiosity about the land, and the two go ashore. Shortly afterwards, Tohoropuga's boss Tutepoganui arrives, having journeyed from his underwater home in Ruahatu (here, the Tuamotuan Hawaiki)[24] to search for two of his subjects, the whale and the turtle, which have been detained by the people of the land. While Tohoropuga heads off to lead the search, the sea-god explores the island and encounters an old acquaintance, the elderly woman Hina, and her canine companion, Ri. (Ri was apparently played by an actual dog, which bristled and barked on cue when a stagehand pulled his tail.)[25] In a lengthy monologue, Hina relates her many voyages and vicissitudes since leaving Ruahatu: her forced marriage to Tuna (Eel) and her journey from island to island to escape him, her deliverance by the demigod Maui and their subsequent marriage, then her infidelity and Maui's revenge by turning her lover into a dog. Tohoropuga then reappears and reports that the whale and turtle have been restored. Tutepoganui pardons the land-dwellers and promotes Tohoropuga, they all perform a dance of joy, and the sea deities return forever to their realm.

It is difficult to determine the precise dramaturgies activated in and by this performance in its historical context, or even, through Caillot's filter, to discern the proper form of the play. (Is the script's five-act structure, for instance, something that Caillot observed organically in the performance and tried to translate, something he imposed upon the recorded performance to aid Western readers' understanding, or something that he wove into the record in an act of more-or-less genuine good faith based on how the performance appeared legible to him?) But of special relevance here are the ways in which *Te Reko no Tutepoganui* evokes and enfolds an oceanic identity as well as a range of established and emergent (trans-)indigenous mobilities in its form, content, production, and circulation, and which readjust and reassert themselves in relation to European permeations. The play's narrative arc, focusing on the maintenance of harmonious relationships between the land-dwellers and the ocean-dwellers, situates the seafaring performers within a holistic epistemology that respects the sea and its denizens as sometimes oppositional and unpredictable, yet also recognizes reciprocal and genealogical ties between human and non-human entities. This mutual ontology is inscribed particularly through the figure of Tutepoganui: half-man and half-fish, and a legendary progenitor of the Tuamotu people,[26] his ancestral presence reinforces the identity of the fisher-folk as not only people of the land but also people of the sea.

References to pan-Polynesian mythological places and figures such as Hawaiki, Maui, and Hina serve to bind the play's local traditions to larger geo-cultural and cosmological schemes. Maui, the quintessential Polynesian trickster and culture hero, features in the legends of most island groups; similarly, his strong female counterpart

Hina (Hine, Ina, Sina) is "the goddess most recognized throughout all of Polynesia,"[27] with stories about her stretching from Hawai'i to Rēkohu (the Chatham Islands).[28] Hina is frequently cast as a sojourner (or the wife, sister, or mother of epic voyagers): sometimes a famous navigator sailing her *vaka* (canoe) throughout the islands and/or to the moon; at other times in exile or on the run, or on a romantic quest, crossing the ocean with the aid of sea creatures.[29] Notably, scholars have pointed out the "remarkable blending" of Tuamotuan, Māori (Aotearoa), and Samoan versions of Hina myths in this drama,[30] which denote widespread interactions and mixed influences between Pacific Islanders both historically and via modern routes galvanized by travel on foreign vessels to different parts of Oceania.

Beyond its formal commonalities with indigenous dramas produced in the Society Islands and the Cooks group,[31] the performance's conventions and circulation highlight other connections between communities in eastern Oceania. *Te Reko no Tutepoganui* is a good example of how a marine industry like pearl fishing provided the stimulus and sustenance for theatrical performance. The Tuamotu atolls (known in the nineteenth century as the "Pearl Islands") were the scene of the South Pacific's principal pearl fisheries, especially Hikueru, which had the richest reefs and was the site of its greatest operations. Although pearl diving, working mother-of-pearl shell, and trading pearl products has a long pre-contact history in the archipelago, these networks were both regulated and intensified by the infiltration of foreign entrepreneurship during the 1800s, which ramped up exports to Chile, the United States, and to major markets in France, Britain, Germany, and Austria. Records from the time of Caillot's study note that during the pearling season up to 5,000 people from several archipelagoes would convene at Hikueru, many traveling distances of 500 miles and camping together in temporary accommodation.[32] These interactions created the conditions for various cultural customs and practices—already in a process of melding and adapting—to enter into dialogue, including the mask that formed the focal prop in the play.

According to Hiriata Millaud, masks of Tutepoganui were used traditionally by Tuamotuan fishermen, who would invoke the ancestral sea god before a deep-water fishing expedition. An actor would wear the mask in a theatre performance staging the planned fishing trip, during which he would become invested with the spirit of Tutepoganui, who would speak through the actor to give the fishermen tips for finding fish and staying safe on the ocean.[33] In *Te Reko no Tutepoganui*, which moves from ritual to a more intercultural dramatic presentation in honor of the god and his products, the fabrication of the Mangarevan-made mask for the Hikueru performance (625 miles away) showcases trans-indigenous cultural traffic in the manufacture of theatrical properties. In addition to non-indigenous materials that may have represented recent modifications to a customary mask design, Tutepoganui's mask was the result of local artistic exchanges; mother-of-pearl decoration is not a feature of traditional Mangarevan ornamentation, but in modern times Mangarevans were possibly inspired by Tuamotuans to use or imitate it.[34] Taken together, the textual and material records of the *reko* suggest how ocean passages of various kinds— linking the local and global—were essential to the content and form of the drama, as well as to the theatrical and social infrastructures that supported it and to which it related.

As *Te Reko no Tutepoganui* slips into script and moves into material objects in processes of archiving and activation, it reminds us that its intercultural history is still in the making. The mask from the 1912 performance survives today, in deteriorated condition, at Te Fare Manaha/Musée de Tahiti et des Îles near Pape'ete, Tahiti's capital. In 2012, Raitia Teihotaata, a Tahitian carver and graduate of the Centre des Metiers d'Art, fashioned a mask of Tutepoganui inspired by the original, of tinted and painted coconut wood and real clam and nacre shells, which is currently displayed in the collection of the Assembly of French Polynesia. In its evocation of a textured intercultural past in the context of contemporary Pasifika arts, Teihotaata's labor enacts new trans-indigenous rapprochements across time and space, performing a diachronic interculturalism that retraces the earlier mask's itineraries. His design registers the impact that wear and display has had on the mask over time, implicitly tracking its transfer and adaptation from artisan to actor to anthropologist to Catholic Father to museum authorities and back to the artist again.[35] By enlivening, transforming, and relocalizing the museal artifact, Teihotaata recalls, like the play a century before, the Pacific's heterogeneous and networked histories and, in so doing, to quote Chadwick Allen, "defin[es] Indigenous identities as the result of ancient and ongoing *processes* of making, trading, moving—in a word, of *be-coming* or coming into being."[36]

The next case study follows lines of flight that route through and out from Tahiti. Pursuing the dialectic between groundedness and movement and the focus on the processual entanglements of cultures-in-relation, I consider a contemporary example of how the intercultural can inhere in notions of indigeneity, and how performance becomes a means of registering the historical making and remaking of Pacific communities and of expressing their claims in the present.

THE *MUTINY ON THE BOUNTY SHOW*, NORFOLK ISLAND

Every week at the Salty Theatre in Anson Bay, Norfolk Island, descendants of one of the early colonial Pacific's most vivid events stage the *Mutiny on the Bounty Show*, which re-enacts the iconic story from the islanders' perspective and ends with a coda that links those ancestors to the present-day inhabitant-performers.[37] Norfolk, a 13½-square-mile volcanic island in the northern Tasman Sea, situated equidistantly between Australia, New Zealand, and New Caledonia, is home to 1,400 residents, almost half of whom descend from the twenty-eight British sailors and Tahitian women who fled to remote and unpopulated Pitcairn Island in the wake of the 1789 mutiny against Captain William Bligh. Over several generations, the group produced a closely interrelated and growing population of mixed European and Polynesian heritage, which, by the 1850s, had become too large for their 2-square-mile home. In 1856, the community was granted leave by the British government to relocate to the more spacious Norfolk, previously uninhabited except for recently abandoned British convict settlements.[38] Narratives of the (in)famous mutiny have been told and retold for the past 230 years in many modes and media—and immortalized cinematically by the likes of Clark Gable, Marlon Brando, and Mel Gibson—but as Anne Salmond observes, while these versions have typically focused on the *Bounty*'s shipboard dynamics and the impact on Bligh's career, the island peoples and histories have had less prominence. Salmond rightly points out the need to work more fully across disciplines and cultural traditions to form a more holistic, insightful picture of the event and its significance. As she argues:

> [T]he tale of the mutiny on the *Bounty* and its aftermath is not just a Western story. At its heart, the historical and mythical trajectories of Britain and the South Pacific intersect, transforming lives on the islands as well as on board the ships and back in Europe. This is an episode in the history of the world, not simply the history of the West; and the Pacific protagonists were as real as their British counterparts, helping to shape what happened.[39]

And helping to shape what happened afterwards. In this performance by the Norfolk Islanders (or the Pitcairners on Norfolk), the story is resignified from the point of view of a Pacific society whose cultural identity was fundamentally impacted and mutually transformed by this encounter, and who continue to defend their right to their autonomy in the face of neo-colonial intrusions.

The ninety-minute *Mutiny* show, presented as a corrective to Hollywood's mythmaking,[40] is performed somewhat in the style of a living history program, with in-character dialogue interspersed with monologues by self-conscious narrators who provide historical context and commentary. It offers us a specifically intercultural *mise-en-scène* in its purpose-built, outdoor amphitheatre, in which most of the "stage" consists of an expansive pool of water, wide and deep enough to row a dinghy across, which represents the Pacific Ocean. Dominant fixtures are (to our left) a large, detailed replica of the *Bounty* vessel and, opposite, across the water, Matavai Bay in Tahiti, complete with huts and outrigger canoes, banana trees, palms, and other lush vegetation. Visually and acoustically, as the opening soundscape of the English port merges with the tropical sounds of Tahiti, the two spaces are positioned to cross-refer to each other from the beginning, evoking, as in the bodies of the descendants, an understanding of the two places as always happening, in process, and in co-imbrication.

The show cites the many beach crossings whose legacies are intimately interwoven into the community's identities, giving these interactions—unsurprisingly—a heroic spin that valorizes resistance to hegemonic structures and emphasizes the superior social vision forged from the community's cross-cultural componentry. It sows the seeds for justifying the mutiny from the outset when our interlocutor Peter Heywood (a historical figure condemned to death as a mutineer but subsequently pardoned) criticizes the *Bounty*'s naval-commercial mission—to transport breadfruit from Tahiti to feed enslaved laborers in the Caribbean—as motivated by profit, greed, and injustice. On the voyage, Bligh's "true colors" soon emerge, leading to the gradual breakdown of morale on the ship and growing tension between Bligh and his second-in-command, Fletcher Christian. These schisms are entrenched with new exchanges of desire that take place during the sailors' twenty-three weeks in Tahiti and their developing bonds with local women; the drama pays special attention to the love match between Christian and Chief Hitihiti's niece, Maimiti (Mauatua, Isabella), who would later become his wife. Maimiti is portrayed as a woman of intelligence and insight rather than as a naïve and seductive "dusky maiden"; indeed, despite the story's privileging of institutional and familial patriarchies (which this show largely replicates), it would be the Tahitian women who would keep the new community together during its turbulent early years on Pitcairn.

Throughout, the rowboat traverses the watery space between the ship and the shore, tracking materially and symbolically the processes by which each side gradually takes on aspects of the other's cultures. Notably, these cultures were plural, given that the sailors came from many parts of the British Isles and midshipman Edward Young was from the West Indies, and the women were from several islands in the group, not just Tahiti. These liaisons, sharpened by historical hindsight, increase our sympathy for the sailors forced to sail away under Bligh's severe command and set the scene for the mutineers' righteous capture of the *Bounty* and Bligh's casting adrift. Rather than focus (as other versions have done) on Bligh's epic longboat voyage to Timor and his subsequent quest for revenge, the final scene features the actor playing Fletcher Christian atop a set piece depicting the stern of the *Bounty* (modeled after Robert Dodd's famous painting of 1790). He gives us the names of the mutineers, relating their passage back to Tahiti and thence to Pitcairn and eventually to Norfolk, where their names remain still, he declares, as testament to repressive naval authority and to those who rebelled against it in the hope of finding a better life.[41]

Mutiny is the flagship performance offering of Pinetree Tours, Norfolk Island's premier tourist organization, and is one of several theatrical presentations in which the islanders' unique and noteworthy history is packaged to visitors as the community's prime export. On a small island that has little other economic infrastructure, and where most residents work several jobs to support themselves, it is common for locals to take roles as actors playing their forebears, capitalizing on their identities as "actual descendants." As Michael Ritzau notes, on Norfolk the *Bounty* myth is "a competitive advantage to be highlighted in almost all business, signage and documentary material on, and relating to, the island";[42] and for many, this "partial commodification of culture helps reinforce and enhance the viability of Pitcairn-descendant 'being' on-island."[43] Curiously, partway through experiencing the *Mutiny* show, I realize that the dialogue—not just the ambient sounds and music—is pre-recorded, meaning that the actors are lip-syncing their lines. A representative of Pinetree Tours explained to me that the community asked a theatre company in Sydney, Australia, to script and record the show, mainly for practical reasons of audibility on a windy island in an outdoor, seaside venue. It also enables the long-running show (operating since 1993), featuring 98 percent direct descendants, to function as a primary industry that residents can enter easily from a young age; many begin as teenagers, with the boys cast as sailors and the girls on Tahiti, working their way up to major roles with experience.[44]

But there is also a symbolic valence in this choice of performative presentation, in which specialized artistic skills are subordinated to the "authentic" aura of the descendant. On the one hand, this is an expedient form of tourist performance with its familiar conflation of being and doing in an encounter that is frequently theorized as ethnographic. But on the other hand, putatively appearing *as* instead of acting *as if* functions as a strident statement of pride and identity that is important in the context of Norfolk Island's struggles to maintain an autonomous existence vis-à-vis the neo-colonial ambit of the Australian nation-state. So far, I have emphasized the community's intercultural nature, emerging from a plural mixture of European and Polynesian influences, and being relocated and relocated again in a multi-stepped journey of adaptation and creolization. Yet in Norfolk's case, these fused trajectories have led, over time and across space, to new claims of indigeneity. The Pitcairn settlers' understanding, once Norfolk Island had been formally separated from Van Diemen's Land (Tasmania) in 1856, was that their new home would comprise a "distinct and separate settlement" from Australia,[45] and that the islanders would enjoy self-government on an island ceded to them in perpetuity by Britain. However, the community soon became subject to political incursions over land and legislation by the government of New South Wales and, after federation in 1901, the Commonwealth of Australia, resulting eventually in the federal authority's Norfolk Island Act 1913. The Act annexed Norfolk as an external territory of Australia and heralded Australia's new role in the southwest Pacific as an alternative to the old imperial order.[46]

The subsequent century has been marked by contention with the "mainland," with Norfolk Islanders' calls for greater freedom and independence, including their 1994 declaration as the indigenous people of Norfolk. This avowal is based on claims that they are the first whole people to settle Norfolk Island as a permanent, intergenerational homeland, that they have a surviving culture developed on Pitcairn by their ancestors that continues to evolve, and that they maintain their own official language, Norfolk (or Norf'k, descended from Pitkern), a creole forged from eighteenth-century English and Tahitian dialects.[47] From this perspective, Norfolk Islander belonging, akin to many other iterations of Pacific indigeneity, is "grounded" in movement and change: as certain residents argue, like early Polynesian settlers on their *vaka*, they sailed to an island and over time became a new and separate people. Moreover, they came to a place that was not Australia and that only later administratively became "Australia," and thus they became a people indentured into an Australian identity in a manner that parallels First Nations experience elsewhere.[48] These claims have been rejected by the Australian government, which doubled down in 2015 when the parliament made the bipartisan decision to revoke Norfolk Island's autonomy, under which the island had been governed by its own legislative assembly since 1979.[49] The period since the takeover has been marked by economic crisis for the small community, as well as intensified protests by pro-independence activists, including appeals to the British Parliament and a petition to the United Nations,[50] and the branding of the island's new Canberra-appointed administrator as a "modern-day Bligh."[51]

Read in this context, the *Mutiny on the Bounty Show* potentially takes on a different intercultural aspect as a statement of indigenous belonging. While it is important to acknowledge that there is a great deal of variation among Norfolk Islanders in terms of this identification, and different levels of investment, advocacy, and expression,[52] it is possible to interpret the performance as a politicized site of resistance that refuses elision into the Australian national imaginary through an assertion of an alternative genealogy that foregrounds the intercultural relationship between the performers and the audience (80 percent of tourist arrivals in Norfolk Island are Australians).[53] The show's depiction of Fletcher Christian as a valiant founding father and leader—as celebrated in many of the island's dramas—is important in this light, especially his portrayal as a noble character defending his honor against Bligh's unfair strictures and imperiously acidic tongue. In contrast to James Cook, the European "forefather" of settler Australia, who represents the orthodoxy and discursive reach of British imperialism with his faithful, serial accomplishment of government-sponsored missions, Christian is a counter-discursive forefather who usurps the authority of naval command and its commercial-colonial complicities through an act of bold rebellion (inflected with imperial anxieties about miscegenation and "going native") to found a new polity figured as the quest for a new and better form of freedom and justice. This championing of Christian asserts the community's own identity and analogizes its "political indigeneity" as a population oppressed by a larger settler culture[54] in an ongoing struggle for self-determination.

Harking back to the "Taahiishan Formadhas" and the "Myuuteniya Forfaadhas" (Tahitian Foremothers and the Mutineer Forefathers),[55] the community exhibits and activates a range of linked practices and genealogies that bring Britain, Tahiti, Pitcairn, Norfolk, and Australia into layered arrangement. Whereas James Clifford locates processes of "indigenous becoming" in "adapting and recombining the remnants of an interrupted way of life" by "reach[ing] back selectively to deeply rooted, adaptive traditions" in contemporary performances of endurance and renewal,[56] the blended history of Norfolk Island suggests how new indigeneities might be inaugurated within modern contexts as well. By making a claim to autochthony born of multiplicity, which, significantly, becomes possible only through further relocation, the community and its *Mutiny on the Bounty Show* positions the Pacific as a dynamic space of mixing, merging, and re-emerging from within and without, and reveals how these cultural intersections influence and are influenced by the boundaries of Oceania as they are shaped and reshaped.

CONCLUSION: OCEANIC INTERCULTURALISMS

These performances from the Tuamotu Archipelago and Norfolk Island do not represent conscious aesthetic experiments in blending, exchanging, or interweaving two or more (performance) cultures, but demonstrate, in their stories of community genealogy, how intercultural formations are already there as part of networked chains of engagement that stretch back centuries and that continue to work themselves out in the present. In this respect, they demonstrate a principle of island life in the Pacific, which does not deny the distant and small-scale existence of many communities, yet nevertheless demands that we pay attention to their deeply ingrained circumstances of contact with other cultures within and beyond the region. From a methodological standpoint, tracking these itineraries requires historically situated and carefully contextualized analyses that deploy archival and ethnographic methods, as well as an interdisciplinary optic that brings approaches in (at least) folklore, cultural studies, linguistics, history, politics, economics, and geography to bear on theatre and performance. It asks that we trace intercultural dynamics not only on the stage but also between performers and audiences, and in/through the structures that make performance possible. Such research also requires, as Margaret Werry adroitly observes, "a shift of a profoundly conceptual character, from static and territorial methodologies of analysis to those modes of categorization, narration, and thought premised on mobility."[57] "Thinking Oceanically" instead of continentally foregrounds alternative concepts of time, space, ownership, knowledge, and representation, positing the sea as a "tapestry of pathways and entry points that extend over both time and space" and privileging "ways of recognizing affiliation and kinship in histories defined by constant motion."[58]

This perspective invites research that goes beyond charting exchanges between clearly defined cultural groups to limn the striations and multiplicities that inhere within cultures. *Te Reko no Tutepoganui* expresses a wide-ranging and multidimensional indigenous world that extends deep into the ocean and its marine resources and cosmogenically to the other-world of gods and mythic heroes. It speaks to an early twentieth-century Tuamotuan culture invested with multiple local practices and exchanges and with multiple Western influences borne by the motilities of globalization. The contemporary re-indigenizing and trans-indigenizing of the mask of Tutepoganui tracks and augments these histories in a political statement that negotiates webs of affiliation and difference. Also stemming from the West's desire to exploit raw materials from eastern Oceania (this time, breadfruit instead of pearl), the story of *The Mutiny on the Bounty Show* tracks the dramatic and multi-staged passage of plurality into indigeneity, standing as a performance that embeds multiple interculturalisms and that serves as a current political statement against neo-colonial assimilation. Both case studies operate at the interface between micro- and macro-level social operations, proving how Pacific islands and islanders are not passive spectators of, but rather active participants in, world-historical processes. In their relevance to discourses on diaspora, indigeneity, and cultural transmission, the performance cultures of Oceania, still little known beyond the Pacific, have much to offer studies of world performance.

NOTES

1. Epeli Hau'ofa, "Our Sea of Islands," in *We Are the Ocean: Selected Works* (Honolulu: University of Hawai'i Press, 2008), 36.

2. Katerina M. Teaiwa, "Our Sea of Phosphate: The Diaspora of Ocean Island," in Graham Harvey and Charles D. Thompson Jr. (eds.), *Indigenous Diasporas and Dislocations* (Aldershot: Ashgate, 2005), 173.

3. Teaiwa, "Our Sea of Phosphate," 176.

4. Leo Cabranes-Grant, *From Scenarios to Networks: Performing the Intercultural in Colonial Mexico* (Evanston, IL: Northwestern University Press, 2016), 8–9.

5. Cabranes-Grant, *From Scenarios to Networks*, 5.

6. Ric Knowles, *Theatre & Interculturalism* (Houndmills, UK: Palgrave Macmillan, 2010), 59, 61. See also Knowles, *Performing the Intercultural City* (Ann Arbor: University of Michigan Press, 2017), 1–20, *passim.*

7. See Knowles, *Theatre & Interculturalism*, 70.

8. New Zealander of European descent.

9. Cabranes-Grant, *From Scenarios to Networks*, 8, emphasis in original.

10. Cabranes-Grant, *From Scenarios to Networks*, 5, 13.

11. Historical sources offer a variety of spellings for local names and places. Unless otherwise indicated, I have followed the orthography of each original source.

12. Stewart Firth, "The Pacific Islands and the Globalization Agenda," *Contemporary Pacific* 12, no. 1 (Spring 2000): 182.

13. Firth, "The Pacific Islands and the Globalization Agenda," 181.

14. See A.-C. Eugène Caillot, "Le Parler-Drame de Tutepoganui, Roi des Mers," in *Mythes, Légendes et Traditions des Polynésiens* (Paris: Ernest Leroux, 1914), 95–109. For a rather archaic English version of the play, minus most of Caillot's notes but with different commentary, see the Editors' Review in *Journal of the Polynesian Society* 35, no. 4 (140) (December 1926): 339–43.

15. The Tuamotuan word *reko* has a broad range of definitions, including story, legend, talk, recitation, statement, demand, pronouncement, and articulation, and also describes the language as a whole, as in Reko Pa'umotu or Re'o Pa'umotu (the Tuamotuan/Paumotuan language); compare, for instance, reo Māori (Aotearoa) and reo Mā'ohi (Tahiti). See J. Frank Stimson and D. S. Marshall, *A Dictionary of Some Tuamotuan Dialects of the Polynesian Language* (The Hague: Martinus Nijhoff, 1964), 445. Caillot laments that "La langue polynésienne n'a malheureusement pas de mot pour définir une pièce de théâtre, et c'est pourquoi je me vois obligé de mettre entre parenthèses, dans la traduction française, le mot drame" ("The Polynesian language [sic] unfortunately does not have a word for a piece of theatre [a play], and that is why I feel obliged to put the word 'drama' in brackets in the French translation"), 95. All translations mine.

16. Formerly called "Paumotu" (conquered islands) because of their historical conquest by the Tahitians, in the early 1850s a delegation from the archipelago petitioned the French authorities to change the name to Tuamotu, which was formalized in 1852. See Kenneth P. Emory, *Material Culture in the Tuamotu Archipelago* (Honolulu: B. P. Bishop Museum, 1975), 1.

17. Emory, *Material Culture*, 5.

18. Caillot writes: "On ne pourra manquer d'être surpris de rencontrer chez les Polynésiens actuels, si dégénérés depuis leur conversion au christianisme, une véritable pièce de théâtre; mais l'etonnement sera-t-il moindre quand on saura que cette pièce n'est pas leur oeuvre, mais celle de leurs ancêtres cannibales? C'est pourtant que les indigènes déclarent unanimement, dans les îles où cette pièce est jouée encore de nos jours" (95). In relation to the "cannibal" designation, Emory notes that human flesh was occasionally eaten in different islands, but that these were typically slain enemies who had fallen in battle (7).

19. For a neat summary of some of these records, see Katharine Luomala, "Post-European Central Polynesian Head Masks and Puppet-Marionette Heads," *Asian Perspectives* 20, no. 1 (1977): 131–3. See also Diana Looser, "A Piece 'More Curious Than All the Rest': Re-Encountering Pre-Colonial Pacific Island Theatre, 1769–1855," *Theatre Journal* 63, no. 4 (December 2011): 521–40.

20. Luomala, "Post-European Central Polynesian Head Masks," 134; Caillot, "Le Parler-Drame," 95.

21. Luomala, "Post-European Central Polynesian Head Masks," 146–7.

22. Caillot, "Le Parler-Drame," 95–6.

23. See Te Rangi Hiroa/Peter Buck, *Ethnology of Mangareva* (Honolulu: B. P. Bishop Museum, 1938).

24. Hawaiki (Havaiki, Havai'i, 'Avaiki) is a sacred place of origin and return for many cultures across Polynesia. Its location varies, but it is generally considered the departing point for the ancestral migrations and the destination for the soul after death. Hawaiki is also often situated as a mystical and primordial world where demigods and heroes carry out superhuman and supernatural exploits. Robert D. Craig, *Handbook of Polynesian Mythology* (Santa Barbara, CA: ABC-CLIO, 2004), 131.

25. Caillot, "Le Parler-Drame," 103.

26. Hiriata Millaud, "Tūtepoganui," flyer produced for the Assembly of French Polynesia, Pape'ete, 2012, not paginated.

27. Craig, *Handbook of Polynesian Mythology*, 167, 132.

28. H. M. Chadwick and N. K. Chadwick, *The Growth of Literature* (Cambridge: Cambridge University Press, 1940), Volume III, 285.

29. See Craig, *Handbook of Polynesian Mythology*, 132–5.

30. Editors' Review, *Journal of the Polynesian Society*, 343.

31. Te Rangi Hiroa/Peter Buck, *Ethnology of Manihiki and Rakahanga* (Honolulu: Bishop Museum, 1932), 203. See also Editors' Review, *Journal of the Polynesian Society*, 343.

32. George Frederick Kunz and Charles Hugh Stevenson, *The Book of the Pearl: The History, Art, Science, and Industry of the Queen of Gems* (New York: Century Co., 1908), 190–2.

33. Millaud, "Tūtepoganui."

34. Luomala, "Post-European Central Polynesian Head Masks," 151.

35. Caillot obtained the mask after the performance on Hikueru and gave it to the Musée des Frères des Écoles chrétiennes in Pape'ete; later, Frère Alain passed it on to the Musée de Tahiti (Luomala, "Post-European Central Polynesian Head Masks," 144).

36. Chadwick Allen, *Trans-Indigenous: Methodologies for Global Native Literary Studies* (Minneapolis: University of Minnesota Press, 2012), 246, emphasis in original. Although Cabranes-Grant does not cite Allen, his "investment in the becoming of objects and events" (8) is similar.

37. Thanks to the University of Queensland for the Australian Research Council Grant Application Support Scheme funding that enabled my research in Norfolk Island.

38. Shortly afterwards, some of the islanders elected to return to Pitcairn, where a separate but related community of about fifty people remains today. Pitcairn Island is a British overseas territory.

39. Anne Salmond, *Bligh: William Bligh in the South Seas* (Auckland: Penguin, 2011), 21.

40. For an insightful reading of some of these filmic representations, as well as the overall theatricality of the mutiny, see Greg Dening, *Mr. Bligh's Bad Language: Passion, Power and Theatre on the Bounty* (New York: Cambridge University Press, 1992), esp. 339–67.

41. Response based on my viewing of the *Mutiny on the Bounty Show* by Pinetree Tours, Salty Theatre, Anson Bay, Norfolk Island, December 10, 2013. It is worth noting that there are also tourist offerings in Tahiti that capitalize on the *Bounty* myth and that remember the Tahitian descendants of these events who remain in Tahiti. See, for instance, "1er International Bounty Festival a Tahiti du 25 au 27 Octobre 2013," Press Kit. *Tahiti News*, http://tahitinews.co/wp-content/uploads/2012/12/DP-FESTIVAL-BOUNTY-2013.pdf.

42. Michael Ritzau, "'Indigenous' Sense of Place and Community in a Small Island: Norfolk Island and the Pitcairn-descendant Population," Hons. thesis, School of Geography and Environmental Studies, University of Tasmania, 2006, 54.

43. Ritzau, "'Indigenous' Sense of Place and Community in a Small Island," 55.

44. Personal communication with the Office Manager of Pinetree Tours, Burnt Pine, Norfolk Island, December 13, 2013.

45. Merval Hoare, *Norfolk Island: A Revised and Enlarged History, 1774–1998* (Rockhampton, QLD: Central Queensland University Press, 1999), 72.

46. Maev O'Collins, *An Uneasy Relationship: Norfolk Island and the Commonwealth of Australia* (Canberra: Pandanus Books, 2002), 5, 15, 145.

47. Ritzau, "'Indigenous' Sense of Place and Community in a Small Island," iii.

48. Ritzau, "'Indigenous' Sense of Place and Community in a Small Island," 33–4.

49. Melissa Davey, "'We're Not Australian': Norfolk Islanders Adjust to Shock of Takeover by Mainland," *Guardian*, May 21, 2015, https://www.theguardian.com/australia-news/2015/may/21/were-not-australian-norfolk-islanders-adjust-to-shock-of-takeover-by-mainland.

50. Brad Norrington, "Norfolk 'Crushed' By Takeover," *The Australian*, November 20, 2017, https://www.theaustralian.com.au/news/norfolk-crushed-by-takeover/news-story/c985135252a294c7eb8e19b5eeb34ca1. Melissa Davey, "Norfolk Islanders go to UN to Fight Australia Over Right to Self-Govern," *Guardian*, March 12, 2018, https://www.theguardian.com/australia-news/2018/mar/13/norfolk-islanders-go-to-un-to-fight-australia-over-right-to-self-govern.

51. Mark Willacy and Alexandra Blucher, "Norfolk Mutiny Brewing Against Island's Australian Administrator amid Claims of Intimidation," *ABC News*, December 7, 2016, http://www.abc.net.au/news/2016-12-07/norfolk-mutiny-brewing-against-islands-australian-administrator/8096096.

52. Ritzau, "'Indigenous' Sense of Place and Community in a Small Island," 9.

53. "Norfolk Island Tourism Industry," SGS Economics and Planning, Australia, page 2, http://www.emaa.com.au/uploads/4/6/3/2/46326229/norfolk_island_tourism_industry_research.pdf.

54. Ritzau, "'Indigenous' Sense of Place and Community in a Small Island," 62.

55. Alice Inez Buffett, *Speak Norfolk Today: An Encyclopaedia of the Norfolk Island Language* (Norfolk Island: Himii Publishing Company, 1999), 97, 65.

56. James Clifford, *Returns: Becoming Indigenous in the Twenty-First Century* (Cambridge, MA: Harvard University Press, 2013), 7.

57. Margaret Werry, "Oceanic Imagination, Intercultural Performance, Pacific Historiography," in Erika Fischer-Lichte, Torsten Jost, and Saskya Iris Jain (eds.), *The Politics of Interweaving Performance Cultures: Beyond Postcolonialism* (New York: Routledge, 2014), 102.

58. Werry, "Oceanic Imagination, Intercultural Performance, Pacific Historiography," 102–3.

CHAPTER SIX

Subversive Immigrant Narratives in the In/visible Margin: Performing Interculturalism on Online Stages

ROAA ALI

Immigrant Americans, particularly Arab and Middle Eastern minorities, are often positioned in the margins not only of whiteness, but also the American religious and political mainstream sphere. Theatre artists of these communities have struggled to "speak" within the limitation of a cultural political discourse that often frames their voices as "ethnic." Critics of multiculturalism as a social model have accused it of allowing "minority" cultures to "speak," while perpetuating their ethnic categorization and thus marginalization. They challenge it as being a model that maintains racial hierarchy whilst advocating racial harmony.

This chapter aims to theoretically investigate the criticism against multiculturalism, and the call for interculturalism to replace it. It will examine Chicago's Silk Road Rising (SRR) as a case study for a theatre company that is culturally carving a space for minority artists, and politically advocating interculturalism as a model of practice. The company has provided a platform for Middle Eastern and Asian voices since its creation in 2002 as a response to 9/11. Through harnessing new technologies, it is attempting to create unrestrictive spaces for its artists by engaging the online public sphere in the making and distribution of projects that seek "the intersections of cultures without denying the specificities of cultures."[1]

CHICAGO'S SILK ROAD RISING (SRR)

SRR materialized out of the vision of artistic director Jamil Khoury, a Christian Arab American, and his husband, executive director Malik Gillani, a Muslim Pakistani

American. The directors characterize the company and its creation as an "intentional and creative response" to 9/11, explaining their vision:

> to counter negative images and stereotypes of Middle Eastern and Muslim peoples with representation grounded in authentic, multi-faceted, and patently human experiences. We'd center politics that were anti-racist, anti-colonial, and pro-feminist, and tell stories that were by us, about us, and for all.[2]

Responding to a static discourse of a clash of civilizations, which demarcated races and cultures in a power dynamic advantageous to white Western superpowers, the company aimed to operate a dynamic dialogue between different immigrant cultures in the US. Although the initial aim of the company was to present artists from the Middle East, this vision soon expanded to include artists from the Silk Road, a geographical area stretching from Japan to Italy that was historically known for its silk trade and cultural interaction. Defining its mission, the company's directors state, "We promote the sharing of stories that are rooted in our unique cultural experiences; stories that challenge both mainstream audiences and Silk Road communities to reconsider their biases and preconceived notions, and to confront uncomfortable issues."[3] The location of the residence and theatre stage of the company in the historic Temple building[4] of the Methodist Church in Chicago further symbolizes a cultural invitation for dialogue between conflicting discourses of religion, race, and sexuality.

One of the core issues that motivated the creation of SRR is the lack of visible self-representations by Middle Eastern and South Asian Americans, as well as many minorities from the symbolic Silk Road geographic areas, in the face of countless negative stereotypes. SRR aimed, thus, to provide a stable stage that would cater specifically for artists with such cultural heritage. Given the barriers facing many Arab and Asian American playwrights[5] who seek to challenge a myriad of political, cultural, and social discourses that antagonize them, SRR offers a much-needed platform for self-representation and visibility. From the start, SRR has had a pluralistic cultural vision: while negotiating the cultural politics it operates within, SRR is aiming to activate interculturalism as an alternative model to multiculturalism.

THE "INTER" REPLACES THE "MULTI" IN CULTURALISM

The specific branding of SRR as an intercultural, or polycultural, institution follows a current theoretical debate that distinguishes multiculturalism from interculturalism, or polyculturalism, in essence and practice. In an attempt to define interculturalism, it is imperative to locate it within a discourse that is crowded with many versions of culturalisms. Neither multiculturalism nor interculturalism or polyculturalism has been explicitly and exclusively defined. The three terms are schools of thought that address cultural diversity in a society and its management, and the following will explore the similarities and differences between these models.

Multiculturalism is a model developed to accommodate the changing ethnic and cultural composition of Western societies, and it has been adopted in the majority of Western Europe, the US, Canada, and Australia, although its implementation in social policy and governance is different in each of these regions. It is a political and belief system "based on the idea of 'difference'"[6] that acknowledges and values diverse ethnicities and cultures in one society, and "has become the preferred perspective on diversity . . . in political debate."[7]

In recent years, however, many critics have highlighted the limitation of this cultural system. While multiculturalism was the offspring of liberal cultural and political theorists, its application in social governance is facing increasing criticism. According to historian Vijay Prashad, multiculturalism "assumes that people come in cultural boxes that are hermetically sealed, that their culture is a thing that is immutable and pure."[8] Prashad's problematization of multiculturalism stems from his view that cultures cannot be marked with either geographic or ethnic borders, but are rather constantly interacting and evolving. As the cornerstone of multiculturalism lies in acknowledging racial and cultural difference, some critics argue that multiculturalism led to segregation,[9] and others think it caused "undue disturbance of the health of society, and that social problems have mounted that outweigh the recognised benefits."[10] Allowing "minority" cultures to "speak" while perpetuating their ethnic categorization and status represents another flaw of multiculturalism, investigated by Sneja Gunew in her *Haunted Nations: The Colonial Dimensions of Multiculturalisms*, who criticizes multiculturalism for being a model that maintains racial hierarchy while advocating racial harmony.

In response to such criticism, a move towards a new cultural conceptualization, as well as a social/political system, of multi-ethnic nations appears to be in demand. Interculturalism has been suggested as a new model that "seeks to replace multiculturalism and provide a new paradigm for thinking about race and diversity . . . Interculturalism is about changing mindsets by creating new opportunities across cultures to support intercultural activity and it's about thinking, planning and acting interculturally."[11] Nasar Meer and Tariq Modood argue that interculturalism is "something greater than coexistence, in that interculturalism is allegedly more geared toward interaction and dialogue than multiculturalism,"[12] and this distinction is echoed in most scholarly thinking on the issue. The conceptual variance between multiculturalism and interculturalism seems to lie in their respective treatment of cultural difference: multiculturalism sees it as something to be preserved, while interculturalism views it as a point of negotiation. These debates on how diverse cultures negotiate and mediate have particular significance for what interculturalism means for theatre and performance studies.

In their formative article "Toward a Topography of Cross-Cultural Theatre Praxis," Jacqueline Lo and Helen Gilbert introduce definitions for a list of theatres including multicultural theatre and intercultural theatre, summarizing the differences:

> Whereas multicultural theatre is often the effect of state-determined cultural management and/or a grassroots response to the "lived reality" of cultural pluralism . . . intercultural theatre is characterized as a "voluntarist intervention circumscribed by the agencies of the state and the market."[13]

The categorization of multicultural theatre as an activity mandated by the state's social agenda brings into question the artistic and cultural authenticity of works commissioned for this purpose. It is also unclear how multicultural theatre is different from intercultural theatre in practice—the assumption here is that they both refer to works of art that incorporate markers of more than one culture. However, it is vital to note that interculturalism, rather than multiculturalism, has been the preferred term in referencing and theorizing works that cross the boundaries of one culture. For example, in his insightful *Theatre & Interculturalism*, Ric Knowles makes a conscious decision to choose "intercultural" as opposed to other terms including "multicultural" in his analysis:

> I prefer "intercultural" to the other terms available—cross-cultural, extracultural, intracultural, metacultural, multicultural, precultural, postcultural, transcultural, transnational, ultracultural, and so on—because it seems to me important to focus on the contested, unsettling, and often unequal spaces between cultures, spaces that can function in performance as sites of negotiation.[14]

Knowles's acknowledgment of the "unequal spaces" that permeate cultures when they meet is vital. There are power structures that govern the interaction of cultural selves and signs in the space of a theatre or a performance work, which were either unrecognized or uncontested in early intercultural theatre of the 1980s. Knowles perceptively and eloquently gives and analyzes many examples of performances that introduced, borrowed, or appropriated markers of other cultures, highlighting the flows of many previous practices. In assessing some modernist theatre practices such as that of William Butler Years and Antonin Artaud, which incorporated elements of Eastern cultures such as Japanese theatrical traditions, Knowles notes that they enacted a "cannibalisation of forms without respect for the cultures that produced them," a strategy that "directly participated in the west's colonisation of the world's cultures and peoples."[15]

Discussing Peter Brooks's 1985 *The Mahabharata*, which was adapted from a sacred Hindu text in India, Knowles indicates that the majority of praise for this seminal work originated from white Western critics and audiences, while non-white scholars criticized the work's inattentiveness to the Indian culture. Through this, Knowles stipulates that "intercultural performance had unwittingly participated in the commodification of the 'other.'"[16] Most critics of early intercultural theatre[17] or intracultural theatre[18] accuse the movement of appropriating non-Western cultural markers, fetishizing the Other and mirroring it with its ethnocentric image. Daphne P. Lei coined the term "hegemonic intercultural theatre" to refer to frames of thinking and artistic practices that compound "First World capital and brainpower with Third World raw material and labour, and Western classical texts with European performances traditions."[19] Daryl Chin argues that "To deploy elements from the symbol system of another culture is a very delicate enterprise. In its crudest terms, the question is: when does that usage act as cultural imperialism? Forcing elements from disparate cultures together does not seem to be a solution that makes much sense, aesthetically, ethically, or philosophically."[20] The risk of cultural colonization and imperialism stemming from intercultural theatre practice, which Chin explores, is undoubtedly great and sometimes unavoidable. However, the problematic assumption here is that cultures are pure, and that individuals of any culture are pure products of their own culture rather than a collective of countless, sometimes unconscious, constituents of other cultures—this is particularly true in the digital age.

Earlier intercultural theatre practices, which appropriated rather than negotiated cultural signs in performance, seem to face similar criticism aimed at multiculturalism. Arguably, both discourses need a new interculturalism geared towards dialogue and negotiation of the politics of power, identity, and place. It is noteworthy that earlier discourses of interculturalism in theatre have mostly been about Western white[21] theatre practitioners portraying elements of other cultures in their performance. Until recently, the discourse of interculturalism was amiss regarding theatre practitioners considered non-white, such as first- and second-generation immigrant artists, where interculturalism occurs, more often than not, organically rather than being an experimental exercise. Charlotte McIvor offers a detailed and elegant study of interculturalism in Ireland,[22] exploring it through individual art initiatives led by minority ethnic and migrant communities who enforce the practice from the bottom up, and introduce their intercultural art as a soft power that enables a reimagining of the nation. Similarly and to reframe the narrative of interculturalism, Royona Mitra theorizes an "interventionist approach to new interculturalism" forged from the practices of intercultural British Asian minority artist Akram Khan: "Driven by the lived experience of diasporic realities, which necessitates subjects having to simultaneously negotiate multiple cultures, new interculturalism is a life-condition as much as an aesthetic and political intervention."[23]

This new interculturalism is similar to polyculturalism. Recently, and particularly in the US, polyculturalism has been gaining prominence as a new cultural model. As advocated by historians Robin Kelley and Vijay Prashad, polyculturalism sees cultures constantly fusing and merging, and thus any cultural Self is "a tangled skein of cultural influences, even if we identify with a single cultural group."[24] According to Robert Winder, writer and former literary editor of *The Independent*, polyculturalism "suggests a mixture of ingredients too closely entwined to be distinct, a whole greater than the sum of the parts" and emphasizes "the connections rather than the barriers between 'cultures.'"[25] In essence, theorists who promote polyculturalism attribute to it the same characteristics as new interculturalism, and they similarly define it by its departure from multiculturalism. Prashad draws the distinction between multiculturalism and interculturalism/polyculturalism: "A polyculturalist sees the world constituted by the interchange of cultural forms, while multiculturalism (in most incarnations) sees the world as already constituted by different (and discrete) cultures that we can place into categories and study with respect."[26]

These theoretical reflections are particularly relevant to understanding how dominant cultures interact with marginal cultures and the role of the minority artist in crossing and challenging the divide. In her analysis of Akram Khan's dance performances, Mitra demonstrates how the intercultural Self of a minority artist cannot be separated from the artistic practice, necessitating a continuous negotiation of identity and socio-political power structures. The debate on interculturalism in theatre and performance studies has been positively expanding to include the voices of minority artists, which is not only essential to enriching the discipline, but also necessary to locate the inherent political urgency of intercultural theatre. SRR is one example of a company that publically identifies itself as polycultural/intercultural, but whose practices aim to contest hegemonic whiteness, marginalization, and cultural appropriation, at the same time as encouraging cultural intersection. SRR is attempting to produce an artistic vision of interculturalism that is organically formed from the cultural Selves of its artistic team, and promote this vision in Chicago's theatre circle, where it operates.

MULTI MEETS POLY IN SRR

Introducing the vision of SRR, a statement on its website reads, "Silk Road Rising understands that cultures are inherently linked . . . And we strive to create a world that values art over ideology and inquiry over dogma."[27] The focus on the "intersections of culture" as a starting point for creativity, dialogue, and self-introspection introduces this company, in essence, as intercultural or polycultural— Much of the content and practices produced by SRR supports that intercultural vision. The company's creation as an artistic response to 9/11 and the culturally divisive rhetoric which ensued and continues to the present, as well as its negotiation of different cultural representations on its stage and within the wider local Chicago area, contextualize interculturalism as an artistic need and response to political and cultural turmoil.

The motivation behind SRR as an intercultural—or polycultural, as the creators prefer to call it—artistic initiative resounds clearly in *Multi Meets Poly: Multiculturalism and Polyculturalism Go on a First Date* video-play. The video-play model is a new project undertaken by SRR to widen its reach by employing dramaturgical language and referencing theatre as its location, while being filmed by a cinematic lens and placed on the company's webpage as an open access source. *Multi Meets Poly* is brilliantly scripted, employing humor and wit while bringing the abstract ideas of multiculturalism and polyculturalism closer to the audience. Playwright Jamil Khoury personifies the two theoretical schools of multiculturalism and interculturalism/polyculturalism, injects them with gender characteristics and sexual tension, and then sets them on a date. The video-play is a testament to the importance of this cultural dialogue to a company that represents immigrant American voices and operates within an ethnocentric cultural setting. The following dialogue presents some of the main differences between multiculturalism and polyculturalism as the playwright envisions them:

> **Multi**   You said that I sequester cultures in their own little silos.
>
> **Poly**   February is African American month. March is Women's History month. May is Asian American month. September 15 through October 15 belongs to Latinos. I'm sorry. It's problematic.
>
> **Multi**   As opposed to all twelve months belonging to white folks?
>
> **Poly**   You had your month, now go away. We ate your food. We watched you dance. We loved your ethnic costumes.[28]

The play is a dramatic translation of the cultural debates preoccupying its author as a playwright and an artistic director of SRR. It is almost a confessional piece about the inner workings of the company as a cultural institution. Here, the vision of a theatre company is, perhaps for the first time, dramatized in an online video-play. While the play does not present either of the two cultural models as triumphant, it definitely encourages the maturation of interculturalism/polyculturalism at the expense of multiculturalism. In the following exchange, polyculturalism is clearly presented as a future certainty:

> **Poly**   I integrate. You segregate. I welcome. You polarise. I facilitate. You regulate. I encourage. You impose. I ask. You accuse. I emerge. You force. I accept. You tolerate.
>
> **Multi**   In other words, I'm serious and you're a suggestion. You're a helpful hint.
>
> **Poly**   No, I'm a destination, and you're a temporary weigh station.[29]

During the workshop sessions,[30] the artistic director invited the actors and the creative team to both rehearse the play and respond to it personally as part of the development stage. In these workshops, *Multi Meets Poly* stirred endless discussions between the two actors who each, on a personal level, believed in only one of the two cultural ideologies. The play thus appeared as an extension of the actors' consciousness, as much as a statement of the company's inner working. The discussions incorporated stories of personal experiences, which reflected on the successes and failures of multiculturalism in the face of racism, sexism, and homophobia in the US. These workshop sessions became cultural laboratories evaluating policies and unsettling established practices in the American context. In *Multi Meets Poly*, cultural politics are anthropomorphized because they represent a vital organism that affects the daily lives of all the ethnic artists of SRR.

Because of its intercultural vision and the new practices it has adopted, SRR presents a rich example of what interculturalism looks like in practice. In welcoming plays from playwrights of the Silk Road (Japan to Italy), SRR is focusing on empowering representations of the under- and misrepresented in the US, rather than promoting a racial alliance to a specific or exclusive race or culture. The company is not specifically Middle Eastern, even though it caters for many Arab and Middle Eastern American works; and it is not particularly South Asian despite hosting many playwrights with this cultural affiliation. This fluidity in welcoming many cultures, even if they collide, allows a more organic dialogue between cultures and their translation in theatre.

The first live play to be staged at SRR was an example of how the company's artists envision theatre as a mediating space between clashing cultural discourses of nationalism. This was Jamil Khoury's 2002 *Precious Stones*, which boldly dramatized the Palestinian–Israeli conflict. The play's subject was the uncompromising discourses of two nations, whose existence depend on the denial of the other, but the dramatic treatment of this conflict was an open negotiation. The story of the conflict was presented through the love affair of a Palestinian American woman and an Israeli-sympathizing Jewish American woman. The play presents the possibility of crossing national and sexual borders to initiate a seemingly unimaginable dialogue between two women, whose national belonging is dividing, but whose sexual belonging is unifying. Although the play ends with an unresolved argument between the two heroines, the final line—"we will figure this out"[31]—is an open invitation to continue the cultural dialogue and eventually reach a resolution.

INTERCULTURALISM AS PRACTICE

To accommodate its intercultural vision, SRR has for the past fifteen years experimented with a company model that has offered subversive narratives to a Western white cultural center, brought invisible Othered cultural representations into view, and experimented with modes of delivery and artistic distribution. Essential to all these activities is the idea of producing one's own self-representation: that is, subverting Orientalist discourses in which Middle Eastern and Asian voices, bodies, and narratives were imagined and negatively stereotyped. SRR nurtures new Middle Eastern and Asian playwrights by reviewing script submissions and inviting a number of playwrights each year to develop their plays in SRR's physical space in Chicago. These plays are then cast and produced in SRR either as staged readings or main productions. Typically, the live theatre program of SRR is seasonal, with many of the productions developing as premieres, with a number of reproductions of plays from inside and outside the US. The company operates as a non-profit theatre funded through grants, sponsorship, and donations, while ticket sales from live theatre returns only 15 percent of production costs.[32] The company's online program is more fluid and each work has its own production process. The audience for both the live and online shows are integral to the artistic work, and are often consulted through organized workshops and after-show discussions, while their input is enlisted as a contribution to the development of online works, as will be discussed below.

SRR is a small company that is politically vocal in its representation of voices from the Middle East and Asia, voices often portrayed as the Other to the American mainstream public. Marginalized by a "war-on-terror" political and social discourse, the voice of most of the artists and characters represented by SRR belong to the periphery, and can be described as "subaltern," to borrow Gayatri Spivak's terminology. Although Spivak objects to its indiscriminate appropriation, the term is generally understood to refer, in postcolonial studies, to the oppressed "objects" who are located in a "space of difference" outside of the hegemonic discourse.[33] It is in this context that most Middle Eastern and Muslim American voices are arguably subaltern. Their representation in the American mass media has been the product of an Orientalist discourse that frames them as the Other, and which has continued with ferocity after 9/11. The Trumpian rhetoric of "America First" has further mutated the othering of Middle Eastern and Muslim Americans, particularly singling out Muslims in America as outsiders and suspects, firmly located in a distrusted space of national and cultural difference.

Artists who are Middle Eastern and South Asian migrants in the US carry markers of both their cultural heritage and their present everyday American culture. They represent the intercultural Self, with an ability to put interculturalism into practice if an intercultural space were to be provided. According to Spivak, "To do a thing, to work for the subaltern, means to bring it into speech."[34] Since its inception, SRR has been producing intercultural works that challenge cultural binaries and bringing into visibility those voices that have been systematically marginalized. For example, in 2010 the company commissioned seven ethnically-diverse contemporary playwrights[35] to contribute short plays that were assembled into one piece titled *The DNA Trail: A Genealogy of Short Plays about Ancestry, Identity and Utter Confusion.* Each playwright took a DNA test and responded to the result with a creative piece that interrogates one's own identity and its relationship with the identity of the other co-creators. In 2017, the company produced and hosted the "Semitic Commonwealth," a week of enhanced stage readings. It featured three plays by Arab playwrights and three plays by Jewish playwrights,[36] and aimed to again negotiate the Palestinian–Israeli conflict through a creative intercultural perspective rather than barren political confrontation.

SRR has also involved powerful cultural voices from outside the US in the production of *Wild Boar* (2017), written by award-winning Chinese playwright Candace Chong and adapted by the esteemed David Henry Hwang, and *Invasion!* (2013), by Tunisian Swedish playwright Jonas Hassen Khemiri. These plays and others brought a multitude of cultural voices to a stage in the center of Chicago, and stimulated a critical engagement with these voices and their cultural and political standings. Presenting a diversity of cultural perspectives is not always without risk, and can casually provoke or upset communities or audience members who are opposed to the dramatization of culturally sensitive issues. In 2005, Yussef El Guindi's *Ten Acrobats in an Amazing Leap of Faith* was met with a storm of criticism from the Arab American community because it represented a gay Muslim son and his atheist brother. Distressingly, SRR received a small number of threatening emails[37] and some members of the audience left the theatre during the performance. Nevertheless, this delicate interrogation of cultural difference and the controversies this approach may inspire are essential to cultural dialogue and the activation of interculturalism on the stage.

BEING SUBVERSIVE

The enterprise of being interculturally vocal while still being demarcated as a minority artist or theatre is a delicate and arduous one. Even when subalterns are brought into speech, their voices are typically resisted and subdued because they are potentially capable of unsettling the "imperial cultural" or hegemonic discourse. In this context, an intercultural theatre can confront the dominant culture and its sometimes damaging practices. A number of incidents and altercations that took place between SRR, as an intercultural company that represents immigrant and marginalized voices, and representatives of the Chicago mainstream cultural center exemplify the disparity between the two theatrical spheres, and the complexity of representing the voice of the cultural Other.

In anticipation of the 2013 premiere of *The Jungle Book* at the established Goodman Theatre in Chicago, Catey Sullivan interviewed the theatre's celebrated Director in Residence, Mary Zimmerman, who adapted and directed the show. The interview included questions about the director's treatment of Kipling's politics of representation, racism, and misogyny, which Zimmerman declares to be "pretty terrible and pretty undeniable."[38] However, when asked whether she was concerned that *The Jungle Book* could perpetuate racial stereotypes, especially with King Louie's character, Zimmerman answered:

> Yeah, it was a concern. But I've decided to make it not a concern . . . I know what the lyrics . . . ["I Wanna Be Like You"] say, but look at the original—it's sung by Louis Prima. He's the King of the Swingers. It's something I think where the racism is in the eye of the beholder, you know?[39]

Zimmerman was most likely speaking with the best of intentions, but her understanding of racial discourses proved rather problematic. Her quick and reductive dismissal of racism was indicative of a "privileged" denial of an Orientalist and colonial past. This was further supported when, in reference to the legacy of colonialism in India, she stated, "You have to remember the past, but you don't have to live in it."[40] This interview provoked a strong reaction from the artistic director of SRR, who wrote an impassioned response.[41] He admitted that he had often felt the need to exercise self-censorship in the past in the face of theatre or cultural discourses that he felt problematic, presumably because the politics of both representation and business would not welcome his critical voice. In his response, Khoury refuted Zimmerman's interpretation of the colonialist legacy as short-lived, and listed examples of the struggles which colonized lands and peoples had to endure. Responding to Zimmerman comment that "You go over [to India] and you see that the British occupation was so short in the history of the country. No one is sitting around moping about the Raj. You have to remember the past, but you don't have to live in it,"[42] Khoury wrote:

> Zimmerman's flippant, aloof dismissal of the brutality and cruelty of the British Raj is as astonishing as it is infuriating. Human injustice of such epic magnitude just shrugged off. Let's see: partition, a nation ripped into three pieces, the forced "transfer" of millions of people, the untold numbers who died, the wholesale destruction of property, the loss of identity and security. But who has time for details?[43]

Khoury especially contested Zimmerman's light-hearted engagement with the issue of stereotypical racial representations and the discourse of racism in general, attributing such views to "unexamined white privilege and American privilege."[44]

Khoury's response highlights the disparity between the two directors' understanding of theatre and its relationship to culture and race. Theatre for Zimmerman represents a vocation informed by artistic experimentation, while for Khoury it symbolizes a rare space for artistic expression of a politically and culturally contested identity. Zimmerman's interview and Khoury's subsequent response demonstrate the discrepancy between the cultural and political spaces the two directors occupy. Khoury made this clear in a follow-up interview with Zimmerman: "I think it fair to say that Silk Road Rising's philosophical and political approaches to storytelling and cultural representation are markedly different than Mary Zimmerman's. We assimilate context and historicity differently. We define authenticity differently. In short, we inhabit a radically different world than Mary Zimmerman."[45]

Khoury's article generated several discussions about theatre's relationship with othered cultures, races, and representations. While comments supporting Khoury and thanking him for "speaking up" were abundant, many were also critical of Khoury personally and SRR generally. The *Chicago Tribune*'s Chris Jones described Khoury's essay as "strikingly personal"[46] in an attempt to question its intellectual and critical legitimacy, while defending Zimmerman and her vision. Some denounced the essay as a promotional stunt for Khoury and his company, describing it as a "full-career slam,"[47] while others argued that Khoury aggravation of the issue lacked substance or accused him of unprovoked racial sensitivity. Both directors eventually reconciled, but many in Chicago's theatre circles deemed SRR's response to be an "unwise" attempt to criticize the politics of representation and race in the work of such an established director as Zimmerman.

Another episode that drew similar attention to SRR and discourses of representation was the premiere of the critically acclaimed *Invasion!* (July 30–September 15, 2013) at SRR. As noted above, this play was the intercultural effort of Tunisian Swedish playwright Jonas Hassen Khemiri, together with translator Rachel Willson-Broyles and director Anna Bahow. *Invasion!* confronts its audiences with the myth of the "threatening" Arab male and deconstructs it by exposing stereotyping and racial profiling as the real culprits that hold language, culture, and humanity hostage at the center of this myth. *Invasion!* stirred heated debate in Chicago theatre circles, which escalated after theatre critic Hedy Weiss wrote a review of the play in the *Chicago Sun-Times*.

Weiss praised the play for its aesthetic and artistic content, but refused to "buy" its argument, concluding her review with implied support for racial profiling against Muslims: "But despite Khemiri's passion, those still thinking of the horrific terrorist attacks at the Boston Marathon might well be tempted to ask: What practical alternative to profiling would you suggest?"[48] The article demonstrated an inability to engage or negotiate with the myriad of cultural signs and settings that grounded the play and informed its argument; they were still deemed cultural Others to Weiss. SRR and its artistic director Khoury responded immediately with an article condemning the "praise" for racial profiling expressed in Weiss's article.

A torrent of social media activity followed, exhibiting both support for and abuse of Khoury and SRR. The *Chicago Reader*'s Michael Miner defended Weiss's review[49] and suggested that problematizing the racial context of Weiss's article was simply motivated by Khoury's desire for publicity. The view that Khoury and SRR were needlessly politicizing cetain artistic issues because of "unprovoked" cultural sensitivity, or worse still, for publicity's sake, was echoed in theatre social circles and through social media posts. Khoury cut an isolated figure in challenging Weiss and her endorsement of institutionalized Islamophobia. In 2017, Weiss faced fresh accusations of harboring bigoted views after her review of *Pass Over* by Antoinette Nwandu at the Steppenwolf Theatre Company. The play addresses the problem of structural racism and police brutality from the perspective of two black men sitting on a sidewalk in a *Waiting for Godot*-esque land. This time, Weiss's apparent racism crossed a line, enraging Chicago's theatre community and resulting in a petition against inviting Weiss to further plays in Chicago.[50] Commenting on the affair and explaining his company's support for the petition, Jeremy Wechsler, Artistic Director of Theatre Wit, reflected on the fact that he had not made a stand earlier:

In 2013, I watched Jamil Khoury at Silk Road Rising confront a strikingly similar review in the *Sun Times*. At the time, I was relieved I didn't have to pick a fight. "I can lay low," I thought. "The review is awful, but it isn't my show. I can avoid this confrontation." ...

I was relieved that I didn't have to threaten this income source by offending a critic. It's a decision I regret; silence, in retrospect, was complicity.

Part of the reason for my inaction then was that the role for response by a "third party" theater was undefined. Thus, Silk Road was left to argue its case in the public square alone.[51]

Wechsler's commendable honesty provides one example of the isolation that SRR faced when confronting such bigotry. The difference between the responses of the Chicago theatre circle to both incidents warrants critical reflection as to why collective action was not initiated when SRR raised concerns over Weiss's apparent prejudice.

These critical responses highlight two points: first, the role of SRR in producing subversive plays, which render alternative cultural points of views visible; and second, the sensitive and sometimes problematic reception by an ethnocentric center of cultural representations of the Other. In this context, SRR as an intercultural theatre has the potential to unsettle dominant configurations of culture and introduce to the cultural center that which has been placed in the periphery. The center's resistance to voices from the periphery has been discussed by Russell Ferguson:

As historically marginalized groups insist on their own identity, the deeper, structural invisibility of the so-called center becomes harder to sustain. The power of the center depends on a relatively unchallenged authority. If that authority breaks down, then there remains no point relative to which others can be defined as marginal. The perceived threat lies partly in the very process of becoming visible.[52]

As Ferguson highlights, power relations are key to understanding the dominance of some cultures at the expense of others: in the case of SRR, a mainstream American white culture at the expense of non-white immigrant cultures. To succeed in challenging this power structure, it is not enough to simply present markers of othered cultures or races—we must also question their flawed cultural positioning, as in the case of Zimmerman's *The Jungle Book*. An intercultural performance needs to fully understand and interrogate its composite cultural elements and provide offer new cultural understandings or cultural positionings through the work. Similarly, an intercultural theatre must acknowledge the existence of the socio-political inequalities inherent in the cultural representations it produces in order to destabilize the status quo and effect change.

CREATIVITY WITH RESOURCES: ONLINE VENTURES

As an ambitious but small company with an intercultural vision, SRR needed to create new venues for theatre production that would liberate it from the traditional demarcations of cultural center/margin. It needed to operate in an unrestrictive space to experiment with ideas, cultural interaction, civic engagement, theatremaking, and distribution. Well aware of the limitations of its eighty-seat physical stage, Khoury and Gillani wanted to widen the company's outreach and intercultural possibilities. In September 2011, the pair revitalized their company by introducing a new website as an additional stage for their theatrical initiatives.

This provided the company with a digital space for various artistic articulations comprising online theatre, video essays, and a new playwriting process that invites virtual audiences to partake in the artistic creation. Paired with the company's desire to experiment with elements of "cyberperformance,"[53] the move was strongly driven by an urge to broaden the company's civic engagement and intercultural agenda. Cyberspace was an option that would, if used wisely and innovatively, rid the company of both the restriction of a small theatrical space and a prescribed cultural invisibility. SRR's directors have said of the rationale that drove their decision, "Beyond our own organization, we see the rising up of new arts and aesthetics, including the rise of the Internet as a leading medium for arts engagement . . . In taking this world as our own, we celebrate the rise of a virtual Silk Road that is artistic, egalitarian, democratic, and visionary."[54] This celebration of a virtual Silk Road represents the company's acknowledgment of its virtual cultural agents and their adaptability to new digital ways of communication and distribution that cross national borders.

With caution, one can arguably identify the internet as a new public sphere that offers, albeit still controlled by organizations and funding agendas, a site where individuals from different cultures might share their views and express their aspirations and frustrations. One can argue that the virtual space encourages the creation of "counterpublics," which Michael Warner defines as spaces "formed by their conflict with the norms and contexts of their cultural environment."[55] According to theatre scholar Janelle Reinelt, "counterpublics" are "alternative publics that come into being creating an alternative or rival public culture."[56] In this context, SRR's online stage becomes an intercultural counterpublic with audience members as cultural agents partaking in the production and consumption of "alternative" or subversive intercultural works.

THE CULTURAL OTHER TAKES CENTER STAGE

Ownership of distribution introduces a more fluid interaction with subject matter and artistic expression. By incorporating the online space as a venue of distribution, SRR managed to ease the pressure of season restriction, ticket sales, and producing content that would probably have high salability. It also meant that SRR would have more freedom to engage with cultural discourses that might be too problematic for a traditional theatre stage. Many of SRR's projects owe their inception and execution to the fact that they are online projects: examples include the documentary film *Not Quite White: Arabs, Slavs and the Contours of Contested Whiteness*, and the online project *Mosque Alert*. Through their online presence, both attempt to create a resistant intercultural discourse.

Not Quite White is an online documentary that investigates whiteness and redefines it through Arab American and Polish American lenses. Disrupting the narrative of whiteness with these different cultural experiences challenges a monolithic understanding of race and culture and advocates interculturalism as an alternative. As suggested by earlier analysis, SRR is a small company that operates from the periphery of a "white" mainstream center. By offering its platform to ethnic voices, it inevitably challenges a white discourse of superiority. Definitions of whiteness are constantly renegotiated in almost every SRR performance, but are most notably pronounced through *Not Quite White*. The documentary can be viewed as an attempt to appropriate the production of knowledge and meaning to reflect minority voices.

Khoury accompanies the documentary with a video essay titled "On Whiteness," and through both, he utilizes cyberspace as a platform not only to reshape knowledge about whiteness, but also to localize it within his own Arab and Slovak experience. Khoury problematizes whiteness outside the dichotomy of whites/non-whites to introduce a category specific to Arab Americans: the "not quite white."[57] *Not Quite White* addresses the role of whiteness in creating power relations that translate to problematic cultural politics: "whiteness as a constructed social and political category, a slippery slope that has historically played favorites, advantaging northern and western European immigrants over immigrants from Eastern and Southern Europe and the Middle East. We maintain that whiteness has victims: non-white victims, not quite white victims, and white victims."[58]

Through this documentary, SRR transforms what is normally an academic debate into a dramatic form, with the company's website as a place of viewing. By employing performative and audio-visual tools, this knowledge is disseminated outside scholarly circles to a more general audience. *Not Quite White* incorporates segments of a film (*W.A.S.P.*) produced by SRR, archival material and photographs, interviews with academics, and music to render knowledge about whiteness accessible, localized, and distributable. Uploaded simultaneously to SRR's website and YouTube, *Not Quite White* has been viewed almost 15,000 times,[59] with audiences commenting on their racial identification as well as their relationship to whiteness as a system of privileges.

This contested relationship with whiteness is negotiated artistically and symbolically through SRR as a theatre company with its own problematic relationship with a white mainstream center. Regarding the trouble with whiteness in relation to the immigrant experience, the documentary states that "we are resentful of how whiteness erases our respective backgrounds, negates our cultures, our family histories, all that is unique and particular about our stories."[60] It is here that the perseverance of alternative voices becomes urgent, as the experience of immigrants introduces organic interculturalism as a way of living. As the company's first online documentary, *Not Quite White* probed the racial positioning of immigrant Americans, problematizing racial and cultural categorization in the US, and producing a counter-discourse to whiteness.

Mosque Alert is another online project that has been a focal point for SRR for the past five years. The project introduces an innovative playwriting process, developed in part to enable its virtual audience to participate in the process of playwriting. One of the aims of the project is to activate its audiences to generate an intercultural response to Islamophobia. *Mosque Alert* as a play dramatizes the tension between three families (two Muslim and one Christian) over the building of a new mosque in Chicago's western suburbs of Naperville. The play examines and contests Islamophobia in the US and its frenzied manifestation whenever the subject of mosque construction arises. Motivated by the controversy that followed New York City's proposed "Ground Zero Mosque" ten years after 9/11, the play destabilizes the negative semiotics surrounding mosques as Islamic cultural markers. It also challenges the stereotypical preconceptions of what family, women, and homosexuality mean in Islam.

Mosque Alert proposes a new model of playwriting in which the playwright, Khoury, introduces his ideas on the plot, characters, and conflict scenes in vlogs on the company's website.[61] Virtual audiences view these segments and enter a dialogue with the playwright by posting their comments in response to questions from the playwright or by introducing their own thoughts on various aspects of the play. Khoury takes these comments as a backbone on which to draft his script, after which SRR produces the live play. Finally, the company produces an edited version of the play suitable for online viewing, and presents it online on a webpage (www. mosquealert.org) specifically designed to facilitate further interaction with the virtual audience. This process maximizes civic engagement with virtual audiences and invites a multitude of cultural voices to address Islamophobia and the cultural reception of Muslims in the US. Actor and director Shishir Kurup responded to the project as a member of its virtual audience, described the approach employed in *Mosque Alert* as an "inclusive way of making art and proliferating personal investment in the writing process. It takes the idea of community-based art making in a meaningful new direction."[62]

The development process for *Mosque Alert* took five years, during which audiences (physical and virtual) were consulted and their input collated into the final draft of the play. At each step, characters were developed as a response to audiences' and commentators' ideas of what cultural identity means. Imam Mostafa is one of those characters, representing the progressive Muslim trying to communicate that his faith is not a threat, but rather in accord with his American identity. In one scene (Act 1, Scene 11), Imam Mostafa, a Pakistani American Muslim, advocates the building of the mosque during a meeting with members of the community. While some of those members encourage him and call him a "hero," others find him culturally un-American:

Mostafa I'm an American by choice and I choose to be an American Muslim. Because Islam is found in American institutions and in the American way of life.

Audience Member #1 Remember 9/11! . . .

Mostafa I'm very much at home in America as a Muslim, because the ideals that we have as Americans are the same ideals we have as Muslims. If you have concerns, if you have doubts, if you are simply seeking knowledge, please know that I am available to you. Here tonight or any other time.

Audience Member #1 We don't want you here! Go back to Iran!

Mostafa I happen to be from Egypt.

Audience Member #1 Go back to Egypt!

Audience member #3   (to Audience Member #1): How about you go back to Alabama?

Ted   How about we all stay put here in Naperville and learn how to behave?[63]

Within the scope of the play, there are a multitude of voices representing both progressive and conservative cultural views placed in scenarios where they have to engage in dialogue. By doing so, the play uses interculturalism to confront xenophobia and "de-Other" the Muslim American. It specifically promotes the view that diverse facets of identity can coexist without erosion or conflict, promoting a positive transgression of the established either/or dichotomy.

Mosque Alert's vlogs have already been viewed over 25,000 times inside and outside the US, including the likes of Canada, the UK, France, Iraq, India, Pakistan, Saudi Arabia, Israel, Columbia, Spain, and Greece, according to statistics gathered from SRR's website. It was translated into German for a stage reading at the Lichthof Theater in Hamburg, and into Arabic with the aim of producing it on Arab stages. *Chicago Reader's* Deanna Isaacs followed *Mosque Alert* from its digital inception to its production as a live play at SRR's physical stage, and posed the question "Did an audience of millions turn up?"[64] Isaacs answered in the negative, but also noted that "the videos did attract 25,000 viewers from all over the 'world, including from countries where—if authorities had been aware of them—the subject matter might have been censored. About 200 of those viewers interacted with Khoury through e-mails or online comments."[65] A large number of virtual audiences did indeed view and engage with the work, which in itself was a positive and promising outcome. *Mosque Alert* demonstrated that intercultural practice needs innovative approaches to civic engagement and distribution if it is to create the sought-after "loud and impactful noise" beyond the physical limitation of theatre spaces.

SRR's approach with *Mosque Alert* can potentially inspire others to promote new vistas for intercultural engagement. It makes possible the presentation of intercultural American immigrant experiences to individuals' cultural spaces of origin, albeit requiring the translation of American cultural specificities and possible adaptability to homeland cultural sensitivities. Ultimately, SRR's working method provides a useful model that might further expand the scope of intercultural practice led by minority artists in other national diasporic contexts.

CONCLUSION

As an example of an intercultural theatre, SRR has used the immigrant experience of its artists and audiences as a stepping stone to negotiate cultural identity and its representation. It has unsettled rigid stereotypes by hosting Middle Eastern and Asian artists who have brought typically invisible cultural representations to the heart of Chicago's theatre scene, and has done so by incorporating different and sometimes opposing cultural voices and inviting audiences to be collaborators in some of its online projects. The company's decision to incorporate virtual space in its operation has enabled it to reach audiences outside the walls of a theatre and beyond national borders.

SRR's approach invites theatremakers in the wider field to rethink interculturalism both as an idea and as a practice. As an idea, interculturalism must address the power dynamics at play between the different cultures it engages, and as a practice, it can benefit from embracing new avenues of production and distribution to circumvent the structural inequalities it seeks to dismantle. Perhaps interculturalism in theatre is best defined by its ability to create positive cultural interventions. Ideally, no cultural sign in an intercultural practice should be superior to another due to its racial, national, religious, or sexual affiliation; rather, practitioners should constantly seek to destabilize structural power relations and privileges. Intercultural theatre can be a powerful tool against structural and institutional exclusion that often hinders the visibility of minority artists and their access to mainstream cultural spaces. In that sense, intercultural theatre can effectively act as a progressive response to global social and political challenges originating from cultural misunderstanding and impasses.

NOTES

1. SRR website, "Our History," https://www.silkroadrising.org/our-history.

2. SRR website, "Our History."

3. SRR website, "Our Mission," https://www.silkroadrising.org/mission.

4. According to SRR website, "The First United Methodist Church of Chicago pre-dates the incorporation of the City of Chicago by six years, tracing its origins to 1831 . . . Celebrated as one of Chicago's most diverse congregations, members hail from every ZIP Code in the city as well as 80 suburbs."

5. See Roaa Ali, "Arab American Theatre: Still a Struggle for Visibility," *Al Jadid* 21, no. 72 (2017): 12–13.

6. Tariq Modood, *Multiculturalism* (Cambridge: Polity Press, 2013).

7. Nick Haslam, "Cultures Fuse and Connect, so We Should Embrace Polyculturalism," *The Conversation*, June 6, 2017, https://theconversation.com/cultures-fuse-and-connect-so-we-should-embrace-polyculturalism-78876.

8. Vijay Prashad, "Interview with Vijay Prashad," 2009, http://www.frontlist.com/interview/PrashadInterview.

9. Eric Uslaner, *Segregation and Mistrust: Diversity, Isolation, and Social Cohesion* (New York: Cambridge University Press, 2012).

10. Max Farrar, Simon Robinson, Yasmin Valli, and Paul Wetherly (eds.), *Islam in the West: Key Issues in Multiculturalism* (London: Palgrave Macmillan, 2012), 2.

11. Ted Cantle, "About Interculturalism," 2012, http://tedcantle.co.uk/publications/about-interculturalism/.

12. Nasar Meer and Tariq Modood, "How does Interculturalism Contrast with Multiculturalism?" *Journal of Intercultural Studies* 33, no. 2 (2012): 4.

13. Jacqueline Lo and Helen Gilbert, "Toward a Topography of Cross-Cultural Theatre Praxis," *Drama Review* 46, no. 3 (2002): 36.

14. Ric Knowles, *Theatre & Interculturalism* (London: Palgrave Macmillan, 2010) 4.

15. Knowles, *Theatre & Interculturalism*, 12.

16. Knowles, *Theatre & Interculturalism*, 22.

17. See Parice Pavis (ed.), *The Intercultural Performance Reader* (London: Routledge, 1996).

18. See Rustom Bharucha, *Theatre and the World: Performance and the Politics of Culture* (London: Routledge, 1993).

19. Daphne P. Lei, "Interruption, Intervention, Interculturalism: Robert Wilson's HIT Productions in Taiwan," *Theatre Journal* 63, no. 4 (December 2011): 571.

20. Daryl Chin, "Interculturalism, Postmodernism, Pluralism," in Bonnie Marranca and Gautam Dasgupta (eds.), *Interculturalism and Performance: Writings from PAJ* (New York: PAJ Publications, 1981), 83–95.

21. By white, I refer to an ideological whiteness.

22. Charlotte McIvor, *Migration and Performance in Contemporary Ireland: Towards a New Interculturalism* (London: Palgrave Macmillan, 2016).

23. Royona Mitra, *Akram Khan: Dancing New Interculturalism* (London: Palgrave Macmillan, 2015), 11.

24. Haslam, "Cultures Fuse and Connect."

25. Robert Winder, *Bloody Foreigners: The Story of Immigration to Britain* (London: Abacus, 2004), 467.

26. Vijay Prashad, *Everybody was Kung Fu Fighting: Afro-Asian Connections and the Myth of Cultural Purity* (Boston: Beacon Press, 2001), 66–7.

27. Prashad, *Everybody was Kung Fu Fighting*.

28. Jamil Khoury, *Multi Meets Poly*. Directed by George Bajalia, USA: Silk Road Rising (2015), http://www.silkroadrising.org/video-plays/multi-meets-poly-multiculturalism-and-polyculturalism-go-on-a-first-date.

29. Khoury, *Multi Meets Poly*.

30. I attended the workshop for *Multi Meets Poly* during a research trip to the SRR company in July 2013.

31. Jamil Khoury, "Precious Stones," in Michael Malek Najjar (ed.), *Four Arab American Plays* (Jefferson, NC: McFarland & Co, 2013), 86.

32. Figures were collected during a funders' meeting that I attended during a research field trip in 2013.

33. Leon De Kock, "Interview with Gayatri Chakravorty Spivak: New Nation Writers Conference in South Africa," *A Review of International English Literature* 23, no. 3 (1992): 45.

34. De Kock, "Interview with Gayatri Chakravorty Spivak," 46.

35. The seven playwrights are Philip Kan Gotanda, Velina Hasu Houston, David Henry Hwang, Jamil Khoury, Shishir Kurup, Lina Patel, and Elizabeth Wong.

36. For more details on the Semitic Commonwealth, see https://www.semiticcommonwealth.org/.

37. These details were communicated to me via a personal interview with Jamil Khoury in 2013.

38. Catey Sullivan, "How Mary Zimmerman Handled Kipling's Racism and Misogyny in a New the Jungle Book Musical," *Chicago Magazine*, May 15, 2013, http://www.chicagomag.com/Chicago-Magazine/C-Notes/May-2013/Mary-Zimmerman-Race-Gender-Jungle-Book.

39. Sullivan, "How Mary Zimmerman Handled Kipling's Racism and Misogyny."

40. Sullivan, "How Mary Zimmerman Handled Kipling's Racism and Misogyny."

41. Jamil Khoury, "The Trouble with Mary," SRR website, June 11, 2013, http://www.silkroadrising.org/news/the-trouble-with-mary.

42. Sullivan, "How Mary Zimmerman Handled Kipling's Racism and Misogyny."

43. Khoury, "The Trouble with Mary."

44. Khoury, "The Trouble with Mary."

45. Jamil Khoury, "Mary Responds: My Interview with Mary Zimmerman," SRR website, June 14, 2013, http://silkroadrising.org/news/mary-responds-my-interview-with-mary-zimmerman.

46. Chris Jones, "'The Jungle Book' at Goodman Theatre: When Mary Met Walt (and Rudyard)," *Chicago Tribune*, June 14, 2013, http://www.chicagotribune.com/ct-ae-0616-jungle-book-preview-20130614-column.html.

47. Rob Weinert-Kendt, "Catch-Up," *The Wicked Stage*, June 17, 2013, http://thewickedstage.blogspot.co.uk/2013/06/catch-up.html.

48. Hedy Weiss, "'Invasion!' Arrives at Divisive Time in the World," *Chicago Sun-Times*, August 7, 2013.

49. Michael Miner, "Hedy's Review was a Rave—Why is Everybody so Upset?," *Chicago Reader*, August 9, 2013.

50. See Diep Tran, "The Review That Shook Chicago," *American Theatre*, June 27, 2017, https:www.americantheatre.org/2017/06/27/the-review-that-shook-chicago/.

51. Jeremy Wechsler, "Our Press Response Policy," *Wit's End: Theater Wit's Own Blog*, August 9, 2017, http://theaterwit.tumblr.com/post/163994540172/our-press-response-policy.

52. Russell Ferguson, "Introduction: Invisible Centre," in Russell Ferguson, Martha Gever, Trinh T. Minh-ha, and Cornel West (eds.), *Out There: Marginalization and Contemporary Cultures* (New York: MIT Press), 10.

53. Helen Varley Jamieson, "Cyberformance," MA diss., Queensland University of Technology, Queensland, 2008.

54. Jamil Khoury, "Our Name," SRR website, July 15, 2011, http://www.silkroadrising.org/pages/our-name.

55. Michael Warner, *Publics and Counterpublics* (New York: Zone Books, 2002), 63.

56. Janelle Reinelt, "Rethinking the Public Sphere," *Performance Research* 16, no. 2 (2011): 18.

57. The term is borrowed from Helen Hatab Samhan, "Not Quite White: Race Classification and the Arab-American Experience," in Michael Suleiman (ed.), *Arabs*

in America: Building a New Future (Philadelphia: Temple University Press, 1999), 209–26.

58. Jamil Khoury, "On Whiteness," SRR website, July 15, 2011, http://www. silkroadrising.org/pages/our-name.

59. Count of YouTube views of the documentary was 14,971 on June 3, 2019.

60. Count of YouTube views of the documentary was 14,971 on June 3, 2019.

61. For further analysis on SRR's *Mosque Alert* project and its online model, see Roaa Ali, "Digitizing Activist Art: Widening the Platform for Civic Engagement," *Journal of Arts & Communities* 7, no. 3 (2016): 47–61.

62. Shishir Kurup, "Mosque Alert Comments," SRR website (n.d.).

63. Jamil Khoury, *Mosque Alert*, unpublished script (2017), 59–60.

64. Deanna Isaacs, "Silk Road Rising's Mosque Alert is Alarmingly Relevant," *Chicago Reader*, March 28, 2016, https://www.chicagoreadercom/chicago/silk-road-rising-mosque-alert-play-relevant-xenophobia/Content?oid=21560780.

65. Isaacs, "Silk Road Rising's Mosque Alert is Alarmingly Relevant."

PART THREE

Interculturalism as Practice

Beyond HIT: Towards Regional Interculturalism through Puppetry in Southeast Asia

JENNIFER GOODLANDER

In December 2015, several puppeteers from around Southeast Asia gathered by the large pool in one of the indoor theatre spaces at the National Puppet Theatre of Vietnam.[1] They were discussing how to combine puppets made to perform in the water and puppets made to perform on land together in one production for the finale of the ASEAN (Association of Southeast Asian Nations) Puppet Exchange (APEX). This task was made more difficult because many of the "dry" puppets would fall apart if exposed to moisture. Mann Kosal, the artistic director of Savanna Phum, a puppet company from Phnom Penh, Cambodia, proposed that perhaps a floating apparatus might be constructed to hold the puppets safely atop the surface of the water. Another puppeteer interrupted that maybe the group needed to focus on creating the story before worrying about which puppets to use. All agreed there was much to do in the week before the scheduled public performance—the stage was not ready, the musicians were still waiting for the story to be completed so they could begin working, shadow puppets being used in the production had to wait until dark to be visible on the outdoor stage—but all were excited to see old friends and meet new ones as part of this endeavor. The artists had met in Hanoi for *APEX One*,[2] the last of a series of workshops bringing together artists from different countries to collaborate and create a theatrical production representing their regional community of Southeast Asia.

Methods and ideas about intercultural theatre have changed drastically since Patrice Pavis proposed the iconic hourglass model depicting artistic practice and culture moving from a source culture (often non-Western) to a target culture (often Western).[3] Artists and artistic practices now travel and work globally, training in different genres, borrowing different approaches, and complicating national or ethnic divisions of performance practice. The power dynamics inherent within such artistic practices remain a central concern for many scholars writing about intercultural performance.[4] In her article describing Hegemonic Intercultural Theatre (HIT), or "a specific artistic genre and state of mind that combines First World capital and brainpower with Third World raw material and labor, and Western classical texts with Eastern performance traditions," Daphne P. Lei proposes that successful intercultural performance requires a careful negotiation of aesthetics, culture, and economics. She observes that the model of HIT extends beyond the West and is adapted by Asian and other cultures hoping to make a mark on the international theatre scene. Lei's model for understanding intercultural performance practices foregrounds the power relationships within and expressed by such work; her definition of HIT emphasizes material hierarchies between East and West—First Word capital is combined with raw material from the Third World. She argues that HIT also offers an opportunity for Eastern theatre artists to revitalize dying forms and to gain recognition on global stages—but what happens when the West is not present within an intercultural performance project? What kinds of networks of hegemony are created or reproduced within an Asian theatrical space?

Audiences attend productions touted as "intercultural" with particular expectations regarding to style. Companies seek a place to showcase traditional genres of performance within a global context—as Lei writes, "Intercultural theatre requires an artificial intervention, by which I mean a calculated interpretation of cultural flow that makes possible the manufacture of an end product—a theatre performance."[5] The artists of APEX performances purposefully worked towards creating something that might be recognizable as this kind of global intercultural performance, and therefore could reach audiences as a commodity representing regional identity. Recognizing that performance is intentionally designated/created as a commodity is not necessarily a purely negative thing, but rather foregrounds the economic forces that make artistic exchange and collaboration possible. The artists each grew from the experience in various ways, but this kind of nuanced learning and sharing must be translated into something to make it economically viable. APEX needed to produce a product.

In this chapter I expand the principles of Lei's HIT in order to understand the work of APEX—a multi-year project to create a performance that strives to articulate the developing ASEAN Community. Marionette, rod, and shadow puppeteers from ten countries came together to create sections of a multilayered work called *One ASEAN*. This chapter is based primarily upon my own observation and participation in the collaborative process of the exchange in Hanoi, Vietnam in 2016, but draws from the workshops and performances that have also taken place in Indonesia, Brunei, Myanmar, and Malaysia. I focus on rehearsals and other parts of the creative process to examine the superstructures around intercultural performance making that are less often examined, in order to interrogate how aesthetics, language, tradition, and modernity come together within a new kind of intercultural performance. Inspired by Lei, I use a framework that establishes how people, places, and materials must necessarily coalesce to negotiate cultures, media, and economies.

ASEAN AND APEX—FORGING COMMUNITY

For the citizens of ASEAN to become truly regional, it will be necessary to know other cultures outside of their own community and country.[6]

Community, in the context of the puppet exchange and ASEAN, must be understood as a commodity with economic and societal value. The goals of APEX mirror those of ASEAN in that both wish to create a strong community for a wider benefit. The creative methods of *One ASEAN*, therefore, strove to dramatize the values of the ASEAN Community in a public performance and to draw from those same ideals in its creation. The ten countries that compose the Association of Southeast Asian Nations, or ASEAN—Brunei, Cambodia, Indonesia, Laos, Malaysia, Myanmar, the Philippines, Singapore, Thailand, and Vietnam—make up one of the most diverse regions in the world. Many different religions, ethnicities, languages, and political systems leave the region especially vulnerable to exploitation and instability.[7] With this challenge in mind, the original founders of ASEAN[8] met in 1967 to declare their intention to work together for a variety of common purposes, including settling regional disputes, corporative economic growth, social progress, and cultural development. In 2003, the leaders of ASEAN renewed their commitment towards creating a strong regional community based upon three pillars: economic, peace and security, and socio-cultural. They also articulated plans to increase cooperation with other key Asian countries such as China, Japan, and Korea. The aims of each pillar interrelate to the others, recognizing that economics, security, and culture are closely intertwined and interdependent. The specific goals and time frame of the ASEAN Community constantly shift, but at ASEAN's core is the committment "to achieve the limited purpose of maintaining regional order."[9] The aspirations of ASEAN rely on creating a sense of a shared identity—as stated in the 1997 document, *ASEAN Vision 2020*: "We envision the entire Southeast Asia to be, by 2020, an ASEAN Community conscious of its ties of history, aware of its cultural heritage, and bound by a common regional identity."[10] This goal became more focused when ASEAN released its Initiative for ASEAN Integration in 2000.[11]

A strong regional identity is viewed as key to developing ASEAN and its member nations into economically developed, just, and politically secure countries,[12] but few, if any, scholars account for how the arts might serve and reflect this developing identity. Michael Jones recognizes that attention should be paid to "what it takes to integrate individual citizens of diverse cultural and ethnic identities into the wider regional identity or regional citizenship."[13] To work towards this goal, the ASEAN Foundation[14] was established in 1997 and hosts programs in education, media, community building, and arts and culture. The arts and culture program focuses on artists and arts institutions who can experience and express "ASEAN awareness and community."[15]

The ASEAN Puppet Exchange, or APEX, is a key way the ASEAN Foundation engaged with regional artists to realize the goals of community, which translate into the ideals of regional strength and power. The ASEAN Foundation believes that puppets offer a unique vehicle for expressing and exploring shared identity because puppets have an over 4,000-year history in the region, employ multiple artistic skills such as craftsmanship, storytelling, and performance, appeal to people of many ages and backgrounds, and offer a place where heritage and modernity intermingle within contemporary performance. The first exchange in 2014 included artists from Thailand traveling to Laos to coach and advise the Laotian puppeteers in order to develop their work further. August 2015 marked the first exchange where puppeteers from all ten nations came together in Indonesia to create a performance around a theme for the celebration of ASEAN Day in Jakarta.[16] Subsequent exchanges in Cambodia, Brunei, Myanmar, and Malaysia further developed the group's methods of working, and added music to the exchange. The December 2016 finale in Hanoi, Vietnam, *One ASEAN*, coincided with the first anniversary of the 2015 declaration of the ASEAN Community.[17] The process and performance of *One ASEAN* exemplifies the goals and processes of creating a regional community, especially shared leadership, language, and expression.

PEOPLING THE EXCHANGE—POWER AND POLITICS

In many ways, the approaches and desires for the ASEAN Community could be considered an intercultural project that is echoed by the work done in APEX. Bonnie Marranca writes that interculturalism is an attitude—a way of approaching performance, not just the product. She states that "Interculturalism is linked to world view, practice, and theory/criticism—that is, the mental attitude that precedes performance, the performance process, and the theoretical writing that accompanies performance . . . a state of mind, as much [as] a way of working."[18] Scholars have often noted that the Asian, or specifically Southeast Asian, worldview differs from Western-centric models. Power, especially political and economic power, is not seen as a top-down construction; rather, power is by association and cumulative over time—"people infer its presence by its signs."[19] The puppeteers and their work function like signs pointing back to their home nations and the region indicating power.

Many of the artists who participated in *One ASEAN* were already working in or connected to global networks of performance in various ways. Organizations such as the regional ASEAN Puppet Association (APA) and the Union Internationale de la Marionnette (UNIMA) host festivals that bring puppeteers and audiences together; governments support artist participation because of the potential to win prestigious awards.[20] APEX founder, Terence Tan, conceived of the puppet exchange projects while participating in the 2011 APA puppet festival. He wanted to create opportunities for artistic exchange and development around the region. The puppeteers Tan invited to participate often came from companies that already traveled abroad occasionally to share their work and represent their nation through puppetry. Sometimes the government limited which puppeteers could be invited. For example, Indonesia has a national puppet association (Sekretariat Nasional Pewayangan Indonesia, or SENA WANGI) that controls who can go abroad to participate in such events, while in Thailand the recent death of the king meant that the puppeteers from the Joe Louis Puppet Company, who had participated in past APEX, could not come to Hanoi because they were needed for official events. Many of the companies, however, strove to bring puppeteers for whom this would be a unique experience so that their artists would learn and grow.

The number of participants in *One ASEAN* from each country varied, and included a number of puppeteers, musicians, translators, and sometimes administrative heads of the companies represented. For example, the group from Cambodia included the director of the company (Mann Kosal), two performers who were both puppeteers and dancers (Hanf Sarmon and Sor Sophal), a musician (Soun Sophak) and a translator (Nang Yanna). Sometimes the roles of the participants would become blurred—translators often were asked to perform alongside the other artists, indicating how integral they were to the process. The number of artists and others made *One ASEAN* the largest exchange in APEX's history.

Not all of the people involved with *One ASEAN* were from Southeast Asian countries, and this also affected the process and outcome of the exchange. Part of the funding for the exchange came from the Japanese ASEAN Solidarity Fund (JASF) and as part of this funding they required Japanese artists to participate in the exchange. Erina Ogawa, a puppeteer from the Utervision company in Tokyo, participated in several exchanges. She was often accompanied by a translator, Moe Shoji, a PhD student from Japan writing her dissertation on contemporary British theatre. Erina sometimes expressed concern about finding a balance between contributing ideas to the artistic collaboration and a desire to allow the artists from Southeast Asia to find their own way. Jodi Theile, a theatre artist originally from Australia who now lives and works in Singapore, often gave structure to the rehearsal process and worked to facilitate communication. I was also aware of my own role in the creative process—I have worked as a theatre director and am trained in Balinese *wayang kulit* (shadow puppetry), but was at *One ASEAN* to observe. I provided my field notes to the organizers, and they used them both in planning and reflecting on the process. Each of us navigated a desire to contribute to the project while cautious that we might overly influence the work because of our perceived status as artists or academics.

The official working language of the exchange, as with ASEAN, was English. Since its inception, ASEAN officially uses English as its sole official language. This has many implications for language policy and education around the region. Some countries, such as Singapore, Brunei, the Philippines, and Malaysia, use English as the primary language in schools, while others only have English language instruction in elite schools. English was a colonial language in some places, and today learning English threatens the rich linguistic terrain of Southeast Asia, where many people already speak a local ethnic language such as Javanese together with a national language such as Indonesian. Among the people living in ASEAN, there is often discussion and criticism regarding the use of English as the official ASEAN language.[21] For example, language professors in Indonesia have been moving for Indonesian to become another official language for ASEAN, possibly replacing English. They argue that it is spoken by more people than any other Southeast Asian language, is similar to and understood by most speakers of Malay, and is one of the most linguistically developed in terms of language resources for instruction.[22] Others argue for the importance of having a common language that comes from within ASEAN, rather than from outside.[23]

APEX demonstrates the difficulty of fostering cultural exchange when there are many different languages in an organization. Some groups had skilled translators who had experience working in performance, but others did not, or the translators had difficulty with the specialized language of theatre. This reflected both the level of language instruction available in those countries, the ability and time the artists have to learn a foreign language, and whether the group could financially support a person to act as translator. For example, Thet Thet Htwe Oo, a young puppeteer from Myanmar, a country that does not offer English in public schools, could speak English. This reflected the value her father, the head of the company—but who was not present at this exchange—placed on arts, culture, and foreign language. Her father, Khin Maung Htwe, was not from a family of artists, as was the tradition for *yokethay*, or stringed-marrionette puppets. At one time, these puppets were the honored artistic form for the court, but that changed during the twentieth century with changes in the government and as puppetry also had to compete with television and movies to attract an audience. The repressive military government made it difficult for puppet companies to survive,[24] and the group, Htwe Oo Myanmar, depended on foreign tourists to come and see their shows. Learning English to communicate has been necessary for their economic survival, but also part of a larger desire to find ways to preserve Burmese heritage.

Performers who could speak English or who had adept translators had more power in the collaborative process. Wandi from Singapore would often share his ideas, while the puppeteers from Laos and Thailand had a much more difficult time. Some artists spoke limited English and were hesitant to use a translator, but this sometimes led to misunderstandings. For example, Mann Kosal spoke relatively good English and preferred to work without the group's translator. He was the head of the group from Cambodia, Sovana Phum, so the group's translator would hesitate to step in to correct misunderstandings, which sometimes resulted in frustration among several people. In contrast, the two performers from northern Thailand spoke almost no English. Thai, especially in that part of the country, is linguistically similar to Lao, so they were able to manage by working with the performers from Laos. English as the lingua franca impacted my research as well; there were some conversations that I could better follow than others, as I speak Indonesian/Malay and so was able to communicate and listen to performers from Brunei and Indonesia.

Each performance created within APEX aspired to tell its story through movement and the physical objects of the puppets, and not depend on language for the audience to understand. Steve Tillis writes about how puppets have their own language—that puppets communicate through the various aesthetics of size, scale, color, shape, and method of manipulaton.[25] Many of the puppet genres in ASEAN also rely on traditional conventions that offer meaning to a knowledgeable audience. For example, in several forms of *wayang* (found in Malaysia, Singapore, and Indonesia), most characters exist on a continuum of *alus* to *kasar*, or refined to unrefined. Refinement is a desirable trait and is often indicated by a small body, narrow eyes, small nose, closed mouth, and a downward gaze. A *kasar* puppet would have bulging eyes, a large nose, an open mouth with large teeth showing, and sometimes a very large body. The nuances of this sign system would be meaningless, however, to audience members from a country with a different tradition.

The ability to comprehend language, whether spoken or performed, shaped the dynamic of the exchange. Rustom Bharucha warns that the power differences between First and Third World countries can result in cultural inbalance, erasure, and appropriation.[26] All of the participants might be from Southeast Asia, but because the region includes both some of the richest and poorest countries in the world, there was still a threat of replicating the kind of East–West division that Bharucha describes. This might be especially true in a top-down creative process, such as Lei described, but the process of *One ASEAN* strove to be different.

The artists actively worked to bridge the differences in language, both spoken and communicated through the puppet, in deciding what story and ideas they desired to convey to the audience. On the second day of *One ASEAN*, the performers discussed what issues they hoped to focus on through the performance, and to think about the story. For example, previous APEX performances focused on social issues such as the environment, gambling, and the role of the arts in society. Amihan Ramolete, the director for Teatrong Mulat from the Philippines, helped guide this discussion by asking what message did they wish to communicate to the audience about ASEAN. Central to the discussion was the question of how the puppets might be able to communicate these ideas through performance without language, verbal or aesthetic. Tan reminded them that as a group they spoke many languages, but the puppets could be one common language. Phannaly Thepptiavongsa, the president of the Vulnerable Youth Development Organization from Laos, agreed, saying that through custom and culture, as might be expressed in puppetry and dance, people would be able to understand each other. Kosal countered, saying that sometimes he felt the traditional puppets were "nothing" and expressed a desire to "create something new on the stage." Kosal imagined a performance where they created new puppets that no longer represented each nation, proposing that maybe it would be better for one puppet to represent many aspects of ASEAN culture. He concluded, "my idea is maybe in the future we will have a new puppet for ten countries." Time and resources, however, did not allow for the creation of a new puppet. Rather, the bodies of the performers and puppets came together to form a collage of images representing many different ideas and relationships.

AROUND ASEAN—OVERCOMING DIFFERENCE

Each APEX Exchange has had different puppets, cultures, and performance spaces. Often the location would both inspire and limit the creative process. Sometimes these differences manifested in logistical difficulties—traffic jams, rain, and intermittent electricity have all shaped some of the exchanges. The performers have tried various approaches to overcome these many differences. Each APEX also has included time for cultural exchange and exploration, which has taught the participants about each host country, given them time to get to know each other, and sometimes inspired the creative work.

The first day of APEX in Hanoi was in the water—literally. The participants were able to watch a performance by the members of the National Puppet Theatre in the beautiful outdoor water theatre. The venue can seat about 400 people and is often packed each afternoon for several shows targeted at international tourists who arrive by the busload. This unique form of puppetry had originally developed in the countryside, but has become more international—going from a focus on inward-facing local group identities and solidarity to outward-facing articulation of national identity for international audiences.[27] The puppets are made from wood and are mounted on a long pole that extends back to the "backstage" or pagoda area where the puppeteers are masked from the audience by a screen. The puppeteers must stand in the water to operate the puppets, which often depict fish, fishermen, cows, dancers, dragons, or other symbols of Vietnamese mythic and rural life. Comic characters and folk tales are a feature of village performances, but in the cities there is very little dialogue or story as the audiences there generally speak many different languages and come from many different places.

Local audiences in Hanoi more often attend "dry puppet" performances, and that branch of the theatre is considered more innovative. During the APEX in Hanoi, we were able to watch members of the company rehearse a dynamic Spanish-inspired piece with music, dancing, and puppets on strings and with rods swirling around. This number was for performance both internationally and for the National Puppet Theatre's anniversary celebration at the end of the year. The troupe also often takes shows out to the villages to teach topics such as hygiene and health care. Dry puppets are typically used for these because of the expense and difficulty of traveling with a water tank large enough to stage a water puppet performance.

The participants from Vietnam were excited to finally be able to include water puppets in an APEX performance; the logistics had made it impossible before *One ASEAN*. The selection of the water puppets for use in APEX reflects the ideology of who constitutes the ASEAN Community; official national identities are typically represented through heritage over local, ethnic minority, or popular ones. Jones warns that if ASEAN emphasizes only dominant identities "the governing structure will remain exclusionary, perhaps even elitist, and not representative of ASEAN ideals."[28] In the May 2016 exchange in Myanmar, Vietnam did not bring water puppets, but rather brought elaborate marionettes that needed to be operated from many feet above the stage. These puppets were not used in the final performance for that APEX because of technical limitations, and the Vietnamese artists expressed disappointment that it was too difficult to bring the "better" water puppets.

For *One ASEAN*, the National Puppet Theatre's large water stage offered a picturesque setting for APEX, visually evoking rural Southeast Asia in the heart of the city. The stage was massive compared to the small spaces that many of these companies typically used for a performance. For example, Htwe Oo had a small stage in their home, often putting on performances for only fifteen people. The large *sbeik thom* (leather shadow puppets) from Cambodia often used a large stage, but with a fabric screen that would have obscured the rest of the playing area. The artists had to think about how to combine puppets of different scales effectively together in the space.

For rehearsals and a performance involving many different kinds of puppets, the location was also a challenge. Many of the rod and string puppets from the other ASEAN countries could not be allowed to get wet, an issue that became even more evident on a day when it rained. The delicate costumes, animal hair, and sometimes papier-mâché would not survive even a little moisture. Even the shadow puppets, made of leather, could not tolerate immersion in the water. To make the National Puppet Theatre's outdoor stage work, innovation was required. The technical staff at the theatre created a larger front stage connected to a platform on either side. Tall screens were erected on each side that could be used as shadow screens. These limited horizontal movement for the shadow puppets, but the artists could manipulate the position of the puppet and light in order to create an impressively tall shadow—about ten feet tall. Across the front of the upstage pagoda, another shadow screen was constructed in place of the curtain. Now all kinds of puppets might appear onstage at the same time, albeit sometimes in separate places and spheres.

The construction work necessary to make the stage accessible to all the different puppets delayed progress. However, waiting for the technical team to ready the space gave the puppeteers opportunities to explore Hanoi, learn about Vietnamese culture, and spend time together. Like the rehearsal process, these excursions exposed both some of the advantages and difficulties of creating a community, whether regional or artistic, from people from so many diverse cultures. For example, on the third day, instead of rehearsal, the participants were given an opportunity to meet together for lunch and explore the city. The group met at one of the many street-side food stalls, with tables and small stools covering the sidewalk and local noodles with meat served in piping hot bowls. Several of the participants from Singapore, Indonesia, and Brunei, however, were Muslim and could only eat halal food. They were not able to join the group for lunch, and spent the day separate from the others doing their own shopping and sightseeing.

Food offers a way to experience culture and create community, and might be seen as just as important in creating an intercultural production as the actual rehearsal process. Mary Douglas applies structural linguistic theories to decipher the meaning of a meal. She argues that food is a social activity—what people eat and how they eat it indicates social structures and cultural patterns of behavior.[29] The certification of food as halal, meaning it adheres to Muslim food restrictions and rules, has become increasingly important, especially in Southeast Asia. The consumption of halal food indicates more than simply following religious doctrine, becoming an essential part of identity and culture.[30] In Muslim majority countries this restriction does not present a problem, but in Vietnam, where most people follow some form of Buddhism, there are very few halal options, even in a big city such as Hanoi. Similar to how language often acted as a barrier to collaboration, food also included some while excluding others. It is difficult to form a community when not everyone can sit together at the same table.

The weather also proved difficult in Hanoi, further demonstrating differences between the countries involved in this enterprise. Vietnam gets quite cool in December through February, and it is common for temperatures to dip down to 50 degrees Fahrenheit. Other countries in Southeast Asia never experience weather this cold, except for perhaps in the mountains. Members of the Vietnamese company brought coats, gloves, and hats to share with their cast mates from other countries. The weather was especially difficult for the artists from Myanmar, where the climate is typically hot and humid; the country's weak infrastructure means that many people live without air conditioning as well. On one very cold day, space heaters were placed around the theatre, which benefitted those sitting nearby, but because the theatre was outdoors, they did not make a significant change for most other participants. It was difficult for everyone to be outside working on such a very cold day, but the weather also provided opportunities for the hosts to demonstrate their kindness and support for their visitors. Practical, rather than cultural, situations sometimes create strong opportunities for exchange and support.

INTERCULTURAL MATERIAL

Each APEX is about the interactions of people in different places, which often reflect different hegemonic formations within ASEAN. The material of the performance includes the story, the actual puppets, and the ways of working with and around these two things to create the final show.

Story

Developing a cohesive story was the most difficult and perhaps most important part of the collaboration. Unlike many other well-known intercultural collaborations, APEX does not use a pre-existing story. Jodi often led the groups through prompts to think about story and movement. She explained to me that she did not seek to direct the production, but rather guide the process and collect and synthesize the group's ideas. On the second day the group had to meet in the smaller water puppet theatre that was indoors. Another group was rehearsing outside and the crew was busy building platforms for the main stage. All together the space felt crowded and chaotic. Yanna, the translator from Cambodia, suggested that perhaps it would be too difficult to work as one large group, and that it would be better to divide into smaller groups to initially generate ideas.

The puppeteers broke into smaller groups of two or three countries together. The new format stimulated conversations, because of the differing abilities with English. The translator did not have to move between multiple groups and sometimes the translator acted as a group's de facto leader, while at other times and in other groups, one of the artists, because of a stronger personality, would guide the conversation. The configuration, however, also emphasized the relationship between nation and identity. Ideas were generated to represent Laos or to represent Singapore, rather than encouraging artists to think and work as individuals coming together in one community. For example, Laos wanted to focus on issues relating to poverty, while artists from Singapore felt that pollution might be more relevant. National differences were emphasized rather than reduced.

Different members of the group offered ideas for the story that might incorporate the concerns of all the ASEAN nations. Phannaly suggested that the story should focus on solidarity, explaining that at one time people and animals lived in harmony—there was enough to eat and everyone was joyful—but then other people came and destroyed the land with illness and pollution. She wanted to create a story that described how the ASEAN countries might come together and address the issues of the environment and education. Phannaly's story reflected a desire for a better society through working together across the region.

Others offered story ideas that might utilize common characters or ideas in traditional stories. Not all of the artists worked with a creative director in their home countries, but tradition dictated the story and style of the performance. Participants from Vietnam and the Philippines thought the story could be about a turtle because they each had turtle puppets and turtle characters in their folklore. Other common characters were dragons, monkeys, and birds. Nature was a common theme in several past APEX Exchanges. *APEX Fire* in Cambodia primarily used shadow puppets to explain that fire has the power both to destroy and to give life. *APEX Earth* told a story about a boy and healing for a forest. The group also discussed the purpose of the exchange and the stories—whether they were meant to solve a problem or just offer the possibility of working together for a better future.

The idea for what would become the main framework of the story came from a legend in Brunei. This story was explained by Ak. Al Muiz Bin Pg. Hj. Bakar, or "Muiz" for short. He said that in the story there were two kings who used chickens to fight for power. The chickens fought to the death, and when one died the other one flew over the sea and transformed into an island. The island was safe from floods as long as the king was safe. The moral of the story was to warn against the dangers of gambling and greed. The group liked the idea as it had the potential to dramatize conflict, it included water and land, and it conveyed a strong moral lesson. Some members of the group wanted to change parts of the story, with many ideas offered, including using the island for a love story; replacing the chickens with different animals; and introducing parts of the *Ramayana*.[31] The challenge was then how to combine these suggestions into a single narrative that could be performed by the puppets available and that would be comprehensible to the audience.

After much deliberation, the story was imagined in several distinct parts in order to address the concerns and wishes of the multiple groups. It was eventually agreed that the performance would open with the creation of the earth, including the people and the animals living together. From peace would come conflict as the two kings fought each other for power. In this sequence, the characters transformed into animals who battled each other for dominance. Finally, at the battle's end, an island was created and the world would again be at peace. The overriding aim was to make the story simple and comprehensible to the audience even without words.

Puppets and Dancers

In many intercultural productions, theatrical languages from one culture must be adapted to "fit the established temporality and locality of the existing performance text."[32] Even though the APEX text could, and sometimes did, change in accordance with the material reality of the puppets and the traditions they came from, the puppets themselves often had to adjust, much like *jingju* or *kabuki* might be adapted to tell a play by Shakespeare. The story attempted to represent the ideas of multiple countries and people, but even when the artists agreed about elements in the story, there was disagreement on how best to execute each moment theatrically. Traditional aesthetics and rules were not always the guiding force; rather, it was often a desire for spectacle that influenced the staging decisions.

The battle between the bird and the snake provided an opportunity to put on show many of the puppets around the region. The bird and snake are important theatrical figures that appear in a variety of ASEAN cultures, hence many of the puppeteers brough puppets of these creatures to the event. Myanmar had a large *naga* (mythic snake) puppet and an angel character that could represent a bird. The group from Laos had a large snake that was manipulated by holding the body and twisting the creature around the stage. Santi Dwisputri, a dancer and the lone representative from Indonesia, brought a costume of a golden mythic bird. Even though the performance focused on puppets, one of the most dynamic moments was a dance/battle between Santi and a dancer from Cambodia, Sor Sophal. They were each an expert dancer, and the traditional movements from both Cambodia and Indonesia complemented and contrasted well. Sophal also wore a lavish gold costume. The scene offered an exciting collage of different puppet forms and aesthetics that visually highlighted the differences and similarities between the many cultures of the region.

Several of the performances at the end of the APEX exchanges have included a mixture of dance and puppetry. In some genres, this comingling is commonplace, exemplified by the group from Cambodia, Sovanna Phum, which often combined the two in their stage performances. Because the *sbeik thom* puppets are not articulated, even in traditional performances the puppeteer must dance to animate the puppet. Other forms also have a strong connection to dance, even though the two are rarely performed together. In Myanmar, numerous traditional dances are done in the style of marionettes, and Htwe Oo used to showcase these side by side, or teach dance as a way to help a new student understand puppet movement.

CONCLUSION

Lei concludes her article by noting that "Self-orientalization has gotten the East this far, and now it is time to think outside of the oriental box."[33] *One ASEAN* demonstrates one such attempt and some of the difficulties, and successes, of such work. The artists and organizers never referred to their work as "intercultural," even though their endeavor was mindful of the kind of developments happening in international festivals and large-scale spectacles that are marketed towards tourists and often acknowledged as intercultural. Since Patrice Pavis published his now almost monolithic hourglass[34] approach to intercultural performance, many studies of such performances have considered the ways that different types of performance have mixed or failed to blend. Certainly it is useful and interesting to understand the relationships between Shakesepare and *kathakali* presented on a recreated Globe stage for an international audience located in London.[35] In a recent rethinking of intercultural performance, Pavis has revisited the different categories of intercultural performance, but it is difficult to locate where *One ASEAN* would fit in this framework. For example, it might be considered to be "syncretic theatre"[36] because is includes music, text, and visuals from several cultures—but *One ASEAN* does not mix European forms or address postcolonial issues. Pavis argues that multicultural theatre "does not exist" because it denies "salutary contacts and exchanges between different cultures."[37] *One ASEAN* might also be considered community theatre because it is "working for a local or regional community in the broad sense of the term,"[38] but this concept does not take account of the ways the artists worked or the combination of puppets, bodies, and story.

The artists planning APEX are drawn to the universal appeal that artists such as Singaporean Ong Keng Sen capitalizes on for his international performances, but they are wary of losing artistic control and the specificity of their own traditions. Is it possible for these Asian artists to create satisfying work while consciously grappling with a Western paradigm of intercultural performance? While pondering the overall value of HIT, Lei hopes that "despite the inevitability interrupted cultural flow into these productions, self-reflection, recognition, and appreciation of one's own culture would form a continuous flow *out of* the productions and back *into* the cultural reservoir for future theatrical endeavors. Furthermore, the discourse from the East should contribute to the theorization of intercultural theatre and thus to the overall well-being of the intercultural environment."[39]

As intercultural performance, APEX was both a success and perhaps a missed opportunity. The final performance that might tour in the region and beyond has yet to be realized. The constraints of time, artistic differences that were exacerbated by economic and social hierarchies, and a lack of funding kept the project from ever developing a final product that could be marketed globally to represent the ASEAN Community. The successes were on a different scale. The artists were challenged to use their traditions in new ways, to consider how symbols or characters communicate to a variety of audiences, and learn new methods through the exchange. They are able to take this experience home and apply the ideas to their own creative process and traditions. Finally, the artists and organizers continue to talk about and consider process. They are not following set methods, but forging their own. Each APEX Exchange has involved different people working in different ways—there is an attempt to keep ideas and approaches that work while continuing to experiment. As I continue to follow these artists through social media and in person, I am inspired by the kind of community that has resulted from the experience. They keep in touch and continue to see each other at festivals and events—even though those occasions are not often structured for artistic exchange, the artists from APEX seek each other out.

POSTSCRIPT

Many of the artists of *One ASEAN* were invited back to Hanoi one year later. They were asked to perform for the fiftieth anniversary of ASEAN and were again hosted by the National Puppet Theatre. The process of this performance was structured quite differently, and highlighted again how APEX worked to overcome hegemonies. The National Puppet Theatre of Vietnam is a well organized company with a clear hierarchy of duties among the administrative and artistic staff. Nguyen Tien Dung, one of the leading directors of the company, served as the project's director. In contrast to the consciously collaborative process that APEX engaged in, slowly developing a story and staging, Dung approached his role with a clear vision—clearly an auteur. The difference in approach, and the visually arresting production he created, demonstrated one of the clear strengths of HIT—an ability to develop a production that was cohesive, even if the nuances of cultural difference were ignored or unknown.

In rehearsal, the other artists had limited opportunity for input into the story or staging. In one instance, the puppeteers from each country were asked to submit ideas for a symbol of their respective nations that would be recognizable to the Vietnamese audience. For example, the twin towers of Kuala Lumpur were used as the symbol for Malaysia, Angkor Wat represented Cambodia, and a golden pagoda indicated Myanmar. After the symbol was selected, the stage designers at the National Puppet Theatre created a two-dimensional image, about two or three feet high and wide, that could float on the water during that country's scene. Dung then directed each country's puppeteers to create a short scene that showcased their puppets—on the water puppet stage! The final show was an innovative collage of puppets from around the region performing in or near the water.

As theatre artists and audiences become more global, the possibilities for intercultural performance will continue to expand beyond the model of HIT, as APEX and the production of *One ASEAN* demonstrate. The economics of collaboration must remain an active concern in order to increase opportunities for artists from both sides of the resource divide. Artistic value sometimes appears beyond the final staged production.

NOTES

1. Water puppets are the most well-known kind of puppets in Vietnam. These wooden puppets perform on the surface of a lake or pool and are manipulated through a long stick that leads back from the puppet to puppeteer. The National Puppet Theatre has two stages for water puppets and one stage for "dry" puppets.

2. Each APEX was organized around a different theme, such as "water," "earth," or "live." The theme became the name of that exchange as well as the name of the workshop production that was given a public performance at each exchange's end. Throughout this article I use *One ASEAN* to refer to the exchange that happened in Hanoi in 2016, and to the final performance.

3. Patrice Pavis, *Theatre at the Crossroads of Culture* (London: Routledge, 1992), 4.

4. The historiography of intercultural theatre has emerged as a rich and varied field within the last thirty years. For an excellent overview of this field, see Ric Knowles, *Theatre & Interculturalism* (London: Palgrave Macmillan, 2010), or the "Special Issue on Intercultural Acting and Actor/Performer Training" in *Theatre, Dance, and Performance Training* 7, no. 3 (2016).

5. Daphne P. Lei, "Interpretation, Intervention, Interculturalism: Robert Wilson's HIT Production in Taiwan," *Theatre Journal* 63, no. 4 (2011): 574.

6. Michael Ernest Jones, "Forging an ASEAN Identity: The Challenge to Construct a Shared Destiny," *Contemporary Southeast Asia* 26, no. 1 (2004): 147.

7. Rodolfo C. Severino, "The Association of Southeast Asian Nations: Ten Countries, One Region in ASEAN," in Rodolfo C. Severino, Elspeth Thompson, and Mark Hong (eds.), *Southeast Asia in a New Era* (Singapore: ISEAS-Yusof Ishak Institute, 2009), 244.

8. Indonesia, Malaysia, the Philippines, Singapore, and Thailand all signed the first ASEAN declaration. Over time the other countries in Southeast Asia have joined, the only exception being East Timor, which hopes to join the association, but a final decision is still pending.

9. David Martin Jones and Michael L. R. Smith, "Making Process, Not Progress: ASEAN and the Evolving East Asian Regional Order," *International Security* 32, no. 1 (2007): 149.

10. The entire ASEAN Vision 2020 and its supporting documents can be found at http://asean.org/asean/about-asean/.

11. See http://asean.org/asean-economic-community/initiative-for-asean-integration-iai-and-narrowing-the-development-gap-ndg/overview-2/.

12. Certainly each of the pillars of the ASEAN Community represent complex categories, both in how ASEAN formulates them, but also within larger global discourses. Looking back on the first fifty years of ASEAN, Joseph Chinyong Liow recognizes the regional organization as key to fostering economic growth and maintaining peace and security within the region. Joseph Chinyong Liow, "Southeast Asia in 2017: Grappling with Uncertainty," *Southeast Asian Affairs* (2018): 59.

13. Jones, "Forging an ASEAN Identity," 143.

14. To learn more about the ASEAN Foundation, visit their website at http://aseanfoundation.org/.

15. http://aseanfoundation.org/.

16. For more details and an analysis of the performance in Jakarta in 2015, see Jennifer Goodlander, "Intercultural Theatre and Community in Southeast Asia: The ASEAN Puppet Exchange in Jakarta," *Asian Theatre Journal* 36, no. 1 (2018): 27–52.

17. ASEAN declared the formation of the ASEAN Economic Community near the end of 2015 (although it is generally just referred to as the ASEAN Community). Most officials acknowledge it as a "work in progress," but the declaration has become an important benchmark for regional celebrations of identity and achievements.

18. Bonnie Marranca, "Thinking About Interculturalism," in Bonnie Marranca and Gautam Dasgupta (eds.), *Interculturalism and Performance: Writings from PAJ* (New York: PAJ Publications, 1991), 11.

19. Shelly Errington, *Meaning and Power in a Southeast Asian Realm* (Princeton, NJ: Princeton University Press, 2014), 10.

20. I participated as a puppeteer in the UNIMA Asia-Pacific International Puppetry Festival in Nanchong, China, in June 2014. Artists from all over the world gathered to share performances—but performance spaces were spread out around the city, making it difficult to see other performances or develop artistic partnerships. Many of the companies participated in order to showcase their work for other international producers who might book them to come and perform or teach workshops.

21. See Andy Kilpatrick, "English as an ASEAN Lingua Franca: Implications for Research and Language Teaching," *Asian Englishes* 6, no. 2 (2003): 82–91.

22. "Expert Supports Bahasa Indonesia to be the Language of ASEAN," *Tempo*, January 4, 2016, https://en.tempo.co/read/news/2016/01/08/055734251/Expert-Supports-Bahasa-Indonesia-to-be-Language-of-ASEAN.

23. Felicia Putri Tjasaka, "Bahasa Indonesia as the Common ASEAN Language?" *Global Indonesian Voices*, September 21, 2015, http://www.globalindonesianvoices.com/22608/bahasa-indonesia-as-the-common-asean-language/.

24. Democratic elections in 2015 resulted in a drastic change, and possible opening-up of the government in Myanmar. Time will tell how these changes affect puppetry and other arts going forward. Htwe was hopeful that this would allow for more performances, especially in the public schools, to teach Burmese schoolchildren about their culture.

25. Steve Tillis, *Toward an Aesthetics of a Puppet: Puppetry as a Theatrical Art* (New York: Greenwood Press, 1982), 118.

26. Rustom Bharucha, "Negotiating the 'River': Intercultural Interactions and Interventions," *TDR* 41, no. 3 (1997): 33.

27. Kathy Foley, "The Metonymy of Art: Vietnamese Water Puppetry as a Representation of Modern Vietnam," *TDR/The Drama Review* 45, no. 4 (2001): 134.

28. Jones, "Forging an ASEAN Identity," 152.

29. Mary Douglas, "Deciphering a Meal," *Daedalus* 101, no. 1 (1972): 65–6.

30. Johan Fischer, "Branding Halal: A Photographic Essay on Global Muslim Markets," *Anthropology Today* 28, no. 4 (2012): 18.

31. *The Ramayana* is a Hindu epic that came to Southeast Asia via India. Many countries in the region have their own version of this famous tale about Prince Rama, Princess Sita, and the monkey king Hanuman.

32. Lei, "Interpretation, Intervention, Interculturalism," 577.

33. Lei, "Interpretation, Intervention, Interculturalism," 585.

34. I am not terming Pavis's hourglass as "monolithic" because I believe it is the one correct way of understanding intercultural performance, or even applicable in all cases. Rather, I want to acknowledge that it is the place from which most considerations of intercultural performance begin, even if the conclusion is that the model is lacking or false.

35. Diane Daugherty, "The Pendulum of Intercultural Performance: 'Kathakali King Lear' at Shakespeare's Globe," *Asian Theatre Journal* 22, no. 1 (2005): 52–72.

36. Patrice Pavis, "Intercultural Theatre Today," *Forum Modernes Theater* 25, no. 1 (2010): 8.

37. Pavis, "Intercultural Theatre Today," 8.

38. Pavis, "Intercultural Theatre Today," 8.

39. Lei, "Interpretation, Intervention, Interculturalism," 585.

CHAPTER EIGHT

Acts of Loving: Emmanuelle Huynh, Akira Kasai, and Eiko Otake in Intercultural Collaboration

SANSAN KWAN

In February 2013 I was in Toulouse, France, to attend a performance of *Spiel*, a collaboration between Vietnamese French contemporary dance choreographer Emmanuelle Huynh and Japanese butoh artist Akira Kasai. The evening of the performance began with a long wait in the vestibule of the theatre as the audience slowly assembled, squeezing into the shrinking space. At last we were released into the theatre. The seats were arranged on risers along three sides of a black marley stage. Ushers stationed at the edges of the stage pointedly warned us not to step on the marley as we took our seats. Watching audience members file into the theatre was a performance in itself. Repeatedly, people walked onto the marley to get around to a seat. The ushers, and then eventually other audience members, would admonish them. This process became a kind of lighthearted game we all watched and participated in: noting people who stepped onto the marley and cautioning them collectively.

I note this pre-performance event because I think it suggests something intriguing about each of the two pieces I want to analyze in this chapter. The second piece, *Talking Duet*, is another collaboration Emmanuelle Huynh initiated, this time with Eiko Otake. In *Spiel*, the boundary established and transgressed that evening in Toulouse reminds us of the performative nature of the duet to come and thus highlights it as a tripartite, rather than simply dual, exchange. The third space in this encounter thus becomes an important component of study. I'll elaborate on this a bit later, but first let me introduce some of the broader questions I want to explore.

In our era of accelerated global contact and mobility, cross-cultural encounter and exchange are more and more a part of all forms of cultural practice. Here in 2019, during the Trump presidency, the ongoing Brexit process, and rising xenophobia in Europe and the United States, it is imperative that we explore as many ways as possible to resist fear and hatred and to encourage understanding across difference. Interculturalism is a contemporary fact and a necessary dilemma. What are the limits and the possibilities of mutual understanding? How do we connect with our cultural others? I contend that the practice and performance of dance serves as a revelatory site for working through the intercultural. Body-to-body interaction on the stage carries the potential to model everyday encounters with alterity in the polity. This is why the space for the audience in Toulouse becomes so important.

I write that interculturalism is a contemporary fact. At the same time, of course, interculturalism has a long history in theatre and dance. One of the most prolific periods in this history is the 1980s and 1990s, a time when a number of European and American artists engaged in large-scale projects that assimilated Western and Eastern forms, performers, staging conventions, epic stories, *mise-en-scènes*, or texts. Artists from that period include Peter Brook, Ariane Mnouchkine, and Richard Schechner. Daphne P. Lei has termed the monumental projects of that period HIT, or "Hegemonic Intercultural Theatre,"[1] a form of production that largely followed a colonialist model of appropriation and exploitation by prominent Western auteurs who drew upon non-Western artistic material and labor. Since that moment and the subsequent criticisms that were directed at HIT productions, particularly via the incisive writing of Rustom Bharucha and others—what William Peterson has called "classic intercultural theory"[2]—artists have made efforts at more reciprocal, more fluid, messier forms of intercultural collaboration.[3] In the 2000s and 2010s, scholars such as Leo Cabranes-Grant, Ric Knowles, Charlotte McIvor, and Royona Mitra began to note a "new interculturalism" that complicated the earlier, more reductive notions of predefined cultural traditions encountering each other across fixed hegemonic maps. For example, Knowles and McIvor began examining intercultural projects that were developing not across national boundaries, but locally across different cultural communities within nation-state borders.[4] Their research teases out the complexities across multiculturalism, postcolonialism, ethnic and racial difference, intraculturalism, and interculturalism.

This chapter enters the interculturalism conversation after the HIT period and the period of "classic" intercultural theory, and as a companion to recent discussions about "new interculturalisms." The choreographers I study here are elite artists who, while not mounting epic productions that stage collaborations across grand national cultural traditions, are also not necessarily representing particular local minority communities either. For example, Huynh's collaborative work has been funded by the French Institute Alliance Francais and by the French Institute of Japan, so there is no denying that she represents "French Culture" in her international projects. Still, the intercultural collaborations I discuss here beg examination not as encounters of difference across established monolithic traditions ("French Culture" or "Japanese Culture" with capital letters), but as *processes* of discovery that are as much interpersonal as intercultural. As processes, I borrow from Cabranes-Grant's notion that intercultural encounter is an "engine of emergence,"[5] rather than just a contact zone at which two statically defined cultures meet (though, as I discuss later, I am more interested in the engine than the emergence). Furthermore, the broader artistic forms in which these dancers work (butoh, European contemporary dance) are deeply inextricable from their personal aesthetics as individuals. I look at duets in this chapter, rather than large group productions. In contradistinction to studies of HIT work, it is the personal approach to interculturalism that animates my analysis, even while I argue that these individual experiences provide a kind of pedagogy of cross-cultural encounter for spectators, a wider lesson in intercultural comportment.

This chapter also adds to the conversation on new interculturalism in dance particularly. Following Royona Mitra's book on Akram Khan, this chapter likewise examines the work of an elite Asian European choreographer seeking out collaborations with other Asian artists, acknowledging the postcolonial, transnational complexities of representations of Westerness and otherness in contemporary intercultural work where the boundaries between the West and the rest are not always so clear.

One of the issues I am interested in examining here is the efficaciousness of different modes and methodologies for intercultural collaboration in dance. *How* do dancers choose to collaborate? What forms of exchange do they use? In what languages do they communicate? What creative processes do they try? And which of these methods seems to work? That is, which forms of collaboration bring the artists, and/or the audiences, to some place of greater cross-cultural understanding? *Spiel* utilizes both movement improvisation and occasional talking. In *Talking Duet*, as the title suggests, Huynh and Otake verbalize even more and also improvise movement. I am curious about this multi-modal approach. Why do these dancers turn to language in their collaborations? Is talking somehow a more effective mode of cross-cultural comprehension? Why dance at all then? What does talking accomplish that dancing does not? And vice versa? Or is the combination of both talking and dancing a more complete model of collaboration?

In addition to thinking about modes of intercultural exchange, I also want to examine ideas of love and loss, potentiality and failure, and, as I suggested earlier, third spaces. In both pieces the spectators constitute an important element of the exchange. I will explore the ways that the triangulation of these performances opens up a form of understanding not available in a private duet. That is, performance creates a site for modeling exchange more broadly. Making these duets social is a way to make visible the potentialities and also the failures that happen across difference: the losses in translation between the dancers, but also the sincerity and the love. To conclude, I will consider love as the guiding principle for a relationship of idealized potentiality, of never fully realized but ever sought genuine exchange and mutual understanding.

SPIEL

I will begin with *Spiel*. *Spiel* is a mutual improvisation between two artists with different cultural backgrounds, different formal training, different genders, different native languages. When Huynh and Kasai first met they used neither French nor Japanese (nor Vietnamese), but another language, German, in order to communicate. This is what Homi Bhabha would term an "enunciation" across the "Third Space" of cultural difference, an enunciation that articulates the hybridity of all culture in a postcolonial world.[6] In addition to talking with each other during the creative process, the two artists engaged each other in a game of choreographic "playback" (borrowed from contact improviser Lisa Nelson), where each would copy the movements of the other. In her artist's notes, Huynh discusses this process as an opportunity to "step into each other's movement 'houses,' visiting them, crossing certain thresholds together." She describes their work as an experience of "transubstantiation" and of climbing "inside the skin of the other person." At the same time, she also acknowledges that there is a gap between original movement and copy, recognizing it not as a loss but as "an interpretation." Their work together becomes a form of "speaking across the gap."[7] Huynh's descriptors shift between spatial or corporeal metaphors and verbal metaphors. Likewise, Bhabha's Third Space of enunciation also combines a spatial and a verbal metaphor to theorize postcolonial encounter. Philosopher Emmanuel Levinas describes the site at which our necessary relationship to an other occurs as a face-to-face encounter.[8] For Levinas, the face is the other that confronts us in its unassimilability and requires us to speak to it.[9] Here, again, we can note a combination of corporeal and verbal metaphors in a theory of intersubjective encounter. Levinas, Bhabha, and Huynh, too, each describe cross-cultural engagement as a space between two bodies that is bridged by speech. I think that speech in these cases can be figurative for various mediums of transmission across difference, including kinesthetic exchange. When Huynh talks about making "a grammar of understanding"[10] or "speaking across the gap"[11] she is referring to the playback process, connecting via reperforming each other's movement. But what is the nature of this in-between space and can it truly be bridged, whether through talking or dancing? Let me describe the piece that resulted from the playback process.

With the house lights still up, Huynh and Kasai sit upstage center in two chairs. They are both wearing black pants and black blazers, with red lipstick and red fingernails. Huynh rises, walks to center stage, and turns to face Kasai. She nods to him, then begins a short phrase, drops it, and casually returns to her chair. Kasai rises and takes Huynh's place. He returns her nod and then copies her phrase, adding his own before returning upstage. Huynh steps forward and copies Kasai's phrase, subsequently adding her own. This exchange continues for several cycles. The stark differences between the dancers become evident. He is slight and wiry; his movements jumpy, staccato, gnarled. She is broad jawed and broad shouldered; her dancing attenuated while also square and methodical. He is seventy; she is fifty. She imitates his movements more faithfully, at least in shape, though she can't quite approach the frenetic quality of the original. He picks up on a few of her moves, but gets to them in his own way and shapes them according to his more tightly wound body and jerky tempo.

Gradually, the house lights dim and both dancers move into the stage space. They begin to improvise on their own. Each of them seems to occupy his or her own territory on the stage, often with their backs turned to one another, involved in their own actions. Kasai is focused on engaging the audience. He runs frantically from one bank of the three-sided stage to the other, dancing right up to the edge of the marley, flinging his body around, slapping himself loudly, banging his knees to the floor repeatedly. He peels off layers of clothing until he is in just a dance belt. Even that he toys with removing. He looks out at the audience, working to get a reaction. He speaks directly to them, using short phrases in English. "The river!" he says, referring to the theatre, Theatre Garonne, which is located on the bank of the Garonne River. "Je t'aime!" (I love you), he proclaims. On a few occasions, he touches a spectator. Huynh, meanwhile, dances in the spaces opposite Kasai. She does not address the audience either physically or verbally, but she does seem attentive to Kasai's actions, following him in her peripheral vision. Huynh's dancing is measured, her phrasing punctuated. She performs a sequence of several moves, pauses, perhaps faces another direction, performs another sequence. She dances alone but with awareness, gauging Kasai, marking the time.

Every so often the dancers call out to each other—short exchanges using a few German, English, or French words. "Dance or spiel," Huynh says. "Akira," she calls. A few times there would seem to be some cue and they would improvise together or perform a set phrase for a brief period and then dance away from each other again. Over time Huynh, too, removes her pants and jacket and dances in a camisole and panties. By the end they have both changed into white, silky slips. The dance draws to a close when Huynh gradually makes her way back upstage to stand against the back wall; Kasai eventually follows her and the lights go to black.

THIRD SPACE: LAG, DISPLACEMENT, REMAINS

In considering Huynh's aims as stated in her artist's notes, I wonder whether the dancers manage to "climb inside each other's skin." It seems to me that their efforts to imitate one another, to inhabit each other's movement styles and bodily habitus, is not fully seamless. Even the attempt simply to connect with one another and dance together is not always successful in this piece.

In Bhabha's formulation of the Third Space of postcolonial encounter he describes the notion of time lag as the disruption that occurs when the cultures of the colonizer and the colonized confront each other.[12] This confrontation jars the discourse of progress falsely presumed by modernity. In *Spiel*, Huynh's Vietnamese French identity, the intercultural legacy of Western modern dance, Kasai's Japanese identity, the intercultural heritage of butoh, all of this combined with the dancers' linguistic, age, and gender differences, produces a clash of multiple time-spaces, bodily epistemologies, and colonial histories. Their collaboration could never be a smoothly synchronous event; it is necessarily a collection of lags.

Dance scholar Deidre Sklar discusses kinesthetic remembering as an endeavor that is both immediate and displaced.[13] The playback process is just this kind of kinesthetic remembering. It both brings another person's actions into immediate subjective experience and is, at the same time, a temporal, spatial, and corporeal dislocation. As Huynh embodies Kasai's movement sequence, re-membering it as her own, she simultaneously decomposes it—importing it to another time, another place, another body. This effect brings to mind Cabranes-Grant's use of the term anaphora (borrowing from Étienne Souriau) to describe his theory about the "networked" nature of intercultural encounter. In linguistics, anaphora is the repetition of certain words or clauses that refer back to other terms, or the replacing of a noun with a pronoun. As Cabranes-Grant explains, "Anaphora expands its range by reappearing at different locations; it creates lines of continuity by introducing variations and informative transfers. Metonymy amplifies proximity; metaphor mixes and conflates its elements; anaphora *moves away* in order to *come back*."[14] Anaphora thus allows us to understand interculturalism as a web of displaced connections.

Huynh acknowledges the displacements in *Spiel* when she says, "It's all about differences and not being able to communicate and being able through impossibility to understand each other."[15] Here she expresses a paradox: understanding through impossibility. Huynh is aware that she and Kasai do not achieve mutual understanding, that total empathy is an impossibility. Still, she insists that they try. She says, "So it's a process, [an] open process, so that people can understand that we are building our relationship environment, that we are building our understanding."[16]

The thing to note here is Huynh's description of the piece as an *open* process designed so that *other people* can recognize their efforts to build understanding. This work is not meant simply as a private exercise between Huynh and Kasai: it is a dance meant to be watched by others. And it is this relationship between the performers and the audience, the space between the marley stage and the spectators' seats, that I argue carries some further potential for intercultural knowledge. Going back to my opening anecdote, this is why I find the admonitions about not stepping onto the marley so revealing. Paired with Kasai's efforts to reach through to the audience and Huynh's efforts to bring Kasai back into collaboration with her, these boundaries and boundary-crossings highlight the potential that exists in that liminal space between interlocutors.

The third space between Huynh and Kasai is the gap in translation, the lag in the playback, the anaphora, the displacement between two bodies, that, I argue, is detectable by the audience. Borrowing from Rebecca Schneider's work on performance re-enactments, playback might be called a practice of "performing remains." Schneider argues that the presence of an audience at a re-enactment serves as the reminder of those remains, of the "leak" of time in reperformance. In her discussion of Civil War re-enactments she writes, "My presence and the presence of others who did not cross-temporal-dress . . . always served as a reminder that it was not, or not *entirely*, 1861, 62, 63, 64, or 65."[17]

As an audience member, I do not experience the internal kinesthetic remembering that would result from doing Kasai's or Huynh's phrases on my own body. Instead I observe, from outside, the residue, the stuff that Huynh does not manage to pick up from Kasai. I see that Kasai does not achieve the length of Huynh's lines or the flow of her phrasing. Huynh does not capture the multidimensionality of Kasai's shapes or the quirkiness of his timing. Kasai does not tune into a collaborative mode through much of the piece and I notice the ignored cues, the pregnant but empty space between the two dancers, their backs to each other, on the stage. It is precisely my position on the other side of the marley that allows me this perspective. In fact, Dee Reynolds, in her book *Kinesthetic Empathy*, argues that "the dance's body" is that entity precisely between performer and spectator. The "body" of the dance, then, does not exist solely with the dancers, but in the relationship with their audience.[18]

In addition to their intercorporeal efforts on stage, words were an important element of Huynh's and Kasai's process of getting to know one another. Huynh says that in rehearsal they would dance for ten minutes and talk for an hour. She recorded all their conversations. As a companion to the performances of *Spiel*, Huynh has been working on a book that chronicles her process with Kasai. In going back to audio from their sessions, however, she has encountered the problem that she only recorded the interpreter's translations of Kasai's words from Japanese into French, not Kasai himself speaking. Now, as a remedy, Huynh has commissioned another translator to retranslate the French back into Japanese as a way to get back to Kasai's original words. And Kasai has been listening to these translations and editing them as "his words." Thus, in both the piece and the subsequent book, in both the corporeal and the textual modes of engagement, we see multiple efforts at playback, or anaphoric chains, and, consequently, multiple sites of disjunction and loss.

Whether described temporally as lag, or spatially as displacement, intercultural encounter is never commensurable. Emmanuel Levinas built a philosophy of ethics around the assertion that the essence of our being is our debt to an other that will always be irreconcilable to us—a subjectivity built upon the impossibility of intersubjectivity, or, as Huynh phrases it, "understanding through impossibility." Ultimately, Levinas does not prescribe an answer to the problem of intersubjectivity. What he offers is a recognition of its limits. For Levinas, we are resigned to the awareness that, even as our own selfhood is built upon a will to know the other, that other is always irreducible to us—and that this is as it should be. I suggest that the audience is necessary in *Spiel* not to witness the successful attainment of mutual understanding between two people, but to note evidence of the impossibility of communion in intercultural encounter, to observe the lag, the dislocations and deformations, the pregnant emptiness of the space of exchange—even as the dancers keep trying.

TALKING DUET

Despite the impossibility, Huynh is ever persistent in her efforts to connect with others. In 2013 she initiated a collaboration with Eiko Otake. Otake is a Japanese butoh-style dancer who has worked in the United States in deep partnership with her husband, Takashi Otake (they are called "Eiko and Koma") for forty years. In 2014, Otake began performing solo work as well as collaborations with other artists. Huynh was introduced to Otake during a trip to New York and became eager to learn about Otake, her artistry, and her life experiences. Together, Huynh and Otake developed a structured improvisation called *Talking Duet*, which they have since performed in Brussels (May 2015), New York (June 2015 and February 2016), and Berkeley (April 2016). As with *Spiel*, *Talking Duet* employs dancing and talking in a multi-modal endeavor at mutual understanding. Unlike *Spiel*, the talking does not happen only primarily in rehearsal—as the title implies, talking is a central element of the performed work. In what follows, I describe the piece and examine its combination of verbal and corporeal methods, its failures and losses, and the triangulated third space of the "dance's body." My analysis follows much the same path I follow with *Spiel*. To conclude, however, I shine a light on the hope and love that both pieces ultimately evoke.

I participated in and observed *Talking Duet* when it was performed on April 19, 2016 in the Bancroft Studio at UC Berkeley. Bancroft Studio is a converted church, with a soaring ceiling, gleaming wood floors, tall paned windows on the south side, and a huge round window on the west side. It is late afternoon and amber light streams through. The audience is seated across two long rows on the north and east sides of the studio. Otake and Huynh have placed two ballet barres at angles along the west side of the space. A large swath of red fabric lies across the floor on the northeast side. Otake's grandmother's purple kimono lies northwest of center. Newspapers are scattered across the stage perimeter on the east and north sides. Finally, Otake has set a large glass bowl of water (borrowed from Anna Halprin's house) at the southeast side.

I am the emcee and an interlocutor in the piece. I open by introducing the dancers' biographies and the context for the piece and explaining how the structure will proceed, including the fact that audience members are invited to write out questions for the dancers and pass them to me. During this time, Otake and Huynh are already on stage, moving casually. Huynh does a series of yoga poses and stretches; Otake sits on the floor. This is their warm-up.

When I finish talking, the dancers begin to move through the space in silence. They come together and lay beside one another on the floor, head to foot. Slowly they float their limbs in the air. They begin to roll over one another, move around one another, remaining in contact, pausing, then moving, then pausing again. (The improvisational rule they are following is to start and stop together, and then to start when the other stops or stop when the other starts; the idea is to feel each other and get attuned.)

This duet is lovely. The dancers are attentive to one another. Huynh seems solicitous of Otake. She is strong and lithe while Otake seems brittle and dainty (she is neither). At one point they hold each other's heads; they trade off gently bearing each other's weight on different parts of their bodies. Huynh is in her early fifties, Otake in her mid-sixties. Huynh wears a form fitting red T-shirt and black shorts; Otake wears black pants and a loose gray and black sweater. There is delicacy and caring in the duet and it is mesmerizing to watch them "listen" to each other and to see what they will do next in relation to one another.

I interrupt the dancing: "Emmanuelle, I have a question for you: What is your artistic obsession?" Otake remains stationary on the floor and Huynh takes the stage space. She answers in bits and pieces, her sentences broken by pauses, speaking one word or phrase at a time. Her movements parallel this rhythm. She dances through a short phrase, stops in a position, talks, then performs another phrase, walks through the space. She offers lots of extended limbs, lunges, and big shapes. She tells us that her artistic obsession is linking things together, or "making life enter art"; she adds that she has been thinking a lot about how to make immigrants feel welcome in Europe.

I ring a bell to indicate the end of this response and then I direct a question to Otake: "Eiko, tell us a memory of your father." Otake slowly begins to sit upright and Huynh exits. Otake takes her time, eventually raising her arms and bringing them to her mouth. Then, sliding her hands to the sides of her head, she says, "He was a communist." Carefully she moves to standing, takes a few steps, arms extended above her. She looks at me and says, "I'm done."

I go on to ask a question of Huynh, then Otake again, then a question for both of them, which they answer in turn. Then more questions for each, drawing a few from a predetermined list, my own list, and questions passed to me from the audience.

One of the questions from a spectator for Otake is about the ghosts of history in the room. In another exchange, Huynh recounts when she first learned that her psychoanalyst was killed during the Charlie Hebdo terrorist attacks in Paris in 2015. Eventually, I ask them to "keep talking," which is a cue for them to begin asking questions of one another. At this point they face each other across the stage on the diagonal and begin to mirror and respond to each other's moves. A silent conversation. Eventually, they begin to verbalize, asking each other questions.

After three exchanges I interrupt and say, "Eiko and Emmanuelle, I have one last question for you: What was your first experience with death?" At this point Otake is slung over Huynh's back and they linger there for a moment. Otake comes down and begins to talk about her grandfather. Then Huynh shares her story. Then silence. They stay in contact with one another, moving slowly as they reattune to one another's movement choices. Huynh is on her back on the floor with her legs in the air. Getting up from the floor and moving a few feet behind Huynh, Otake steps out of her pants and stands in her loose, long sweater. Huynh walks back and stands next to her. Shoulder to shoulder they pause. Then they bow and the audience applauds.

TALKING AND DANCING AS MODES

As the interlocutor, it was a privilege to watch Huynh and Otake rehearse and to be a part of their choice-making process. We decided on some of the possible questions I would ask during the performance by starting with a list from postmodern dance pioneer Anna Halprin, whom they had met earlier in the week. Then we added some of our own. Huynh and Otake liked a mix of difficult personal questions and a few lighter ones. In rehearsal, it was clear that they found it hard to answer questions comprehensively and to dance at the same time—tough for their minds to focus on both actions simultaneously. It was decided that answering partially, or even just pronouncing words for the sound they made, was still artistically compelling.

During the performance, Huynh and Otake approach the combination of talking and dancing differently. Otake never really reveals herself in her talking. She gives us words, phrases, images. They are disjointed. Her most expressive moments are in movement, when the smallest gesture with her fingers can be achingly articulate. True to her aesthetic, she moves slowly, with the aim seemingly not to hold shapes but to evolve from one shape to another. Sometimes she moves in a more pedestrian fashion, pouring water from the glass bowl onto the floor, moving the ballet barres, tearing up newspaper, or simply walking around the space.

Huynh provides more earnest and literal answers to the questions. She narrates memories and shares emotions. Meanwhile, her movements are outstretched and she steps with deliberation from one pose to another. In addition, for Huynh, taking a moment to walk quickly through the space seems to give her time to think so that she can then re-establish herself and verbally offer a new thought with a new set of movements.

During the talkback after the performance the two artists reveal their different approaches. Otake claims that she does not like talking. She says that it "conflicts" with her dancing; it takes her out of the transformative place that she likes to be when dancing. She explains that as soon as she talks, especially because she is speaking English, too much of her identity (Japanese, female, older) is revealed.[19] Of course, I would argue that these identity markers are revealed through her body, too. Still, I understand her point; normally the aesthetic aim of Otake's work is to transport the performance space to somewhere non-mundane, non-literal, to create a surreal experience. Otake is a butoh-trained artist—to talk is to break the otherworldly effect of the work. She admits that throughout the performance she "ducks" the questions asked of her, or gives partial answers, or tries to turn her utterances primarily into sound.[20]

These vocalizations put me in mind, again, of Levinas, or of Levinas as understood through Judith Butler. In the last chapter of *Precarious Life*, Butler wonders about the efficacy of the humanities to foster empathy across otherness (she is responding to a comment made by a university president that the humanities have nothing more to offer our times). She goes to Levinas to consider this question. Levinas uses the idea of the face as the other that addresses me and makes a moral demand on me. Butler draws on a Levinas essay, "Peace and Proximity," in which he refers to another text, Vassili Grossman's *Life and Fate*, that describes a woman waiting in line for news of a relative who is a political detainee. The scene depicts the woman's emotions as read through her back and the suffering sounds that are not words that emit from her. Butler writes:

> So we can see already that the "face" seems to consist in a series of displacements such that a face is figured as a back, which, in turn, is figured as a scene of agonized vocalization. And though there are many names strung in a row here, they end with a figure for what cannot be named, an utterance that is not, strictly speaking, linguistic.[21]

What is important for my purposes is that the "face," a metonym for the body, expresses itself physically and vocally, but the utterance of the face is non-linguistic. It exceeds the limits of the verbal. Butler continues:

> The face, if we are to put words to its meaning, will be that for which no words really work; the face seems to be a kind of sound, the sound of language evacuating its sense, the sonorous substratum of vocalization that precedes and limits the delivery of any semantic sense.[22]

In rehearsal, Huynh and Otake agreed that their answers did not always need to make coherent sense. In performance, Otake, especially, allows single words and phrases to hang in the air. Kasai does this in *Spiel* as well. Thus, the body does what language cannot do, but the voice, also, expresses itself both as something inherently physical and as something beyond the literalness of language. In their utterances they communicate, but they do not necessarily talk, neither are they specifically dancing. Butler, via Levinas, helps me to understand that there are actually three modes in *Talking Duet* and in *Spiel*: talking, corporeal movement, and utterance. These three modes are distinct, but also deeply tied; they are the physical-vocal expressions of the face-body of the other.

Huynh recognizes the intertwining of the physical-vocal. While she concedes Otake's point that the literalness of language can "conflict" with the expressive capacities of the body, she maintains that she still appreciates the possibilities they afford when put together. She says that sometimes in performance when she has been stuck and then she throws out a word, a "crystallization of sense" happens that she could not have reached otherwise.[23] Interestingly, Huynh likens this experience of crystallization to psychoanalysis, which utilizes a "talking cure" to verbalize and thereby to draw out some psychic disorder that is often manifesting itself somatically. For Huynh the combination of verbalizing and moving becomes a fruitful method of realization. Unlike the fantastic dream worlds that Otake is known for creating, Huynh's aesthetic is pared down, human, matter-of-fact; it deliberately exposes its own process.

As for Otake's comment about how speaking onstage makes her too real, it is, in fact, Otake's real persona, and her life experiences, that Huynh is interested in knowing, through both dancing and talking together. Huynh says of talking in their piece, "And it's now a way or so of meeting because that's true, I'm curious, profoundly curious of Eiko, as a woman, as a person, as an emigrant, all what we say. Yeah, so. It's not an added, it's another tool."[24] Otake grants that she remains interested in, if daunted by, the challenge of talking onstage,[25] while Huynh views talking as one strategy towards greater comprehension. Otake is reluctant about being fully revealed while Huynh remains curious and continues to insist.[26]

As in *Spiel*, a great deal of talking also occurred in rehearsal, in the various coffees and meals shared, the communications and negotiations that happen in order to coordinate the logistics of meeting, or even just sitting in the taxi on the way from the airport.[27] Still, while the dancers did lots of discussing throughout the process, in the end, the goal was to experience one another intercorporeally. Otake argues that there was too much verbalizing and she felt that the structured improvisation was a way to engage differently: "But this is, again, how to get out of our dinner conversation, our lunch conversation. We wanted to have a structure. We are talking but we are not moving. So it's one of those things we have to always think about . . . because we can be talking forever." Huynh agrees that the movement improvisation was a way to "train us in something common," even while "knowing that anyway we will be very different, very separate."[28]

In his book on embodied technique, Ben Spatz takes some time to compare language and embodiment. He argues that language requires a "low ratio between effort and articulation." In other words, the act of speaking allows for a wide range of varied articulations with very little physical expenditure. Nevertheless, talking is still an embodied technique, just one in which "symbolic meaning takes precedence over the meaning of effortful embodied production."[29] So while we learn from Levinas that the physical and the vocal are figured in each other, at the same time, Spatz cautions us not to use "language" as a metaphor for embodied practice. This metaphorization is a temptation because we want to emphasize the ways that embodied technique is epistemic, is a form of knowledge production and communication. Recall that even Huynh, in describing the work of *Spiel*, refers to their dancing as "speaking across the gap." Of course, she also describes their duet as a form of "transubstantiation" and a way to climb "inside the other person's skin."[30] Spatz insists that dance is different from speaking:

Dance is linguistic only to the extent that we fail to recognize the physical work it entails: not just the effort involved in a single performance, but the long-term effort of training and rehearsal . . . When we "read" embodied practice in terms of signification alone, we ignore much of its meaning, which is located not in the relationship between signs but in the quantity and quality of embodied effort that goes into the enactment of technique.[31]

I think that it is this difference that compels Huynh and Otake, as well as Huynh and Kasai, to combine modes in their efforts to comprehend one another. Talking and dancing, and even non-linguistic vocalizing, offer interfigural but still distinct forms of expressing and of knowing that, combined, tell more than their sum.

THE DANCE'S BODY

While they could have been "talking forever" in rehearsal and over dinner, the obligation to produce a work, and the repeated performances of that work, are essential elements of Huynh and Otake's collaboration. Performing for an audience makes social a process that was previously private. It should be noted, however, that although the production of a publicly shown work is the goal for Huynh and Otake, the improvisational structure of the piece ensures that Talking Duet retains the processual, exploratory character of their chats and rehearsals, with the audience invited into the act of in-the-moment creation. In my analysis of Spiel I argue that the audience is key to recognizing the losses in translation between Huynh and Kasai. I think this is also true in Talking Duet. In fact, in this piece the audience becomes an even more explicitly acknowledged element of the performance. Even though it is called a "duet," in fact, it is a trio.

The fact that Talking Duet invites the audience to engage with the dancers is a recognition of the spectators' vital role in cross-cultural understanding. It gives the work of mutual comprehension broader socio-political implications, rather than simply personal ones. Referring back to Dee Reynolds, the "dance's body" is a triangulation. My position as interlocutor symbolizes this tripartite relationship. During the talkback, Huynh explains:

We all know that a triangle is different from a face to face. So the context for the insertion of SanSan, the fact of teaching, both of us, and knowing that we are in a transmission place made us think of it a bit differently . . . And inviting SanSan made us really think that this place that SanSan is having belongs to this work . . . We feel like going on, but not going on just being the two of us. It's going on being attached to some context that we want to choose and work with the context of this place.[32]

When Huynh refers to "the fact of teaching" and "the context of this place," she means that she and I, and Otake, too, are teachers, and she highlights the fact that the Berkeley performance is held on the university campus, primarily for students. For Huynh, it is important that her work with Otake, their duet-plus, is pedagogical, that it transmits across to others, and thus that it matters beyond her and Otake.

Spatz argues, contrarily, that the efficacy of embodied practice to transform does not require an audience.[33] What is key, however, is that he distinguishes embodied performance from embodied technique, reducing performance to mere representation or spectacle and emphasizing technique as practice, as a form of embodied pedagogy with the power to enact change. It is certainly true that Huynh and Otake, like Huynh and Kasai, learn a great deal through their intercorporeal transmissions in rehearsal and over lunch, and that they come to comprehend in a way that their audiences cannot. I argue, however, that the goal in *Talking Duet* and in *Spiel* is not only for an encounter to be experienced by the two practitioners, but for an audience to bear witness to this transmission, to have the privilege to make determinations about it, and, further, for an audience to participate in this modeling of intercultural exchange.

POTENTIALITY AND FAILURE

What, however, is modeled for the audience? What do we learn about intercultural collaboration? Although Otake claims to prefer dancing to talking, during the talkback she confesses that she also "faked" parts of the movement improvisation.[34] By way of explanation she says that she is "not very good in rules."[35] It turns out then that Otake both ducks the verbal questions, as well as fakes the improvisation structure. Thus, as in *Spiel*, the dancers are sometimes at odds with one another in their process of exchange, no matter the mode of communication. Where Kasai misses Huynh's cues in *Spiel*, Otake resists following the structure in *Talking Duet*. Where Huynh fails to attain Kasai's idiosyncratic movement style, Otake evades Huynh's questions. Regarding *Spiel* I argue that the audience, situated beyond the marley boundary, is particularly poised to identify the losses in translation between Huynh and Kasai. Similarly, Huynh and Otake chose a question-and-answer format for their duet because they understand that their work is pedagogical. What the audience learns along with the dancers, I think, is the very struggle of learning, the misses and failures across mutual understanding, the refusals as well as the earnest efforts.

Huynh is undaunted by the losses and resistances as they are revealed in performance. She acknowledges that there will be separation and yet she persists through the ducking and faking in *Talking Duet*, as she does through the lags and displacements in *Spiel*. Returning to Butler's disquisition on Levinas, we are reminded that the face of the other is always unattainable:

> For Levinas, then, the human is not *represented* by the face. Rather, the human is indirectly affirmed in that very disjunction that makes representation impossible, and this disjunction is conveyed in the impossible representation. For representation to convey the human then, representation must not only fail, but it must *show* its failure. There is something unrepresentable that we nevertheless seek to represent, and that paradox must be retained in the representation we give.[36]

It is impossible for Huynh and Kasai or Huynh and Otake to become fully attainable to each other, whether through movement or through talking. It is through the effort, the process, the repetition, even despite the ultimate acknowledgment of unassimilable difference that tells us something about ethical collaboration. As Butler explains,

> It is worth noting, however, that identification always relies upon a difference that it seeks to overcome, and that its aim is accomplished only by reintroducing the difference its claims to have vanquished. The one with whom I identify is not me, and the "not being me" is the condition of identification.[37]

Perhaps a more optimistic way to think about the persistence-amidst-failure that characterizes these intercultural collaborations is through an idea of potentiality. Bojana Kunst theorizes collaboration as both a strategy of coercion in a neoliberal society and as having the potential for a more liberated future. First, she critiques the current demand for teamwork and cooperation as "part of the obsessive administration of the neoliberal subject" and contemporary capitalistic production's emphasis on efficiency, time management, flows, goals, and deadlines. She wonders, "Can we also collaborate with no revolutionary, corporative, metaphysical deadline on the horizon?"[38] Then, interestingly, Kunst turns to dance; she references choreographer Eleanor Bauer discussing the current predicament of the freelance performing artist and the imperative of the dancer to be flexible labor:

> Could this not be precisely the description of the contemporary collaborative worker, equipped for continuous high performance? That of the always critical and active labourer, whose subjectivity is totally subjected to the modes of contemporary capitalistic production?[39]

Kunst suggests here that even the arts have been co-opted by the neoliberal impulse. She goes on to consider, however, what a genuine exchange might be like:

> We have to think about the future of collaboration in the rupture between the impossibility of the refusal of the collaborative processes in which we are already implemented, and the possibility of genuine exchange, which has yet to happen.[40]

For Kunst, truly transformative collaboration is necessarily conditioned by failure and unactualized potentiality. In fact, it must only ever be yet to happen:

> Potentiality can come to light only when not being actualised: when the potential of a thing or a person is not realised. A certain failure, an impossibility of actualisation, is then an intrinsic part of potentiality. At the same time, only when the potential is not being actualised, one is opened to one's being in time, to one's eventness. In this openness one experiences the *plurality of ways* that life comes into being and is exposed to the plurality of possible actions.
>
> Through collaboration, we condition our future lives together, which of course means that, in order to open up the time, we have to take time out of the obsession with presence and participate in the time what has yet to happen.[41]

This idea of collaboration as unrealized potentiality is, of course, emblematized by Huynh's work. I repeat here her description of her partnership with Kasai: "It's all about differences and not being able to communicate and being able through impossibility to understand each other."[42] And of her "non-stop talking" with Otake: "But then that's the part of going on, and insisting since two years. And I feel like insisting more."[43] Huynh recognizes that earnest intercultural collaboration is not about goals but about insistence and repetition, not about full comprehension but about potentiality.

Interestingly, Kunst's own collaborator (in their research on collaboration), Ivana Muller, likens this potentiality to theatre:

> It is like theatre. When we make theatre, we prepare ourselves for the moment of the meeting with the spectator; that moment in the future that will become our mutual here and now. Days and days in advance . . . trying to imagine how it is all going to be. Rehearsing that moment over and over again. Rehearsing its potentiality, its accuracy, its power, even, absurdly, its Authenticity. So in fact, a big part of working in theatre is conditioning our future together.[44]

Recall, of course, the importance of the marley as boundary between audience and performers in *Spiel* and my role as interlocutor in *Talking Duet*. These structures remind us of the performative nature of these pieces. They emphasize the repetition and rehearsal that collaboration requires and, importantly, the idealized moment of meeting the other in performance. Huynh and her collaborators know about the potentiality of the stage for conditioning futures together.

LOVE

If collaboration requires the recognition of unrealizable potentiality, however, then what compels collaborators to keep collaborating? Why persist in the effort if it is necessarily going to fail? I like to think through this conundrum via a notion of love. First, an anecdote.

A while back I was chatting with another parent in the little league stands. We were bonding over our experiences in interracial marriages. I asked this father how he would describe his experience being a Jewish American guy married to a Chinese American woman. In a word, he said, "miscommunication." He went on to describe various experiences he had had, for example, of being with his in-laws and not understanding how or why decisions got made even as they were discussed, in English, right under his nose. Or why his wife would sometimes make certain choices, inexplicable to him, when her parents were around that she would never make when they were not. Obviously, every family is its own micro-culture and not all quirks of a particular family can be attributed to ethnicity. One of my favorite passages from Maxine Hong Kingston is, "Chinese-Americans, when you try to understand what things in you are Chinese, how do you separate what is peculiar to childhood, to poverty, insanities, one family, your mother who marked your growing with stories, from what is Chinese?"[45] Still, I think there are unique challenges that come with working across ethnic cultures, misunderstandings that cannot be ameliorated via explanation, or pedagogy, or even direct experience.

I share this personal anecdote because it helps me to think through this question about why and how we continue striving to understand each other across cultures, despite the ducking and the lags. I want to suggest that *love* is key to the work of interculturalism. After all, isn't love the thing that impels us toward union, towards externality, towards care for another, while also requiring us to honor our separate selves?

One of Huynh's earlier works, *A Vida Enorme/episode 1* (2003), evokes this idea of love as conditioned by separation. For the piece, she sought the linguistic help of Nuno Bizarro, a contemporary dancer from Portugal, because she wanted the sensuous poems of Portuguese poet Herberto Hélder to be dictated aloud alongside her French translation. Huynh says that she fell in love with Bizarro, now her husband, partly through listening to him speak a language she did not understand. Obviously, Huynh has a long abiding interest in trying and failing to understand the other as an act of love.

In watching *Spiel* I note close mutual attunement between the dancers, but also many moments in which Kasai moves away from Huynh, addressing himself to the audience, hamming it up, while Huynh waits patiently for him on the other side of the stage. In an interview, Huynh admits to sometimes being frustrated with Kasai, feeling like a mother having to scold and cajole. But she also proclaims deep respect for Kasai. She says that she loves him.[46] Likewise, Kasai proclaims, "J'taime!" repeatedly during the performance. I know that he was deeply committed to working with Huynh. In *Talking Duet*, Huynh and Otake are similarly tender with each other. Although Otake claims to fake the improvisation, it is clear that she attunes herself to Huynh. The section in which they alternate gently bearing each other's weight is delicate and full of care. Huynh is clearly devoted to Otake and continues to want to know her and connect with her. Otake, while she plays at ducking and faking, also says that her job for this performance is "to make myself totally available to her."[47] I am not referring here to romantic love between Kasai and Huynh or Otake and Huynh, but love as the impulse to understand, to care for, to connect with.

Alain Badiou describes love as the experience of the world from the point of view of difference. Love, he says, is woven from experience with otherness.[48] For Badiou, desire for the guarantee of sameness is not love. Interestingly, he likens love to theatre. He offers that theatre is a moment at which thought and body are exposed to each other such that you cannot separate them: in theatre, "The two [body and idea] are mixed up, language seizes the body, just as when you tell someone, 'I love you': you say that to someone living, standing there in front of you, but you are also addressing something that cannot be reduced to this simple material presence, something that is absolutely and simultaneously both beyond and within."[49] So I argue that love is what structures these two dance collaborations. These duets are deliberate engagements with difference; engagements with the body *as* comprehension. The playback process in *Spiel* is precisely that mixing up of body and idea, where Huynh and Kasai use their bodies as simultaneously form and content. Through the embodied method of playback they both make themselves present to one another and strive to comprehend each other. Likewise, in *Talking Duet*, the go–pause improvisation paired with the conversational exchange are also intimate meetings of body and idea that require multi-modal "listening" in order to engender mutual creative expression. These two duets are professions of love in that they are each an engagement with two presences created by two individual bodies, but also with an affective, experiential moment that is created through them and beyond them. We, as spectators, are privileged to bear witness to this mutual effort and joint creation.

I do not intend to be excessively utopian about love as the ultimate answer to the difficulties of intercultural collaboration. Love sometimes involves threat, coercion, hurt, and power. Even as the power differentials between these pairs of artists do not match the kinds of gaps we saw in the HIT productions of the 1980s and 1990s, between Huynh and Kasai there are certainly gender, age, language, and national differences. Between Huynh and Otake there are differences in age, language, and immigrant versus native-born experience. And I saw both pieces on Western soil, sitting amongst a Western audience with all the presumptions spectators might bring about Asia and Asian artists. I am not arguing that love overcomes these imbalances of power. In fact, I contend that thinkers on love precisely understand that any engagement with an other is inherently unbalanced. Love is the thing that both acknowledges and strives to *accept* differentials.

Erika Fischer-Lichte, in her formulation of "interweaving performance cultures," imagines a utopian potential for intercultural work to eventually give rise to future self-transformations.[50] In his book on interculturalism in colonial Mexico, Leo Cabranes-Grant argues that "intercultural exchanges tend to increase the legibility of certain types of poiesis."[51] One of his key ideas is that interculturalism can be an "engine of emergence." That is, he posits interculturalism as a form of creation, of becoming. While I am drawn to these visions of the productiveness of interculturalism, my turn to love is a way not to emphasize what new forms arise from the intercultural process but to describe the impulse that brings people to the collaborative process, indifferent to its result. As I write above, my interest in love is a focus on engines more than on emergence.

Badiou writes that "love contains an initial element that separates, dislocates and differentiates."[52] And love is that which struggles over "the hurdles erected by time, space and the world."[53] In "Shattered Love," Jean Luc Nancy suggests that love exposes the self as an openness to the excess that is beyond being.[54] And in the exposure it reveals both self and other as endlessly plural, shattered. Love is the constancy to remain receptive even through the comings and goings of understanding, the shatteredness of being. The lags, the dislocations, the pregnant spaces, the ducking and the faking between Huynh and Kasai, Huynh and Otake, are excesses that are nevertheless the condition for ongoing acts of love.

NOTES

1. Daphne P. Lei, "Interruption, Intervention, Interculturalism: Robert Wilson's HIT Productions in Taiwan," *Theatre Journal* 63, no. 4 (2011): 571.

2. William Peterson, "*Amazing Show* in Manila: 'Fantasy-Production' and Filipino Labor in a Transnational, Transcultural, Transgendered Theatre Enterprise," *Theatre Journal* 63, no. 4 (2011): 587.

3. See SanSan Kwan, "Even as We Keep Trying: An Ethics of Interculturalism in Jérôme Bel's *Pichet Klunchun and Myself*," *Theatre Survey* 55, no. 1 (2014), 186–9.

4. See Ric Knowles, "Multicultural Text, Intercultural Performance: Performing Intercultural Toronto," in D. J. Hopkins, Shelley Orr, and Kim Solga (eds.), *Performance and the City* (Basingstoke, UK: Palgrave Macmillan, 2009), 73–91; Ric Knowles, *Theatre & Interculturalism* (Houndsmill, UK: Palgrave Macmillan, 2010); Charlotte McIvor, *Migration and Performance in Contemporary Ireland: Towards a New Interculturalism* (London: Palgrave Macmillan, 2016).

5. Leo Cabranes-Grant, *From Scenarios to Networks: Performing the Intercultural in Colonial Mexico* (Evanston, IL: Northwestern University Press, 2016).

6. Homi Bhabha, *The Location of Culture* (Abingdon: Routledge, 2004), 55.

7. Emmanuelle Huynh, *Speil* (2010).

8. Emmanuel Levinas, *Totality and Infinity: An Essay on Exteriority*, trans. Alphonso Lingis (Pittsburgh, PA: Duquesne University Press, 1961/1969).

9. Emmanuel Levinas, *Otherwise Than Being or Beyond Essence*, trans. Alphonso Lingis (The Hague: Martinis Nijhoff, 1974/1981).

10. "Grid_lab @ EXTRA 11 festival 2011: Interview with Emmanuelle Huynh, Akira Kasai," YouTube video, uploaded by dancetechtv, May 20, 2011, https://www.youtube.com/watch?v=7VPE4lk9fh8.

11. Huynh, *Spiel*.

12. Bhabha, *The Location of Culture*.

13. Deirdre Sklar, "Remembering Kinesthesia: An Inquiry into Embodied Cultural Knowledge," in Carrie Noland and Sally Ann Ness (eds.), *Migrations of Gesture* (Minneapolis: University of Minnesota Press, 2008), 85–112.

14. Cabranes-Grant, *From Scenarios to Networks*, 15.

15. "Grid_lab @ EXTRA 11 festival 2011."

16. "Grid_lab @ EXTRA 11 festival 2011."

17. Rebecca Schneider, *Performing Remains: Art and War in Times of Theatricality* (New York: Routledge, 2011), 9.

18. Dee Reynolds, "Kinesthetic Empathy and the Dance's Body: From Emotion to Affect," in Dee Reynolds and Matthew Reason (eds.), *Kinestetic Empathy in Creative and Cultural Practices* (Bristol, UK: Intellect Ltd., 2012), 121–38.

19. *Talking Duet*. Live performance, Emmanuelle Huynh, Akira Kasai, and SanSan Kwan, April 19, 2016, Berkeley, CA, University of California, Berkeley.

20. *Talking Duet*.

21. Judith Butler, *Precarious Life: The Powers of Mourning and Violence* (New York: Verso, 2006), 133.

22. Ibid., 134.

23. *Talking Duet*.

24. *Talking Duet*.

25. "So that's why I ducked. But I didn't want to refuse it. So sometimes ducking is . . . the words, the voice, as part of the body." *Talking Duet*.

26. "Eiko: We have been talking non-stop." *Talking Duet.*

27. "Em: I think I will sleep a lot on the plane! But then that's the part of going on, and insisting since two years. And I feel like insisting more." *Talking Duet.*

28. *Talking Duet.*

29. Ben Spatz, *What a Body Can Do* (New York: Routledge, 2015), 49.

30. Huynh, *Spiel.*

31. Spatz, *What a Body Can Do*, 50

32. *Talking Duet.*

33. Spatz, *What a Body Can Do.*

34. It was not clear to me from the audience perspective how exactly she was not faithful to the improvisation guidelines, nor was it obvious to Huynh, who expressed surprise when Otake confessed to faking.

35. *Talking Duet.*

36. Butler, *Precarious Life*, 144.

37. Butler, *Precarious Life*, 145.

38. Bojana Kunst, "Prognosis on Collaboration," in Gabriele Brandstetter, Kai van Eikels, and Sybille Peters (eds.), *Prognoses über Bewegungen* (Berlin: B-Books, 2009), http://www.ivanamuller.com/contexts/bojana-kunst-prognosis-on-collaboration/.

39. Kunst, "Prognosis on Collaboration."

40. Kunst, "Prognosis on Collaboration."

41. Kunst, "Prognosis on Collaboration."

42. "Grid_lab @ EXTRA 11 festival 2011."

43. *Talking Duet.*

44. Ivana Muller, "Letter to Bojana For the Conference on Future," in *The Congress: Prognoses on Movements(s): 10 Future Scenarios: Performances and Lectures*, June 2008, Berlin, http://www.ivanamuller.com/contexts/ivana-muller-letter-to-bojana-for-the-conference-on-future/.

45. Maxine Hong Kingston, *The Woman Warrior: Memoirs of a Girlhood Among Ghosts* (New York, Vintage: 1989), 6.

46. Emmanuelle Huynh, interviewed by author, October 10, 2015.

47. *Talking Duet.*

48. Alain Badiou with Nicolas Truong, *In Praise of Love*, trans. Peter Bush (London: Serpent's Tail, 2012), 36.

49. Badiou, *In Praise of Love*, 85.

50. Erika Fischer-Lichte, "Introduction: Interweaving Performance Cultures—Rethinking 'Intercultural Theatre': Toward an Experience and Theory of Performance beyond Postcolonialism," in Erika Fischer-Lichte, Torsten Jost, and Saskya Iris Jain (eds.), *The Politics of Interweaving Performance Cultures: Beyond Postcolonialism* (London: Routledge, 2014), 11.

51. Cabranes-Grant, *From Scenarios to Networks*, 3.

52. Badiou, *In Praise of Love*, 28

53. Badiou, *In Praise of Love*, 32.

54. Jen-Luc Nancy, *Inoperative Community*, trans. Peter Connor, Lisa Garbus, Michael Holland, and Simona Sawney (Minneapolis: University of Minnesota Press, 1983/1991), 103–4.

CHAPTER NINE

ReORIENTing Interculturalism in the Academy: An Asianist Approach to Teaching Afro-Haitian Dance

ANGELINE YOUNG

INTRODUCTION

Phillip Zarrilli, T. Sasitharan, and Anuradha Kapur argue that while intercultural performance scholarship has produced a wealth of analyses on productions, little attention has been given to the nuanced processes of exchanges and "interweavings"[1] that occur at the "micro-level"[2] of interaction in the intercultural performance training studio. Zarrilli et al. identify that our "global, urban, multi-, inter-, intra-cultural realities"[3] make intercultural encounters *the norm* in twenty-first-century performance training settings such as university classrooms. However, they also contend that the privileging of Western training regimes in our intercultural classrooms reinscribes European colonial imperatives that produce cultural hegemony and sustain a discrepancy between our intercultural realities and university training practices. In summation, the alarming domination of Western ideologies in our twenty-first-century performance training classrooms is an urgent call for educators to take center stage with critical intercultural pedagogies that engage the productive tensions of our intercultural realities in the university classroom.

This chapter grapples with an intercultural performance teaching project that pulses at the critical juncture of dance training and post-secondary education. I discuss an action research study that explores teaching Afro-Haitian dance from an Asianist perspective at Arizona State University (ASU). I used action research methodology to explore the productive tensions of intercultural performance training in the academy, and from this study three strategies for productively engaging those tensions emerged: explicit acknowledgment, elastic discourse, and multidirectionality. While I provide dance teaching examples of these strategies, they apply widely to intercultural performance training educators in a variety of settings including community workshops, private studios, and international teaching collaborations. Moreover, these strategies are suitable for all intercultural arts practitioners as we continue our collective moves in praxis toward more inclusive, democratic, and ethical approaches to intercultural learning in the twenty-first century. The following two questions shape this chapter: How can one create a critical intercultural pedagogy in performance training? What is at stake here?

To engage these questions thoroughly, I begin with an overview of existing intercultural models. I follow by defining my terms *reORIENTation* and *Asianist* and I clarify why I used them in my teaching. Next, I give a definition of *intercultural education*, connecting it to human rights initiatives. I then outline the landscape of global intercultural arts education and I describe the context in which I taught my course. Next, I discuss the ethical and political complexities of assuming the labor of interculturalism as an Asian body at ASU, one of the largest universities in America with a predominantly white demographic. In that section I consider how the residues of Arizona's history as a politically conservative territory of the United States impacted my experience as a racial minority and intercultural arts educator; I do this to demonstrate how the geopolitics particular to each teaching context influence the process of critical self-reflection required of intercultural arts educators in twenty-first-century classrooms.

After contouring the general challenges of this intercultural arts teaching project, I suggest action research methodology as an appropriate response by giving an overview of its history and its purpose. From there, I transition into a discussion on applying action research at the critical juncture of intercultural dance performance and education in the university. Finally, I detail the three themes of explicit acknowledgment, elastic discourse, and multidirectionality which emerged from the action research study, providing examples from my experience teaching Afro-Haitian dance from an Asianist perspective. In my conclusion I revisit the successes and challenges of this study and provide reflection on the future implications of this work.[4]

EXISTING INTERCULTURAL PERFORMANCE MODELS

Intercultural collaboration models all share a common concern for cultural encounter, however they derive exclusively from investigations of performance. Presently, there are no intercultural performance teaching models that explicitly engage the ethical and political implications of intercultural exchange in the classroom. Even so, existing intercultural collaboration models provide an informative genealogy of conflict and resolution that offers intercultural educators a theoretical foundation from which to consider the ethics of exchange that underpin encounters in the classroom. Patrice Pavis's famously controversial "hour glass"[5] theory depicts a unidirectional flow in intercultural collaboration. Scholars have widely criticized the "hour glass" model for neglecting the political dimensions of Western hegemony and intra-ethnic dynamics in intercultural collaboration. In response, Jacqueline Lo and Helen Gilbert suggest a "spinning disk"[6] model to account for bidirectional cultural flow. Similarly, Li Ruru and Jonathan Pitches defy the "hour glass" and describe intercultural collaboration as a series of concentric circles that represent "layered experimental intercultural exchange."[7]

Clearly, the existing debates on ethics and interculturalism require that intercultural performance educators design pedagogies that engage learners in stabilizing just economies of cultural flow in the classroom. The central mission should be to establish group mechanisms for the collective practice of democracy in the intercultural classroom. The distinct particularity of each intercultural teaching project is best described by Li and Pitches who write that "each intercultural project must define itself on its own terms, naturally resisting any linear models of communication and instead negotiating the layers of cultural complexity uniquely each time."[8] If we approach intercultural performance training through this lens, we can understand how a flexible pedagogy is vital to generating inclusive economies of intercultural exchange in the classroom.

I acknowledge that my specific pedagogical model cannot be reproduced by instructors without the same training and knowledge. Rather, I suggest that each individual's intercultural pedagogy evolve out of their own unique skillset in conversation with the three strategies of explicit acknowledgment, elastic discourse, and multidirectionality to produce the fluid parameters in which a learning community engages the labor of interculturalism as a practice of democracy, accountability, and social justice.

DEFINITION OF TERMS

My social justice intentions influence my pedagogical lexicon. I reclaim the word *Orient*, a pejorative appellation that has been used to categorize Asians as objects and as the "Other." I deploy the term *reORIENT* as an intervention on Western regimes that have long overprioritized Eurocentrism in dance and performance training. My *Asianist* rhetoric draws on Edward Said's theory of Orientalism[9] and signals the work of Brenda Dixon-Gottschild, who first coined the term *Africanist* to describe the African aesthetics that have shaped US dance history, choreography, and performance and training practices.[10] Similarly, Asian American dance studies scholars have produced evidence that the lineage of US modern dance and somatic movement training has deep ties to Eastern aesthetics, philosophies, and movement practices, yet attribution to Eastern origins remain obscured within the dominant canon.

The custom of erasing Africanist and Asianist genealogies from the Western dance canon is a result of hegemonic intercultural dance "collaborations" carried out by European/Euro-American dance choreographers, performers, and practitioners;[11] unfortunately this pattern of hegemony reproduces itself in Western dance training paradigms. The continued act of expunging Asianist footprints that have labored to construct the Western dance canon should be interrupted with a reORIENTation of perspectives. Daphne Lei contends that interventions of hegemonic intercultural practice that make use of Eastern traditions should be an "interruption of the interruption of cultural flows" and make "adequate reconnection to Eastern sources."[12] My term *reORIENTation* acknowledges that my pedagogy manifests itself in a Western context, as the teaching environment is an American university.

However, I adapt Lei's process of interruption and reconnection to the Eastern sources that inform my pedagogy by explicitly acknowledging the Asianist sources operating within my intercultural performance training paradigm. Later, I discuss reORIENTation as applied in a classroom setting, where it describes the fluid process of relocating one's perspective in response to shifting matrices of historical, cultural, geopolitical, and corporeal perspectives in the twenty-first-century classroom.

INTERCULTURAL EDUCATION

Twenty-first-century education specialist Panagiotis Maniatis reminds us that intercultural education is a human right, pointing out that it is through "[the] process of the meeting of cultures and their mutual interaction"[13] that intercultural education assumes a multiplicity of cultural traditions, customs, and belief systems of individual cultures as they are predisposed to engendering the practice of compassion, humanity, and shared community. Likewise, the United Nations Educational, Scientific and Cultural Organization (UNESCO) guidelines consider intercultural education a part of their human rights initiatives.[14] Maniatis continues that "the intercultural premise in education involves on the one hand interrogating every traditional aspect of the education process and teaching activity, while on the other hand broadening its targets."[15] If we understand intercultural education within the context of human rights initiatives then we can move with urgency to challenge education policies and practices that sustain social inequalities.

I acknowledge, however, that the social justice initiatives of intercultural education are problematic. Some may argue that intercultural education prioritizes the instructor's political agenda. However, intercultural education does not reify a singular viewpoint but works to privilege multiple positionalities in the classroom. Still others may contend that the leap from theorizing democracy to enacting it in a classroom is at best visionary. Indeed the practice of intercultural education cannot avoid the disputes over power, rights to authorship, and cultural authenticity that often plague intercultural performance collaborations; however, intercultural arts education considers these tensions to be a productive impetus that drive and direct us towards more equitable encounters at the micro-level of the intercultural performance training classroom.

GLOBAL INTERCULTURAL ARTS EDUCATION

The micro-level of the intercultural performance training classroom contributes to a vast constellation of theatre, dance, music, and arts research activity that is the global landscape of intercultural arts education. Likewise the broad field of intercultural arts research includes pedagogical investigations in visual arts and urban projects engaging museums and other civic spaces.[16] Given the interdisciplinary nature of intercultural practice and its inherent international scope, interculturalism occupies a vanguard position in progressive movements to initiate and engage alterity, hybridity, and the in-betweeness of arts learning and global citizenship. However, despite the emphasis on global inclusion, scholars and practitioners from across disciplines often encounter intercultural projects that sidestep the ethical principles of reciprocity in intercultural "collaborations." The result of bypassing ethical principles is the reinforcement of colonial patterns of domination that sustain Eurocentric paradigms.[17] In the field of intercultural theatre, Daphne Lei defines this reinscription of inequity as Hegemonic Intercultural Theatre (HIT), a process by which First World capital employs Third World labor to manifest "the other" through the lens of the European imaginary.[18] Similarly, in the emergent field of intercultural dance studies, scholars, teachers, and choreographers are striving to bring attention to marginalized voices that contribute to intercultural dance projects and inter-geographical dance collaborations.[19] Even still, there remains a paucity of practical models available to intercultural performance training educators.

CONTEXTUALIZING THE COURSE

Without an existing practical model, I taught Afro-Haitian dance for the first time at ASU in Tempe, Arizona, where my department positioned it as a new course for non-dance majors. The fifteen-week course was valued at two credits; we met twice a week for one hour and fifteen minutes and two drummers provided live accompaniment for each class. The course ran with seven students.[20] None of the students had previous formal dance and/or movement training beyond recreational activity, with the exception of one student having studied taiji. All students were female ranging from twenty-three to fifty-two years old. The student group included an ASU faculty member, a doctoral student, three Master's students, and two undergraduate students. The racial make-up was as follows: four white Americans, a mixed/white North African American, and two black Americans.

THE ETHICS OF ASSUMING INTERCULTURAL LABOR

Who is performing the labor of interculturalism? Whose interests does intercultural labor serve? These ethical questions should be asked at the outset of all intercultural projects as they centralize the dynamics of race, power, and profit at the heart of intercultural teaching in the university. As a Master in Fine Art (MFA) Dance student, I taught one dance course per semester in exchange for tuition remission and a stipend. It was during my audition interview that the admissions committee asked if I would teach Afro-Haitian dance upon acceptance. While I understood the department's desire to diversify their dance program, I felt conflicted about their request given the implications of ASU's location in Arizona. ASU is one of the largest universities in America, with a campus-wide commitment to "innovation" and "assuming fundamental responsibility for the economic, social, cultural and overall health of the communities it serves."[21] Despite the progressive goals of ASU, Arizona is a politically conservative state with a history of authorizing the special persecution of non-white peoples;[22] these injustices have also extended to students within the educational system, including ASU students.[23] On the one hand, I felt an urge to teach the course to reinforce racial visibility and cultural diversity; on the other hand, I anticipated complications as an Asian person teaching Afro-Haitian dance at a mostly white university—that I could potentially be contributing to white hegemony in US dance and the uneven power dynamics of HIT.

Anthea Kraut describes US dance history as "also a history of white borrowing from racially subjugated communities . . . [T]he question of who possesses the right to which movement, of who is authorized to borrow from whom, and who profits from the circulation are all entangled in racial injustice."[24] My role as a Chinese American teaching Afro-Haitian dance in exchange for tuition remission and a stipend lies at the irresolvable crux of debates related to Asian labor, cultural appropriation, and the commodification of non-white cultural traditions. I was an Asian body producing an intercultural pedagogy to diversify one of America's largest and most racially homogenous universities; this arguably reflects HIT's dynamic of power imbalance between First World capital (ASU) and Third World labor (me).

The issues of race, power, and profit that surrounded this intercultural teaching project carried several more implications. First, I had to accept that teaching Afro-Haitian dance as a new "ethnic" dance form would mean consenting to its commodification within the university system. Next, I had to accept that I was complicit with assuming the intercultural labor of diversifying the dance program. Since I had no choice but to accept the teaching position, I decided the only way to proceed ethically was to create a curriculum that would push students beyond a tourist concept of Afro-Haitian dance. I designed a dance curriculum that required both movement learning and content learning of Afro-Haitian dance history and exploration of its contemporary practices across geographies. However, doing this without mentorship meant that my intercultural labor proceeded without infrastructural support. The lack of support and absence of awareness of the ethical issues of this project meant that aspects of my intercultural labor remained unaccounted for. In summation, I assumed the intercultural labor that the university implicitly considered important but was somehow not willing or able to carry out themselves. Given these conditions, I turned to action research methodology as a self-supporting framework while also contributing data to the emerging field of intercultural dance teaching.

ACTION RESEARCH AS ETHICAL PRACTICE

Action research is a collaborative mode of inquiry that has developed over time and from an expansive range of disciplines.[25] Early evidence of action research can be located in labor-organizing traditions in the US and throughout Europe as well as in Latin American liberation theology and the works of Paolo Freire.[26] During the 1970s in the UK, the educational action research movement emerged in resistance to developments in education policy that demanded curricular shifts that emphasized the pre-enumeration of measurable learning outcomes.[27] It was in light of this policy shift that the educational action research movement placed ethical emphasis on the philosophy of teaching practice, stressing "process values as a basis for constructing [the] curriculum"[28] as opposed to "technical means-ends reasoning."[29] Thus, action research's emphasis on "process values" is ethical in character because it requires reflection on choosing a specific course of action, considering its particular set of circumstances, and interrogating one's personal and teaching values in light of existing political obstacles. From here, pedagogical action research emerged as an alternative mode of inquiry to support ethical reflection in the domain of practice and has evolved in scope to identify feminist, emancipatory, transformational, and critical approaches to collaborative education research.[30]

Teachers typically apply action research methodology to a specific problem related to their own teaching practice,[31] or related to issues in the school-wide curriculum.[32] While applications of action research methodology vary, the basic action research cycle is a series of four steps: plan, act, observe, and reflect.[33] The repetition of this cycle provides a framework of reiterative inquiry to improve the competence and practice of the teacher-researcher rather than simply produce theoretical knowledge.[34] In action research, the teacher evaluates their own educational practice methodically and scrupulously, engaging in a self-reflective process in which inquiry and discussion are the components of "research."[35]

The fundamental question that drives action research is how to bring about the production of knowledge that is both fruitful and vital to "improving the well-being of individuals, communities, and for the promotion of large-scale democratic social change."[36] In a classroom, action research directly engages students in the co-creation of knowledge. As Hilary Bradbury-Huang writes, "Action research is a pragmatic co-creation of knowing *with*, not *on* people."[37] Based on the history and contemporary practices of action research in relation to "social justice, civil rights, and democracy,"[38] we can understand it as a suitable framework for exploring critical intercultural pedagogies that aim to construct democracy, inclusion, and mutual reciprocity at the intersection of performance and education in the university classroom.

CONNECTING INTERCULTURAL PERFORMANCE AND INTERCULTURAL EDUCATION THROUGH ACTION RESEARCH

Action research methodology was the framework of inquiry through which I engaged the tensions at the crossroads of intercultural performance and intercultural education. I determined the specific problem to be the predominance of Western training paradigms in dance education. I conducted the first action research cycle during a fifteeen-week semester which I divided into four sections, each dedicated to the study of one dance: Weeks 1–4 focused on *Yanvalou*; Weeks 5–8 focused on *Nago*; Weeks 9–13 focused on *Banda*; Weeks 14–15 were dedicated to rehearsing the final performance.

The first step of action research is to "plan." During this phase I conducted interviews, gathered course materials, and designed my syllabus.[39] The second step of action research is to "act." In this phase I commenced teaching the course. I carried out the third step, to "observe," in class, noting student responses in discussions, witnessing their movement and their overall participation throughout the fifteen weeks. I performed the final step, to "reflect," by logging my written reflections and, ultimately, by analyzing the data I collected.

This was the basic action research cycle that spanned the fifteen-week semester, and while conducting the study, I relied on this basic template of plan/act/observe/reflect to process information and make decisions at a micro-level. For instance, I collected and read student journal entries throughout the semester, and their writing informed me as to whether or not the Asianist warm-ups were effective in conveying the somatic concepts related to producing the technical aspects of Afro-Haitian dance movement. I learned to reORIENT my pedagogical approach to address student uncertainties or reinforce concepts that were successful; in the restructured class I observed the results of my changes to the pedagogy. In this way I utilized the action research framework as a functional support system to reinforce my evolving teaching process. Action research in practice requires teacher flexibility to move in accordance with the flows of understanding from different student viewpoints and the curriculum. In an intercultural learning environment where shifting and unsettling is the status quo, action research can be a very useful navigation tool.

REORIENTING INTERCULTURALISM IN THE ACADEMY: THREE KEY STRATEGIES

Three strategies emerged from my action research inquiry into teaching Afro-Haitian dance with an Asianist lens. These strategies guide practitioners toward critical self-reflection and centralize the ethics of reciprocity, inclusion, and student empowerment in intercultural performance training. Explicit acknowledgment, elastic discourse, and multidirectionality are adaptable to a multitude of learning spaces, and practitioners should use them rigorously. These strategies are synergistic: no single tactic will ever operate alone, as the activation of one will inevitably engage at least one other. For clarification, I include qualitative examples from my study to illustrate the ways each concept is a catalyst for more democratic and ethical approaches to intercultural performance training.

Explicit Acknowledgment

Explicit acknowledgment prioritizes crediting cultural sources that inform one's intercultural pedagogy. When an intercultural practitioner credits the cultural traditions, practices, and philosophies at work in their pedagogy, they assume accountability for their borrowing and make transparent their role in the shuttling of cultural capital in the performance training classroom. Explicit acknowledgment accepts that the loaning process is not one of individual invention but a collective practice that recognizes the various secular, religious, spiritual, and diasporic forms of a particular cultural tradition. In this way, intercultural performance training pedagogy builds itself around a multiplicity of temporal and locative viewpoints to accommodate alternative conceptions of "origins" and acknowledges those tensions as assembling the structure of an intercultural pedagogy.

For example, I explicitly acknowledge to the students that I draw on my training in taiji martial arts in my approach to teaching Afro-Haitian dance. When I first introduce the idea of "center" in the body, I refer to the *dantian* and *qi*, two concepts applied in Chinese medicine, philosophy, and martial arts. I explain *qi* as "vital energy" which is centralized in the *dantian*, a region located in the body between the abdomen and the lower back and between the pubic bone and the belly button. I describe *dantian* as a "battery" where their *qi* is stored and I refer to the Japanese equivalent of *hara* (battery/*dantian*) and *ki* (vital energy/*qi*). I acknowledge the concept of *prana* (vital energy/*qi*/*ki*) from Indian Ayurvedic medicine practice to illustrate the interconnectedness of Asianist genealogies of body knowledge.

After explaining *dantian*, from which flows *qi*, students locate their *dantian* by squeezing their right index and middle fingers together and placing them just below their belly button. Then, with the left index finger, they mark where the right middle finger sits on the abdomen and from there, they imagine three-fingers-width beneath the surface of the abdomen to locate the *dantian*. Next, students explore sensing their *qi* moving up and down the body beginning from the *dantian*. Afterwards, I introduce the Ayurvedic concept of *chakras* as vortexes of energy. I explicitly acknowledge the *chakra* system as an alternative paradigm for us to understand landmarks on the body beyond the musculoskeletal system often used in Western dance training. Students explore the *chakras* in order to produce the lyrical body undulation characteristic of Afro-Haitian dance. To do this, they learn to perceive their *chakras* by hovering their hands one or two inches above the body to locate the seven sites of *prana*. All students typically achieve this in the first exploration; most describe shifts in temperature, density, and size of the vibrational field between the *chakras*. After they have located the *chakras*, the students practice moving *qi* up and down through the *chakra* points, replicating this motion with the physical body until they are able to produce the body undulation of Afro-Haitian dance. This happens first on the floor, standing upright in a stationary position, then moving across the floor.

By explicitly acknowledging the traditions that inform my Asianist approach, I convey to students that their performance training activates a nexus of cultural knowledge and reflects a multiplicity of cultural "origins." This acknowledgment is significant because it reinforces the point that multiple paradigms produce body knowledge in dance training. Furthermore, an Asianist, polycentric approach to bodily training reflects Africanist sensibilities; both Asianist and Africanist approaches challenge conventional Western paradigms by suggesting there is always more than one "center" in the body.

When I teach the *Nago* warrior dance, we begin with a review of the content assignments in which students learn that it is a militaristic dance that evolved out of the Haitian Revolution of 1804. The performance of *Nago* was a call to arms that unified the marooned and enslaved Africans to seek emancipation from the slavery imposed by French colonial power. I explicitly acknowledge to the students that I draw from my training in Japanese taiko drumming to teach the feeling of *Nago* as I learned to understand it from my Asianist perspective. In taiko drumming, the percussive vocalization of *kiai!* centers the mind-body and directs intention and energy in performance. *Kiai!* is the vocalization of *ki* (vital force) and arises from the *hara* (*dantian*). I explain that taiko performers vocalize *kiai!* as a source of encouragement for soloists to overcome an apparently insurmountable physical challenge in performance; it is also prevalent throughout martial arts practice and various forms of combat training. I explain that for these reasons, *kiai!* is suitable for learning *Nago* and extends the Asianist body knowledge to intercultural understanding.

The lesson begins with students inhaling into their *hara*/*dantian* and exhaling with a quick percussive contraction to vocalize *kiai!* Then, lunging deeply into the legs with both knees bent, one leg in front of the other, they extend both arms parallel to the floor in front of the torso. In this position both wrists are flexed and palms are facing away from the body. Beginning from the shoulder girdle (or the fifth *chakra*), the right arm swings down and back to gather momentum before a forceful push forward with the same open palm to return the arms to the original position in front of the body, parallel to the floor. At the very moment of directing the momentum forward with the open palm, the students vocalize *kiai!* in unison. Additionally, in a different section of the choreography, dancers draw an imaginary bow, and as they release their arrows at a target ahead of them, they collectively vocalize *kiai!* as they move across the dance floor.

While I have described explicit acknowledgment in a dance context, the strategy applies to any intercultural performance training practice. Explicitly identifying the traditions that shape one's pedagogy allows practitioners to engage an ethics of intercultural performance training by assuming accountability for one's role in the transference of cultural knowledge in the classroom. Making the borrowing process transparent conveys a practitioner's performance training lineage, allowing students to understand that their training is inextricably bound to a nexus of cultural practices that exist beyond the dominant paradigm and across geographic territories.

Elastic Discourse

Elastic discourse is the practice of expanding the learning community's engagement with theoretical, practical, cultural, and disciplinary viewpoints such that the arena of the twenty-first-century classroom facilitates reciprocal intercultural exchange. A defining feature of elastic discourse is student empowerment. In this process, students facilitate the communal practice of building knowledge across disciplines to broaden the territory of discursive understanding in an intercultural arts classroom. As such, they contribute expertise from their fields of study in relation to the course materials and connect the discussion to their personal lived experience. Elastic discourse highlights the interstices between disciplines to strengthen the network of bodies and bodies of knowledge in the intercultural classroom; this reflects Rustom Bharucha's argument that intercultural practice should move toward the heightening of intercontextuality, or the investigation of the interrelationships between contexts.[40] The practice of elastic discourse also reflects the widely held view in global intercultural arts research that interculturalism is inherently interdisciplinary.[41] Karan Barad offers unqualified support for elastic discourse, drawing on Foucault: "Discourse is not what is said; it is that which constrains and enables what can be said."[42] Therefore in a dance training context where the body "speaks," elastic discourse liberates the body from the bondage of dominant training regimes and invites students to contribute to the process of intercutlural exchange. But what does elastic discourse look like in an intercultural performance training classroom?

For intercultural performance education practitioners, elastic discourse at the most basic level is the practice of accountability via gathering learning materials from a variety of disciplines from different ethnic, cultural, religious, secular, and gender perspectives. For students, elastic discourse means engaging course materials from their areas of study and synthesizing their lived experiences to expand the field of discursive understanding in an intercultural classroom. For instance, I designed a pedagogy that interlocks Afro-Haitian dance movement learning with content learning of Haitian culture to push students beyond a tourist conception of Afro-Haitian dance.[43] *Movement learning* describes the kinesthetic practice of producing the technical aspects of dance movement. *Content learning* describes student engagement with written texts, video viewings, reflective journaling, class discussions, and presentations; essentially, *content learning* frames movement learning within a broader sociocultural and historical context. Interlocking movement and content learning reORIENTs student engagement with Afro-Haitian dance within elastic parameters that considers the dance form's development across religious, secular, historical, political, and diasporic contexts.

Elastic discourse and student empowerment emerged in a mini-midterm research project that invited students to investigate a topic of their choice related to Haitian literature, history, film, food, or Afro-Haitian dance and drumming practice. Students presented their findings interlaced with data from their research areas followed by a student-led question-and-answer session. In this study, students elasticized classroom discourse with perspectives from women and gender studies, anthropology, biological science, history, and psychology. One student drew from anthropology by investigating how the contributions from Katherine Dunham's research in Haiti shaped the field of dance ethnography and the US modern dance aesthetic. Another student presented elements of her doctoral research on the function of Afro-Caribbean food traditions as an ethnoculinary performance practice of African diaspora survival; she prepared three traditional Haitian dishes to share and provided a narration of the oceanic migration of each ingredient. A third student traced the musical and medicinal traditions of Afro-Haitian voodoo practice to the Taino indigenous peoples of Haiti who were also displaced by Western colonial expansion.

The mini-midterm project showcased the students' individual ability to inhabit the role of leader and expert in the intercultural classroom. Elastic discourse compels students to combine analytical ways of knowing with personal experience to contribute a unique understanding of the subject matter. bell hooks calls this mixture of analytical and experiential ways of knowing in the classroom a "privileged standpoint"[44] that challenges essentialist practices in which only the teacher holds the "authority of experience." Elastic discourse empowers students to contribute their views, which hooks argues "cannot be acquired through books or distanced observation and a study of a particular reality."[45] The intercultural practitioner must be willing to step aside so that student authority and their transdisciplinary realities can emerge.

Multidirectionality

Multidirectionality anticipates collisions in intercultural education practice as productive encounters. Of the three themes I present in this chapter, I believe multidirectionality has the most potential for democratizing approaches to critical intercultural practices in education and research; for the intercultural practitioner, it is also the most uncomfortable to enact. Multidirectionality defies Pavis's unidirectional hourglass model and builds on Lo and Gilbert's notion of a bidirectional flow. While multidirectionality supports elastic discourse, it differs in that it resists the "add and stir" model of mixing viewpoints to produce diversity and expand talking points. Rather, multidirectionality deepens the practice of elastic discourse by acknowledging the intersectionalities of privilege and oppression inherent to the discursive practice of critical intercultural education. Patricia Hill Collins and Sirma Bilge contend that intersectionality is a tool of analysis that regards individual identity as shaped by a variety of social factors such as race, class, gender, sexuality, and physical ability in "diverse and mutually influencing ways."[46] Intersectionality vigorously posits that an individual simultaneously inhabits a multiplicity of nodes on the intersectional matrix, a conceptual space defined by socially constructed categories that produce multilayered inequalities across temporal-spatial topographies. Intersectional theory problematizes inequities by asserting that oppressions synchronistically operate as privileges depending on the context in which those privileges and oppressions activate. Because intersectionality concerns itself with identifying shifting inequities produced by a number of sociocultural and political factors, it lends itself to reinforcing multidirectionality as a strategy for engaging the inevitable collisions in an intercultural context as moments of productive discovery.

I turn now to highlighting how multidirectionality reflects Zarrilli et al.'s call for an examination of the "micro-level" of exchange as a way of magnifying "our global, urban, multi-, inter-, intra-cultural realities as *the norm* rather than the exception." At the very heart of this final concept is the notion of listening.

One night as I was teaching *Nago*, I used the term *African slaves* to describe the Haitians who ritualized the communal practice of the *Nago* dance as a remembrance of Haitian resilience and triumph against slavery and European colonialism. A student promptly corrected the phrase *African slaves*, replacing it with *enslaved Africans*. She explained that the former term implied that all Africans were slaves, while the latter phrase recognized that the oppression of human slavery was *imposed* on Africans. Multidirectionality demonstrated itself here in the bidirectional flow of power in which a student was able to suggest a more appropriate term, one that we used for the rest of the semester. Multidirectionality also checked me, the teacher. Even with seemingly good intentions to advance social justice initiatives in the intercultural classroom, by using the term, I was reinscribing a racist vernacular that was counterproductive to my efforts and brought offense to the students. In this instance, multidirectionality produced a moment of reverse-mentorship; the student was completely entitled to make the correction and she seized the teaching moment to the benefit of the collective.

It would be naïve to suggest that the discomfort of multidirectionality is quarantined in the classroom. In fact, if intercultural performance training practitioners are interested in advancing social justice, the dissemination of their data is necessary. My first public encounter with multidirectionality was at a popular national dance conference where I was presenting my action research findings. Upon showing a clip of the students' final performance, a black Haitian woman in the front row of the audience said with what seemed like disdain, "That's not any *Yanvalou* that *I've* ever seen." I was uncomfortable. In that moment I did not have recourse to dialogue. I knew that controversy could be a possibility but I was not prepared with a response. As I continued explaining the context in which I was applying an Asianist lens to Afro-Haitian dance as a way of coalition building to challenge Europeanist paradigms of dance training in the academy, she seemed to nod in support.

After the presentation, I thought about how my own Haitian dance teacher would have recognized the students' performance as reflecting her dance lineage from her training with Frisner Augustin in New York, a Haitian-born master drummer often credited with bringing Haitian drumming and dance practice to the United States. The woman's comment was a productive reORIENTation of view for me to consider how migration engenders the reproduction of traditional performance practices to reflect the intercultural collisions that inform the training processes that bring Afro-Haitian dance to life in a new space. I make this point to clarify that on the micro-level, the collisions in my intercultural dance classroom generated a unique movement language that reflected the nuanced intersectionalities of our particular intercultural experience together and I believe that this is true for all intercultural performance training encounters. I also think it is important to remember that altruistic intentions do not safeguard intercultural practitioners from encountering criticism from communities who lay claim to a performance practice or assert that there is only one way to reproduce a dance movement. However, if we are to redefine the ways we engage interculturally, the discomfort of multidirectionality is necessary. These awkward micro-level exchanges reinforce the reality of our shared "global, urban, multi-, inter-, intra-cultural realities" and force our reORIENTations to other viewpoints and modes of thriving.

CONCLUSION

This chapter began with two questions: "How can one create a critical intercultural pedagogy in performance training?" and "What is at stake here?" As I have demonstrated, there are a variety of obstacles and considerations that critical intercultural performance training practitioners will contend with as they design and implement more equitable approaches to intercultural exchange in twenty-first-century classrooms. I have suggested action research methodology as an appropriate response to the shifting landscapes of our intercultural classrooms. The three pedagogical strategies of explicit acknowledgment, elastic discourse, and multidirectionality will help practitioners navigate those geographies to build reciprocity, student empowerment, and mutual exchange in the intercultural learning process. I have also discussed the risks in applying a critical intercultural performance training paradigm in an academic setting, including wrestling with the ethical and political dimensions of one's role as an intercultural educator—a process that requires taking inventory of one's simultaneous privileges and restrictions and considering how the geopolitical territory of one's teaching environment contextualizes their intercultural pedagogy. Another risk is having to debate matters of cultural copyright. Still, I believe braving these risks is crucial to the practice of critical intercultural arts education as it enables us to challenge dominant paradigms and create new legacies of empowerment for voices in the margins. We need to push forward with a heightened awareness that any singular ethnocentric approach lacks the tensile quality needed to account for and accommodate the diversity, interdisciplinarity, and interculturality emblematic of our twenty-first-century classrooms. And to change this, the place to begin is in our own classrooms.

NOTES

1. Phillip Zarrilli, Thirunalan Sasitharan, and Anuradha Kapur, "Special Issue on 'Intercultural' Acting and Actor/Performer Training," *Theatre, Dance and Performance Training* 7, no. 3 (2016): 335–9. Zarilli et al. employ Erika Fischer-Lichte's problematic term *interweaving* as a gesture to recent debates on the process of cultural exchange in performance practice. In 2008, Lichte founded the International Research Center for Advanced Studies on "*Interweaving* Performance Cultures" at Freie Universität Berlin to investigate the possibilities and problems of the "interweaving" of cultures through performance. The website states, "The International Research Center 'Interweaving Performance Cultures' was founded in August 2008 with the aim of opening up a new field of research." In 2011, during a public dialogue between Lichte and Rustom Bharucha, Bharucha incisively reasoned, "if we follow your raison d'être for the naming of the institution—that all the problems associated with 'interculturalism' will somehow disappear with the introduction of 'interweaving'? When you 'interweave' one culture with another, do the problems disappear? Problems relating to the distribution of power, stereotyping, etc. Obviously, they don't. In a sense, the problems could be deflected, or circumscribed—that's one possibility. But they could also engender new problems, which are as yet unanticipated." See www.textures-platform.com.

2. Zarrilli, Sasitharan, and Kapur, "Special Issue on 'Intercultural' Acting," 335.

3. Zarrilli, Sasitharan, and Kapur, "Special Issue on 'Intercultural' Acting," 335.

4. For more details, see Angeline Young, "Risks and reORIENTations: An Asianist Approach to Teaching Afro-Haitian Dance," *Journal of Dance Education* 17, no. 1 (2017): 13–22.

5. Patrice Pavis and Loren Kruger, *Theatre at the Crossroads of Culture* (London and New York: Routledge, 1992).

6. Jacqueline Lo and Helen Gilbert, "Toward a Topography of Cross-Cultural Theatre Praxis," *TDR/The Drama Review* 46, no. 3 (2002): 44.

7. Li Ruru and Jonathan Pitches, "The End of the Hour-Glass: Alternative Conceptions of Intercultural Exchange between European and Chinese Operatic Forms," *Studies in Theatre and Performance* 32, no. 2 (2012): 125.

8. Ruru and Pitches, "The End of the Hour-Glass," 136.

9. For more information, see Edward Said, *Orientalism* (New York: Random House, 1994).

10. Brenda Dixon Gottschild, *Digging the Africanist Presence in American Performance: Dance and Other Contexts*, Contributions in Afro-American and African Studies, No. 179 (Westport, CT: Greenwood Press, 1996).

11. SanSan Kwan, "Even as We Keep Trying: An Ethics of Interculturalism in Jérôme Bel's *Pichet Klunchun and Myself*," *Theatre Survey* 55, no. 2 (April 2014): 186.

12. Daphne P. Lei, "Interruption, Intervention, Interculturalism: Robert Wilson's HIT Productions in Taiwan," *Theatre Journal* 63, no. 4 (December 2011): 574.

13. Panagiotis Maniatis, "Critical Intercultural Education Necessities and Prerequisites for its Development in Greece," *Journal for Critical Education Policy Studies* 10, no. 1 (April 2012): 157.

14. United Nations Educational, Scientific and Cultural Organization, *UNESCO Guidelines on Intercultural Education* (Paris: UNESCO, 2016), 5, http://unesdoc. unesco.org/images/0014/001478/147878e.pdf.

15. Maniatis, "Critical Intercultural Education," 2.

16. Pamela Burnard, Elizabeth Mackinlay, and Kimberly A. Powell (eds.), *The Routledge International Handbook of Intercultural Arts Research* (New York and London: Routledge, 2016).

17. See, for example, SanSan Kwan, "Even as We Keep Trying"; Daphne P. Lei, "Interruption, intervention, interculturalism"; Priya Srinivasan, "The Bodies beneath the Smoke or What's behind the Cigarette Poster: Unearthing Kinesthetic Connections in American Modern Dance," *Discourses in Dance* 4, no. 1 (January 2007): 7–47; and Yutian Wong, *Choreographing Asian America* (Middletown, CT: Wesleyan University Press, 2010).

18. Lei, "Interruption, Intervention, Interculturalism," 571.

19. See Marvin Khoo, "What My Intercultural Training Taught Me," *Theatre, Dance and Performance Training* 7, no. 3 (2016): 490–2; Royona Mitra, *Akram Khan: Dancing New Interculturalism* (New York: Palgrave Macmillan, 2015); Cheryl Stock, "Moving Bodies across Cultures: An Analysis of a Vietnamese/Australian Dance and Music Project," *Australasian Drama Studies* 34, no. 47 (1999): 46–67; and Cheryl Stock, "Adaptation and Empathy: Intercultural Communication in a Choreographic Project," *Journal of Intercultural Studies* 33, no. 4 (2012): 445–62.

20. All students consented to their participation in this study and their permissions remain on file with the International Review Board.

21. See ASU Charter at https://president.asu.edu/about/asucharter.

22. Arizona's conservative, "Red State" politics are tied to its history as a former part of Mexico which was ceded to the United States in 1848 after the Mexican–American War. In 1863, Arizina became a territory and continues to share a bitterly contested border with Mexico. This contest played out in labor discrimination and anti-immigrant laws throughout the nineteenth and twentieth century via the special persecution of Chinese immigrant laborers, the confinement of Indigenous peoples on reservations, and the internment of Japanese Americans during the Second World War. In 2010, Arizona passed State Bill (S.B.) 1070, permitting police officers to apprehend anyone they presumed to be "illegal." In practice, S.B. 1070 mandated racial profiling against Latinos, Asians, and Indigenous peoples. S.B. 1070 was followed by a chain of discriminatory legislative acts, notably, S.B. 1108, an anti-ethnic studies law that prohibited Mexican-American and Indigenous studies

programs in Arizona public schools. S.B. 1108 prompted community activists in Arizona to engage in a seven-year litigation to overturn the bill and it was during this time that I was a graduate student designing my intercultural pedagogy.

23. DREAMers are immigrant students that hold Deferred Action for Childhood Arrivals (DACA) status. DACA is a federal policy that the Obama administration implemented in 2012 to provide temporary work permits and administrative relief from deportation for immigrants that arrived in the US as young children. In 2016, President Donald Trump authorized a nationwide racist, anti-immigrant movement when he campaigned on a platform of discrimination against Mexicans, undocumented immigrants, and revoking the rights of DREAMers. As a result, on April 9, 2018, the Arizona Supreme Court ruled to uphold federal and state laws requiring DREAMers to pay out-of-state tuition for college, making it impossible for many DACA students to continue their post-secondary education. This ruling sets Arizona apart from other US states that offer in-state tuition for DACA students. At present under the Trump administration, the future of DACA and its DREAMers is uncertain. At the time of publication, ASU was one of many organizations that rejected this ruling and continue to support DREAMers with in-state tuition while they seek legal advice to navigate the State Supreme Court ruling. For more information, see University of California at Berkeley, "DACA Information," *Undocumented Student Program University of California at Berkeley*, 2017, https:// undocu.berkeley.edu/legal-support-overview/what-is-daca/; Clarice Silber, "Fight Flares in Arizona over Tuition for Young Immigrants," *New York Times Associated Press*, July 12, 2017; and "ASU's Commitment to DACA Students and all DREAMers," *ASU Office of the President*, November 23, 2016.

24. "ASU's Commitment to DACA Students and all DREAMers," 4, 5.

25. Mary Brydon-Miller, Davydd Greenwood, and Patricia Maguire, "Why Action Research?" *Action Research* 1, no. 1 (2003): 11; and Eileen Ferrance, "Action Research," *Themes in Education*, Northeast and Islands Regional Educational Laboratory at Brown University (Providence, RI: Brown University, 2000), 7.

26. Brydon-Miller, Greenwood, and Maguire, "Why Action Research?" 11.

27. John Elliott, *Action Research for Educational Change* (London: McGraw-Hill Education, 1991), 51.

28. Elliott, *Action Research for Educational Change*, 51.

29. Elliott, *Action Research for Educational Change*, 51.

30. Hilary Bradbury-Huang, "Introduction to the Handbook of Action Research," in *The SAGE Handbook of Action Research: Participative Inquiry and Practice*, 3rd edn. (London: SAGE Publications, 2015), https://actionresearchplus.com/wp-content/ uploads/2015/.../HB_Introduction_final.pdf.

31. Ferrance, "Action Research," Introduction.

32. Ferrance, "Action Research," Introduction.

33. University of Warwick, "Action Research," *Learning and Development Center*, July 10, 2012, https://warwick.ac.uk/services/ldc/resource/evaluation/tools/action/.

34. John Elliott writes in *Action Research for Educational Change*.

35. John Elliott writes in *Action Research for Educational Change*.

36. Brydon-Miller, Greenwood, and Maguire, "Why Action Research?" 11.

37. Bradbury-Huang, "Introduction to the Handbook of Action Research," 1.

38. Brydon-Miller, Greenwood, and Maguire, "Why Action Research?" 11.

39. I conducted interviews with a black American dance instructor and a white American faculty member who had each taught an African diaspora dance course at ASU. I was cautioned about the bureaucratic issues related to low enrollment in a "global" dance course and was also warned about the practice of racial politics in the seasonal hiring of black African instructors to diversify the all-white dance faculty.

40. Rustom Bharucha, *The Politics of Cultural Practice: Thinking Through Theatre in an Age of Globalization* (London: The Athlone Press, 2000). See also Rustom Bharucha, "Envisioning Ethics Anew," *Performance Paradigm* 3 (2007), http://www.performanceparadigm.net/index.php/journal/article/view/36.

41. Burnard, Mackinlay, and Powell, *The Routledge International Handbook of Intercultural Arts Research*.

42. Karen Barad, "Posthumanist Performativity: Toward an Understanding of How Matter Comes to Matter," *Signs* 28, no.3, Gender and Science: New Issues (2003): 819.

43. Doug Risern argues that "tourist" conceptions of non-European and non-Euro-American dance forms in universities is a problem related to the hegemonic practice of eroticizing "the Other;" this eroticization results in superficial engagements with "ethnic" cultural practices. See Doug Risner and Susan W. Stinson, "Moving Social Justice: Challenges, Fears and Possibilities in Dance Education" *International Journal of Education & the Arts* 11, no. 6 (2010): 1–26.

44. bell hooks, *Teaching to Transgress: Education as the Practice of Freedom* (New York: Routledge, 1994), 91.

45. hooks, *Teaching to Transgress*, 91.

46. Patricia Hill Collins and Sirma Bilge, *Intersectionality* (New York: Key Concepts/Polity Press, 2016), 1.

PART FOUR

Testing the Limits of New Interculturalism

Mamela Nyamza and Dada Masilo: South African Black Women Dancer-Choreographers Dancing "New Interculturalism"

KETU H. KATRAK

"New interculturalism" in performance is explored in the creative choreography of noteworthy South African dancer-choreographers Mamela Nyamza and Dada Masilo. Their choreography is innovatively intercultural, mining the in-between spaces of their movement forms—classical ballet (in which they were trained from a young age) and their indigenous South African dance forms denigrated during colonial and apartheid eras, now recuperated as classical Zulu and Xhosa dance with their own vocabularies and rhythms, along with modern, contemporary, jazz, release technique, and, for Nyamza, also gumboot dance and butoh. Both dancers challenge the traditional execution of these styles; in particular they deconstruct, indeed demystify, ballet, presenting it as stripped of its "prettiness" and edgy and relevant for their South African context. Their choreography embodies interculturalism in their singular engagements with dance styles—Western and local—that are personalized and indigenized in their conceptual creations. Both dancers' signature dance styles are deployed to challenge socio-political and gender discriminations based on race, gender and sexuality, colonial and elitist definition of "high art," and state and international funding practices. In their hands, ballet is refashioned in a hybrid presentation with Zulu dance's vigorous hip movements, as in Masilo's renowned *Swan Lake*. Nyamza's *De-Apart-Hate* skillfully interweaves movement, song, and bold social critique of women's subordination under religious patriarchy.[1] I argue that Nyamza and Masilo, as virtuosic dancers, deploy their choreography as artist-activists to evoke issues of social justice and the necessity for social change in the new South Africa, still haunted by apartheid's (1948–94) legacy of racism and sexism endemic in indigenous tradition as well as in colonial (British and Dutch) cultures. An analysis of their creative work opens up the relationship between sexuality—defined by patriarchal cultures and structures of power such as the state and religion—and interculturalism as theory and as performed practice.

Both artists have a high national (in South Africa and on the continent) and international reputation, having performed in France, Germany, and the UK among other locations. Their intercultural choreography is inspired by the autobiographical and sociocultural realities of post-apartheid South Africa, especially issues of gender and sexuality that unfairly subordinate women through the continuing collusion between indigenous and Western patriarchy. Their dance styles also evoke and confront violence against gays and lesbians. It is significant and ironic that although the South African Constitution (the only one on the African continent) crafted under Nelson Mandela in 1994 guarantees equality of gender and sexuality for LGBTQ communities, the realities on the ground are sobering, since violence against the latter continues. Nyamza strongly critiques such discrimination, even the murders of lesbian women by men—who claim, in a chilling phrase, to be trying to "correct them" for their sexual choices—in her co-choreographed work entitled *I Stand Corrected*. The Constitution also ensures racial equality, linguistic equality (there are eleven recognized languages), and respect in the new democracy for all economic classes and political and artistic affiliations.

I draw upon interculturalism as a suitable lens through which to discuss Nyamza's and Masilo's solo and collaborative works with visual artists, dancers, and musicians. Their creative choreography is understood effectively via a "new interculturalism" that is both aesthetic and political, embodied in their danced synergy of multiple movements and cultures, and mediated significantly by their own South African cultural heritage, growing up as the "born frees," namely those who grew up after apartheid officially ended in 1994.[2]

As Royona Mitra argues in her book *Akram Khan: Dancing New Interculturalism*, this British-Bangladeshi dancer layers South Asian movement concepts such as the use of gesture language (*abhinaya*) and emotions (*rasas*) into his unique contemporary dance. Similarly, Nyamza and Masilo draw on their South African movement styles that work in hybrid choreography, stunning both for its technical rigor and its emotional effect. Like Akram Khan, whom Mitra describes as "transforming the landscape of British and global contemporary dance through his own embodied approach to new interculturalism," so Nyamza and Masilo in their own intercultural work "represent a conceptual, processual, embodied lived condition" that is "driven by one's own multiple affiliations to cultures, nations, and faiths."[3] Like the innovative Khan, Nyamza's and Masilo's movement language works "at the interstices" between South African classical dance styles and "eclectic idioms of contemporary dance, theatre, music, visual arts, literature, digital arts and film."[4]

Nyamza's and Masilo's art has evolved in response to the changing political and aesthetic landscape in South Africa and the authority of patriarchy and religion that subordinate women in patriarchal cultures, along with the opening up of a post-apartheid nation with its ideals of *simunye* (we are one) and "the rainbow nation." What is unique about both these artists is their negotiation of their South Africanness with their position as women in this society, reaching for freedom in all avenues of life—away from patriarchal domination, into new job opportunities and new aesthetic ventures. They do not abide by a kind of state-blessed multiculturalism where different races, dance styles, or languages are showcased as a harmonious whole; rather, in embracing the intercultural, they delve into the gaps, the fissures, the cracks and complications among different movement styles; they are interested in exploring how these styles can express and carry the weight of the sociopolitical and gender focused themes that they showcase.

In a world where hybrid identities are increasingly common, it is equally significant to recognize a similar trend in hybrid aesthetic forms. What do intercultural performances in the twenty-first century mean? How can artists and spectators remain vigilant regarding the dominant Western powers (expressed often via funding) and give priority to marginalized knowledges and voices from below? Indeed, how can artists and scholars make space for those who have been historically ignored or silenced? Nyamza's and Masilo's use of Western and African movement vocabularies reveals a significant concern with interculturalism, namely, how different knowledges (such as dance styles) are exchanged across cultures. Their work makes audiences ponder the possible persistence of unequal power relations, as was common in older models of interculturalism.

Interculturalism has been decried when it amounts to a dancer or director based in the West who enters somewhere in the global South to appropriate local stories, epics, or myths for consumption in the West. Egregious examples of such unequal exchanges include Peter Brook's mis/use of the Indian epic *The Mahabharata* for his own purposes of conveying a universal story disconnected from the Indian context. Brook has been critiqued convincingly by Rustom Bharucha,[5] while Robert Wilson has been taken to task insightfully by Daphne P. Lei in her essay "Interruption, Intervention, Interculturalism: Robert Wilson's HIT Productions in Taiwan."[6] Lei asserts that "The most common form of intercultural theater today [essay published in 2011], which I term, 'intercultural hegemonic theater', is a specific artistic genre and state of mind that combines First World capital and brainpower with Third World raw material and labor, and Western classical texts with Eastern performance traditions."[7]

While it is true that unequal power distribution among artists in the global North and South continue to plague artists, Susan Leigh Foster's incisive argument in her introduction to *Worlding Dance* states that scholars should

> examine dance not as a reflection of individual or cultural values, but *as* culture. As culture, dance is in(sinew)ated with power relations. Built bone-deep into the dancing body and permeating its practice and performance, these structurings of power both discipline and pleasure the body. And this cultivation of the corporeal takes place within and as a part of the power relations that operate throughout the body politic.[8]

Foster connects power relations embedded in the dancing body itself to how power functions in the larger sociopolitical framework. For Nyamza and Masilo, the South African political landscape is fraught with inequities and discrimination that are experienced bodily in the lack of basic human needs such as food and shelter.

Several issues of the problematic model of interculturalism and a revised "new interculturalism" are explored usefully in Ric Knowles' *Theatre & Interculturalism*.[9] Knowles prefers the term intercultural to others such as cross-cultural, intracultural, or multicultural since interculturalism focuses on "the contested, unsettling and often unequal spaces that can function in performance as sites of negotiation."[10] Ideally, cultural exchange involves cultural dialogues (where both sides speak and are heard) with the possibility of new knowledges for both sides of the exchange. Often, negotiation and power sharing are needed in performances that involve at least two or more cultures or cultural practices, whether these are in the realm of movement idioms or indigenous ways of moving and knowing along with those of a different culture.

MAMELA NYAMZA

Mamela Nyamza is a multiple award-winning dancer and choreographer, a remarkable teacher, and an artist-activist. In 2011 she won one of the highest honors for South African dancers: the Standard Bank Young Artist Award for Dance. Most recently, Nyamza was appointed Artist of the Year for 2018 by the National Arts Festival in recognition of her cutting-edge creative choreography over the past two decades that was celebrated at the event (July 2018). Nyamza is the first dancer to receive this award; in previous years, it was given to musicians, theatre directors, and playwrights. Nyamza was pleased, since for years she has spoken out about artists like herself being more appreciated in European festivals than in their own home country. She remarked, "This accolade is a great honour. It shows that my work is being seen. Dancers in SA often feel like we're not being looked at. I'm excited."[11] A profile of Nyamza noted that she planned to use her new status to premiere new material and revisit old work "with her matured body and an evolving dance vocabulary," as it "is a time to reflect on the past, present and future with material that has made her a formidable artist-activist refined at condensing personal and socio-political issues into bold artistic expressions . . . Her movement style has grown into a strong, conceptual signature, which can be an intellectual exercise for audiences."[12]

A member of a large family, Nyamza grew up in the 1980s in Gugulethu, a black township on the outskirts of Cape Town. Her origins in Gugulethu continue to have a profound influence on her artistry and her commitment to social justice art. She recalls being surrounded by music in this environment, and connected with dance as a means to understand the world around her. She remarks, "I used my body as the instrument to reach to all forms of sound, whether it be playing, crying, or watching all sorts of things that one can imagine happened in Gugulethu in the '80s" (*Real Magazine*, 2009).

Nyamza was born on September 22, 1976, a historic year in South Africa's violent history with the Soweto student uprising and massacre by security forces unleashing violence against blacks. The students were rallying against the state-imposed Bantu education which mandated Afrikaans, a language of Dutch origin, rather than English, a world language, to be the medium of instruction.[13]

At age eight, in 1984, as apartheid's racist policies were increasingly challenged, Nyamza started ballet classes at the Zama Dance School in Gugulethu with a white Jewish woman, Arlene Westergaard. Nyamza then completed a national Diploma in Ballet at the Pretoria Technikon Dance Department. Like other black women aspiring to ballet, Nyamza faced the usual prejudices against not having the thin body, a near-must in ballet, and not slender but large hips. But she was not deterred, explaining in an interview in *Real Magazine*, "I developed an attitude of 'I am going to do it' and that has helped me be where I am today and has proven wrong those who tried to de-motivate me."[14]

Nyamza won a scholarship in 1998–9 to study at the Alvin Ailey American Dance School in New York City, prestigious for its showcasing of black dancing bodies. She notes that for the first time in her life as a dancer "no one said you have a big bum and for the first time I felt the essence of being light as woman."[15] The renowned South African journalist Adrienne Sichel points out in her essay "Legacies of Violence" (which she describes as a "think-piece") that "Fabrice Herrault choreographed a personalized *The Dying Swan* (for Nyamza) initially titled *The Black Swan* which is now part of her repertory."[16]

A black lesbian dancer and choreographer, Nyamza's works are in line with artists whom I term "chore-activists" such as South African choreographer, theatre director, and curator Jay Pather, who is also Artistic Director of the Siwela Sonke Dance Theatre Company (SSDT; "siwela sonke" translates from isiZulu as "crossing over to a new place altogether") and South African scholars Gerard Samuel and Lliane Loots, who advocate for differently abled dancers. Loots is also Artistic Director of Flatfoot Dance Company and of the yearly JOMBA! Contemporary Dance Experience Festival in Durban. Nyamza, like Loots, is a "feminist choreographer" whose work, as Loots puts it, "emanates from her body"; Nyamza is "the embodied 'I.'"[17] Nyamza, like Loots and Pather's Siwela Sonka, is committed to community educational work through dance. She has been project coordinator for the University of Stellenbosch's Project Move 1524, which uses dance movement therapy to educate community members about HIV/AIDS, domestic violence, and drug abuse. She believes passionately in empowering youth through dance training, from teaching ballet in Mamelodi to doing volunteer work at Thembalethu Day School for the Disabled.

Nyamza's own mother was raped and killed, a horrifyingly scarring experience for the daughter who began to use her autobiographical material as she developed her own strong, unique signature style. "After my mother died" remarks Nyamza, "I could feel her in my dreams telling me to use my dance to tell real stories. I also later came out of the closet and I started experiencing discrimination in society and that's when I thought, 'You know, I'm an artist so let me be the voice that addresses all these issues.'" In an interview, Nyamza remarked that she had "forced" herself "to live the model life women are expected to have, that of getting married and having a child. But I realized I was not myself . . . I came out as a lesbian and left my husband for a woman . . . Since then I blossomed into the artist I have always wanted to be."[18]

Nyamza's work is overtly political, taking inspiration from her own body to explore social and gender issues facing black women, their traditional roles as wives and mothers—often forced upon them (as was true for Nyamza)—unseen and unrecognized domestic labor, and other forms of commodification of female bodies. Nyamza remarks that she "loves her art" and that "this powerful tool speaks to all without a word."[19]

Since 2006, Nyamza's choreography in *Hatch*, *Hatched: The Meal*, and *Kutheni* has drawn on autobiographical material. All these works have been featured at Johannesburg's Dance Umbrella. *Hatched: The Meal*, like *Hatch*, effectively challenged the norms of ballet. Nyamza has performed *Hatch* (choreographed in 2008), which deals with domestic violence, at schools around Durban and Cape Town as well as in the Netherlands, where she took it to shelters for abused women.

Nyamza describes *Hatch*, which she began in 2007 and later morphed into *Hatched*, as a way of connecting to her mother who suffered a brutal rape and was then murdered. In *Hatched*, Nyamza herself is a mother who performs at times with her son, Amkele. *Hatched* was also part of the UK's Dance Umbrella in 2011. Nyamza writes in her Artist Statement that "This movement piece seeks to convey deeply personal and challenging issues of culture, tradition and a woman's evolving sexuality within the customary rites and rituals of marriage, until she realizes her true identity."[20] *Hatched* opens with a body backing onto the audience with a bare back, wearing a long skirt with clothes pins, and a tin bucket filled with clothes on a bald head. Then the body rises up onto pointe shoes previously hidden, moving across the stage with hips wiggling. *Hatched* "tells the story of a woman faced with a life of dualism: she is a South African performing in the UK, but also a dancer who is a mother."[21] Domestic chores appear to consume her time: scrubbing the floor, arranging the clothes. Her son performs with her. Initially, he is covered "by a giant red cloth, as if still enclosed within the safety of her womb. He barely notices her. But, as she potters about, her movement is peppered with moments of miniaturized ballet, performed with frantic, joyful release. Nyamza is battling with her new identity as a mother, while still clinging on to her life as a performer."[22] The work uses movement and music from Western and African cultures.

Nyamza's site-specific work entitled *Kutheni* (meaning "why" in isiZulu), which is set in a parking lot, is a tribute to HIV and lesbian activist Sizakele Magasa, age thirty-four, and her partner Salome Masasa, age twenty-three, of Meadowlands, who were both murdered in Soweto on July 7, 2007. Nyamza's Artist Statement on her website remarks, "I read their stories and other stories were coming up about lesbians who were killed, so that inspired me. I needed to talk about that in my work. I was scared to talk about that in my work."[23] Sichel traces the genealogy of *Kutheni*:

This work was performed first as a duet in the backyard of a Gugulethu shebeen in 2009, then moved up to Johannesburg to Dance Umbrella. The performance started in The Wits Theatre foyer where the two performers (professional Jazzart dancers Refilor Magoje and Phindile Khula) were holding hands and kissing, moving into the theatre with the audience. On stage, they jived to Mbaqanga music, Ladysmith Black Mombazo's *Amazing Grace* and included other facets of South African cultural history. Protest placards were suspended over the stage.[24]

After the performance in Johannesburg, Sichel recounts that the "next morning art and real life met on the pavement outside the High Court" to protest the postponement (twenty-three times) of the trial of eight men who had allegedly raped a pregnant woman, Buyisiwe, in Tembisa in October 2005. Protestors banged against the closed high court doors; they handed out flyers titled "Justice for Buyisiwe—Raped Again by the Justice System!" and sang protest songs.

Marginalization and Violence against
LGBTQ Communities: I Stand Corrected (2012)

One of Nyamza's most hard-hitting choreographies, entitled *I Stand Corrected*, created collaboratively with UK-based, British-born Nigerian-Dutch artist Mojisola Adebayo, represents issues of homophobia and rape, based on the murder of two lesbians. Below, I discuss this work which challenges the horrific concept of "corrective rape," used to justify violence against lesbians. In 2012, funded by the British Council, Nyamza and collaborator Adebayo created a stunning work, *I Stand Corrected*, which Nyamza describes as "dark, strange, witty and absurd" (*Real Magazine*, 2009). In it, Nyamza is killed for being a lesbian, and is coming back to "correct herself."[25] In her essay "Legacies of Violence," Sichel observes that "*I Stand Corrected* weaves a theatrical spell through a fractured, dramatic narrative which succinctly choreographs an epitaph for ordinary people textured with love, pain, loss, brutality and dignity,"[26] and continues:

> A passionate artistic response to an epidemic of hate rape and murder in South Africa . . . *I Stand Corrected* is a landmark dance theatre work which marries the skills, experience, sensitivity, sensuality and artistry of two African artists— a theatre director, actor and playwright and an uncompromising dancer and choreographer. The final message is love is stronger than death.[27]

Sichel describes "corrective rape" as "rape and often gang rape to turn a lesbian into a woman."[28] Nyamza dances with a metal trash bin in which the bodies of the two lesbians were stuffed. She puts her head all the way into the bin as if to discover what could have led to such brutality. Sichel records that this work was staged at the Oval House in London in 2013 and was nominated for several Offies (Off West End) awards.

Yutian Wong's expression "performative autoethnography" is useful in analyzing *I Stand Corrected* and in thinking through the multiple uses of "representation" and "performance."[29] Wong builds on Dorinne Kondo's argument in her book *About Face* that performance should hold a "status as ethnographic practice, and in which ethnographies through performance conventionally defined and through performative writing strategies, *can count as theory and as political*."[30]

Despite the Standard Bank Award in 2011 exposing her to a larger audience in South Africa, Nyamza has yet to perform in some of South Africa's big theatres. She says that it worries her that the only way black artists can secure a spot in national theatres is by collaborating with international artists. Recently, though, her dream came through when she was invited to perform her piece *I Stand Corrected* at the Soweto Theatre. She says the experience was like coming back home after being away for a long time: "I believe the township is where real art comes from. Even though I still haven't performed on some stages, I have performed in Soweto and because of that I'm the proudest artist ever."[31]

A Bold Critique of Religious and Patriarchal Domination: De-Apart-Hate (2016)

Nyamza's brave and hard-hitting choreography in *De-Apart-Hate* resolutely takes on religious platitudes and traditional practices imposed on women, which result in physical and mental violence. This extraordinary work premiered at the Cape Town Fringe Festival in 2016 before it was presented at other venues in South Africa. I saw it at JOMBA! in 2017.[32] The performance begins before we see Nyamza. Church hymns in Xhosa and English are distributed to the audience and they are encouraged to sing. As Nyamza enters the stage, urging the audience to raise their voices in prayer, she is a spectacle to behold, dressed in a long, tight-fitting black and grey dress of stretchy fabric that reaches a few inches above her ankles. It has a large white collar (commonly worn by women who attend church; Nyamza removes it in certain scenes) and a white trim of around ten inches on the dress's bottom. She dances onto the stage wearing white/silvery gold high-heeled shoes and keeps them on throughout the work when she dances, moves, crawls on all fours, and enacts other challenging movements. With her is a male dancer, Mihlali Gwatyu, dressed in a black suit with a white shirt, who later plays a preacher. In his review of the piece, David Fick comments that the two performers, "through the use of dance, movement, stillness, spoken language, allusion, symbolism, sound and silence, build an intensely emotional experience."[33]

The single prop on stage is a bench on the far right-hand side, painted in the colors of the post-apartheid "rainbow nation," but also recalling the "iconic apartheid bench" that clearly demarcated whose body (white or non-white) could sit on it.[34] The bench is also colored in the gay flag colors of red, blue, yellow, and orange (excluding white and black). Spectators soon realize that this is an unsteady bench with see-saw-like movements—as Nyamza and Gwatyu sit on it, they embody who is up and who is down. Another purpose this wobbly surface serves is to represent the very passage of time—from apartheid to post-apartheid, which involved a long struggle and a waiting of many years to achieve democracy. The waiting is recreated in the theatre via an extended silence of nearly two minutes. I recall the audience being spellbound, then getting fidgety as it waited for something to happen. Such lengthy time lapses in performance, when purposeful, as in *De-Apart-Hate*, demonstrate Nyamza's mature artistry. The potent gap of time, with its silence, in between the action begun on the bench resonates with the political uncertainty in 2016 and continuing into 2017, when calls for the South African president to step down—"Zuma must fall"—along with calls that "fees must fall," "Rhodes must fall," were heard in the activist movements at several South African universities. Zuma did step down in February 2018, but only under the threat of impeachment.

Suddenly, the two bodies on the bench change places, then they repeat the motion; they get up and sit down in quick succession as if in church; they get up and turn around and sit down, as the bench gets shakier and more unsteady, "gradually dismantling into the absurdity of it all."[35] As Nicola van Stratten writes, "The bench is not the only aspect of this performance that is dismantled. Through the piece, the performers create a rhythm that builds, crescendos and collapses. This happens repeatedly in different and surprising ways."[36] A fascinating comment by David Fick sheds light on another purpose served by the bench, namely, that it seems to move autonomously, increasingly unbalanced, but in fact it is "a construct. Like apartheid. Like the rainbow nation. Like colonialism. Like reconciliation."[37] De-Apart-Hate's political weight is conveyed with so much artistry that one might miss the serious critiques of unreliable preachers, politicians, and laws that do not protect the vulnerable, such as gays and lesbians. The work conveys the dangers of abiding by any ideology, political or religious, that can manipulate. Fick takes his commentary about the bench as "a construct" further by arguing that "when we try to dismantle a construct, it may transform; when the bench is separated from its hinge, it becomes variously a barrier, a crutch, a trap, maybe even a grave."[38]

Among several challenging moves, Nyamza at one point is on all fours as Gwatyu climbs on her back, stands, and begins shouting the bible verse Ephesians 5.6. He takes on the persona of an evangelical preacher, repeating his words vehemently as if to make a point but "in the repetition" his words "begin to lose all meaning . . . hollowed out, emptied as the scripture itself warms."[39] Van Stratten quotes the words from Ephesians 5:6 that say as much: "Let no one deceive you with empty words, for because of such things God's wrath comes on those who are disobedient."[40] Nyamza responds like a congregant, compliantly providing "Amens" and "Hallelujias," until the pace builds to such an extent that the "bench" provided by Nyamza's back collapses and the preacher is thrown off.

As Nyamza's very body participates in the religious dogmas that she critiques, her work takes on "tradition," exerted oppressively on women, who are regarded as its "guardians." Indeed, cultural anthropologists such as George Marcus and James Clifford contend in Writing Culture: The Poetics and Politics of Ethnography that cultural traditions are slippery, porous, and not fixed as hegemonic patriarchies like to assert.[41] Rather, their instability and the fact that the "practices are themselves in motion" are highlighted by Homi Bhabha's concept of the in-between, and Arjun Appadurai's notion of "scapes," which is developed by dance scholars to include "bodyscapes."[42] Nyamza puts her body on the line in De-Apart-Hate as she undertakes incredible labor such as physically lifting the wooden bench vertically and placing it like a coffin over the preacher lying on the floor.

Symbolically, Nyamza is rejecting institutional platitudes repeated ad nausea to keep the congregation "contented" with their lives—lives which are dire for the majority of black South Africans, with over 27 percent unemployment, substandard housing in the townships, and other social inequities. As she creates the coffin on stage, she turns to face the audience and makes fierce eye contact. Then she lifts her tight-fitting dress, opens her legs, and sits on the upside-down bench with the preacher in the "coffin." In one riveting move, when all eyes are on her center stage, she touches her crotch, revealing a Bible that has been there all along. It is incredible that she managed to move so freely with it held between her thighs. She opens her stocking-covered legs wide in a grand plié in second position, with her feet in shiny silvery-gold shoes. She calmly and courageously opens the Bible at her crotch. As she challenges the audience with her strong stare, she sticks out her tongue to its full length, takes her time to then lick her fingers, and turns the page, intoning "It never ends" as she recites significant dates, such as 1872 (when the Cape of Good Hope was accorded "Responsible government" diminishing British power; white settlement began around 1652). The pace quickens as she begins to repeat Leviticus 18.22: "Do not have sexual relations with a man as one does with a woman; that is detestable."[43]

Next, in this continuing in-your-face segment, she pulls her dress down and keeps the Bible between her thighs, as "something to be lived with and endured."[44] Now that the audience knows that the Bible is held inside by Nyamza (something they did not know until the book was shown), it evokes a penis thrusting itself into the woman's body as she shakes her hips as if having sex, then drops the book as if indicating that the man is done while the woman's face shows continuing passion. Nyamza's stunning commentary via movement and the use of the Bible as a prop is both audacious and subtle, inspiring the audience to question religious and sexual oppression, especially for women. In a classic repetition of "Amen," Nyamza tellingly intones, "Ah, men."

Doubtless, Nyamza's *De-Apart-Hate* includes multiple meanings interwoven among the symbols, images, and narrative. For Fick, himself a queer theatremaker:

> Nyamza offers some ideas . . . about what we can do with the things to which we cling, that we keep clenched in the most vulnerable and intimate parts of ourselves . . . It meant everything to me as a queer person who was taken in by a society that works very hard to pretend that a queer voice has the same value as a straight voice, and who consequently has to learn to speak all over again. I think DE-APART-HATE will mean a lot to everyone who is trying to engage with what is going on in our country at the moment. Because the mystery of what will rise once what must fall has fallen, what lies beyond decolonisation is what is at the heart of this piece, and Nyamza's recognition of that makes her a visionary.[45]

Ultimately, *De-Apart-Hate* is about a search for personal freedom, especially for a black, gay woman who seeks liberation from the dominance of patriarchy, religious dogma, and political platitudes. As noted in *Afrovibes*, Nyamza "explores the limits of dance, performance and provocation."[46] In her conceptual choreography, she boldly crosses the disciplinary boundaries of movement, dramatic dialogue, and the use of props; she also transcends gender delineations of her own traditional Xhosa, patriarchal culture via her chosen lesbian identity and ethic. Nyamza's interculturalism breathes through all her work as showcased in her dancing ballet with South African dance rhythms, and interculturalism is also in evidence in Nyamza's black body as it is showcased on European stages.

DADA MASILO

> I don't want to be [just] a body in space. I want to open up conversations about issues like homophobia and domestic violence, because those are the realities at home.[47]

Dada Masilo, like Nyamza, trained in ballet and contemporary dance, as well as traditional South African dance, and choreographs in the interstices of these styles, at times creating an eclectic fusion of classical and contemporary Western and African dance. Born in 1985 in Soweto, a township on the outskirts of Johannesburg, when apartheid was still in force, she was nine years old at independence in 1994; hence, she grew up in a relatively "free" atmosphere. Masilo danced with her neighborhood children, and when they were offered formal ballet and contemporary dance training, she notes, "I was bitten by the bug right away. I fought very hard to be able to dance; my family did not like it one bit. They wanted me to be a lawyer or accountant, something stable."[48] Masilo studied at the Braamfontein National School for the Arts, where Suzette le Seuer, Director of the Dance Factory School, saw her and invited her to train professionally. Seuer has since then been Masilo's mentor. Today, Masilo is artist-in-residence at the Dance Factory School.

In 2008, at age twenty-three, Masilo won the prestigious Standard Bank Young Artist Award. To date, she has created ten original works, including her own versions of ballet classics—*Romeo and Juliet* (2008), *Carmen* (2009), and *Swan Lake* (2010). She has performed internationally in France, Germany, and the US, among other locations.

Masilo was drawn to the classics because she liked the stories and the characters. She is renowned for deploying her ballet training to deconstruct classics and exemplify the crossing of cultures—namely, ballet as a symbol of the white bastion of culture, especially in South Africa during apartheid, now used to challenge white ownership of this art form. Masilo has masterfully and radically re-envisioned classics such as *Swan Lake* as a hybrid of arabesques executed with bare feet and free flowing traditional African hip movements. "My approach," remarks Masilo, "is to show that contemporary African dance and ballet can co-exist. It is about finding an innovative way of fusing the two. I believe that we can collapse the barriers between them."[49] Masilo is startlingly adept at interrupting the beauty and flow of the ballet body, as in her performance of *Swan Lake* presented at the Lyon Biennale in 2012 and in Canada (Ottawa and Montreal) in 2016. Visually, the audience admires an impeccable ballerina who startles with her signature blending of this European form with traditional South African dance in her original choreography in which her hip bounces up and down, as does her tutu. At other moments, Masilo interrupts perfect pirouettes with sudden, grounded African dance stamps. The black female body with prominent hips also makes a statement against the compulsory thin white female body as the ideal for ballerinas.

Masilo's *Swan Lake* quite distinctly takes on significant sociopolitical and cultural issues, especially those oppressing women in South African society even during the post-apartheid era. Her intention in rechoreographing the classics is hardly to recreate stories of women needing to be rescued by men, but rather to evoke strong contemporary women who face domestic violence and sexual discrimination. Masilo stirs controversy since she makes audiences uncomfortable with interpretations that turn gender and racial stereotypes on their heads. In "Dada Masilo: South African Dancer who Breaks the Rules," Robyn Cumow remarks, "Think 'Swan Lake' with strong homosexual overtones and a tutu-wearing man playing one of the female leads, or 'Romeo and Juliet' with a multi-racial Capulet family. Re-envision a more erotic 'Carmen' in Masilo's attacking style of dancing."[50] Masilo's unique approach to choreography includes overtly sexual movements, particularly showcasing homosexual relationships. In her rechoreography of *Swan Lake*, "the male dancers joined the women in wearing tutus and Odile, one of the female leads, was played by Boysie Dikobe, a male friend of Masilo's in real life."[51] Cumow quotes a reviewer who described Masilo's *Swan Lake* as "agonizingly beautiful . . . an African homophobe's worst nightmare and a dance lover's delight."[52]

Masilo uses a combination of Tchaikovsky's original score and music by American composer Steve Reich and Estonian composer Arvo Part. She plays with the classical tradition by dancing barefoot herself along with her dancers and, in gender-bending representations, having bare-chested males wear tutus. The original love story is transformed by the theme of homophobia and social discrimination against AIDS. These serious realities along with social prejudice persist in South Africa despite the fact that it is the only African nation in which LGBTQ communities are accepted as equal with other sexualities. Masilo's *Swan Lake* has been well received in South Africa at the National Arts Festival in Grahamstown, in France at the 2012 Biennale de Danse de Lyon and Paris, and in London at Sadler's Wells, among various performances.

Masilo has been described as "shocking and captivating at the same time" by Diana Vernon of *Culture Trip* in her article "Dada Masilo, South Africa's Star Choreographer."[53] Like Nyamza, Masilo defies social codes, gender inequality, and Western notions of beauty. In terms of her dance form, she creates choreography that pushes the boundaries of classical ballet.

Her *Giselle* is reimagined in a South African context, remarks Masilo in an interview with Zama Luthuli in Grahamstown that she wanted to make this work to be "edgy" and relevant in South Africa and get away from the "prettiness of ballet."[54] *Giselle* bears her signature style of moving between barefoot balletic and African movements, portraying a strong female who, when she is betrayed by her lover, seeks revenge. Her dancers, in bright-red long tutus, confront the lover and kill him. Masilo's face is deeply expressive of passion, something she "enjoyed performing," as she notes in the interview. In recreating *Giselle*, Masilo wanted "to push her story-telling," adding that "the *Giselle* I made fits very well into what is happening around the world. I never really go into the political root when I am making a work, but themes of revenge and not forgiving are all around the world." Luthuli notes that Masilo's *Giselle* is "not only a retelling of a classical ballet but a re-imagining of ballet itself."[55]

Giselle received high praise from *New York Times* reviewer Gia Kourlas in "A Reimagined 'Giselle,' With South African Roots." In the original story, when Giselle loses her mind her tidy hair is let loose and "frames her face like a sticky, sweaty halo. She unravels—physically, emotionally, mentally—and eventually collapses and dies."[56] Masilo is "boldly and magnificently bald" and she comments that she "wanted to go deeper than 'messy hair' and 'create Wilis that are really vicious.'"[57] The Wilis are "a spooky sisterhood" who exact revenge/ death from the men who have betrayed them. Kourlas remarked that "Ms. Masilo's *Giselle* is a feminist." In this production, although the original score by Adolphe Adam "is referred to, the score is a contemporary one by the South African composer Philip Miller."[58]

Another adaptation of a classic by Masilo was *The Bitter End of Rosemary*, based on Ophelia in *Hamlet*, which was performed at the 2012 Infecting the City Public Arts Festival in Cape Town and curated by Jay Pather. Masilo also choreographed *Death and the Maidens*, set to Schubert's music for the same Public Arts Festival.

Masilo's unique collaboration with internationally acclaimed South African artist William Kentridge, best known for his charcoal drawings, prints, and animated films, demonstrates her creative acumen and openness in extending her form. As Gia Kourlas noted in her *New York Times* article, Kentridge "was immediately intrigued by the eroticism and unconventionality of Ms. Masilo's work, and its blend of dance styles. There are a lot of very good dancers and choreographers in South Africa but to have someone who is engaged with tradition, who is playing against expectations, and has the openness to allow all things to come into the dance was something I was in sympathy with."[59]

Masilo dances to Kentridge's multimedia artistry which includes adventurous portrayals in his drawings onstage and a cacophony of sounds made by unique instruments, intermingled with text by Shakespeare, with a further layer added via the live bodies of dancers, singers, and, at times, puppets. Such a collage of materials mixed with music and dancers was showcased at Johannesburg's Market Theatre in a two-week festival of his work entitled *Refuse the Hour*. Masilo dances in *Refuse the Hour*, which has been described as

> a chamber opera . . . [which] recounts a tale that begins with the myth of Perseus and ends with Einstein's visionary findings. Speaking backwards and forwards in the midst of a Dadaistic landscape, surrounded by spinning dancers, megaphoned singers, live musicians and projected animation, Kentridge himself is the narrator, delving into the nature of time as he delivers a fragmented lecture about procrastination, myth, entropy, empire and black holes. With choreography by South African dancer and choreographer Dada Masilo, video design by Catherine Meyburgh, and dramaturgy by science historian and physicist Peter Galison, *Refuse the Hour* takes us on an elliptical journey to the outer edges of science, theater and art that is both playful and profound . . . [Masilo's] movement is stunning, her performance quality is electric.[60]

Masilo, in her early thirties, is at the height of her career in her reinventions of ballet classics. Interestingly, she comments that after having done "flamenco, Zulu dance, West African dance," she is "now learning the dance of my own Tswana culture. It is very delicate and intricate, with a lot of complicated rhythms and footwork with rattles."[61] Pausing, she added, "I'm thinking, 'Giselle.' "[62]

Both Nyamza and Masilo have pushed interculturalism in new directions with their innovative, hybrid choreography, working with movement styles and musical traditions that challenge sociocultural discrimination against women and LGBTQ communities. These artist-activists deploy their art to create unusual layerings of African and Western dance styles. Their signature dance styles which take on social ills provide models of synergistic and socially relevant creative work for audiences within South Africa and beyond.

NOTES

1. I was an audience member viewing *De-Apart-Hate* in Durban, South Africa, at the Elizabeth Sneddon Theatre in September 2017 at the JOMBA! Contemporary Dance Experience Festival.

2. The term "new interculturalism" entered the scholarly arena in 2002 with Una Chaudhuri, who identified a need to refine the use of the word "interculturalism" that was challenged increasingly by scholars such as Joanne Tompkins, Rustom Bharucha, and Johannes Birringer. Ric Knowles further theorized "new interculturalism" in his path-breaking book, *Theatre & Interculturalism* (2010). Since then, the term has been used by scholars in theatre and dance including in Royona Mitra's *Akram Khan: Dancing New Interculturalism* (2015) and Charlotte McIvor's *Migration and Performance in Contemporary Ireland: Toward a New Interculturalism* (2016). My work is inspired by noteworthy dance studies scholars who include interculturalism in their analyses of different cultural forms of dance within the US and from across the world. These include Marta Savigliano, *Tango and the Political Economy of Passion* (1996); Ann Cooper Albright, *Choreographing Difference: The Body and Identity in Contemporary Dance* (1997), and co-editor of *Moving History/Dancing Cultures* (2001); Melissa Blanco Borelli, *She is Cuba: The Genealogy of the Mulata Body* (2015); Ramsay Burt, *The Male Dancer* (1995, revised 2007); Pallabi Chakravorty (ed.), *Dance Matters: Performing India* (2010); Urmimala Sarkar Munsi (ed.), *Dance Transcending Borders* (2008); Janet O'Shea, *At Home in the World: Bharatanatyam on the Global Stage* (2007); Alexander Carter and Janet O'Shea (eds.), *The Routledge Dance Studies Reader*, 2nd edn. (2008, 2010); Susan Leigh Foster, *Worlding Dance* (2009); Anthea Kraut, *Choreographing Copyright: Race, Gender and Intellectual Property Rights in American Dance* (2015); Yatin Lin, *Choreographing a Flexible Taiwan: Cloud Gate Dance Theatre and Taiwan's Changing Identity, 1973–2003* (2004); Yutian Wong, *Choreographing Asian America* (2010); Ananya Chatterjea, *Butting Out: Reading Resistive Choreographies Through Works by Jawole Willa Jo Zollar and Chandralekha* (2004); Carolyn Merritt, *Tango Nuevo* (2012); Peter Manuel (ed.), *Creolizing Contradance in the Caribbean* (2009); Stephanie Burridge and Fred Frumberg (eds.), *Beyond the Apsara: Celebrating Dance in Cambodia* (2010); Jennifer Fisher and Anthony Shay (eds.), *When Men Dance: Choreographing Masculinities Across Borders* (2009); Hari Krishnan, *Celluloid Classics: Early Tamil Cinema and the Making of Modern Bharatanatyam* (forthcoming, Wesleyan University Press), and co-editor of *Dance and the Early South Indian Cinema* (forthcoming, Oxford University Press); and SanSan Kwan, *Kinesthetic City: Dance and Movement in Chinese Urban Space* (2013).

3. Royona Mitra, *Akram Khan: Dancing New Interculturalism* (Basingstoke, UK: Palgrave Macmillan, 2015), 15.

4. Mitra, *Akram Khan*, xiv.

5. Rustom Bharucha, *Theatre and the World: Performance and the Politics of Culture* (London: Routledge, 1993).

6. Daphne P. Lei, "Interruption, Intervention, Interculturalism: Robert Wilson's HIT Productions in Taiwan," *Theatre Journal* 63, no. 4 (2011): 571–86.

7. Lei, "Interruption, Intervention, Interculturalism," 571.

8. Susan Leigh Foster, "Worlding Dance—An Introduction," in Susan Leigh Foster (ed.), *Worlding Dance* (Basingstoke, UK: Palgrave Macmillan, 2009), 7.

9. Ric Knowles, *Theatre & Interculturalism* (Basingstoke, UK: Palgrave Macmillan, 2009).

10. Knowles, *Theatre & Interculturalism*, 4.

11. Kgomotso Moncho-Maripane, "Mamela Nyamza's Alchemy of Anger into Grace at National Arts Festival," *Business Day*, June 11, 2018, https://www.businesslive.co.za/bd/life/arts-and-entertainment/2018-06-11-mamela-nyamzas-alchemy-of-anger-into-grace-at-national-arts-festival/.

12. Moncho-Maripane, "Mamela Nyamza's Alchemy of Anger into Grace."

13. The Soweto Uprising in 1976 at the height of apartheid was a political rally led by students inspired by Steve Biko's Black Consciousness Movement. This was only one of several anti-apartheid struggles by the majority black population of South Africa. The year 1976 features in Nyamza's choreography *19 Born 76 Rebels*, which I saw as an outdoors performance in Grahamstown, South Africa, at the National Arts Festival in 2015.

14. Mamela Nyamza, "Interview," *Real Magazine* (2009).

15. Levern Botha, "A Critical Appraisal of Mamela Nyamza's *Kutheni* That Aims to Identify and Investigate Emerging Features Unique to her Choreographic Style," research essay of B.Mus. (Hons.) Choreography, University of Cape Town School of Dance, 2009, 10.

16. Adrienne Sichel, "Legacies of Violence/Art Resolution: Mamela Nyamza and Fellow Trailblazers," unpublished essay, presented at the Open Participate Enrich Negotiate (O.P.E.N) conference in Singapore, June 27, 2014. I am grateful to Sichel for providing a copy of this essay.

17. Lliane Loots, "TRANSMISSIONS: A South African Choreographer Uses Language to Reflect on the Gendered 'Embodiment' of Writing with and on the Body," *Southern African Linguistics and Applied Language Studies* 24, no. 4 (2009): 453.

18. Nyamza, "Interview."

19. Brand South Africa, "Mamela Nyamza: The Body as Instrument," May 4, 2011, http://www.southafrica.info/about/arts/mamela-nyamza.htm#.VEG5KeeXszV.

20. A clip of *Hatched* is available online: https://www.youtube.com/watch?v=Nid-0fN9PAA.

21. Lucy Jarvis, "Hatched," MamelaNyamza.com, http://mamelanyamza.com/creations/hatched.html.

22. Jarvis, "Hatched."

23. "Kutheni," MamelaNyamza.com, http://mamelanyamza.com/creations/kutheni.html.

24. Sichel, "Legacies of Violence."

25. See clip on this site: https://www.youtube.com/watch?v=DWpcpCym-RY.

26. Sichel, "Legacies of Violence."

27. Sichel, "Legacies of Violence."

28. Sichel, "Legacies of Violence."

29. Yutian Wong, *Choreographing Asian America* (Middletown, CT: Wesleyan University Press, 2010), 5.

30. Dorinne Kondo, *About Face: Performing Race in Fashion and Theater* (New York: Routledge, 1997), 20, emphasis added.

31. Brand South Africa, "Mamela Nyamza."

32. See clips at these links: https://www.youtube.com/watch?v=U10UUYZ8XyQ; https://www.facebook.com/afrovibes/videos/10154803607185703/.

33. David Fick, "BWW Review: Mamela Nyamza's DE-APART-HATE is First Rate Dance Theatre from a Visionary Artist," *Broadway World*, October 8, 2016, https://www.broadwayworld.com/south-africa/article/BWW-Review-Mamela-Nyamzas-DE-APART-HATE-is-First-Rate-Dance-Theatre-from-a-Visionary-Artist-20161008.

34. Nicola van Stratten, "Mamela Nyamza: De-Apart-Hate," January 12, 2017, https://peoplearedancing.wordpress.com/2017/01/12/de-apart-hate-mamela-nyamza/.

35. Van Stratten, "Mamela Nyamza: De-Apart-Hate."

36. Van Stratten, "Mamela Nyamza: De-Apart-Hate."

37. Fick, "BWW Review."

38. Fick, "BWW Review."

39. Van Stratten, "Mamela Nyamza: De-Apart-Hate."

40. Van Stratten, "Mamela Nyamza: De-Apart-Hate."

41. See George Marcus and James Clifford (eds.), *Writing Culture: The Poetics and Politics of Ethnography*, 2nd edn. (Berkeley: University of California Press, 2010).

42. Foster, "Worlding Dance," 7–8.

43. I rely on van Stratten's quotation of Levictus 18.22.

44. Fick, "BWW Review."

45. Fick, "BWW Review."

46. https://de-de.facebook.com/afrovibes/videos/trailer-de-apart-hate/10154803607185703/

47. Roslyn Sulcas, "Dada Masilo Turns Tchaikovsky on His Head in 'Swan Lake,'" *New York Times*, February 1, 2016.

48. Diana Vernon, "Dada Masilo, South Africa's Star Choreographer," *Culture Trip*, June 20, 2016, https://theculturetrip.com/africa/south-africa/articles/dada-masilo-south-africas-star-choreographer/.

49. Vernon, "Dada Masilo."

50. Robyn Curnow, "Dada Masilo: South African Dancer who Breaks the Rules," *CNN*, November 2, 2010, https://web.archive.org/web/20120528213747/http://articles.cnn.com/2010-11-02/world/south.africa.dada.masilo_1_ballet-moves-classical-ballet-international-dance-world?_s=PM%3AWORLD.

51. Curnow, "Dada Masilo."

52. Curnow, "Dada Masilo."

53. Vernon, "Dada Masilo."

54. "Dada Masilo's Giselle," YouTube video, published by CueTube1, July 3, 2017, https://www.youtube.com/watch?v=BeNGUq_i9eo.

55. "Dada Masilo's Giselle."

56. Gia Kourlas, "A Reimagined 'Giselle,' With South African Roots," *New York Times*, April 4, 2018, https://www.nytimes.com/2018/04/04/arts/review-dada-masilo-giselle-joyce-theater.html.

57. Kourlas, "A Reimagined 'Giselle.'"

58. Kourlas, "A Reimagined 'Giselle.'"

59. Kourlas, "A Reimagined 'Giselle.'"

60. Jessica Emmanuel, "Dada Masilo in William Kentridge's Refuse the Hour," Mothership LA, November 7, 2017, https://mothershipla.org/2017/11/07/dada-masilo-in-william-kentridges-refuse-the-hour/.

61. Vernon, "Dada Masilo."

62. Vernon, "Dada Masilo."

CHAPTER ELEVEN

The "Dis-/De-" in the Hyphen: The Matrix and Dynamics of Displacement in Intercultural Performance

MIN TIAN

In an attempt to displace the dominant theoretical perspectives of intercultural theatre and performance developed in the twentieth century, the new century saw the emplacement of some "new" theoretical perspectives. These perspectives prescribe in different formulations a seemingly universal/utopian/egalitarian vision that seeks to overcome and transcend the complexities and contradictions of the predominantly Occidental-centered globalization of theatre and performance driven by an inevitable displacement of the differences and identities of culturally and aesthetically specific traditions worldwide.

A decade earlier, I presented my critique of the theories and practices of twentieth-century intercultural theatre.[1] I believe that the core of my critique still applies to these new variants of the twentieth-first century. This chapter offers a critical examination of these perspectives and proposes a different, historically grounded perspective. An attempt to reassert the historical differences and identities of different theatrical cultures and traditions, it maintains that intercultural performance is a socio-politically, culturally and aesthetically centered process of inter-displacement and re-placement of historically, culturally, and aesthetically conditioned and differentiated theatrical forces, cultures, and traditions.

THE HYBRIDIZATION OF INTERCULTURAL PERFORMANCE

In recent decades, hybridization has been one of the most prominent postmodern and postcolonial positions on intercultural theatre and performance. Naturally, one of the most profound influences on the hybridizing position has been Homi K. Bhabha's notion of cultural hybridity. As such, the hybridizing position shares the inherent contradictions of Bhabha's theory, as exemplified by Jacqueline Lo and Helen Gilbert's model of intercultural theatre and Erika Fischer-Lichte's idea of "interweaving performance cultures." On the one hand, Bhabha argues that it is in the "inter"—"the inbetween space" or the "Third Space"[2]—or "in the emergence of the interstices—the overlap and displacement of domains of difference"—that the difference, value, and meaning of culture are articulated and negotiated.[3] On the other hand, Bhabha sees in the same "liminal" space "the possibility of a cultural hybridity that entertains difference without an assumed or imposed hierarchy."[4] Thus, Bhabha still clings to a utopian vision of cultural exchange, which transcends the displacement of domains of difference and which fails to account for the inevitable assumption or imposition of hierarchy and the ultimate recentering of the self in "the inbetween space." Although Bhabha asserts the emphasis of "Hybrid hyphenations" on "the incommensurable elements" as "the basis of cultural identifications," his notion of cultural hybridity essentializes "the performative nature" of differential cultural identities and turns the process of "the regulation and negotiation" of those in-between or third spaces into a performative autonomy that is cut off from their origins and histories.[5] As Bhabha's "interstitial future" is essentially an abstract and ahistorical utopian space whose emergence "in between the claims of the past and the needs of the present"[6] is not defined in a concrete historically conditioned and socio-politically structured relation to the past and the present, it in effect deprives cultural differences and identities of their origins, traditions, and histories. Thus, in spite of its self-conscious attempt to underscore its differentiatedness, postcolonial cultural hybridity is haunted by the postmodern abhorrence of originality, historicity, and authenticity that define and distinguish the identities of different cultures and thereby the differentiatedness of cultural hybridity. For me, the difference that emerges from the in-between space is the result of the differentiated self's displacement of the pre-existing difference of the Other and of its self-centered re-placement in relation to the Other. Thereby the structure of the differentiated hybridity remains hierarchical as its differentiation is ultimately conditioned by the self's past and present.

Integral to his theory of hybridity is Bhabha's notion of cultural translation. According to Bhabha, his theory of culture is close to a theory of language, and cultural translation, like linguistic translation, is "a process of alienation and of secondariness *in relation to itself*."[7] Here Bhabha's seemingly anti-essentialist argument performs an ahistorical essentialization of hybridity or otherness, making it internal and essential to a culture's self-translation and constitution, a process of self-alienation, cut off from its own histories and from its translational relations to other cultures. For Bhabha, "the importance of hybridity is not to be able to trace two original moments from which the third emerges"; hybridity is rather the "third space" that "enables other positions to emerge" and that "displaces the histories that constitute it, and sets up new structures of authority, new political initiatives."[8] For me, however, this third space is the result of the displacement by the first space (the self) of the second (the Other) space or the result of an inter-displacement of the first and the second space. Such an act or process of inter-displacement, at once productive and destructive, is not a self-enclosed and traceless play of performativity but is ultimately conditioned by the histories of the first and the second space. Consequently, the "new" structure of the third space as a re-placement of the histories it displaces is inevitably recentered in its (op)positional relation to the other spaces.

Jacqueline Lo and Helen Gilbert have reminded us that "It is vital that intercultural theatre's potential to cross cultures is not co-opted and neutralized by the 'weaker' forms of postmodernism, which tend to result in an abstract, depoliticized, and ahistorical notion of 'difference,' or, in effect, a masked 'indifference.' "[9] In this respect, however, it is ironical for Lo and Gilbert to subscribe, conclusively, to Bhabha's notion of postcolonial hybridity as "a workable model for an ethics as well as an aesthetics of cross-cultural engagement."[10]

According to Lo and Gilbert, their two-way flow model "not only foregrounds the dialogic nature of intercultural exchange but also takes into account the possibility of power disparity in the partnership."[11] It rests on "a notion of differentiated hybridity"[12] and is designed to outline "some of the ways in which the mise-en-scène can be politicized and the notion of cultural hegemony relativized."[13] It is necessary to note that such an attempt to relativize (Western) cultural hegemony was also underlined in Patrice Pavis's "hourglass" model.[14] However, in such an intercultural transfer, as a result of a series of displacements by the target culture of the source culture, the emplacement of the target culture is not relativized but recentered in relation to the source culture. For instance, in Eugenio Barba's Eurasian or intercultural *mise en scène* on *Faust* presented to and experienced by a Western audience, Pavis observes that "there is always a double displacement of the Japanese or Indian source cultures" and that "the codes of oriental theatre are both as foreign and as displaced *in our* [Western] *direction.*"[15]

As a theoretical displacement of Pavis's model, Lo and Gilbert's hybridity model seeks "to adapt what is essentially an appropriative/assimilationist model into a more collaborative/negotiated one."[16] In my view, however, given the socio-political and cultural-economic conditions, artistic creation in intercultural performance is fundamentally a process of translation, appropriation, and assimilation, in which collaboration/negotiation is necessary not for the construct of an equalized playing field but insofar as it is instrumental in the ultimate accomplishment of such a creative/destructive process. Furthermore, such an (one-way or two-way) intercultural process is not truly "dialogic" in nature as envisioned by Mikhail Bakhtin[17] or Bhabha in their performative imagination of a utopia of heteroglossia or hybridity, but is inevitably a centered and hierarchical inter-displacement of both the source culture and the target culture. In Barba's work as seen through Pavis's model, there is at once a displacement of the Japanese or Indian culture (the source culture) and a displacement of Christopher Marlowe's and Goethe's *Faust* (the target culture). In Lo and Gilbert's model, this process is exactly driven by the same inter-displacement by the target culture of the two source cultures (A and B) that are consequently subject to a series of displacements. In this process, positioned or emplaced in either source culture A or B in its inter(re)action with/against other cultures, the target culture becomes the center of the process and thus dictates its hierarchical structure, which is ultimately conditioned by the historical (the past and the present) emplacement of the target culture. Thus, looked at through either Pavis's model or Lo and Gilbert's model, this process of inter-displacement, ultimately, does not decenter or relativize the central position of the target culture but recenters it in its re-placement in relation to other cultures.

Most recently, Bhabha invokes Goethe's concept of "world literature" in his further argument—in agreement, at least perceived by Fischer-Lichte as such, with the latter's concept of "interweaving performance cultures"—for a hybrid cultural space and hybridized intercultural translation and exchange.[18] Bhabha's translational use of Goethe—or what I call his hybridizing interiorization of Goethe's Eurocentric idea of world literature—is, again, ahistorical as it focuses on the translational intercultural exchange as a contingent and performative processual moment of cultural performance, (violently) cutting it off from the origins, histories, and traditions of the translated and exchanged cultures. Bhabha's performative imagination of a utopia of hybridity fails to expose but conceals the inherent hegemonic nature of such a translational relation between different cultures. I would argue that the practice of such an intercultural hybridization necessitates an intercultural translation and transposition—an inter-displacement that is inherently hierarchical in its structure, at least in the sense that it is necessary for an artist to assert his/her creative hegemony, and that is at once constructive/productive and deconstructive/destructive.

WHAT IS NOT "NEW" IN THE "NEW INTERCULTURALISMS"?

After a survey of different theories of intercultural performance, Ric Knowles proposes the use of the term "new interculturalism," calling for a reconstruction of Western hegemonic intercultural performance, not from the perspectives of the dominant Western and colonizing cultures but from those of the historically colonized, marginalized, and diasporic cultures. In Knowles's imagination, the "new interculturalism" involves "collaborations and solidarities across real and respected material differences within local, urban, national, and global intercultural performance ecologies"; these performance ecologies function as "heterotopias"—not "merely as sites of semiotic intersection, or as postmodern collages" but as "political sites for the constitution of new, hybrid, and diasporic identities in space."[19] Similarly, Charlotte McIvor posits her idea of "a new interculturalism" in her study of migration and performance in contemporary Ireland.[20] Primarily an ethnographic and socio-cultural-political study of "Irish social interculturalism" as embodied in the Irish community art and performance projects, McIvor's work examines "a range of minority-ethnic subjects in Ireland"[21] and underlines Irish social interculturalism as minority-ethnic "community praxis"[22] as opposed to the Occidental-centered practice of globalized/globalizing interculturalism.

In my view, like Rustom Bharucha's counter-globalist and counter-neocolonialist "intracultural" position,[23] invoked both by Knowles[24] and by McIvor,[25] the socio-political stance of this diasporic-centered or minority-ethnic-centered "new interculturalism" represents an inverse of the logic of the Western hegemonic interculturalism. However, as long as it is hybrid, in between, or hyphenated with "inter," "trans," or "hetero" in the ecological environment of globalization, such "new" interculturalism cannot escape the hauntings of the "old" interculturalism as its performance ecologies remain fundamentally conditioned by the same underlying mechanism of intercultural displacement. Indeed, such mechanism inheres in and undergirds Knowles's "new interculturalism" defined by what he calls "strategic reappropriation"[26] and "diasporic transnationalism and transindigeneity."[27] Likewise, it underlies the two Irish intercultural performances of John Synge's *Playboy of the Western World*, rigorously examined by McIvor from the perspective of the Irish new interculturalism.[28] While the Sinicization of the Irish classic represents, in its treatment of Synge's play as material, an inverse of the Eurocentric approach of twentieth-century Western intercultural theatre, the "new" African-Irish "synergy"[29] representation of Irish social interculturalism entails the same mechanism of displacement and inter-displacement.

In her study of the Bangladeshi-British dancer Akram Khan, Royona Mitra uses the term "new interculturalism" to describe Khan's dance performances. According to Mitra, Khan's "new interculturalism" is characterized by his "syncretic aesthetic" that "translocates" South Asian dramaturgical principles of *abhinaya* and *rasa* "onto" his contemporary dance vocabularies[30] and is driven by his "transposition" of such principles "onto" the landscape of contemporary dance.[31] Mitra repeatedly emphasizes Khan's decontextualizing and "deconstructive" transpositional use of the dramaturgical principles or coded language of *abhinaya* and *rasa* as "a vital mechanism" in the generation of his own aesthetic of "new interculturalism" that "simultaneously rewrites both Western and South Asian dramaturgies."[32] For me, however, as Khan's "multistitial" "embodiment" (the "new" in his "new interculturalism") is "fundamentally intercultural,"[33] it cannot escape the logic of the "inter" and it is still driven by the underlying mechanism of intercultural displacement. Khan's dance is not an organic fusion but a "confusion"[34] of *kathak* and contemporary dance as a result of their inter-displacement. Mitra speaks, albeit affirmatively, of the clash of "the rigid stylisation of *kathak*" with "the improvisatory nature of Western contemporary idioms"[35] and of "the deconstructionist possibilities inherent in the condition of [Khan's] confusion."[36]

Mitra views Khan's "new interculturalism," or rather Khan's practice as seen through the lens of her theory of "new interculturalism," as generative and productive. What is missing, however, is an account of the inevitable destructive effect of Khan's deconstructive "confusion" approach to *kathak* on the viewer's understanding of this particular dance form and the aesthetic of South Asian theatre as a whole. Mitra contends that Khan's "innovative experimentations with *abhinaya* and his intercultural channelling of *rasa*" serve as "important reminders" that "the *Natyashastra* is by no means a static and permanent dictate, but one that needs constant reconsideration in light of our current social milieu, in its call to create art that mirrors and comments upon today's society."[37] Such being the case, how is Khan's "new interculturalism" truly *different* and *new* in contrast to Peter Brook's "old" interculturalism, if we accept as valid Rustom Bharucha's argument against Brook's hegemonic appropriation of Indian classical traditions, which for me evokes Bertolt Brecht's secularizing and sacrilegious approach to classics, European or Asian?

THE IDEA OF "INTERWEAVING PERFORMANCE CULTURES"

In her critique of the concept of "intercultural theatre" or "intercultural performance," Erika Fischer-Lichte debunks some of the main assumptions underlying this predominantly Occidental concept that privileges the centered placement of the dramatic text, or rather a Western dramatic text, in terms of the ownership, universality, and authority of the text.[38] Against the assumptions, Fischer-Lichte proposes the replacement of the concept with what she calls "interweaving performance cultures" (IPC)—a translation of the German phrase, *Verflechtungen von Theaterkulturen.*" This metaphoric concept treats different performance cultures as "diverse strands and threads" to be interwoven into "a piece of cloth" in such a way that these components are no longer "recognizable individually" and that each strand cannot be traced back to its "origin."[39] At the same time, it defines the act of interweaving as a process that "does not necessarily result in the production of a whole," thus underlining "culture's inherent processual nature with its continuous production of new differences" that "are not understood as opposites but seen within an 'as well as' logic, that is, the logic of interconnectedness."[40] Furthermore, Fischer-Lichte emphasizes "the *utopian dimension*" at the very core of her new concept, celebrating the moving within and between cultures as "a state of in-betweenness."[41] Thus, for her, processes of IPC generate "a new kind of transformative aesthetics" that defines "forms of utopian and transformative experiences" ignored by theoretical approaches of postcolonial theory as well as intercultural performance.[42]

In his "anti-utopian realist registers," Rustom Bharucha has questioned the materiality of IPC's metaphoric thinking, exposing its limits in its account of the material and sociopolitical dynamics of the complex act of "interweaving."[43] I wish to argue that the material and practical interweaving of different cultural threads displaces those cultural threads out of their pre-existing fabrics (contexts) and re-places them in the recentered and hierarchical structure of the in-between space in which differences that define and differentiate the identities of those cultural threads are inter-displaced and homogenized in the processual generation of "new differences." Moreover, the idea of IPC is not only immaterial but is largely divorced from the reality of the historical and contemporary practice of intercultural theatre, which was conditioned by the matrix and dynamics of displacement of culturally and aesthetically differentiated theatrical forces. It is ironic for Fischer-Lichte to refer to Brecht's treatment of the texts as material in support of her repudiation of the Occidental text-centric assumptions that she thinks underlie the outdated concept of intercultural theatre. Brecht's practice of refunctioning the texts as material in disregard of their historical and cultural authorships and particularities effaced the differences and identities of the texts and was fundamentally hegemonic as it served his overriding ideological as well as aesthetic interests.[44]

Fischer-Lichte has acknowledged "the homogenization of discourse" in the studies of "interweaving performance cultures," as researchers are working with a terminology and with concepts originating in Western theory largely written at Western academic institutions.[45] Bharucha finds "at once sad and oppressive" the continuing dominance of the existing "imperialism" and Eurocentrism in theatre and performance studies—the Euro-American theoretical paradigms—in the discourses of the "intercultural" and "interweaving," where "'the non-West' continues to provide the material, and 'the West' continues to frame this material within theories that assume a universal legitimacy."[46]

According to Bharucha, in her conceptualization of "the transformative power of performance" as "a new aesthetics,"[47] Fischer-Lichte essentially reads "today's performativity" within "a very rich spectrum of European philosophical ideas" and is "still working very much *within* the complexities" of what she embodies in her own tradition.[48] Indeed, Fischer-Lichte's idea of IPC as a "new" transformative aesthetic is firmly rooted in European, particularly German, aesthetic and cultural—not just linguistic and conceptual—traditions. It does not transcend European traditions and remains Eurocentric, as historical and contemporary practices of intercultural theatre and performance—Western and non-Western—are (dis/re-) placed and approached from IPC's predominantly European perspective.

A conceptual displacement from the text-centric concept of Western intercultural theatre and from her previous notion of "interweaving cultures in performance,"[49] Fischer-Lichte's definition of IPC clearly indicates that IPC deals with the interweaving of performance ideas, forms, styles, genres, techniques, and devices, decidedly divesting the process of interweaving of its cultural, political, ideological, and social significance. I want to emphasize that IPC is essentially "intercultural" (even in the narrow sense of performance cultures) and that performance ideas, forms, styles, genres, techniques, or devices cannot be cut off from their original cultural contexts without deforming, de-authenticating, and ultimately effacing the differences that differentiate and define their identities. Regardless of its conceptual displacement, the process of IPC in its "in-between" space reaffirms the self's dominance in its emplacement of its own identity by displacing other performance cultures out of their original historical and cultural contexts, effacing their differences and identities.

Daphne P. Lei has succinctly termed the Western dominant form of intercultural theatre as "Hegemonic Intercultural Theatre" (HIT). She believes that in today's globalized world such a Western-dominated form of HIT can be neutralized with the active participation of the East as "an equal partner" in the creation of intercultural theatre.[50] Granted that possibility, it is my belief that, not being "Oriental" or self-Orientalized but being truly "Asian," an Asiacentric or Asianizing approach leads inevitably to an Asian HIT form. In his critique of Ong Keng Sen's "New Asian" intercultural project, *Desdemona*, an adaptation of *Othello*, Bharucha argues that "Asiacentricity" is "the other side of the same coin as Eurocentricity."[51] Here Bharucha refers to the misappropriation of South Asian cultural (and performance) traditions in Ong's work. For me, more importantly, it is Ong's directorial appropriation (inter-displacement) of Shakespeare's text as well as various Asian performance traditions and his hegemonic (new) Asiacentric production of Shakespeare's text in such displaced Asian forms that constitute an inversion of the hierarchical binary—the text-centric West versus the performance-centric East. An Asiacentric (performance-centric) deconstructive appropriation of Shakespeare (or any other Western text) such as Ong's *Desdemona* and *Lear* remains "intercultural," hierarchical, and hegemonic. Carol Fisher Sorgenfrei's historical and context-specific study brings to light Itō Michio's "Japancentrism" in his "interweaving" dance performance that Sorgenfrei argues demonstrates "the triumph of strategic unweaving that strips the Japanese body of imported Otherness, denying the in-betweenness that Fischer-Lichte maintains is inherent in interweaving."[52] I want to add that, inversely, Sorgenfrei's argument is also true with respect to an alternative reading, or "a gross misunderstanding,"[53] of Itō's performance as an embodiment of "Orientalism" (a form of Western HIT). Thus, both the Western HIT and an Asian HIT underline the ultimate unreality and impossibility of a utopian aesthetic of interweaving and the reality and inevitability of unweaving in the practice of interweaving conditioned and driven by the matrix and dynamics of displacement.

THE NETWORKING OF INTERCULTURAL PERFORMANCE

Globalization, with the rise of the network society, has a profound impact on the theorization of intercultural performance in the twentieth-first century. According to Brian Singleton, with globalized networked communication that transcends local and national boundaries, cultural communication is no longer concerned with origins and meanings per se but with the process and structure of meaning.[54] Relating this phenomenon to intercultural performance and bringing into contrast the projects of those old-fashioned Western orientalists and interculturalists, Singleton considers Fischer-Lichte's IPC a new paradigm that enables a potential liberation of intercultural performance and scholarship from the trap of the Anglo-Saxon (or European/Western-centered) discourse of the postcolonial and a focus on the transformative power of performance between cultures.[55]

Singleton's point of view was also championed by Leo Cabranes-Grant, who, a few years earlier, had put forth his main idea on the networking of intercultural performance.[56] According to Cabranes-Grant, his "main purpose is to explore the possibility of finding an analytical language that honors, as effectively as possible, the *becoming* of performance itself"—the performative process and the relational structure of intercultural performance scenarios.[57] In his view, the existing critical models of intercultural theatre "posited hybridity as an *effect* of intercultural encounters, never as its source; as a result, they repressed the heterogeneous history of those same cultures, enforcing a strategic essentialization of them."[58] Cultures are "moving targets," he argues, and the prefix "inter" in "intercultural" should emphasize "their becoming, not their decidability,"[59] while "all renditions of intercultural performativity need to be conceptualized as narratives of coeval, and frequently evanescent, networks."[60]

Cabranes-Grant's idea is heavily indebted to the French sociologist Bruno Latour's social constructivist theory, Actor-Network Theory (ANT),[61] and it shares the latter's inherent contradictions. Like ANT, in its attempt to avoid the essentialist and determinist traps, Cabranes-Grant's idea ignores outside, pre-existing structures and discourses of performance cultures and traditions without which the end of the processing or becoming cannot ultimately be determined. The assumed equality of elements in this "network" is a theoretical construct; it is coeval only in the sense that the elements coexist but not in the sense that they coexist as equals; it is always self-centered and hegemonic in its becoming of itself and in its structuring displacement and re-placement of cultural and performance sources. Hybridity is at once a source of the becoming of performance within the network and an effect of intercultural encounters (displacement and re-placement) of the sources pre-existing outside the network of intercultural performance. Moreover, the process of "becoming" (and, I want to add and underline, the un-becoming) in the network is not autonomous, as it is driven by the dynamics of displacement and is ultimately conditioned by the elements' cultural positions or placements outside the network.

The performative turn of IPC or of the intercultural network turns its postmodern aversion to essentialism, historicism, and determinism into a passion for structural or processual essentialism and determinism. In its conscious attempt to avoid the pitfalls of essentialism, historicism, and determinism, it falls into the blind loop of structural or processual essentialism and determinism. IPC or the intercultural network essentializes the creative (or productive) process of intercultural performance as something in itself, something becoming of itself, something perpetually generating by itself, without origin and history (social, cultural, as well as artistic), something phenomenologically performative, empty of essence and devoid of originality, authenticity, and historicity. The "in-between" or the "liminal space" in IPC and in the intercultural network is an aesthetic and performative closure—self-contained, self-referencing, and self-generating—or what Fischer-Lichte calls an "autopoietic feedback loop,"[62] which draws on the originally biological concept of "autopoiesis," as opposed to approaching art as a social and cultural system. Fischer-Lichte places her emphasis on the "autopoietic feedback loop" on the interaction and movement (the movement in the in-between space) between the actor and the audience. For me, however, this in-between space is not sealed off from the outside space, and the bodies and their embodiments in the in-between space are pre-enculturated and their interaction and movement cannot be immune from, but is conditioned by, the pre-enculturation of the actor and the audience. In agreement with Latour that "performance is not something that reflects or illustrates a social network: performance *is* the armature of the network itself,"[63] Cabranes-Grant intends to reassert the ontological being of the "in-itself" of the "in-betweens" in intercultural performance.[64] The purchase IPC or the intercultural network offers on intercultural performance remains theoretical and academic and its teleology of a progressive, productive, and transformative aesthetic remains imaginative and performative.

THE "DIS-/DE-" IN THE HYPHEN OR
THE ACT OF "MURDER"

The idea of displacement has often been associated with postmodern and postcolonial theories, especially Jacques Derrida's theory of deconstruction. Derrida's idea of displacement can be traced back to Sigmund Freud's theory of psychoanalysis. In Freud's theory, displacement and condensation are the two operations of distortion or refraction by the dream-thoughts represented in the dream-work. "In its implications," Freud states, "the distortion of a text resembles a murder: the difficulty is not in perpetrating the deed, but in getting rid of its traces."[65] Thus, according to

Freud, the word "*Entstellung*" (distortion) should be lent "the double meaning" of deformation/disfiguration and displacement/de-positioning:

> It should mean not only "to change the appearance of something" but also "to put something in another place, to displace." Accordingly, in many instances of textual distortion, we may nevertheless count upon finding what has been suppressed and disavowed hidden away somewhere else, though changed and torn from its context.[66]

Drawing on Jacques Lacan, Gayatri Chakravorty Spivak notes that "condensation" and "displacement" may be "rhetorically translated as metaphor and metonymy."[67] Spivak speaks of "Derrida's often implicit Freudianism" that surfaces in his use of metaphor and metonymy: "Metaphor and metonymy are rhetorical translations of 'condensation' and 'displacement,' two major techniques, as Freud pointed out, of dream-distortion."[68] Derrida once acknowledged that he used the word "deconstruction" with the sense that he "was translating and deforming a word of Freud's and a word of Heidegger's."[69] Indeed, Derrida maintains that metaphor is "the *analogical* displacement of Being"[70] and that "[t]he history of metaphysics, like the history of the West, is the history of these metaphors and metonymies."[71] Thus, for Derrida, universal history is a history of metaphorical displacement of Being. In Emmanuel Levinas's critique of Edmund Husserl's phenomenology, Derrida finds "a displacement of concepts"—a displacement of "the concept of history."[72] In Levinas's critique of G. W. F. Hegel's phenomenology, Derrida observes "the displacement of the concept of historicity," which constitutes "the necessary condition" for the fulfilment of Levinas's "anti-Hegelianism."[73] Likewise, in Georges Bataille's reinterpretation of Hegel's own interpretation, Derrida discerns "a barely perceptible displacement" that "disjoints all the articulations and penetrates all the points welded together" by the Hegelian discourse.[74] When Derrida speaks of the generation of "the ghostly" in the movement of European history ("*Kant qui genuit Hegel qui genuit Marx*"),[75] he underlines, in effect, the movement of its very *déplacement*, a movement I describe in the direction of *Marx qui déplaça Hegel qui déplaça Kant*. In general, Derrida observes "a metaphorical displacement" in "the history of the concept of structure" that is as old as Western science and Western philosophy.[76]

Now as part of the history of Western thought, Derrida's deconstructive approach was driven by a discursive displacement of Western metaphysics. Drawing a distinction between "dissemination, seminal *différance*" and "polysemia," Derrida opposes displacement to dialectics. For him, "a teleological and totalizing dialectics" that must permit "the reassemblage of the totality of a text into the truth of its meaning" annuls "the open and productive displacement of the textual chain" that forbids "an exhaustive and closed formalization of it."[77] Derrida's observation applies equally to intercultural performance. The open and at once productive and destructive displacement of a performance text makes impossible the dialectical reassemblage of the totality of it into "an exhaustive and closed formalization" of it in any particular saturating theory or model.

Ethnology, which has a particular relevance to the theory and practice of intercultural performance, is one of the human sciences that Derrida thinks occupies a privileged place in the history of Western thought. Derrida argues that "the critique of ethnocentrism—the very condition of ethnology—should be systematically and historically contemporaneous with the destruction of the history of metaphysics."[78] Without such a decentering displacement and destruction and as long as ethnology as a scientific discourse "borrows from a heritage the resources necessary for the deconstruction of that heritage itself," there is no escaping ethnocentrism (Eurocentrism as ethnology is "primarily a European science") and thereby the necessity that "the ethnologist accepts into his discourse the premises of ethnocentrism at the very moment when he denounces them."[79] For Derrida, "this necessity is irreducible; it is not a historical contingency."[80] For me, however, "irreducible" as it is, it is at once discursive/metaphoric and historical in the sense that it is historically conditioned.

Like Derrida's deconstructive approach, Michel Foucault's ahistorical and counter-humanist approach to the history of Western thought was underpinned and driven by a mechanism of discursive displacement underlying the historical movement of Western thought. In his investigation of the Western order of things, Foucault discovers an epistemological break or discontinuity in the history of Western thought between the eighteenth and the nineteenth century, "a minuscule but absolutely essential displacement, which toppled the whole of Western thought" in terms of the relation of representation to being.[81] In his view, the "Kantian critique" or "Kantian doctrine" that marks the threshold of Western modernity is "the first philosophical statement" of "this displacement of being in relation to representation."[82] With what he calls "this displacement of the question of transcendence," Foucault subsequently performs "a fourfold displacement in relation to the Kantian position."[83] In fact, as Foucault later acknowledged, in his "historical" and "philosophical" investigation into the "histories" of Western thought from the archaeology of knowledge to the history of sexuality, "a theoretical displacement" was necessary for him to analyze and problematize what he calls "the games of truth" played out in the domains of knowledge, power, and subjection.[84]

In the domain of the theatre, the Foucauldian order of things represents a displacement of the Western classical idea of the theatre as mimesis and representation. For Foucault, in the theatre there is no representation, only what he calls "liberated simulacrum."[85] The Foucauldian theatre is a theatre of heterotopia. It is a theatre of difference that stages, without the past and the future, "the present as the recurrence of difference, as repetition giving voice to difference," affirming "at once the totality of chance."[86] It is a theatre of displacement that "brings onto the rectangle of the stage, one after the other, a whole series of places that are foreign to one another."[87] Foucault's spatialized view of history and society is in accord with his idea of the theatre.[88] For Foucault, like the theatre, the space in which we live "is also, in itself, a heterogeneous space ... a set [ensemble] of relations that delineates sites [defines emplacements] which are irreducible to one another and absolutely not superimposable on one another."[89] In Foucault's spatialized—not temporalized/ historicized—imagination, this "ensemble of relations" is not historically conditioned and defined; it is purely spatial and non-hierarchical. The Foucauldian theatrical take on the order of things has an uncanny affinity with our postmodern (Foucauldian) turn to the performativity (fictionality) of representation in the theatre. For me, however, displacement is not only spatial in that it takes place in an open (not self-enclosed and autonomous) network ("ensemble of relations") that is at once heterogeneous and hierarchical, but also temporal in that it takes place in a historical context. This is especially true with the in-between space of hybridity and heterogeneity of intercultural theatre and performance. Thus, the postmodern notion of displacement that denies a dialectical sublation or a syncretic universalism that transcends the performance of difference must be historicized: cultural differences, displacements, and emplacements are historically grounded and their theorization must be historically contextualized in the rootedness as well as the alterity and hybridity of cultures.

As in the histories of Western thought, the dynamics of displacement underlay the historical movement of Western theatre. Before the turn of the twentieth century when intercultural theatre began to take shape, it was constituted by an internal displacement and emplacement of historically different theatrical forces and trends in theory and practice. Around 1930, writing of "[t]he way to a great contemporary theatre," Bertolt Brecht, whose Marxist idea of history was drastically at odds with Foucault's, provided a Foucauldian reading of the history of European bourgeois theatre, which was marked by a movement of reactional displacements:

> In the sphere of variants, there is no tradition; there are only action and reaction, that is, there are only reactions. The pendulum swings back and forth. What appears to lead is the opposition, and it owes its existence to oversaturation [Übersättigung]. Classicism and Romanticism, Impressionism and Expressionism are reactions.[90]

In Brecht's view, these "reactions" or trends were merely "variants" intrinsic to the system of European bourgeois theatre, to be consumed by "this oversaturated and appetiteless body," the bourgeois superstructure based on its "economic system of variants," as the bourgeoisie "no longer have the possibility to design entirely new basic plans or to discuss them."[91] Thus, for Brecht, these "variants" were not truly revolutionary or consequential.

In contrast, Brecht argued, "tradition is necessary" for his idea of the epic theatre as it was concerned with "true, revolutionary continuation."[92] "If we extract the epic style of representation among the many trends out of the dramatic literature of the last hundred years (1830–1930)," Brecht maintained, "we do so in search of a tradition."[93] Thus, for instance, by bringing the great bourgeois (French and Russian) novels to the stage, "naturalism transported some epic elements into the drama," albeit "very much against its will."[94] In spite of his attempts to find the tradition of the epic style of representation in European literature, including naturalistic novels and dramas, Brecht was keenly aware of the need to find, as far as form was concerned, models, not merely to extract and transport (displace) some epic elements, for his revolutionary theatre. Realizing that such models certainly cannot be found "in our spatial or temporal surroundings," Brecht turned to Asia and felt the need to prove that he had "the 'Asiatic' model."[95]

In fact, at the turn of the twentieth century, European avant-garde theatre, or what Jerzy Grotowski and Eugenio Barba call "the Great Reform"[96] of the theatre in Europe, turned to the East in its reactional movement against the dominant trends of naturalism and commercialism. As early as 1916, W. B. Yeats spoke of "the circle" many European arts ran through and thereby of the pressing need for the Europeans "to copy the East."[97] This movement, or rather displacement, continued decades into the twentieth century. During the last three decades of the century, intercultural theatre as part of this movement reached a historical crescendo. As a reaction to the practices and theories of the late twentieth century, new theories were put forward in the new century. Notwithstanding their different spatial and temporal detours, these theories, as I have demonstrated previously, present, ultimately, a predominantly Occidental approach to the condition of the Occidental-centered globalization of theatre and performance that is driven by an inevitable displacement of the differences and identities of culturally and aesthetically differentiated theatrical traditions.

Ultimately, to use Freud's psychoanalytical analogy, the distortion (in any form) of a text (dramatic, performance, as well as cultural) in intercultural performance resembles a "murder": the difficulty lies not in perpetrating the sacrilegious and violent act of deforming/disfiguring a text, but in displacing it out of its context, disintegrating it as a whole, effacing its difference and identity, and integrating or interweaving it, tracelessly, in the in-between text. The in-between text cannot escape the haunting of the ghostly afterlife of the "murdered" text, whose uneffaceable traces lead inevitably to the deconstruction of the act or process of hybridizing or interweaving and to the unweaving of the fabric(ation) of the in-between text that is supposedly traceless and teleologically productive, capable of creating "new" places or identities. The intercultural act or process of hyphenating a text necessitates displacement; the matrix and dynamics of displacement render impossible any syncretic, sublational, transformational, or transcendental approach to such acts or processes. This is exactly the underlying condition for the twentieth- and twentieth-first-century Western (or non-Western)-dominated intercultural theatre and the twenty-first-century emplacements of the "new" aesthetics of intercultural performance and of the variants of "new" interculturalisms in the theatre.

NOTES

1. Min Tian, *The Poetics of Difference and Displacement: Twentieth-Century Chinese-Western Intercultural Theatre* (Hong Kong: Hong Kong University Press, 2008).

2. Homi K. Bhabha, *The Location of Culture* (London: Routledge, 2004), 56.

3. Bhabha, *The Location of Culture*, 2.

4. Bhabha, *The Location of Culture*, 5.

5. Bhabha, *The Location of Culture*, 313.

6. Bhabha, *The Location of Culture*, 313.

7. Homi K. Bhabha, "The Third Space: Interview with Homi Bhabha," in Jonathan Rutherford (ed.), *Identity: Community, Culture, Difference* (London: Lawrence & Wishart, 1990), 210–11 (emphases in original).

8. Bhabha, "The Third Space," 211.

9. Jacqueline Lo and Helen Gilbert, "Toward a Topography of Cross-Cultural Theatre Praxis," *Drama Review* 46, no. 3 (2002): 49.

10. Lo and Gilbert, "Toward a Topography of Cross-Cultural Theatre Praxis," 49.

11. Lo and Gilbert, "Toward a Topography of Cross-Cultural Theatre Praxis," 44.

12. Lo and Gilbert, "Toward a Topography of Cross-Cultural Theatre Praxis," 45.

13. Lo and Gilbert, "Toward a Topography of Cross-Cultural Theatre Praxis," 48–9.

14. Patrice Pavis, *Theatre at the Crossroads of Culture*, trans. Loren Kruger (London: Routledge, 1992), 5.

15. Pavis, *Theatre at the Crossroads of Culture*, 172 (emphases added).

16. Lo and Gilbert, "Toward a Topography of Cross-Cultural Theatre Praxis," 44.

17. M. M. Bakhtin, *Speech Genres and Other Late Essays*, trans. Vern W. McGee (Austin: University of Texas Press, 1987), 1–7.

18. Homi K. Bhabha, "Global Pathways," in Erika Fischer-Lichte, Torsten Jost, and Saskya Iris Jain (eds.), *The Politics of Interweaving Performance Cultures: Beyond Postcolonialism* (London: Routledge, 2014), 259–75.

19. Ric Knowles, *Theatre & Interculturalism* (Basingstoke, UK: Palgrave Macmillan, 2010), 59.

20. Charlotte McIvor, *Migration and Performance in Contemporary Ireland: Towards a New Interculturalism* (London: Palgrave Macmillan, 2016), 4–20.

21. McIvor, *Migration and Performance in Contemporary Ireland*, 2.

22. McIvor, *Migration and Performance in Contemporary Ireland*, 15.

23. Rustom Bharucha, *The Politics of Cultural Practice: Thinking Through Theatre in an Age of Globalization* (Hanover, NH: Wesleyan University Press, 2000), 6. For my brief critique of the "intracultural," see Tian, *The Poetics of Difference and Displacement*, 5.

24. Knowles, *Theatre & Interculturalism*, 32–3.

25. McIvor, *Migration and Performance in Contemporary Ireland*, 6.

26. Knowles, *Theatre & Interculturalism*, 63.

27. Knowles, *Theatre & Interculturalism*, 68.

28. Knowles, *Theatre & Interculturalism*, 55–73.

29. McIvor, *Migration and Performance in Contemporary Ireland*, 67.

30. Royona Mitra, *Akram Khan: Dancing New Interculturalism* (Basingstoke, UK: Palgrave Macmillan, 2015), xiv.

31. Mitra, *Akram Khan*, 6.

32. Mitra, *Akram Khan*, 37–8, 155, 156, 158.

33. Mitra, *Akram Khan*, 23.

34. Mitra, *Akram Khan*, 9–10.

35. Mitra, *Akram Khan*, 43.

36. Mitra, *Akram Khan*, 73.

37. Mitra, *Akram Khan*, 159.

38. Erika Fischer-Lichte, "Introduction: Interweaving Performance Cultures—Rethinking 'Intercultural Theatre': Toward an Experience and Theory of Performance beyond

Postcolonialism," in Erika Fischer-Lichte, Torsten Jost, and Saskya Iris Jain (eds.), *The Politics of Interweaving Performance Cultures: Beyond Postcolonialism* (London: Routledge, 2014), 7–9.

39. Fischer-Lichte, "Introduction," 11.

40. Fischer-Lichte, "Introduction," 11.

41. Fischer-Lichte, "Introduction," 11–12.

42. Fischer-Lichte, "Introduction," 12.

43. Rustom Bharucha, "Hauntings of the Intercultural: Enigmas and Lessons on the Borders of Failure," in Erika Fischer-Lichte, Torsten Jost, and Saskya Iris Jain (eds.), *The Politics of Interweaving Performance Cultures: Beyond Postcolonialism* (London: Routledge, 2014), 180, 184.

44. For my examination of Brecht's refunctioning of Chinese and Japanese theatre, see Min Tian, *Mei Lanfang and the Twentieth-Century International Stage: Chinese Theatre Placed and Displaced* (New York: Palgrave Macmillan, 2012), 175-213; *The Use of Asian Theatre for Modern Western Theatre: The Displaced Mirror* (Cham, Switzerland: Palgrave Macmillan, 2018), 239-62.

45. Fischer-Lichte, "Introduction," 15.

46. Bharucha, "Hauntings of the Intercultural," 195.

47. Erika Fischer-Lichte, *The Transformative Power of Performance: A New Aesthetics*, trans. Saskya Iris Jain (New York: Routledge, 2008).

48. Erika Fischer-Lichte and Rustom Bharucha, "Dialogue: Erika Fischer-Lichte and Rustom Bharucha," August 6, 2011, http://www.textures-platform.com/?p=1667. (Emphasis in original)

49. Erika Fischer-Lichte, "Interweaving Cultures in Performance: Different States of Being In-Between," *New Theatre Quarterly* 25, no. 4 (2009): 391–401.

50. Daphne P. Lei, "Interruption, Intervention, Interculturalism: Robert Wilson's HIT Productions in Taiwan," *Theatre Journal* 63 (2011): 585.

51. Rustom Bharucha, "Foreign Asia/Foreign Shakespeare: Dissenting Notes on New Asian Interculturality, Postcoloniality and Re-colonization," in Dennis Kennedy and Yong Li Lan (eds.), *Shakespeare in Asia: Contemporary Performance* (Cambridge: Cambridge University Press, 2010), 257.

52. Carol Fisher Sorgenfrei, "Strategic Unweaving: Itō Michio and the Diasporic Dancing Body," in Erika Fischer-Lichte, Torsten Jost, and Saskya Iris Jain (eds.), *The Politics of Interweaving Performance Cultures: Beyond Postcolonialism* (London: Routledge, 2014), 219.

53. Sorgenfrei, "Strategic Unweaving," 210.

54. Brian Singleton, "Performing Orientalist, Intercultural, and Globalized Modernities: The Case of *Les Naufragés du Fol Espoir* by the Théâtre du Solei," in Erika Fischer-Lichte, Torsten Jost, and Saskya Iris Jain (eds.), *The Politics of Interweaving Performance Cultures: Beyond Postcolonialism* (London: Routledge, 2014), 82–4.

55. Singleton, "Performing Orientalist, Intercultural, and Globalized Modernities," 84–6.

56. Leo Cabranes-Grant, "From Scenarios to Networks: Performing the Intercultural in Colonial Mexico," *Theatre Journal* 63, no. 4 (2011): 499–520.

57. Leo Cabranes-Grant, *From Scenarios to Networks: Performing the Intercultural in Colonial Mexico* (Evanston, IL: Northwestern University Press, 2016), 34. (Emphasis in original)

58. Cabranes-Grant, *From Scenarios to Networks*, 9 (emphases in original).

59. Cabranes-Grant, *From Scenarios to Networks*, 34.

60. Cabranes-Grant, *From Scenarios to Networks*, 35.

61. Cabranes-Grant, *From Scenarios to Networks*, 19–25.

62. Fischer-Lichte, *The Transformative Power of Performance*, 50.

63. Cabranes-Grant, *From Scenarios to Networks*, 44 (emphasis in original).

64. Cabranes-Grant, *From Scenarios to Networks*, 34.

65. Sigmund Freud, *The Standard Edition of the Complete Psychological Works of Sigmund Freud*, vol. 23 (1937–9), *Moses and Monotheism: An Outline of Psycho-Analysis and Other Works*, trans. James Strachey et al. (London: Hogarth Press and the Institute of Psycho-Analysis, 1964), 43.

66. Freud, *Moses and Monotheism*, 43.

67. Gayatri Chakravorty Spivak, "Translator's Preface," in Jacques Derrida, *Of Grammatology*, trans. Gayatri Chakravorty Spivak (Baltimore, MD: Johns Hopkins University Press, 2016), lxvi–lxvii.

68. Jacques Derrida, *Of Grammatology*, trans. Gayatri Chakravorty Spivak (Baltimore, MD: Johns Hopkins University Press, 2016), 371, n. 18.

69. Quoted in Herman Rapaport, *Heidegger and Derrida: Reflections on Time and Language* (Lincoln: University of Nebraska Press, 1989), 8.

70. Jacques Derrida, *Writing and Difference*, trans. Alan Bass (Chicago: University of Chicago Press, 1978), 27. (Emphasis in original)

71. Derrida, *Writing and Difference*, 279.

72. Derrida, *Writing and Difference*, 88.

73. Derrida, *Writing and Difference*, 94.

74. Derrida, *Writing and Difference*, 260.

75. Jacques Derrida, *Specters of Marx: The State of the Debt, the Work of Mourning and the New International*, trans. Peggy Kamuf (New York: Routledge, 1994), 3, 9.

76. Derrida, *Writing and Difference*, 278.

77. Jacques Derrida, *Positions*, trans. Alan Bass (Chicago: University of Chicago Press, 1981), 45.

78. Derrida, *Writing and Difference*, 282.

79. Derrida, *Writing and Difference*, 282.

80. Derrida, *Writing and Difference*, 282.

81. Michel Foucault, *The Order of Things: An Archaeology of the Human Sciences* (New York: Pantheon Books, 1970), 238–9.

82. Foucault, *The Order of Things*, 242, 245.

83. Foucault, *The Order of Things*, 323.

84. Michel Foucault, *L'Usage des Plaisirs*, vol. 2 of *Histoire de la Sexualité* (Paris: Gallimard, 1984), 12.

85. Michel Foucault, "Theatrum Philosophicum," in *Language, Counter-Memory, Practice*, ed. Donald F. Bouchard and trans. Donald F. Bouchard and Sherry Simon (Ithaca, NY: Cornell University Press, 1977), 171.

86. Foucault, "Theatrum Philosophicum," 194.

87. Michel Foucault, "Of Other Spaces," trans. Jay Miskowiec, *Diacritics* 16, no. 1 (1986): 25.

88. Thomas R. Flynn, *Sartre, Foucault, and Historical Reason*, vol. 2: *A Poststructuralist Mapping of History* (Chicago: University of Chicago Press, 2005), 125.

89. Foucault, "Of Other Spaces," 23; Michel Foucault, "Des espaces autres," in *Dits et Ecrits 1954–1988*, vol. 4, 1980–1988 (Paris: Gallimard, 1994), 755.

90. Bertolt Brecht, "Der Weg zu grossem zeitgenössischem Theater," in Werner Hecht et al. (eds.), *Werke: Große Kommentierte Berliner und Frankfurter Ausgabe*, vol. 21 (Berlin and Weimar: Aufbau; Frankfurt am Main: Suhrkamp, 1992), 379.

91. Brecht, "Der Weg zu grossem zeitgenössischem Theater," 377–8.

92. Brecht, "Der Weg zu grossem zeitgenössischem Theater," 379.

93. Brecht, "Der Weg zu grossem zeitgenössischem Theater," 379.

94. Brecht, "Der Weg zu grossem zeitgenössischem Theater," 379.

95. Brecht, "Der Weg zu grossem zeitgenössischem Theater," 379–80.

96. Jerzy Grotowski, *Towards a Poor Theatre* (New York: Simon and Schuster, 1968), 24; Eugenio Barba, *The Moon Rises from the Ganges: My Journey through Asian Acting Techniques*, ed. Lluís Masgrau and trans. Judy Barba (Holstebro, Denmark: Icarus Publishing Enterprise, 2015), 38, 173.

97. W. B. Yeats, "Introduction," in *Certain Noble Plays of Japan: From the Manuscripts of Ernest Fenollosa, Chosen and Finished by Ezra Pound, With an Introduction by William Butler Yeats* (Churchtown, Dundrum, Ireland: Cuala Press, 1916), ix. For my examination of Yeats's interest in the Japanese Nō drama, see Min Tian, *The Use of Asian Theatre for Modern Western Theatre: The Displaced Mirror* (Cham, Switzerland: Palgrave Macmillan, 2018), 69–97

CHAPTER TWELVE

Interculturalidad: (How) Can Performance Analysis Decolonize?[1]

LISA JACKSON-SCHEBETTA

In 2007, the Culiacán Botanical Garden, located in the center of the capital city of Sinaloa, Mexico, embarked on a program to expand the garden's collection of plant life. They simultaneously began commissioning and collecting major works from contemporary artists, with the goal that these works, resident within the garden and its spaces, would also be accessible to visitors.

One of the first artworks supported by the garden was Mexican artist Pedro Reyes's *Palas por pistolas* ("Shovels for guns") in 2008. At the time of Reyes's commission, Culiacán had long been a city convulsed with violence, home to the Sinaloa cartel led by "El Chapo" Guzmán, and a key territory in the militarized "War on Drugs," as waged by the cartels and the Mexican and US governments. From 2006 to 2008, Mexico's homicide rate increased by 55.5 percent. From 2006 to 2011, the homicide rate in Mexico grew by over 190 percent, averaging "20,000 people per year, more than 55 people per day, or just over two people every hour."[2] As Heinle et al. point out, "No other country in the Western Hemisphere saw such a large increase either in its homicide rate or in the absolute number of homicides over the last two decades."[3] Culiacán, as a beating heart of the Sinaloa operations, suffered from the increased violence. Despite Mexico's stringent gun laws, many of the homicides in Culiacán could be tracked to firearms, often trafficked into Mexico across the US border.

Reyes, with the support of the Culiacán Botanical Garden, launched a television and radio campaign asking local citizens to surrender their firearms in exchange for electronic and household appliances (microwaves, radios, and the like). As a result, 1,527 firearms were voluntarily surrendered.[4] Reyes melted the 1,527 guns in a foundry and from them created 1,527 shovels. A handful of the shovels permanently reside in the Botanical Garden, arranged in a straight line on an exterior wall, as a permanent installation. But other shovels travel around the world and are used to plant trees. Reyes for years would travel with, or send in advance of his arrival, a shovel to wherever he was doing an exhibit, giving a talk, or creating work in Mexico and beyond: Vancouver, Paris, Houston, London, San Francisco.[5] He requested that he and his hosts use the shovel to plant a tree. The shovels have also been distributed to art institutions and public schools, again with the request that they be used to plant a tree, transforming through use, as Reyes says, "an agent of death" (the gun) into "an agent of life" (the shovel).[6] Each shovel bears a label detailing its origin.

In this chapter, I argue that *Palas por pistolas* imagines—and partially enacts a performance of—*interculturalidad*, and thus also, per the theorization of Catherine Walsh, decolonization.[7] I suggest that the concept/practice (for it is both, resulting in what Walsh deems a "logic," a way of thinking, relating, doing, and behaving) of interculturalidad contributes to Erika Fischer-Lichte's critique of intercultural performance.[8] I additionally articulate the exigencies that interculturalidad brings to scholarship: that we orient our work towards decolonization by contouring our postcolonial discourses with those of modernity/coloniality.[9] Walsh, whose articulation of interculturalidad I rely on here, has long committed herself as a scholar to working with Ecuadorian indigenous movements. Walsh writes:

> Although I work in the university, I seldom identify as an academic. I identify rather as a militant intellectual, an intellectual activist or activist intellectual, and always as a pedagogue. The latter I understand not in the formal educational sense of teacher who transmits or imparts knowledge, but as facilitator; as someone who endeavors to provoke, encourage, construct, generate, and advance with others critical questionings, understandings, knowledges, and actionings; ways of thinking and doing.[10]

In this chapter I ask if there are ways of analyzing performance, as scholars, that also carry out decolonizing labor, minor though it may be.

INTERCULTURALIDAD, MODERNITY/ COLONIALITY, AND DECOLONIZATION

Interculturalidad, writes Walsh, is "more than a simple concept of inter-relation." Interculturalidad "signals and signifies processes of constructing other ways of knowing, of other political practices, of other social power, and of another society; distinct forms of thinking and being, in relation to and in contrast to modernity/ coloniality."[11] There are two key points in this statement that I wish to examine, and then situate in relation to intercultural performance, before I move on to an analysis of *Palas por pistolas*: first, the concept of modernity/coloniality, foundational to Walsh's thinking; and, second, the articulation of interculturalidad as a process, the goal/work of which is not only the imagining but the enacting of worlds other than—yet (and this is key) in relation to—those of the present and past.

Modernity/coloniality posits that modernity and coloniality, as epistemologies and ontologies, are co-constitutive of one another.[12] Modernity/coloniality developed in the fifteenth century (with the Atlantic trades, the ascent of capitalism, the development of the nation state, and imperial projects and desires) but persists to the contemporary moment. That is, modernity cannot be thought, written, or lived on its own, but is always already modernity/coloniality. Coloniality, in turn, is neither solely colonial nor postcolonial.[13] It persists past the postcolonial, precisely because modernity (and its necessary hierarchies of class, race, gender, sexuality, governance, economics, religion, and thought) depends upon it. Broadly, a newly independent geography (or space/time, per Anibal Quijano) may be classified as postcolonial.[14] Though discourses of the postcolonial track and critique legacies of colonialism—including the inequalities of race, class, gender, and language (among other markers) that persist through multiple times—modernity/coloniality offers an additional critical orientation. Modernity/coloniality demands that we repeatedly confront the fact that legacies of colonialism *must* persist in order for modernity to exist, even as modernity attempts to occlude what Walter Mignolo terms its dark side: coloniality.[15] That is, the desires of a newly independent time/space to become a nation state require participation in modernity and its Eurocentric processes of not only government and economics (and modernity/coloniality's critique of Eurocentrism includes Marxist as well as capitalist philosophy, as both are embedded in colonial relations of power), but knowledge production, ways of thinking, and ways of being—which are (and have long been) reliant on the devaluation of the colonized, including indigenous values, governance, and cosmologies. Modernity/coloniality's insistent marking of the devaluation of indigenous worlds enables decolonial thinking: the acknowledgment of the (past, present, and future) viability of those worlds, and, in turn, acceptance that the world we have known since the fifteenth century (that of modernity/coloniality) is but one option among many (including more just) worlds. Decolonization is action taken to enact these *other* options, to change, as Mignolo has written, not only the conversation but its very terms.[16]

Interculturalidad, as a project of the Confederación de Nacionalidades Indígenas de Ecuador (Confederation of Indigenous Nations of Ecuador, or CONAIE), is borne of and with decolonial thought. It also enacts decolonization. CONAIE's interculturalidad, as Walsh documents, is founded in indigenous forms of knowledge production. And yet, the project of interculturalidad, as demonstrated by CONAIE, is not a reverse of power, nor a toppling of the established state of Ecuador in favor of an indigenous state (which would change the conversation but not, necessarily, its terms). Rather, CONAIE's projects imagine, and enact, transformations that take into account, account for, and utilize indigenous and non-indigenous worlds. Walsh explains that "the logic of interculturalidad" is not "isolated" from "dominant paradigms and structures," but, rather, "knows" these structures, cannot but know them, due to the processes of modernity/coloniality.[17] It is through this "knowing" that interculturalidad is able to forge other ways of knowing, being, and thinking.

For example, foundational to the practices and politics of the CONAIE is the concept of the Estado Plurinacional (the Plurinational State),[18] a process of transition as well as an objective, in which the structures and processes of governance, value systems, and decision-making are both shared and transformed. That is, the Estado Plurinacional does not develop through the inclusion of indigenous peoples in established, Western and Northern forms of governance. Gestures of inclusion do not change the structure of the governing institution, nor its value systems, nor do they erase the lived experience of marginalized peoples and cosmologies. But neither does the Estado Plurinacional require the complete rejection of established governance. Rather, in the Estado Plurinacional, indigenous ways of knowing and being recontour practices of governance. The Estado Plurinacional demands multiple actions: the restructuring of education to position indigenous languages on equal curricular ground to Spanish; the restructuring of educational institutions to organize not in departments but in centers of learning, reflective of indigenous ways of structuring time and space; the redistribution of water and land rights; and the reconceptualization of agrarian and mining practices through indigenous technologies.[19] Interculturalidad is directed towards structural and socio-historical transformation. It does not seek incorporation in the state as the state exists, but rather a restructuring of the state in which difference is not "additive" but rather "constitutive."[20]

Interculturalidad is not interculturality, an English term that has, as Robert Aman (working from within the Bolivian context) writes, "come to dominate the debate on cultural diversity" within and between "supranational bodies such as the European Union and the United Nations Educational, Scientific, and Cultural Organization."[21] Aman explains that "UNESCO advocates interculturality as a method of facing the cultural challenges of every multicultural society by uniting around shared values," while the EU has viewed interculturality as a "tool with which member states can promote cultural cohesion."[22] Interculturalidad, in contrast, is not founded on the idea that "all cultures are already . . . mixed with one another; but, rather, in terms of the fact that some cultures are recognized by the state while others are not."[23] Interculturalidad, then, "is intertwined with an act of restorative justice for the way in which, for centuries, the nation-state has turned indigenous populations into its blind spot."[24] It is this restorative justice that fuels the projects of the CONAIE, situating interculturalidad as decolonizing.

Interculturalidad (and its distinction from interculturality) resonates, to an extent, with Erika Fischer-Lichte's suggestion that theatre and performance studies replace "intercultural performance" with "interweaving performance cultures." Fischer-Lichte articulates the ways in which intercultural performance has, by default, neglected its colonialist presumptions centered on the privileging of Western cultural aesthetics and values. Intercultural performance, Fischer-Lichte argues, relies on a "notion of equality that almost always requires the west to be involved," while simultaneously "[implying] a sharp" (and staid) "division between 'our' and the 'other' culture."[25] In contrast, as Fischer-Lichte avers, "interweaving" accounts for the dynamic interaction that can happen between cultures in performance, reacknowledging "performances as sites of in-betweenness," which are able to constitute "fundamentally other, unprecedented realities—realities of the future."[26]

The Estado Plurinacional might be characterized as such an interweaving, but only if explicit objectives of decolonization, restorative justice, and structural transformation are part of the term, a possible shortcoming of the term that Fischer-Lichte acknowledges. Drawing upon Khalid Amine, Fischer-Lichte asks us to "stay vigilant and alert," reminding us to question, for example, how "emancipation from postcolonial cultural codes generate new inequalities."[27] In contrast, interculturalidad, bound with modernity/coloniality, denies the possibility of emancipation from either the colonial or the postcolonial. Interculturalidad does not ask us to consider "new" inequalities, but, rather, to take inequality as certain, and to seek, imagine, and enact transformation. To, in essence, decolonize, with the recognition that decolonization in the American hemispheric context (and translatable to other time/spaces) requires structural change forged through state-devalued indigenous (and, as Walsh notes, African descended) cosmologies.

Interculturalidad, as Aman and Walsh articulate and as I have examined here, is bound to governmental practices, to restorative justice, and to decolonizing the state. Interculturalidad is borne of indigenous movements, influenced by indigenous-African alliances in Latin America, and contoured, in particular, by the unique socio-historical contexts of Andean Latin America. I pause here to voice my trepidation in attempting to move interculturalidad into the academy and into conversation with intercultural performance, to utilize interculturalidad as a method of performance analysis, and to carry out that analysis within (though not, notably, *with*) a time/space (Culiacán, as origin point) distinct from the Ecuadorian, Bolivian, and indigenous contexts. I hope to enact a small decolonization with my work in this chapter: to center and use non-Western theory to examine ostensibly Western (certainly non-indigenous) performance, in order to offer a nuanced analysis of hemispheric injustice and restorative possibility (if not action). I offer this intention not as a justification, but in order to be transparent, to admit my own misgivings, and, in doing so, to invite critique—and other ways of doing.

I turn now to *Palas por pistolas*, which, though a sculptural art project, was conceptualized and created through performance. As the shovels travel, dig, and plant, *Palas por pistolas* remains deeply performatic.[28]

PALAS POR PISTOLAS

In 2015, the Culiacán Botanical Garden was named one of the ten best gardens in North America. It is run by a private non-profit organization, and admission is free.[29] The garden currently hosts over 1,000 plant species and thirty-nine works of art, varying from large-scale, outdoor pieces to smaller, interior works. The botanical goals of the garden focus on valuable ethnobotanical plants indigenous to Mexico and/or reflective of environmental histories of the geography from before contact to the present. The artists hail from around the globe. Culiacán business owner Agustín Coppel, inheritor, with his brothers, of his father's multi-million-dollar department store chains, sponsors the garden's art collections.[30]

In 2007, Coppel supported the work of Mexico City-born Reyes, not only as a commissioner, but as a participant. Reyes was and continues to be an activist-artist. He creates work that is often participatory and with the intention of contributing to the creation of a more just world. Reyes explained his position in an interview in 2015:

> It's suspected that all art has to be open-ended, no? That all art has to ask questions but not answer them. That if you take a position you are considered messianic, patronizing your audience. I think that's a kind of cliché that is preventing a lot of artists from taking a stand. It limits the agency that cultural production has . . . I don't believe all art should serve a purpose. But if you want art to take a stand, there should be that option. If you want to take action, you should be allowed to do so.[31]

Reyes's work has taken on environmental crises, the ravages of capitalism explicitly and implicitly, the fallacies of democratic governance, human rights, and—with *Palas por pistolas,* and, later, *Imagine* and *Disarm*—the disarmament and demilitarization of cities and communities. "I don't want to have an open position about gun control," Reyes insists. "I want to say that people who invest their money in companies that produce weapons should be culturally rejected like those who invest in child pornography."[32]

For his Culiacán project, Reyes needed guns. Because he was not interested in art for art's sake, but, rather, in using art for disarmament, purchasing guns was not an option. Reyes wanted to recirculate guns already in use, effectively stopping usage before transforming usage. He wanted to use guns voluntarily surrendered by citizens of Culiacán. Coppel agreed to provide vouchers to his stores in exchange for the guns. Donators could use the vouchers to purchase household goods. The Culiacán drive, thanks in part to Reyes' design of and participation in telenovela style advertisements on TV and radio, broke records for voluntary firearms donation.[33] Reyes counted 1,527 firearms as his raw material. He then contracted with the military to steamroll the weapons and melt them in a foundry (thus also inculcating the military in disarmament, if only for a moment). Out of the melted metal, Reyes created 1,527 shovels, with the intention that they would be used to plant 1,527 trees. Each shovel, that is, would plant a tree before its display as a piece of Reyes' artwork.

In a city of 675,000 people, 1,527 guns are not that many, and certainly do not constitute large-scale disarmament. And yet, the public acts of destroying and repurposing firearms changes (and continues to change) what Reyes characterizes as "the polarity" of the weapon—its charge, its meaning, its molecular make-up, a kind of alchemy that, as Reyes explains, is not only embedded in the actual transformation of firearms into shovels, but also carried by the transformed objects. "If you have a shovel that was formerly a weapon," Reyes explains, "and that's being used by a school to plant a tree, there is activity organized around the planting of the tree . . . there's a social event that has a psychological impact—you're winning over a situation that was seemingly intractable and overwhelming."[34] Simultaneously, and in keeping with the tenets of interculturalidad as well as interweaving performance cultures, the gun remains. That is, its material has not been destroyed, but reimagined and re-employed—to such an extent that the "terms of the conversation" are, necessarily, fundamentally different. These facts position *Palas por pistolas* within and as decolonial thought as well as, interpreted from the object's position, decolonizing action. Other worlds are publicly created through the labor of planting a tree in an event that was not imagined before, a use of a weapon in an unimagined way. Though the tree plantings may be circumscribed within a museum or institutionally sponsored context, *Palas por pistolas* elides and escapes the museum's curatorial imagination, ranging through public schools as readily as in permanent display.[35] Reyes contends he is not certain where his shovels have ended up; he has stopped tracking them as their travels accumulated.[36] The shovels defy not only spaces of modernity/coloniality (institutions and their structures), but time as well. The tree planted by one of the shovels, presumably, could continue to grow, a reminder (and future enactor) of deep time, of geological time, of time not determined by humans, of time other than modernity/coloniality.

While my thoughts above point to the decolonizing aspects of *Palas por pistolas*, I would like to spend a bit more time examining how *Palas por pistolas* enacts interculturalidad: a decolonization that transforms structural relations between the US and Mexico. By structural relations, I don't necessarily mean the state apparatus in terms of governance, but, rather, the logic of the War on Drugs and illegal immigration that insists that "threatening" traffic travels from Mexico to the US, a logic that involves and is promulgated by both the states of Mexico and the US. The blind spot of this logic that *Palas por pistolas* exposes and transforms—and reaches towards if not materially enacts restorative justice with—is the travel of firearms across the US–Mexico border, from the US into Mexico.

According to the University of San Diego's Trans-Border Institute's 2013 report, 120,000 people had been killed violently in Mexico since 2006, "many of them with firearms." The authors explain that:

> The majority of reported homicides are committed not with assault rifles, but rather pistols and revolvers. Many are perpetrated by hitmen connected to narco-cartels and rival gang members, or as a result of confrontations with soldiers, police and paramilitaries. What is more, most of these weapons are made in the United States. Yet curiously, an empirically robust treatment of the scale and volume of firearms trafficking from the United States to Mexico has yet to be attempted.[37]

Based on reported and accounted-for homicides, "the government counted nearly 35,000 deaths related to organized crime from December 2006 to the end of 2010, with the number of killings increasing dramatically with each passing year, from 2,826 in 2007 to 15,273 in 2010."[38] In the 1990s, firearms accounted for 10 percent of homicides. By 2011, firearms accounted for more than 50 percent.[39]

And yet, Mexico enforces highly restrictive gun control laws. It is very difficult for a Mexican citizen to purchase a firearm, and gun possession is considered a privilege (not a right) that is largely reserved for the military, for police officers, and for circumscribed hunting scenarios.[40] Accounting for both registered and illegal gun possession, Mexico's ratio of guns per citizen is likely 15 guns for every 100 people, "six times less than the United States."[41] Moreover, there is only "one legal firearms retailer" in Mexico, "compared to around 51,300 retail gun shops and around 7,400 pawnshops with a license to deal in guns in the United States."[42] In the United States, 13 percent of US arms retailers (6,700 out of a total 51,300) were located along the Mexico–US border in Texas, New Mexico, Arizona, and California in 2012, and 46.7 percent of "small arms dealers" in the US depend on demand from Mexico.[43] In 2013, the value of the "illegal arms trade increased substantially to $127.2 million annually." In 1999, its value was $32 million.[44]

Estimates of the number of guns crossing borders each day into Mexico between 2006 and 2012 vary from 600 to 2,000 weapons a day, or between 18,000 and 60,000 firearms per month.[45] The variance can be attributed to the difficulty of tracking trafficked weapons, but even the lower number is remarkable. According to the Centro de Estudios Sociales y de Opinión Pública (CESOP), in 2012 there were 15 million firearms held by civilians in Mexico, 85 percent of which were illegal.[46] Law enforcement in Mexico account for 655,000 weapons and the military for 505,000 firearms, leaving 14 million in the hands of Mexican citizens.[47] While it is difficult to attribute the entire number of circulating guns in Mexico to US sellers, the number of firearms seized at the US border increased by 189 percent between 2006–8 and 2010–12.[48] For *Palas por pistolas*, Reyes collected 1,527 guns, voluntarily donated by citizens of Culiacán. Given the evidence above, most of these firearms had to be illegal, and many, quite plausibly, originated or traveled through US sellers.

Palas por pistolas is steeped in US–Mexico modernity/coloniality. It seeks to transform those relations at ideological and material levels by providing visibility to both the human and the non-human blind spots of Mexico–US relations, reconfiguring a key object of modernity/coloniality (the gun) into another object, in order to reconfigure social relations towards planting trees rather than killing people. The guns (as shovels) spread throughout Mexico and cross back over the Mexican border, but not in a reversal of guns, money, and drugs. *That* conversation can no longer be the conversation. To return to Mignolo, the conversation's terms have been changed, from guns to shovels. And yet—because the materiality of the gun remains—the guns have not been *replaced*. Rather, the shovels (from guns) account for past and present US–Mexico relations centered on guns–drugs–money while simultaneously metamorphosing those relations towards a different future. One of the goals of interculturalidad is restorative justice for the blind spots of the state. In terms of the War on Drugs, the blind spot may be the Mexican civilians, armed with US guns. *Palas por pistolas* does not achieve restorative justice, but it points to a place in need of that work, a site not as seen.[49]

The travels of trafficked weapons, notions and practices of border security, and the hemispheric narcotic and opioid economies might be characterized as complex levels of a spectacular performance of US–Mexico relations. If intercultural means taking place between two cultures, or an exchange between cultures, we might characterize weapons trafficking as an intercultural performance of the social, economic, and political relations and histories of US–Mexico interactions. We might even go a step further and, following Erika Fischer-Lichte, reposition the weapons trafficking as an *interweaving*, rather than an intercultural, performance. Although there certainly are legacies of colonialism, neo-colonialism, and postcolonialism at play, the binary categories upon which intercultural performance history has relied, as Fischer-Lichte articulates, preclude the consideration of the effects of one culture on another.[50] The US and Mexico are both deeply involved in weapons trafficking, and both the Mexican and US cultures of firearms have undeniably influenced and shaped one another economically, culturally, politically, socially, and geographically. I suggest we might go even further, and consider that the imagining—the decolonial thought— carried within and by *Palas por pistolas* is the basis for an interculturalidad, a decolonization of US–Mexico relations. Our task, as scholars, then, becomes to commit to a position of modernity/coloniality; to examine the decolonial thought and action, both realized and potential, of performance; and to think, rather than in terms of the intercultural or the interweaving, in terms of interculturalidad: examining how performance does and does not enact transformation, where difference is constitutive, and restorative justice the process and goal.

NOTES

1. Thank you to Charlotte McIvor, Daphne Lei, and my readers for their thoughtful notes. The initial impetus for writing about Reyes's work was developed within the

University of Pittsburgh's Global Studies Faculty Development Seminar in 2016–17, Dr. Michael Goodhart, director. The seminar supported a visit from Reyes to the university. The visit was organized by Dr. Goodhart, Dr. Mina Rajagopalan, and me.

2. Kimberly Heinle, Octavio Rodríguez Ferreira, and David A. Shirk, "Drug Violence in Mexico: Data and Analysis Through 2016," *Justice in Mexico* (San Diego: University of San Diego, 2017), 6, 2, 7, https://justiceinmexico.org/publications/reports/.

3. Heinle, Rodríguez Ferreira, and Shirk, "Drug Violence in Mexico," 2.

4. Sky Gooden, "Interview: Pedro Reyes Reclaims the Politics in Art," *MOMUS*, January 14, 2015, http://momus.ca/interview-pedro-reyes-reclaims-the-politics-in-art/.

5. Reyes' website tracked initial plantings. In 2016, Reyes noted he no longer can keep track of the shovels and their travels. Pedro Reyes, *Palas por pistolas* (2008), http://pedroreyes.net/palasporpistolas.php. Pedro Reyes, "Lecture: Activism, Art and the Global," Humanizing the Global/Globalizing the Human Lecture Series, Global Studies Center and Humanities Center, University of Pittsburgh, April 18, 2016.

6. Gooden, "Interview."

7. I will not translate *interculturalidad* into English, for reasons I discuss in the first section of this chapter.

8. Erika Fischer-Lichte, "Interweaving Performance Cultures: Re-thinking 'Intercultural Theatre' Towards an Experience and Theory of Performance beyond Postcolonialism," in Erika Fischer-Lichte, Torsten Jost, and Saskya Iris Jain (eds.), *The Politics of Interweaving Performance Cultures: Beyond Postcolonialism* (New York: Routledge, 2014), 40.

9. I am inspired by Ric Knowles's call "to focus on the contested, unsettling, and often unequal spaces *between* cultures, spaces that can function in performance as sites of negotiation." I am not suggesting that discourses of postcolonialism be eschewed for modernity/coloniality. Rather, I offer interculturalidad as an additional tool, originating within minoritarian knowledge production, for decolonization in and through performance (inclusive of theatre) and, potentially, performance analysis. Ric Knowles, *Theatre & Interculturalism* (London: Palgrave Macmillan, 2010), 4. See also Christopher Balme, *Decolonizing the Stage: Theatrical Syncretism and Post-Colonial Drama* (Oxford: Clarendon, 1999), and Rustom Bharucha, *The Politics of Cultural Practice: Thinking through Theatre in an Age of Globalization* (Hanover, NH: Wesleyan University Press, 2000).

10. Catherine Walsh, "Pedagogical Notes from the Decolonial Cracks," *e-misférica* 11, no 1 (2014), http://hemisphericinstitute.org/hemi/en/emisferica-111-decolonial-gesture/walsh.

11. Catherine Walsh, "Interculturalidad y colonialidad del poder. Un pensamiento y posicionamiento otro desde la diferencia colonial," in Walter Mignolo, Álvaro García Linera, and Catherine Walsh (eds.), *Interculturalidad, decolonización del estado, y del conocimiento* (Buenos Aires: Ediciones del Signo, 2006), 21.

12. I have written about modernity/coloniality in relation to theatre history and performance studies elsewhere. See, for example, Lisa Jackson-Schebetta, *Traveler,*

there is no road: Theatre, The Spanish Civil War, and the Decolonial Imagination in the Americas (Iowa City: University of Iowa Press, 2017).

13. Mignolo explains the distinction further: "It is certainly diverse, but few people will confuse decolonial with postcolonial for the distinction between the 'de' and the 'post' is non-negotiable by the self-constituting narrative of each respective universe of meaning. The 'post' and the 'de' belong to different genealogies of meanings, processes, and contexts, having in common an element of content: colonialism." Walter Mignolo, "Looking for the Decolonial Gesture," *e-misférica* 11, no 1 (2014), http://hemisphericinstitute.org/hemi/en/emisferica-111-decolonial-gesture/mignolo.

14. The concept is central to Quijano's article, but is first mentioned on page 535. Anibal Quijano, "Coloniality of Power, Eurocentrism, and Latin America," *Nepantla: Views from the South* 1, no. 3 (2000): 535.

15. Walter Mignolo, *The Darker Side of Western Modernity: Global Futures, Decolonial Options* (Durham, NC: Duke University Press, 2011).

16. Mignolo writes "that it is not enough to change the content; the terms of the conversation must be changed." Mignolo, *The Darker Side*, 122.

17. Walsh, "Interculturalidad," 29.

18. Walsh articulates the historical relationship between state formation and indigeneity in Ecuador and Bolivia: "In the America of the South, State formation has, since its beginnings, found its ground in an alleged homogeneity and unity that is intimately tied to the dominant economic, political, social and cultural order and the interests of capital. As such, the present efforts in countries like Bolivia and Ecuador to transform State, shed it of its colonial, neoliberal and imperial weight, and re-found it from below—from the diversity of peoples, cultures, and historical practices—are transcendental." Catherine Walsh, "The Plurinational and Intercultural State: Decolonization and State Re-founding in Ecuador," *Kult* 6 (Fall 2009): 65, http://www.postkolonial.dk/artikler/kult_6/WALSH.pdf.

19. An example would be the pluriversidad, the Universidad Intercultural Amawtay Wasi, part of the educative and political project of CONAIE. The pluriversidad was approved by the state of Ecuador in 2003. Instruction began in 2005. Walsh, "Interculturalidad," 39–40.

20. Walsh, "Interculturalidad," 34. For a summary of CONAIE's objectives, see Jorge Herrera, Carlos Pérez, Marlon Vargas, and Edison Aguavil, "CONAIE pide a Presidente Moreno construir un Estado plurinacional y una sociedad intercultural," *Ecuador Inmediato*, July 4, 2017, https://www.ecuadorinmediato.com/modules/umFileManager/pndata/2017-06/pedido_de_conaie_a_presidente_moreno_62876.pdf.

21. Robert Aman, "Why Interculturalidad is Not Interculturality," *Cultural Studies* 29, no. 2 (2015): 207.

22. Aman, "Why Interculturalidad is Not Interculturality," 207.

23. Aman, "Why Interculturalidad is Not Interculturality," 208.

24. Aman, "Why Interculturalidad is Not Interculturality," 208.

25. Fischer-Lichte, "Interweaving Performance Cultures," 26–7.

26. Fischer-Lichte, "Interweaving Performance Cultures," 40.

27. Fischer-Lichte, "Interweaving Performance Cultures," 42–3, 45.

28. I use this, following—among other scholars—Diana Taylor, as an adjective for performance. Diana Taylor, *Performance* (Durham, NC: Duke University Press, 2016), 120.

29. Jardín Botánica Culiacán, "Historia," *Jardín Botánica Culiacán*, http://www.botanicoculiacan.org/es/historia.

30. Gooden, "Interview." See also "Top 200 Collectors: Isabel and Agustín Coppel," *ART NEWS* (2017), http://www.artnews.com/top200/isabel-and-agustin-coppel-2/, and Hiroshi Takahashi, "Cómo Coppel inundó (sin querer) con sus tiendas a México," *Forbes México*, November 18, 2015, https://www.forbes.com.mx/como-coppel-inundo-sin-querer-con-sus-tiendas-a-mexico/. Walter Mignolo has cautioned against artist grants as effective instruments of decolonization: "Grants are embedded in the colonial matrix of power. The granting institutions not only have the privilege of setting the rules and appointing the committee that will 'judge' the value of the proposals, but they also create a relationship of dependency that, on the one hand, is humiliating for those who are granted economic support, and at the same time disguises that humiliation (even for the person humiliated) by the 'honor' of being recognized as a valuable person (artists, social scientist, scientist in general) and by being portrayed in the mainstream media if the award is big, or in the home institution if the award is of less national or international relevance." Mignolo, "Looking for the Decolonial Gesture." While it is not my project to analyze Coppel in this piece, in *Palas por pistolas* the role of the benefactor was transformed to simultaneous participant.

31. Gooden, "Interview."

32. Gooden, "Interview."

33. Numbers would be surpassed in later drives. In 2010, the city of Juárez granted Reyes 7,000 donated firearms, which Reyes transformed into playable musical instruments for his projects *Imagine* (2012) and *Disarm* (2013). Pieces of the firearms remain identifiable, but the flute can be played like a flute—and, indeed, an orchestra and musical concert was equipped with the instruments. Groups of instruments also travel to museums for display as self-playing instruments.

34. "Weapon for Change: Interview with Mexican Artist Pedro Reyes," *Evening Standard*, March 26, 2013, http://www.standard.co.uk/goingout/exhibitions/weapon-for-change-interview-with-mexican-artist-pedro-reyes-8549414.html.

35. I am thinking, here, with André Lepecki, "Decolonizing the Curatorial," *Theatre* 47, no. 1 (2017): 101–15.

36. Reyes, "Lecture."

37. Topher McDougal, David A. Shirk, Robert Muggah, and John H. Patterson, *The Way of the Gun: Estimating Firearms Traffic Across the U.S.–Mexico Border* (San Diego: University of San Diego Trans-Border Institute and the Igarapé Institute, 2013), 4.

38. "Neither Rights Nor Security: Killings, Torture, and Disappearances in Mexico's 'War on Drugs,'" *Human Rights Watch America*, November 9, 2011, https://www.hrw.org/

report/2011/11/09/neither-rights-nor-security/killings-torture-and-disappearances-mexicos-war-drugs.

39. McDougal et al., *The Way of the Gun*, 6.

40. "While law enforcement and military personnel are permitted to use firearms by Article 160 of the country's federal criminal code, the Mexican army (SEDENA) oversees the sale of all firearms to private individuals through the Federal Arms Registry. Indeed, person-to-person firearm sales are prohibited by Article 164 of the criminal code. There are also strict penalties under Article 162 of the federal criminal code for ordinary citizens who possess or carry firearms without authorization. There are also restrictions on the caliber of firearms that ordinary citizens may possess, which is limited to .380 or less (.357 magnum and 9mm are also prohibited), and in practice the lawful possession of firearms above .22 caliber is limited by the difficulty of obtaining permits to do so. Hunters and target shooters may obtain licenses for firearm possession, and gun collecting is allowed with some exceptions." McDougal et al., *The Way of the Gun*, 8–9.

41. McDougal et al., *The Way of the Gun*, 6.

42. McDougal et al., *The Way of the Gun*, 6.

43. McDougal et al., *The Way of the Gun*, 6.

44. Ryan Villareal, "Gun Runners For Mexican Cartels Keep US Gun Shops In Business," *International Business Times*, March 26, 2013, http://www.ibtimes.com/gun-runners-mexican-cartels-keep-us-gun-shops-business-report-1150349.

45. David Gagne, "2000 Illegal Weapons Cross US–Mexico Border Per Day: Report." *Insight Crime*, January 22, 2015, http://www.insightcrime.org/news-analysis/2000-illegal-weapons-cross-us-mexico-border-every-day.

46. Gagne, "2000 Illegal Weapons."

47. McDougal et al., *The Way of the Gun*, 9.

48. Gagne, "2000 Illegal Weapons."

49. Reyes himself does not characterize his work as action, but rather as "*suggesting* that we should transform the defense sector to a kind of rescue force for humanitarian needs and managing environmental crises rather than waging conflict." Gooden, "Interview."

50. As Leo Cabranes-Grant articulates, "intercultural criticism has been more focused on unpacking the reception and ideological impact of our performance than in reconstructing the relational webs of labor and maintenance that keep those occasions arising." *Palas por pistolas* exposes "webs of labor and maintenance" that structure long-standing "inter-cultural pressures" of US–Mexico relations and histories. Leo Cabranes-Grant, *From Scenarios to Networks: Performing the Intercultural in Colonial Mexico* (Evanston, IL: Northwestern University Press, 2016), 4–5.

PART FIVE

Interculturalism(s): Mapping the Past, Reflecting on the Future

CHAPTER THIRTEEN

Annotated Bibliography

CHARLOTTE MCIVOR WITH JUSTINE NAKASE

INTERCULTURAL PERFORMANCE THEORY'S WAVES

In the Introduction, we proposed that we must think of intercultural performance's theoretical and practical evolution to the present through a series of ecological metaphors: waves, caves, roots. This theoretical lens grounds intercultural performance practices and practitioner networks within materialist ecologies composed of living and non-living actors that must negotiate constantly shifting social, political, and cultural geographies.

In this annotated overview of key intercultural performance debates and texts, we narrow in on ocean waves as our organizational metaphor to guide readers becoming oriented with the field's genealogy. Using this device, we will outline for readers how attitudes and key concepts within intercultural performance theory as a distinct subfield within theatre and performance studies have shifted over time (as well as recycled central questions and even terms re-presented as 'new' in subsequent waves).

We posit that there have been three key waves within intercultural performance theory whose progression between the twentieth-twenty-first century was catalyzed by the winds of influence whipped up by modernist theatrical practices' influential figures who repeatedly cited theatre and performance practices of the "East" and Global South as direct influences and aspirational models. While the Third Wave has increasingly challenged this modernist genealogy as the origin story of intercultural performance theory, we nonetheless cite its figures here to map the discourse as it evolved in print (in the West). The winds and waves are:

Winds: Modernist genealogies of experimentation (late nineteenth century–1970s)
Wave One: Emergence and backlash (1970s–late 1990s)
Wave Two: Consolidation (early 2000s–2010)
Wave Three: "Other" interculturalism(s) (2011–present)

This annotated bibliography outlines these winds and waves by featuring:

- a summary of each period's main interlocutors, activities and shifts in practice/attitude;
- brief definitions of associated key terms;
- and a chronological listing of key texts with summary.

Our annotated overview does not encompass related critical literatures that have influenced the progression of intercultural performance theory's waves, including but not limited to critical race theory, whiteness studies, postcolonial studies, diaspora studies, indigenous studies, and transnational and/or materialist feminisms. Rather, we focus on how scholars more narrowly focused in theatre and performance studies have made use of interdisciplinary discourses to produce key publications within our discipline over time, articulating how these other points of reference triggered new waves. For a more comprehensive bibliography and consideration of the interplay between other key critical texts outside our field and the development of intercultural performance theory from the 1970s to early 2010s, see Ric Knowles' *Theatre & Interculturalism* (Wave Three).

We choose a chronological approach to animate for readers how scholar/ practitioners have debated with one another across "real" (i.e. linear) time. However, we choose the teleological precisely to problematize it. We invite you to move through this annotated bibliography with a keenly critical eye attentive to patterns and unresolved concerns, particularly as to how a review of this discourse's trajectory now reveals Daphne P. Lei's point in the Introduction, that "intercultural time is always partially repetitive cyclical and overlapping," with the discourse surrounding it sharing this same feature. We were struck, for example, by the first appearance of "interweaving" in the 1980s with Richard Schechner and Victor Turner, not with Erika Fischer-Lichte's recent influential 2010s research and publications on the term, and by "new interculturalism" first being a "new" term in 2002, almost a decade before Knowles' highly influential *Theatre & Interculturalism* which heralded the turn that we now designate as the Third Wave.

As we have worked on this annotated bibliography, we have also been keenly aware that this is an account of intercultural performance *theory* rather than a full inventory of performance *practices* which could be counted as intercultural in form or intent. Therefore, this annotated bibliography is an account of how *discourse* concerning intercultural performance theory has developed over time albeit with its own gaps (through our blindspots, omissions, and the constraints of the word limit). However, we must look to this historical discourse comprehensively in order to chart new directions for intercultural performance theory's expanded and increasingly minoritarian objects/case studies, many of which are being found in the archives. Indeed, the recent historiographical turn within intercultural performance theory's Third Wave as animated by Lei in the Introduction as well as the work of Leo Cabranes-Grant and Diana Looser powerfully challenges Western theatrical modernism as the seminal case study on which intercultural performance theory should be based, instead employing a non-Western counter-genealogical approach enabled by attention to a broader range of performance practices and their traces. These scholars purposefully mine early modern and/or early or pre-colonial/ Western contact with Chinese, Mexican and Australasian archives to expose how intercultural performance theory might be best used now to trace alternative *historical* genealogies which productively challenge the trajectory of intercultural performance theory's development as created primarily in/by Western centers of power.[1]

WINDS: MODERNIST GENEALOGIES OF EXPERIMENTATION

If we are to use the metaphor of waves to structure this annotated overview, we must also account for what *catalyzed* the waves of intercultural performance theory under consideration here to begin rolling forward in the first place. In nature, wind remains the primary cause of most waves, with some exceptional wave events like tsunamis being triggered instead by subterranean earthquakes. We might understand wind's effect on the generation of waves as the force exerted *on* or *in* water that triggers a wave's swelling and crescendo of moving water before its inevitable break at sea or on shore. Likewise, key performance events, approaches, or problems generate individual and/or collective forces that have driven forward the evolution of intercultural performance theory, triggering wave after wave of innovation, contestation, and occasionally repetition.

The multiple waves of intercultural performance theory and practice that have emerged since the 1970s are inflected by the thematic wind arising from genealogies of theatrical modernism (as well as the wider impact of this diverse movement across arts forms in the late nineteenth and early twentieth century). Theatrical modernism in the West, much like its literary counterpart, was heavily influenced by key encounters with Eastern forms. Bertolt Brecht, Gordon Craig, and Vsevelod Meyerhold were inspired by Chinese Peking Opera artist Mei Lanfang, whose performances in 1935 sparked Brecht's conception of the alienation effect and Meyerhold's interest in biomechanics.[2] Similarly, Irish poet and playwright W. B. Yeats's collaboration with Japanese dancer Michio Ito resulted in his Noh-inflected dance plays, while Antonin Artaud's "discovery" of Balinese dancers at the 1931 Paris Colonial Exhibition prompted his philosophy of a purely physical theatrical language, as explored in his influential book *The Theatre and its Double*.[3]

This legacy of Eastern aesthetics rejuvenating Western theatre practice has been read as the original prototype for the primarily Western-driven intercultural projects of the First and Second Wave. Furthermore, the politics of these modernist transactions have also haunted contemporary intercultural practice. The fact that Artaud saw his Balinese dancers at the Paris Colonial Exhibition explicitly links the Western project of colonialism to the modernists' access and relationship to those cultures and traditions that were so influential to their work. This undercurrent of colonialism—with its tensions of access, appropriation, and the politics of representation—anticipates one of the main currents of debate that flows through each of the waves of intercultural performance practice and the theory. Additionally, modernism's desire to access a universal or essential language of theatre through an anthropological survey of foreign theatre practices (itself inflected with Western colonialist assumptions) anticipates the theatrical "laboratories" of many First Wave practitioners. For this reason, Jerzy Grotowski is included here as the bridge practitioner who escalated the stakes and longevity of the performance experiments influentially attempted by earlier twentieth-century practitioners.

Associated Keywords

Orientalism: Introduced by Edward Said and a key theoretical framework of postcolonial theory, orientalism is "the enormously systematic discipline by which European culture was able to manage—and even produce—the Orient politically, sociologically, militarily, ideologically, and imaginatively."[4] Orientalism can be seen as a Eurocentric construction of the East (the Orient) as Other to the West (the Occident), a narrative that both romanticized and infantilized the East and was used to justify Western imperialism and colonialism. Much like interculturalism itself, orientalism as a term has since been applied retroactively to define and describe the impulses guiding Western modernists' Eastern inspiration, as well as the continuing legacy that has haunted intercultural performance from the First Wave onwards.

Primitivism: More frequently applied in fine arts (for example, in the influence of Tahitian art on Paul Gauguin) and music (as in the pagan themes of Igor Stravinsky's *The Rite of Spring*), primitivism rejected Western realism in favor of simplified forms that evoked an "essential" truth, and was often inspired by the artistic cultures of Africa, Asia, and the Americas. Though less frequently used in discussions of intercultural performance, modernist primitivism mirrored its orientalism, and can be seen as a precursor to the project of compiling a universal (or transcultural/precultural) theatrical language.

Theatre of Convention: Vsevolod Meyerhold worked towards a theatre that defied psychological realism and naturalism but sought to portray the real through stylized convention and an emphasis on the grotesque, drawing on the "theatres of the far West (France, Italy, Spain and England) and the far East."[5] He was particularly influenced by the performing career of Mei Lanfang.

Via Negativa: Jerzy Grotowski's belief that actors should remove physical and psychological blocks to becoming fully present onstage in order to act from the most stripped-back version of themselves. There is a connection between this idea and Eugenio Barba's later concept of pre-expressivity, developed in his work with the International School of Theatre Anthropology (ISTA).

Foundational Texts

Artaud, Antonin. *Theatre and Its Double*. 1938. Translated by Mary Caroline Richards. New York: Grove Press, 1994.
Artaud's highly influential collection of essays theorizing a surrealist "Theatre of Cruelty" was directly influenced by his encounter with Asian theatre forms and in many ways anticipates the central themes that will define the First Wave of intercultural performance studies. Artaud proposes a "Theatre of Cruelty," a mystical and ceremonial form of performance that he sets in opposition to bourgeois Western theatre, which he feels is stifled by psychological realism and the written word. Central to Artaud's conception of the Theatre of Cruelty is a purely theatrical language, an "altogether Oriental form of expression" that "ultimately breaks away

from the intellectual subjugation of the language, by conveying the sense of a new and deeper intellectuality which hides itself beneath the gestures and signs."[6] For Artaud, "Oriental" theatre is an "archetypical, primitive theatre" that underlies origins of performance—foreshadowing the transcultural work of practitioners such as Eugenio Barba, Jerzy Grotowski, and Peter Brook. Artaud's dichotomy of "Oriental" and "Occidental" clearly signals the "West and the rest" binary that marks the First Wave of intercultural performance studies that will be increasingly problematized in the subsequent waves of scholarship.

Brecht, Bertolt. *Brecht on Theatre: The Development of an Aesthetic.* **Edited and translated by John Willett. New York: Hill and Wang, 1964.**
In his collected essays, Brecht defines and explores the key concepts that would become central not only to his own practice, but to contemporary conversations of theatre and performance. Most notable for discussions of interculturalism is his essay "Alienation Effects in Chinese Acting," in which Brecht first introduces his idea of the alienation effect (*Verfremdungseffekt*) using the illustrative case study of Chinese theatre. Though Brecht notes that aspects of the alienation effect can be found in a "primitive form" in Western popular culture, the majority of his essay emphasizes an East–West dichotomy contrasting Chinese and Western (Aristotelian) performance. Brecht extensively discusses how the various staging aspects of Chinese theatre enact his ideas of alienation through codified movement, masks, and symbolic costume and scenic design. Unlike Artaud—whose encounter with the Balinese dancers was a pivotal starting point—Brecht had already been developing his ideas of the alienation effect both in practice and in theory before he saw the performances of Mei Lanfang during his visit to Russia in 1935. However, in his incorporation of not only "Asiatic" theatre but also a variety of popular and historic forms of Western performance, Brecht's development of an epic theatre can be seen to echo the First Wave of intercultural projects.

Grotowski, Jerzy. *Towards A Poor Theatre.* **1968. 1st Routledge edition. London and New York: Routledge, 2002.**
Though not as explicitly concerned with interculturalism, Grotowski's work resembles that of other First Wave practitioners in his rejection of Western realism and his search for a precultural, mystical, ritual form of actor training and performance. Significantly, Grotowski was also a mentor of Eugenio Barba (see below) and heavily influenced Barba's own interest in performer training and process across culture as a means of transcultural exploration.

WAVE ONE: EMERGENCE AND BACKLASH

Wave One of intercultural performance theory emerged out of a complex nexus of shifts in theatre practice, theory, and methodology from the 1970s to the 1990s. Key inaugural voices included Richard Schechner, Victor Turner, Eugenio Barba, Erika Fischer-Lichte, and Patrice Pavis. Schechner, Turner, and Barba's approach to intercultural performance was anthropological (though also focused on actor training), while Fischer-Lichte and Pavis prioritized analysis of performances that explicitly blended culturally distinct forms and techniques. In particular, Schechner and Turner's interdisciplinary performance explorations at the intersection of theatre studies and anthropology (which instigated the field formation of performance studies) drove the initial discourse, with an emphasis on the relationship between theatre and ritual specifically. As intercultural terminology took off, it became increasingly applied to the work of Western (and mostly New York City-based) avant-garde artists and companies such as Eugenio Barba, Jerzy Grotowski, Robert Wilson, Peter Brooks, Lee Breuer, Peter Sellars, Elizabeth LeCompte and the Wooster Group, and Ariane Mnouchkine. In tracing those artists' influences, critics also retroactively applied intercultural performance theory to key Western modernist theatre practitioners (see above). Although focused to some extent on non-Western and particularly postcolonial theatre practices, the nascent development of postcolonial theory as a field meant that its full theoretical impact did not coalesce until the Second Wave. However, Peter Brook's landmark and controversial production of the *Mahabharata* (first produced in 1985) was one of the most important touchstones of not only intercultural performance theory but the development of postcolonial performance theory as a coherent discourse central to theatre and performance studies as a wider discipline.

Associated Keywords

Hourglass of cultures: Patrice Pavis's highly influential (and contested) diagram which represents the process of intercultural theatrical exchange as involving a series of steps negotiated between a "source" (usually non-Western) and a "target" (usually Western) culture.

Internationalism: The aspiration that artists and cultural performance forms and techniques would be able to cross borders to collaborate and influence one another's ongoing practice and development, resulting in an eventual de-hierarchization of power structures between nations and their cultures, realized through the transmission of performance.

Intraculturalism: Used by Rustom Bharucha to refer to the "dynamics" of encounter "between and across specific communities and regions *within* the boundaries of the nation-state."[7] This term's nuance challenges the homogenization of "national" cultures and the assumption of a singular shared identity graspable through the exchange of indigenous performance or other practices.

Postcolonial performance: Performance is one of the major ways through which to understand and trace the impact of colonial and imperial occupation on indigenous cultures and the ways in which both sets of cultural actors (colonizer and colonized) changed through their contact with one another. The study of postcolonial performance focuses on work produced by those from formally colonized locations, and frequently focuses on the interplay between imported Western and indigenous or folk theatrical forms which amalgamate to produce new hybrids or the invention of new theatrical forms entirely as a reaction to colonial occupation. Postcolonial performance is thus characterized by a dialectical relationship between the colonizer and colonized which manifests theatrically in content and/or form. It qualifies as a mode of intercultural performance (as cultures designated as distinct mix and blend in the encounter, producing new forms). But as multiple scholars, including Jacqueline Lo, Helen Gilbert, and Erika Fischer-Lichte, identify, postcolonial performance is always characterized by its directly political intent, but the same cannot be said of intercultural performance practice as a broader category.

Postmodernism: This broad theoretical term was used loosely across the First Wave as a description/defense of the impulse by practitioners to combine/splice cultural influences and references particularly along a Global North–Global South exchange axis as arising from the condition of modern life where individuals, cultural practices, objects, and commodities travel, encounter one another, and become reshaped in their meaning. As such, the purity of culture becomes fundamentally destabilized and is constantly being remade by individuals and communities who encounter cultural icons, artifacts, or objects in decontextualized ways. Richard Schechner in particular draws on this term in the late 1970s and 1980s—especially to describe how the pluralism of intercultural/post-modern performance practices can be used to destabilize the nation as a category of political reference. He offers "Interculturalism is replacing—ever so tenderly but not so slowly—internationalism. The nation is the force of modernism; and the cultures—I emphasise the plural—are the force of postmodernism."[8] Other first-wave artists frequently referred to as postmodern include Peter Brooks, Peter Sellars, Robert Wilson, and Ariane Mnouchkine.

Pre-expressivity: Used within theatre anthropology by Eugenio Barba and his followers as a term that connotes certain baseline physical behaviors and gestures common to humanity. This field maintains that "the pre-expressive level is at the root of the various performing techniques and that there exists, independently of traditional culture, a transcultural 'physiology.'"[9] Pre-expressivity is what can be observed of the body anatomically before the performance begins, or in the moment of shift into a performance state. These pre-expressive states or vocabularies may therefore be accessed by studying performance traditions and performers from distinct cultures of origin in relationship to one another and observing patterns in pre-expressive states that recur across cultures.

Social drama: Victor Turner's conceptualization of the process of social change, which he saw as composed of four distinct phases: breach, crisis, redress, and reintegration. Turner used this framework to analyze the use of ritual and public action in social change, while Schechner built on the idea to apply it to a theatrical/ performance paradigm.[10] Investigations into social drama as a theoretical framework were a central preoccupation of Turner and Schechner's 1980s conferences on ritual and theatre (see below).

Theatre anthropology: A comparative study of "human beings' socio-cultural and physiological behaviour in a performance situation"[11] initiated by Eugenio Barba.

Unlike the use of anthropological methods in the wider field of performance studies, theatre anthropology refers to the isolated study of performance forms and methods from across cultures. Barba charges theatre anthropology with isolating "out the principles which the performer must put to work in order to make this dance of the senses and mind of the spectator possible"[12] in a transcultural context. He defends this approach from charges of cultural relativism by claiming that "Theatre Anthropology does not reduce to . . . but concentrates on."[13]

Third Theatre: Eugenio Barba's term to describe disparate theatre movements that he saw emerging in the 1970s. Barba defines this Third Theatre by its marginality— it "lives on the fringe, often outside of on the outskirts of the centres and capitals of culture," and is distinct from both traditional and avant-garde theatres—as well as its ethical imperative to seek new forms of theatre to articulate the present moment as a means of "creating a social cell in which intentions, aspirations and personal needs begin to be transformed into actions."[14]

Key Texts

Fischer-Lichte, Erika, Josephine Riley, and Michael Gissenwehrer, eds. *The Dramatic Touch of Difference: Theatre Own and Foreign.* Forum Modernes Theatre Schriftenreihe, Vol. 2. Tübingen: Gunter Narr Verlag, 1990.
This collection of essays presents a global range of intercultural case studies from First Wave practices to investigate "whether these uniquely remarkable equivalents have emerged independently" as they identify a particular proliferation in the 1970s onwards and whether "similar methods of approach to a production indicate a basic underlying unity, which would make the comparison of this phenomenon both fruitful and meaningful."[15] The book is organized geographically, with sections on North America/Europe, Japan, China, Indonesia/India, and Africa (as evidenced by these section headings, primacy is given to Occidental-Oriental inflected interculturalism). This also results in a focus on how national theatre traditions accommodate or contest intercultural theatre practice. It encapsulates and traces many of the grounding themes of intercultural performance theory: the connection between modernism and contemporary intercultural theatre practice, the link between post/colonialism and interculturalism; the broad strokes of exchange (texts from the West, techniques from the East); and the initial practitioners and theorists (Eugenio Barba, Peter Brook, Erika Fisher-Lichte, Arianne Mnouchkine, Patrice Pavis).

Schechner, Richard and Willa Appel, eds. *By Means of Performance: Intercultural Studies of Theatre and Ritual.* New York: Cambridge University Press, 1990.
This edited collection documents and reflects on the early 1980s series of conferences focused on the "interweavings of ritual and theatre" convened by Victor Turner in collaboration with a group of others,[16] prominently among them Richard Schechner. Contributors to this volume are split between theatre studies and anthropology. Chapters range between the cataloguing and analysis of performance practices and/ or/as ritual and theoretical reflections on performance from the perspective of

practitioners/scholars. Thematic clusters include liminality, audience, the sacred/ profane, and spatiality. While this collection is a key part of the theoretical genealogy of intercultural performance theory, it most strongly captures the foundations of key terminology within performance studies as a broader field as Schechner and Appel note that their intention was to approach different genres of embodied action *as* performance with these conferences. This collection is in fact more concerned with *cross*-cultural exchange rather than intercultural exchange as it becomes further nuanced, particularly by Patrice Pavis (see below). At this point, Schechner in particular was often using interculturalism and internationalism interchangeably and they do not even define "intercultural" in the introduction to the collection.

Barba, Eugenio and Nicola Savarese. *The Secret Art of the Performer: A Dictionary of Theatre Anthropology.* **London and New York: Routledge, 1991.**
Focused on performance technique and training and grounded in theatre anthropology (see above), this illustrated guide draws on a range of global theatrical traditions with the intention of mapping shared common characteristics of performance, or what Barba refers to as pre-expressivity (see above). The volume draws on Barba's decade of research with the International School of Theatre Anthropology (ISTA) in Denmark, which brought together theatre practitioners from around the world and showcases Barba and his collaborators' perspectives on this work. As such, it is a key index of the First Wave's interest in interculturalism as a study of actor training and performance processes as a means of accessing universal performance languages or states. The range of contributions and the precision used by all collaborators to identify points of difference and commonality across forms evidences ISTA's focus under Barba's leadership on deep analysis of the performer's body and physical states in performance across cultures.

Marranca, Bonnie and Gautam Dasgupta, eds. *Interculturalism and Performance: Writings from PAJ.* **New York: PAJ Publications, 1991.**
This collection of writings from *Performing Arts Journal (PAJ)* reconstructs more than fifteen years of the earliest debates about intercultural theatre/performance and its then-related terminologies including transculturation, theatre anthropology, and postmodernism, among others. The spread of contributions makes clear the influence of both contemporary American (and mostly New York City-based) avant-garde performance and the rise of performance studies in intercultural performance theory as a discourse. On the one hand, the collection privileges the work of the American (and European) avant-garde artists discussed above. However, the collection also features analysis of rituals such as Zambia's Kankanga Dances and a Yaqui Easter ceremony in the Southwestern United States, as well as an essay by Victor Turner on his active experimentation with Richard Schechner in bringing anthropological approaches and ethnographic materials to bear on staging drama. This collection communicates strongly that at this early stage of the subfield's development, intercultural performance theory was often used like a "connector" theory which could create bridges between diverse fields including theatre studies, literary studies, anthropology, and music, and unify discussion of wildly different aesthetic and/or social objects. As such, this collection in particular makes clear how intercultural

performance theory in particular enabled the inauguration of performance studies as a much wider field.

Bharucha, Rustom. *Theatre and the World: Performance and the Politics of Culture.* **London: Routledge, 1992.**

Bharucha's forceful monograph deconstructs the politics and ethics of the proliferation of intercultural performance theory from his perspective as not only a scholar, but a professional theatre practitioner. Bharucha indicts Western practitioners, including Richard Schechner, Eugenio Barba, and Peter Brooks, for their appropriation of Indian performance forms without an understanding of their history and ethics, or in the case of Brooks, without reciprocity or respect extended to his Indian collaborators. He treats the explosion of intercultural theatre practices (particularly as led by elite white male theatre practitioners) as a manifestation of neo-colonialism, with postmodernism often being offered as an excuse that fails to take into account the power differentials present within the collaborations and the terms on which they are founded. Bharucha tests his own theories of interculturalism within an *intracultural* context (a term later explored in his second book, see below) by devoting a portion of the book to studying three of his own separate productions of German playwright Franz Xaver Kroetz's one-woman, wordless play in different cities (Calcutta, Bombay, and Madras) with a different local actress in each. Through these performance experiments, Bharucha demonstrates the nuances of local cultural context that impact not only each performer's relationship to the concept personally, but how they use theatrical (or performance) form in collaboration with Bharucha to engage with the structure of the play from their own rooted perspective. The final section of this book focuses on the multiple theatrical genealogies of India, disrupting the homogenization of India and diverse classical Indian theatrical forms that he charges renowned intercultural theatre practitioners with. Ultimately, Bharucha argues for theatre practitioners and theorists to ethically situate their inter/ intracultural inquiries within material grounded local contexts that are cognizant of their colonial/neo-colonial genealogies.

Barba, Eugenio. *The Paper Canoe: A Guide to Theatre Anthropology.* **Translated by Richard Fowler. London and New York: Routledge, 1995. (First published in Italian as** *La Canoa di Carta* **in 1993.)**

Barba's autobiographical account of his theatre research practice and the development of his work with Odin Teatret into ISTA, which he describes as organically emerging from his travels throughout Asia after the founding of the theatre company in 1964. He therefore characterizes his own practice as Eurasian theatre, characterized by "*movement* between East and West."[17] In this book, he outlines his definition of theatre anthropology and the tenets of its practice that ISTA has engaged in since 1979. He distinguishes between North Pole performers "(dancers, mimes of the Decroux school, actors modelled by the tradition of a small group who have elaborated their own personal codifications, actors of the classical Asian theatres, modelled by rigorous traditions)"[18] and South Pole performers who do "not belong to a performance genre characterized by a detailed stylistic code."[19] He characterizes his interest as being in North Pole performance and outlines the interrelationship of performance codes and precepts across forms as diverse as noh, kathakali, Peking opera, ballet, butoh, and the work of individual practitioners including but not limited to directors, actors, and puppeteers Katsuko Azuma, Tokuho Azuma, Bertolt Brecht, Jacques Copeau, Michael Chekhov, François Delsarte, Étienne Decroux, Jerzy Grotowski, Tatsumi Hijikata, Hideo Kanzo, Vsevolod Meyerhold, Sanjukta Panigrahi, Konstantin Stanislavski, and I Made Pasek Tempo. Barba argues throughout the book against claims that his theatrical practice is orientalizing and reductive by weaving together comparative accounts of shared principles regarding presence and theatrical composition particularly across North Pole forms. He maintains that his rigorous attention to detail and dynamic dialogues with living practitioners complicate these charges, and ultimately argues for his practice as an ongoing and mediated engagement of substance and impact.

Fusco, Coco. "The Other History of Intercultural Performance." *TDR: The Drama Review* 38, no.1 (Spring 1994): 143–67.
Coco Fusco's documentation of the reception of her ground-breaking performance, *Couple in a Cage*, with Guillermo Gómez-Peña situates this work within a longer genealogy of intercultural performance as a practice she argues is founded in histories of racism, colonialism, and exploitation of indigenous and non-Western peoples. Fusco and Gómez-Peña's intervention as Chicano performance artists with *Couple in a Cage* intended to satirize historic practices of exhibiting native peoples by playing these parts with a postmodern twist. Fusco argues that audiences' unironic reception of the artists *as* native peoples being displayed by contemporary institutions illustrates that our capacity to consume *and* critique intercultural performance is irreparably shaped by the living afterlife of violence against indigenous and non-Western peoples over centuries. Fusco's prioritization of an "Other" history of intercultural performance (that is *lived* and not just represented by minoritarian subjects) and her insistence on histories of race and racism as central to our understanding of intercultural performance theory clearly foreshadow the critical race-theory inflected "interculturalism from below" of the Third Wave.

Pavis, Patrice. *Theatre at the Crossroads of Culture*. London and New York: Routledge, 1995.
This monograph gathers together essays written by Pavis between 1983 and 1988 as a response to what he describes as an unprecedented explosion of non-Western cultures on Western stages. He argues that current theoretical models are neither flexible enough nor specific enough to truly capture the nuance of what occurs through theatre events that can be described as intercultural, as these represent "the dialectic of exchanges of civilities between cultures."[20] His answer to what he perceives as a lack of precision in the wider field of theatre studies is to centralize his hourglass model (see above) as the unit of analysis which grounds his study as a whole. *Theatre at the Crossroads of Culture* also draws on postmodernism and poststructuralism, as well as assessing the ongoing status of drama as a genre and modality of performance.

Pavis, Patrice, ed. *Intercultural Performance Reader*. London: Routledge, 1996.
This seminal reader indexes the debates that multiplied during the First Wave of intercultural performance theory. Whereas earlier publications reflected the chaos of a field trying to come to terms with the expansiveness of intercultural performance theory as a tool, Pavis's reader influentially imposed coherent organization on prominent threads of inquiry within this subfield, which it notably divides by geographic areas from which the practices emerged. The reader consists of four parts: "Historical contexts," "Intercultural performance from the Western point of view," "Intercultural performance from another point of view," and "Interculturalism, all the same . . ." While tilted towards Western genealogies and perspectives (particularly an extended consideration of Peter Brooks' *Mahabharata* across several chapters), the third part ("Interculturalism from *another* point of view"; emphasis ours) details African, Indian, and Maori perspectives on interculturalism from practitioners and scholars living within those cultures. Pavis's organization seems to suggest that on the spectrum of intercultural performance, that which aspires to a universalist or transcendent point of view offers the most forward-looking and future-oriented perspective.

WAVE TWO: CONSOLIDATION

With postcolonial theory as a primary point of departure, this wave (which spans the early 2000s–2010) also centrally emphasizes a systematic study of globalization as a cultural and economic process that influences the practice of intercultural performance techniques. As such, many major works address the marketing and dissemination of intercultural theatre on global festival circuits, in addition to mapping the power dynamics of formal exchanges between individual artists and groups. Theatre anthropology and the study or exchange of ritual as intercultural performance are de-emphasized (although Barba's work remains ongoing) and celebratory studies of auteur intercultural theatre practitioners continue to be problematized, particularly through postcolonial theoretical lenses. The politics and lived experience of migration (particularly into nations located in the Western hemisphere) by diasporic communities begin to be discussed in relationship to intercultural performance, but performances generated within and between these communities in diaspora or from backgrounds of migration are not yet comprehensively addressed through the lens of intercultural performance theory.

Associated Keywords

Cross-cultural theatre: An umbrella term that Jacqueline Lo and Helen Gilbert use to designate what they see as related but distinct genres of theatre practice: postcolonial, multicultural, and intercultural theatres. While all cross-cultural theatre "entails a process of encounter and negotiation between different cultural sensibilities,"[21] Lo and Gilbert make a distinction between these forms according to crucial differences in political commitment as well as use of form across these three genres.

Globalization: The increased movement of people, money, information, enterprise, jobs, and so on. through deliberate regulation and/or restructuring of national borders/economies, and the cultural, social, economic, and political impacts of these flows on scales ranging from the individual to the transnational. Materialist analysis of the consequences of globalization using intercultural performance practices as a lens became a pronounced strand during the Second Wave of intercultural performance theory, particularly in the work of Jacqueline Lo, Helen Gilbert, Rustom Bharucha, and Una Chaudhuri.

Multiculturalism: Discussed mainly in relationship to its application as a state policy for the management of minority populations in Canada, the United Kingdom, and Australia by Bharucha, Gilbert, and Lo. It is not considered to have produced as coherent a body of artistic work across national contexts as intercultural theatre.

New interculturalism: Although later adopted by Ric Knowles, Royona Mitra, and Charlotte McIvor to describe the aspiration of Third Wave intercultural performance theory approaches, the term was first used by Una Chaudhuri in 2002 to articulate the aims of what we classify here as Second Wave interculturalism. New interculturalism, according to Chaudhuri, "ranges over many genres, subjects, agents, sites and approaches; and like its shadow, globalization, interculturalism challenges all its participants to redefine their cultural identities."[22]

Taxonomic theatre: Intercultural performance practices which emphasize the boundaries or differences *between* cultures. Julie Holledge and Joanne Tompkins trace this performance strategy's deployment through histories from colonialism's use of racial classification to justify expansionist rule and nineteenth- and twentieth-century world fairs and exhibitions, to a late twentieth century "intensification of the global arts markets and the proliferation of international festivals," which they argue reproduced "a vogue for extravaganzas with multicultural casts."[23]

Key Texts

Balme, Christopher. *Decolonizing the Stage: Theatrical Syncretism and Post-Colonial Drama*. **Oxford: Oxford University Press, 1999.**
Balme applies a semiotic reading of postcolonial drama to define what he terms "theatrical syncretism," a process and set of strategies to decolonize the stage "which involve the combination and amalgamation of indigenous performance forms within the framework of the Western notion of theatre."[24] While theatrical syncretism is similar to theatrical interculturalism in that it draws on and combines in the moment of performance multiple cultures and aesthetics, Balme differentiates theatrical syncretism from theatrical interculturalism based on its producers as well as its use of indigenous cultural texts. He focuses his study on text-based, English-language productions originating in former British colonies, including India, Africa, the Caribbean, Canada, Australia, and New Zealand, providing a wide-ranging analysis that is grounded in several key close readings.

Bharucha, Rustom. *The Politics of Cultural Practice: Thinking Through Theatre in An Age of Globalization.* **Middletown, CT: Wesleyan University Press, 2000.**
Bharucha builds on his earlier critiques of intercultural performance practice to more explicitly address the role of both the nation-state and the neoliberal market in intercultural exchange. He defines intercultural theatre as a "voluntarist intervention circumscribed by the agencies of the state and the market"[25] and focuses his analysis on globalization's impact on the creation and circulation of intercultural performance. Grounding his study in an Indian context, Bharucha examines how intercultural performance impacts and is impacted by factors of gender, class, caste, and religion, and extends his consideration of *intra*culturalism as "interventions [that] have the capacity to challenge the generalized tents of citizenship that ostensibly connect all social actors to the idea of 'the nation'" and might better enable "a critical examination of those differences relating to caste and economic inequality that are more often than not evaded in valorizations of 'regional culture.'"[26] In his investigation of these intracultural dynamics, Bharucha signals toward the more intersectional approach to intercultural performance studies that marks the Third Wave.

Chakravorti, Pallabi. "From Interculturalism to Historicism: Reflections on Classical Indian Dance." *Dance Research Journal* 32, no. 2 (2000–1): 108–19.
Chakravorti uses her case study of Indian classical dance to "uproot interculturalism from its location in Euro-American metropolitan centers and restore it to historical specificity within the context of the formation of the Indian nation-state and national identity."[27] She summarizes her subject position as that looking from the periphery to the center, and argues that power relations between the colonizer and colonized must be acknowledged as central to intercultural exchange. She traces the impact of Ruth St. Denis and Ted Shawn's imported works which exoticized India on reinvigorating interest in dance amongst the Indian colonial elite. Looking across the modern development of forms including Bharatanatyam and redevelopment of classical dance repertoires, Chakravorti argues that nostalgic conservativism which reinforces gender norms and limits suffuses modern and contemporary Indian dance as part of a wider nationalist project. She proposes looking to contemporary choreographers who challenge these aesthetic norms as alternative models of intercultural practice: Chandralekha, Kumudini Lakhia, and Manjushree Chaki-Sirkar.

Choudhury, Mita. *Interculturalism and Resistance in the London Theatre, 1660–1800: Identity, Performance, Empire.* **Lewisburg and London: Bucknell University Press, 2000.**
Choudhury's book is perhaps the first full-length intercultural performance historiography as she locates British eighteenth-century theatre as the artistic medium most able to capture "'the exoticism of multiculturalism' (through scenes, images, mise-en-scene) or the 'diversity of cultures' (through gestures, costumes, makeup) present within the culture at this time."[28] Locating her study at the "dawn of imperialism," Choudhury works to "isolate ways in which the London theatre as intercultural undercuts the native constructions of British culture and its ethnocentric

claims of indigeneity, supremacy and purity."[29] Choudhury does not simply focus on East–West binaries in her study, rather she documents the points of contestation regarding the British adaptation of Italian opera and the use of tunes from multiple European (and/or directly colonized subjects) in the quintessentially English opera, John Gay's *The Beggar's Opera*. She also considers the representation of the Ottoman Empire, and the staging of Walter Brimsley Sheridan's *The School for Scandal* in Calcutta among other case studies. Like Holledge and Tompkins (see below), Choudhury also focuses on gender and race as modalities shaping interculturalism and places these relations within deeply materialist theatre economies which enact tensions within the trade markets that they feed back into. Choudhury's detailed exposition of intercultural performance as a historical site of contestation and not just producing evidence of colonial power dynamics, even in London, the center of British Empire, ultimately provides an alternative genealogy of both intercultural theory and performance practice in the West that begins before the modernist period.

Holledge, Julie and Joanne Tompkins. *Women's Intercultural Performance*. London and New York: Routledge, 2000.
One of the first key studies of intercultural performance to dedicate itself to an intersectional approach, Holledge and Tompkins combine intercultural and feminist performance theories in a book that "investigates how culture, feminism, and theatre intersect with one another and with globalism, commodification, and consumption."[30] They define interculturalism as "the meeting in the moment of performance of two or more cultural tradition, a temporary fusing of styles and/or techniques and/ or cultures."[31] However, they reject the idea of a "singular definitive model of interculturalism" as "such a model would risk assuming too many similarities among cultures and theatrical practices."[32] Instead, they advocate for a site-specific approach to theorizing intercultural work on a case-by-case basis, paying particular attention to the shifting cultural and political specificities of each performance and its context. Holledge and Tompkins draw on a global range of performances—from global productions of *Antigone* and *A Doll's House*, to Korean and Warlpiri ritual in Australia, to butoh dance—in chapters focusing on themes of narrative, ritual, space, bodies, and markets. Like many other studies of the Second Wave, they are particularly attuned to the role of an increasingly globalized touring market on the creation and circulation of women's intercultural performance.

Chaudhuri, Una. "Beyond a 'Taxonomic Theater': Interculturalism After Postcolonialism and Globalization." *Theater* 32, no. 1 (Winter 2002): 33–47.
Chaudhuri's review essay formally announces the closure of her characterization of the First Wave of intercultural theatre—what she calls the taxonomic theatre (which she uses interchangeably with theatre anthropology following Julie Holledge and Joanne Tompkins. She reviews four publications (Rustom Bharucha's *The Politics of Cultural Practice*, Johannes Birringer's *Performance on the Edge: Transformations of Culture*, Julie Holledge and Joanne Tompkin's *Women's Intercultural Performance*, and Claire Sponsler and Xiaomei Chen's *East of West: Cross-Cultural Performance*), across which she identifies a proliferation of intercultural performance practices

which destabilizes the more centralized auteur-focused investigations of the First Wave. However, she also cautions regarding the danger inherent in this theoretical and practical expansion of intercultural performance theory if the circulation of bodies and performance practices as commodities is depoliticized. Dwelling particularly on Bharucha, Birringer, Holledge and Tompkin's approaches, Chaudhuri also argues that a critical theorization of the intercultural body in performance begins to emerge during this wave of scholarship which considers overtly individuals' experiences of unstable cultural identities within rooted political contexts. With Chaudhuri's explicit use of the term "new interculturalism" (see above) and her injunction for scholars to turn towards related theoretical formations (including "feminism, queer theory, and postmodernism"[33]), this short review essay most explicitly foreshadows the eventual consolidation of the Third Wave post-2010.

Lo, Jacqueline and Helen Gilbert. "Toward a Topography of Cross-Cultural Theatre Praxis." *Drama Review* **46, no. 3 (Fall 2002): 31–53.**
This conceptual survey article is one of the most pivotal in what we might term the Second Wave of intercultural performance theory in the early 2000s, which took increasing account of globalization's effect on cross-cultural flows and centrally problematized the nation-state as the arbitrating figure of cross-cultural exchange. Lo and Gilbert work to classify performance practices broadly constellated under cross-cultural theatre (see above).

They designate three broad categories within the cross-cultural: multicultural, postcolonial, and intercultural. For Lo and Gilbert, multicultural theatre broadly concerns race, ethnicity, diversity, and/or migration as expressed through the performers' or characters' identities or the themes of the performance. They differentiate between "small 'M' multicultural theatre" (which features "a racially mixed cast" and may "not draw attention to cultural differences among performers" or to "the tensions between the text and performance context") and "Big 'M' multicultural theatre" ("counterdiscursive," aiming to "promote cultural diversity, access to cultural expression, and participation in the symbolic space of the national narrative").[34] "Big 'M' multicultural theatre" is further subdivided still into ghetto theatre (intended for a minority community), migrant theatre (focused specifically on experiences of migration), and community theatre (non-professional, devoted to community activism and committed to democratic principles).

They describe postcolonial theatre as "a geopolitical category designating both a historical and discursive relationship to imperialism, whether that phenomenon is treated critically or ambivalently," an orientation which they argue is highly politicized.[35] This form can be either syncretic—mixing "performance elements of different cultures" in ways that "highlight rather than disguise shift in the meaning, function, and value of cultural fragments as they are moved from their traditional contexts"—or non-syncretic—which "uses imposed imperial genres/aesthetics or, less often, wholly indigenous ones, to voice postcolonial concerns,"[36] though they note that this distinction tends to be one of degree rather than two fully distinct categories.

In contrast to these two other genres of cross-cultural theatre, Lo and Gilbert define intercultural theatre as "a hybrid derived from an intentional encounter between cultures and performing traditions."[37] This broad definition covers a diverse range of performance practices that they further divide into three main subcategories: *transcultural* (work that, like Barba's explorations of pre-expressivity [see above] seeks to "transcend culture-specific codification in order to reach a more universal human condition"), *intracultural* (borrowing Bharucha's term for those "cultural encounters between and across specific communities and regions within the nation-state"), and *extracultural* ("theatre exchanges that are conducted along a West–East and North–South axis").[38]

Crucially, they review the critiques to Pavis's "hourglass" model of intercultural process and respond by proposing their own alternative theoretical model of intercultural exchange. Inspired by a childhood toy of a piece of elastic strung through the middle of a plastic disc that "moves in either direction along the string depending on whether the tension is generated by the left or the right hand," their spinning disc model represents intercultural exchange as a two-way (rather than unidirectional) flow.[39] For Lo and Gilbert, "Both partners are considered cultural sources while the target culture is positioned along the continuum between them."[40] Through this model, they connect theories of interculturalism with postcolonial discussions of hybridity and authenticity. While Lo and Gilbert note that intercultural theatre as a whole has tended to be dominated and over-determined by Western practitioners and theorists, they argue that intercultural theatre is better positioned to "explore and critique alternative forms of citizenship and identity across and beyond national boundaries, although the subjectivities they produce are not wholly free of state mediation."[41]

Watson, Ian and colleagues. *Negotiating Cultures: Eugenio Barba and the Intercultural Debate.* **Manchester and New York: Manchester University Press, 2002.**

This collection addresses multiple dimensions of Eugenio Barba's work from the perspective of colleagues he has worked with over decades from across the world, and also includes Barba's own reflections on the progression of his work. It is divided into three sections which address ongoing work at ISTA (International School of Theatre Anthropology), Barba's focus on performance barter as a tool of cultural exchange, and Barba's network of links in Latin America as they relate to this concept of the Third Theatre. Editor Watson sets out to distinguish between multiple strands within Barba's work: interculturalism, multiculturalism, transculturalism and cultural pluralism. Watson understands interculturalism to be about the mixing and merging of cultures within performance, multiculturalism to encompass the comparison of culturally unique performance practices (such as through Barba's method of lecture-demonstration through ISTA), transculturalism as referring to the pre-expressive states common across cultures and cultural pluralism as that which "includes the possibility of various cultural transactions"[42] across the afore-mentioned range. This collection brings the reader in to ISTA's meetings and working practices over a series of decades, through Watson's and other's first-hand accounts of the insights and tensions experienced through meetings and exchanges. The collection both celebrates and problematizes Barba and ISTA's faith in performance barter as creating an equal playing and learning ground.

Gilbert, Helen and Jacqueline Lo. *Performance and Cosmopolitics: Cross-Cultural Transactions in Australasia*. Houndsmills: Palgrave Macmillan, 2007.

While Gilbert and Lo's book employs cosmopolitanism as its primary theoretical keyword, its thematic concerns and historiographical/methodological approach share much in common with Third Wave intercultural performance theory. They position their study of Australasian performance from the 1830s to the present as an engagement with the potential of "new cosmopolitanism" which seeks to resignify this idea as "a more worldly and less elitist concept" which would include "'cosmopolitans from below'-defined along class and racial lines and encompassing refugees, migrants, and itinerant workers" as well as the "new meritocratic ruling class of transnationals."[43] They press on thin conceptions of cosmopolitanism which flatten individuals' experience across difference by turning to theatre's "material aspects" as a social and economic practice which might "help us apprehend the contingencies of cosmopolitanism as a form of cross-cultural *praxis* as well as a discourse about cross-cultural engagement."[44] This book focuses strongly on themes of migration, displacement and minority ethnic subjects, and places their contemporary Australasian representation within a historical trajectory. They also deeply investigate the impact of the global performing arts markets and the particular pressures of the Australasian region on how intercultural performance forms are received and utilized within and across this cultural landscape.

Tian, Min. *The Poetics of Difference and Displacement: Twentieth Century Chinese-Western Intercultural Theatre*. Hong Kong: University of Hong Kong Press, 2008.

Tian argues powerfully that "intercultural theatre" is a "process of displacement and re-placement of culturally specified and differentiated theatrical forces, rejecting any universalist and essentialist presumptions."[45] For Tian, the incorporation of foreign theatrical forms will inevitably distort these forms' original intentions because they are being reappropriated for use in a new cultural context in which spectators do not share the same semiotic vocabulary or political and social histories. He summarizes this recurring relationship as a dialetic between the Self and Other where "[d]isplacements of the Other by the Self are guided by Self's desires and needs originated within the Self's own specific cultural as well as theatrical context."[46] However, the study outlines that this repetitive process of displacement is not merely limited to Western misrepresentation of Eastern theatrical forms, but rather Tian also details for example how twentieth century Chinese theatre also reworked Western tenets of theatrical realism when adapting these conventions for their own purposes. He also designates four major modes of displacement: displacement by interpretation, displacement by appropriation, displacement by parody, and displacement by translation. The first part of the book offers an in-depth analysis of Mei Lanfang's use by key Western modernist theatrical figures including Bertolt Brecht, Vsevolod Meyerhold, Sergei Eisenstein, Gordon Craig and Peter Sellers. The second part of the book examines twentieth-century Chinese theatre's interpellation of Western realism and avant-garde theatrical techniques (particularly the work of Henrik Ibsen and Konstantin Stanislavski) as well as Chinese adaptations of Greek theatre.

Zarrilli, Phillip. *Psychophysical Acting: An Intercultural Approach after Stanislavski*. New York: Routledge, 2009.

Zarrilli elaborates on Konstantin Stanislavski's key concept of the "psycho-physical" through using his own practice of Asian martial arts and yoga to inform a deeper investigation of the relationship between body and mind in performance, a state he terms "bodymind." He terms his exploration "self-consciously intercultural," drawing directly upon "non-Western philosophies and practices in order to freshly (re)consider a psychophysical approach to acting, East and West."[47] This book consolidates decades of Zarrilli's practice-as-research and vanguard ethnographic approaches to the study and practice of actor training, offering a rigorous counter-model and genealogy for how to understand and practice Stanislavski's teachings according to a dialogical intercultural model based on his own experiences.

Pavis, Patrice. "Intercultural Theatre Today." *Forum Modernes Theatre* 25, no. 1 (2010): 5–15.

Influential critic Pavis's 2010 revisiting of this controversial term declares interculturalism now "a very common thing."[48] He considers the term "intercultural" as not only a matter of aesthetic form or exchange, but also a description of social and political realities—for example, he highlights its cachet as an alternative to multiculturalism's segregating tendencies. In general, he highlights what he perceives to be the diminishing influence of the nation state as a frame of reference despite the need to remain attentive to "the political and economic analysis of the transformations created by globalization"[49] and its implications for theatre practices. He also suggests a move from intercultural "theatre" to "performance" in order to capture the more capacious range of forms that he argues now proliferate.[50] He concludes that "the reflexion on globalization and its impact on theatre" have "allowed us to modify our vision of intercultural performance" which he feels was previously "too obsessed with the legitimacy of representing another culture."[51] Instead, Pavis briefly profiles the recent work of artists including Michael Vinaver, Oriza Hirata, Guillermo Gomez-Peña, and Akram Khan, as well as the ongoing work of familiar figures including Peter Brooks, Robert Wilson, and Robert Le Page. Pavis demonstrates how these theatremakers' staging of characters'/performers' identities and the semiotics of their performance spectacles consistently problematize cultural origins and heritage as a sign of increasingly globalized conditions of living.

WAVE THREE: "OTHER" INTERCULTURALISM(S)

Wave Three is characterized by a proliferation of methodologies and theoretical approaches to the study of intercultural performance with an emphasis on minority-led and/or Asian and/or non-Western artists, projects, events, and experiences, and an even more pronounced focus on intercultural processes including but not limited to actor-training and rehearsal processes. In contrast to early interculturalism which emphasized interplay between source and target cultures, Wave Three studies approach interculturalism as fluid, ephemeral, multi-nodal, and minoritarian. If Wave One interculturalism was catalyzed by Western modernism's lingering influences and Wave Two was the growing critique of these influences' traces, then

Wave Three might be seen as centered on practices that repurpose, replace, redirect, or ignore these traces entirely. Many of the major works here also build on the Second Wave's interest in the impact of globalization on conceptions of cultural exchange. As such, they shift their focus to projects and histories arising from migrant and/or minoritarian practices and practitioners, often in a collaborative and community-based interculturalism-from-below (see below), privileging these over the top-down (primarily white, male, and Western) auteur projects that had so preoccupied the previous waves of study. The Third Wave also sees a rise in intersectional and critical race studies-based analysis that interrogates the impact of multiple identity markers on both the creation and reception of intercultural work.

Associated Keywords

Acoustic interculturalism: Marcus Tan's term for the sonic aspect of intercultural performance. Tan advocates that an analysis of a production's "acoustic texts" in addition to its visual semiotics allows for a fuller understanding of how intercultural exchange operates in the moment of performance.

Asian interculturalism: Models of intercultural theatremaking and practice that emerge from within diverse Asian performance cultures. While in many cases responding to Western genealogies of intercultural theatre practice, scholars such as Min Tian, Marcus Tan, Daphne P. Lei, and Alvin Eng Hui Lim complicate these flows of influence and conclusively demonstrate the impact of these interchanges on both cultural partners.

Hegemonic Intercultural Theatre (HIT): Daphne P. Lei's succinct term which describes elite practices of intercultural theatremaking that are unbalanced in their power dynamics between collaborators, typically led by auteur directors, spectacular in scale, and driven by the West or Western sources of influence and funding.

Interculturalism-from-below: The antonym of HIT, this form of interculturalism resists the hierarchical, Western-dominated, and auteur-driven interculturalism that Lei describes. Rather, interculturalism-from-below is defined by Ric Knowles as marked by collaborative, multiple, and horizontal processes, typically driven by minoritarian practitioners and communities.

Intercultural performative: The Third Wave features an increased emphasis on intercultural encounters through performance as potentially generative or reflective of ongoing processes of identity formation when experienced by individuals in relationship to social, cultural, and political pressures which frame these encounters. Leo Cabranes-Grant puts forward the idea that intercultural performance might be best understood as an "engine of emergence"[52] which manufactures identities rather than confirming them, while Knowles, Royona Mitra, and Charlotte McIvor reflect on how performance captures the identity formation processes of minority ethnic subjects, particularly those working within urban contexts in collaboration with other minorities.

Intersectional interculturalism: Studies of intercultural performance that draw on critical race and intersectional feminist approaches to map how multiple identity factors such as race, gender, sexuality, class, religion, and disability impact the expression and reception of intercultural performance, particularly for migrant and/ or minority ethnic subjects.[53]

Interweaving: Erika Fischer-Lichte's proposed alternative term for the phrase "interculturalism" to describe and define cross-cultural performance practices in an attempt to move beyond often binary discussions of postcolonialism. Fischer-Lichte employs the visual metaphor of weaving, in which disparate threads (cultures) are woven into a cloth (performance) that is both constitutive of the individual threads and yet wholly original and distinct in and of itself.

New interculturalism: Ric Knowles reinvigorates this term introduced by Chaudhuri as a specific description of intercultural theatre practices led by minoritarian practitioners which reveal cultural identities as processes in formation influenced by individual and group encounters with difference in their lived environment.

Performance ecology: Knowles's metaphor to describe the social and material conditions and contexts of interculturalism-from-below in increasingly heterogeneous city spaces. Performance ecologies "can be understood to consist of a shifting and unstable constellation of human and nonhuman actors and factors operating interdependently to constitute an ecosystem."[54] As such, intercultural performances (or individual practitioners or companies) cannot be understood in isolation from one another whether in a local urban context (such as in Knowles's focus on Toronto) or within global networks of contemporary and historical performance practices.

Rhizomatic interculturalism: Gilles Deleuze and Felix Guattari's concept of the rhizome as a model for history centrally influences the Third Wave of intercultural performance theory, particularly through the work of Knowles and Cabranes-Grant. For Deleuze and Guattari, the rhizome resists a teleological and/or hierarchical organization of historical knowledge instead seeking "ceaselessly established connections between semiotic chains, organizations of power, and circumstances relative to the arts, sciences, and social struggles."[55] The rhizome is ultimately characterized by connection, multiplicity, heterogeneity and rupture. A turn towards rhizomatic interculturalism refuses the linear and Western-centric genealogy of intercultural performance theory and practice (again enacted by this annotated bibliography) and instead pushes for the continued mapping of alternative genealogies and heretofore unconsidered sites of investigation. This companion's use of waves as organizing metaphor picks up on rhizomatic interculturalism quite directly. Our waves might be understood as the experience of travel across and between rhizomes over time in the ongoing evolution of intercultural performance practice and theory. Like Knowles and Cabranes-Grant, we call for the ongoing revelation of new branches of the intercultural rhizome through searching cross-temporally and cross-spatially (below as well as above) while advocating that we bring our knowledge from previous waves to bear on these new studies and destabilize our understanding of the earlier waves.

Social interculturalism: Charlotte McIvor uses this term to describe the active use of interculturalism as a named alternative to multiculturalism within state and supranational policy contexts including Canada and the European Union. Social interculturalism connotes a dynamic reformation of identity that supposedly happens when individuals from different cultures meet and interact within civil society across a spectrum of encounters ranging from the everyday to arts and performance practices. In comparison to social interculturalism, multiculturalism carries the negative associations of policies that were seen to encourage ghettoization and maintained difference through a "separate but equal" approach to tolerance and diversity. When used within supranational and national contexts, social interculturalism therefore has a crucially performative dimension which recognizes an individual's ongoing formation of identity across a constellation of factors not only related to race and ethnicity but also including gender, sexuality, religion, and class, and in theory, social interculturalism addresses both majority and minority ethnic groups. However, as theorized by McIvor, this policy usage and its translation into funding streams and projects often erases or minimizes structural differences between minority and majority ethnic groups. Ultimately, social interculturalism can be understood as the transformation of Knowles' new interculturalism into supranational and state policy with far-reaching implications not only for the arts, but also for contemporary civil societies more broadly.

Key Texts

Knowles, Ric. *Theatre & Interculturalism*. Houndsmills: Palgrave Macmillan, 2010.
Ric Knowles' 2010 publication most clearly signals the beginning of the Third Wave of intercultural performance theory. Despite being intended as a survey, he also uses the book to make a powerful argument for the inauguration of a new kind of intercultural performance theory—that driven from below and informed by the practices of minoritarian communities working together across difference by examining the work of Toronto-based companies including the Modern Times Stage Company, Red Sky Performance, the Turtle Gals Performance Ensemble, and Native Earth Performing Arts among others. Knowles also situates intercultural performance theory's trajectory in the context of the development of a number of related critical fields including performance studies, critical multiculturalism studies, critical race theory, whiteness studies, diaspora studies, and critical cosmopolitanisms. Knowles concludes the book with a call for "migrant, diasporic and Indigenous peoples of the world" to gain more control over "funding, spaces, and processes of production."[56]

Farfan, Penny and Ric Knowles. "Special Issue on Rethinking Intercultural Performance." *Theatre Journal* 63, no. 4 (December 2011).
This crucial special issue records for the first time the breadth of the new wave of intercultural performance theory that is emerging post-2010. Some of this wave's most influential articles appear in this issue including Daphne P. Lei's treatment of

Robert Wilson in Taiwan through which she coins the term Hegemonic Intercultural Theatre (HIT) (see above). Also included is Leo Cabranes-Grant's work on networks of performance in colonial Mexico, Diana Looser's analysis of pre-colonial Pacific Island theatre, Katarzyna Jakubiak's examination of 1960s Polish blackface productions of Lorraine Hansberry's *A Raisin in the Sun,* and two articles on performance in the Phillipines: William Peterson's consideration of transgender (bakla) performance and transnationalism (particularly Asian interculturalism) in *The Amazing Show* and Lorenzo Perillo's analysis of the transnational reception of the Cebu Provincial Detention and Rehabilitation Centre's viral adaptation of Michael Jackson's *Thriller* video featuring prisoners. In the issue's conclusion the editors suggest that Lei's term HIT be used to apply to a specific form of intercultural theatre and they ultimately advocate a turn toward "intercultural performance" to designate the wide range of intercultural practices increasingly being assessed in the Third Wave—a charge that this companion takes up actively.

Li, Ruru and Jonathan Pitches. "The End of the Hour-Glass: Alternative Conceptions of Intercultural Exchange between European and Chinese Operatic Forms." *Studies in Theatre and Performance* 32, no. 2 (2012): 121–37.
This article places actor-training and collaborative processes at the center of evolving models of intercultural performance analysis. Li and Pitches' case study focuses on an "experimental intercultural performance laboratory investigating traditions of opera and song-dance theatre," including "European traditions of opera on the one hand and Chinese indigenous forms of song-dance theatre, including *jingju* or Beijing Opera, and *lüju.*"[57] This study was carried out over two years (2008–10) as part of a "large EU-supported project entitled Operatic Encounters, Common Voices (OPENCOV)."[58] Li and Pitches utilize ethnographic and practice-as-research methodologies to critique once more Patrice Pavis's seminal hourglass model of intercultural exchange, using the experience of their work with these performers to call for "a more individualistic conception of intercultural exchange."[59] They stress the need for artists to be "placed centrally and cognizance . . . taken of the complexity of their own cultural backgrounds and trainings, before any intercultural exchange can occur,"[60] a theoretical and methodological turn echoed in the recent work of Royona Mitra, Phillip Zarrilli, and others. They also stress the need for planning for "orientation and awareness-raising of different methodological in influences' in ensembles of diverse collaborators,"[61] also cautioning practitioners that moments of "genuine connection" between individuals or the group may be "fleeting and will be read differently by different audiences," another strong steer towards a necessary polyvocality that challenges Pavis's binary model of intercultural exchange. Instead, they ultimately suggest, any project which utilizes intercultural models of exchange must carefully resist "any linear models of communication . . . instead negotiating the layers of cultural complexity uniquely each time."[62]

Tan, Marcus Cheng Chye. *Acoustic Interculturalism: Listening to Performance.* Houndsmills: Palgrave Macmillan, 2012.
Tan's book makes two major interventions in the field of intercultural performance theory. First, he applies paradigms of intercultural performance theory to the analysis

of sound and music within works of intercultural theatre, arguing that "acoustic texts disclose" additional layers of "cultural contestations and conversations occurring within each performance" (198). Second, he anchors his study as part of what he identifies as a burgeoning field of "Asian interculturalisms,"[63] made visible by the work of directors such as Singapore's Ong Keng Sen, Taiwan's Wu Hsing-Kuo, Japan's Yukio Ninagawa, and China's Lin Zhaohua. Tan ultimately suggests that turning to the complex textures of sound onstage (whether through music and/or language) opens up more layered possibilities for flow and reinvention within intercultural performance, particularly those works created by the cohort of Asian intercultural directors he surveys.

Fischer-Lichte, Erika, Torsten Jost, and Saskya Iris Jain, eds. *The Politics of Interweaving Performance Cultures: Beyond Postcolonialism.* **New York: Routledge, 2014.**

This edited collection brings together many of the central voices of the Second Wave of intercultural theory, including Christopher Balme, Rustom Bharucha, Helen Gilbert, and Jacqueline Lo. Along with the volume's other contributors, they present a truly global range of case studies that engage with the concept of "interweaving" performance cultures, a rhetorical shift advocated by Erika Fischer-Lichte. Fischer-Lichte uses her introduction to propose "interweaving" over "intercultural" as the key term to define and describe cross-cultural performance practices. Tracing the debates of First and Second Wave interculturalism, she sees that term as constrained by assumptions of ownership, universalism, and textual authority. Ultimately, she argues that the concept of "intercultural theatre" is inherently contradictory as it "proclaims equality between the theatrical traditions of all cultures . . . and denies all former hierarchies established by colonialism and cultural imperialism" while at the same time "it hails culture as a fixed, stable, and homogeneous entity."[64] Instead, she proposes the metaphor of "interweaving," where "[m]any strands are plied into a thread; many such threads are then woven into a piece of cloth, which thus consists of diverse strands and threads . . . without necessarily remaining recognizable individually."[65] For Fischer-Lichte, interweaving "captures far more accurately culture's inherent processual nature with its continuous production of new differences," with these differences "seen within an 'as well as' logic, that is, the logic of interconnectedness, as suggested by the metaphor of threads woven into cloth."[66] Interweaving, then, allows for a move beyond "the pervasive binary concepts of Self versus Other, East versus West, North versus South, own versus foreign and the aesthetic (i.e. intercultural performance) versus the political and ethical (i.e. postcolonial theory)."[67] Fischer-Lichte's "interweaving" is both evocative and utopic, and pushes toward the more nuanced, anti-hierarchical, and anti-essentialist impulses of Third Wave intercultural performance practice. However, it is worth noting that even many of the contributors themselves continue to use the term "intercultural" in their engagement with Fischer-Lichte's "interweaving"—signaling the enduring legacy (and productive loadedness) of interculturalism as a key term in these debates.

Kwan, SanSan. "Even as We Keep Trying: An Ethics of Interculturalism in Jérôme Bel's *Pichet Klunchun and Myself." Theatre Survey* 55, no. 1 (2014): 186–9.

Kwan examines failure as a potential ethics within intercultural collaborations by looking at a work created by French avant-garde choreographer Jerome Bel with Thai dancer-choreographer Pichet Klunchun. Bel's resulting work *Pichet Klunchun and Myself* stages a conversation between the two with no choreography and minimal demonstration of technique by either dancer. Kwan places this performance event within an intercultural genealogy of dance practice, citing figures such as Ruth St. Denis, Martha Graham, Merce Cunningham, and Deborah Hay who have also drawn on Eastern aesthetics similarly to more oft-cited HIT figures discussed throughout this companion. Kwan asks whether contemporary intercultural performance might provide "instances of neighbourliness, of careful but productive negotiation across the unevenness of difference,"[68] such as that staged by *Pichet Klunchun and Myself* which "lays bare the miscomprehensions that occur in the encounter"[69] between the two dancers.

Mitra, Royona. *Akram Khan: Dancing New Interculturalism*. Houndsmills: Palgrave Macmillan, 2015.
Mitra draws on postcolonial theory, critical race studies, and dance studies to expand theories of interculturalism as both an aesthetic and a sociopolitical practice. Reading the work of second-generation British-Bangladeshi dancer and choreographer Akram Khan, Mitra develops an understanding of new interculturalism as an embodied and minoritarian practice that moves beyond the "us-them" hierarchies of previous waves. She defines Khan's new interculturalism as "not an intellectual and formulaic exercise but an embodied reality and a political and philosophical stance" that results in "an inherently non-white reality, critique and aesthetic."[70] In his work, Khan draws on his training in multiple movement vocabularies that include South Asian kathak dance as well as "an eclectic palette ranging from classical ballet, Graham, Cunningham, Alexander, release-based technique and contact improvisation, to physical theatre."[71] Mitra compares Khan's interculturalism to that of the HIT model (see above), whose directors tend to favor epic or canonical texts, privilege the theatrical literacy of an imagined Western target audience, and often perpetuate the racial othering of non-white performers or cultures. In contrast, Khan chooses to work with personal stories, eschews the text for "an open-ended corporeal aesthetic that is ambivalent and ephemeral and therefore impossible to fix in its significations,"[72] unapologetically deploys dramaturgical codes and stage elements foreign to Western audiences, and "deploys othering as an aestheticisation process and a conscious dramaturgical strategy through which he and his audience encounter multiple versions of his self."[73] Mitra's study signals the growing interest in intersectional interculturalism, and the Third Wave's focus on minority ethnic and migrant intercultural practice.

Cabranes-Grant, Leo. *From Scenarios to Networks: Performing the Intercultural in Colonial Mexico*. Evanston, IL: Northwestern University Press, 2016.
Cabranes-Grant's study of mid-sixteenth to seventeenth-century Mexican colonial performance engages a "materialist critique with a poesies of emergence"[74] in order to analyze the interplay of individuals, objects, and their environments across this period. Working very closely with Bruno Latour's actor-network theory, he focuses

on the labor of interculturalism as a process of becoming which can be traced across networks of meaning and their interrelationship over time. He also aims to challenge dominant discourses of *mestizaje* within Latin American cultural and literary studies as the primary framework through which to understand hybridity, suggesting his conceptualization of interculturalism as an alternative framework. Cabranes-Grant's objects of analysis include masquerades, pageants, the display of saintly relics, religious festivals, and Sor Juana Ines de la Cruz's 1689 Corpus Christi play, *El divino Narciso* (The Divine Narcissus). He insists on a performance-focused methodology even though he works with archival fragments, proposing that performance is "the suspension bridge that links being to becoming."[75] Cabranes-Grant ultimately offers a mode of intercultural performance analysis that further decentralizes semiotics in favor of processual and archival-focused study.

McIvor, Charlotte. *Migration and Performance in Contemporary Ireland: Towards a New Interculturalism*. London: Palgrave Macmillan, 2016.

McIvor analyzes the use of "interculturalism" as a keyword of both social policy *and* performance practice following the unprecedented changes in racial and ethnic demographics in the Republic of Ireland post-1990s after the "Celtic Tiger" economic boom. Falling in line with wider post-2000s trends in the European Union, Ireland's use of interculturalism over multiculturalism places more emphasis on the individual than the group in order to communicate that *all* cultural identities, and not just those of minority ethnic groups, are continuously in flux. She examines performance practices ranging from the professional to the community-led in order to capture how aesthetic experiences set up as intercultural (in terms of participants or forms used) are meant to catalyze the social processes of interculturalism from the grassroots. She employs ethnographic methodologies as well as more traditional performance and theoretical analysis in order to capture Irish intercultural policy's translation into lived experience for a range of artists and arts participants from both majority and minority ethnic backgrounds. McIvor's focus on Irish-based minority ethnic arts practices and artists ultimately foregrounds the politics of race, ethnicity, and migration in Ireland and Europe today as key contexts for analyzing interculturalism's contemporary valences in both social and aesthetic spheres of influence, further problematizing nation-to-nation contact as the paradigm of analysis for intercultural performance theory.

Tan, Marcus Cheng Chye. "Elephant Head on White Body: Reflexive Interculturalism in *Ganesh Versus the Third Reich*." *Contemporary Theatre Review* 26, no. 4 (2016): 416–28.

Tan coins the term "reflexive interculturalism" through his engagement with Australian Back to Back Theatre's *Ganesh Versus the Third Reich* which he argues is "acutely conscious of its (mis)representation of historical, cultural and ethnic Otherness even as it seeks to interrogate and deconstruct these processes."[76] Tan proposes that this performance represents an alternative model to Daphne P. Lei's HIT through the inclusion of performers with intellectual disabilities and the performance's auto-reflexive metatheatricality, which continually refers back to the audience rather than to the intercultural spectacles being enacted and deconstructed onstage. As Tan argues, "seeing" turns into "a self-conscious act."[77] He also identifies the performance's rejection of an auteur led intercultural theatre through its onstage challenges to the actual "non-disabled, intellectually and physically abled white" male director Bruce Gladwin with an ending that "seems to iterate that collaboration and cooperation, traits of a democratic creative process, are necessary in the act of producing intercultural works or any theatrical piece."[78] Tan argues that this production moves beyond reiterating HIT models even while critiquing them because it compels audience members to assume an "auto-reflexive gaze as it dramaturgically distorts and dismantles the frames of theatricality, meta-theatricality, acting, 'not-acting,' performance and 'real-life.'"[79] This article represents an important intervention in bringing the representation of dis/ability into intersectional intercultural performance theory.

Zarrilli, Phillip, T. Sasitharan, and Anuradha Kapur, eds. "Special Issue on 'Intercultural' Acting Training and Actor/Performer Training." *Theatre, Dance and Performance Training* 7, no. 3 (2016).
This special issue addresses the necessity to consider the impact of globalization, migration and an imbalance in Western-centric curriculums in actor training in a global context. The editors allege that "[c]ontrary to the between-ness of our global realities, the vast majority of professional/conservatory-based training programmes in Europe, the UK, US, and Australia, with a few exceptions have not yet embraced these multi-, inter-, intra-cultural realities in their structure or pedagogical practice."[80] Like Li and Pitches, they push for a focus on the "micro-level of the studio"[81] in order to understand more dynamically how an individual's encounters with Western and/or non-Western training methods are negotiated from the point of view of lived experience and cultural habitus. Zarrilli et al.'s project is to understand how individual practitioners and collectives confront and reshape the genealogies of performance training that they undertake. The contributors to this issue address training undertaken at Singapore's Intercultural Theatre Institute (Giorgia Ciampi); how Japanese post-war experiences impact subjectivity within Tadashi Suzuki's work and training practices (Glenn Odom); the use of butoh methods by Royal Shakespeare company performers (Tanya Calamoneri); Taiwanese jingju actor Wu Hsing-Kuo's experience working with the Cloud Gate dance company to perform *Macbeth* (Jasmine Yu-Hsing Chen); socio-cultural tensions around actor training in South Africa (David Peimer); a reflection on the relationship between Korean and Buddhist cultural concepts they drew on while performing in an intercultural production of Jean Genet's *Playing the Maids* (Sunhee Kim and Jeungsook Yoo); a critique of hidden cultural norms within voice training that must be deconstructed interculturally (Tara McAllister Biel and Electa Behrens); and how leading practitioners in Indonesian "new theatre" such as Arafin C. Noer and Putu Wijaya confront and reshape Western theatrical genealogies (Kathy Foley). This special issue does rehearse many similar themes, methodologies and relational models (East–West, West–East) of the First and Second Waves, particularly in terms of the encounters between forms described. However, Zarrilli et al.'s call to work outwards from the individual performers's dynamic experiences to change wider structural systems of intelligibility and esteem

within actor training processes does aim to redefine the intercultural as a shared value of constant scrutiny within training and rehearsal rooms. This impulse echoes the work of Knowles and Mitra within the Third Wave.

Knowles, Ric. *Performing the Intercultural City*. Ann Arbor: University of Michigan Press, 2018.
Through a sustained analysis of the diverse theatre scene of Toronto, Knowles develops his theories of new interculturalism, interculturalism-from-below, and performance ecology that he introduced in *Theatre & Interculturalism*. He investigates how Canada's official multicultural policies—particularly as interpreted within state funding structures for the arts—have impacted how intercultural work is made, as well as the various and oftentimes resistant dramaturgical models of interculturalism employed in that making. He chooses as his central case studies a dozen established theatre companies and artists that "have contributed significantly to the emergence, over the past few decades, of a vibrant, interdependent ecology of intercultural performance that crosses cultures and performance disciplines, challenges the hegemony of whiteness on the city's stages, and begins to reflect the cultural differences that are visible and audible on the city's streets and streetcars."[82] Through these case studies, Knowles explores the intercultural practices of strategic reappropriation, disaporic transnationalism and trans-indigeneity, and urban interculturalism (what Knowles compares to Bharucha's "grassroots theatrical *intra*culturalism"). Like other Third Wave scholars such as Leo Cabranese-Grant, Charlotte McIvor, and Royona Mitra, Knowles is not purely concerned with aesthetics but is equally interested in an intersection querying of "how individual gendered, raced, and classed subjectivities and community identities within the contemporary multicultural city are not just reflected or given voice but are *constituted* through performance."[83] Furthermore, Knowles' attempts an intercultural research methodology throughout by drawing on both Western and Indigenous frameworks as part of a larger ethics of study.

McIvor, Charlotte and Jason King, eds. *Interculturalism and Performance Now: New Directions?* London: Palgrave Macmillan, 2019.
This edited collection brings together both established and emerging voices in the Third Wave of intercultural studies and indexes new interculturalism as a diverse set of methodologies. There are sections dedicated to new interculturalism as methodology (including the use of digital humanities to trace the routes of touring and transmission of intercultural performance); reconsiderations of central figures and themes of the First and Second Waves of interculturalism including Ariane Mnouchkine, (post-)colonialism, and modernist genealogies; intersectional interculturalism; and migrant interculturalisms. The case studies remain primarily focused on Western contexts such as the US, Canada, Australia, the UK, and European nations, with the exception of Cabranes-Grant's colonial Mexico, Alvin Eng Hui Lim's Asian Shakespeares, and Yvette Hutchinson's South African case studies, signaling the ongoing need to further engage collaborators from the Global South in this discourse, particularly as the terms of the debate and use of intercultural methodologies have shifted so radically in the Third Wave.

NOTES

1. See Leo Cabranes-Grant and Diana Looser, "A Piece 'More Curious Than All the Rest': Re-Encountering Pre-Colonial Pacific Island Theatre, 1769–1855," *Theatre Journal* 63, no. 4 (December 2011): 521–40.

2. For more on the impact of Mei Lanfang on Western theatrical thought, see Mei Lanfang, "Befriending Eisenstein on My First Trip to the Soviet Union," *Opera Quarterly*, 26, no. 2–3 (Spring–Summer 2010): 426–34; Min Tian, "Gordon Craig, Mei Lanfang and the Chinese Theatre," *Theatre Research International* 32, no. 2 (2007): 161–77; Min Tian, "Meyerhold Meets Mei Lanfang: Staging the Grotesque and the Beautiful," *Comparative Drama* 33, no. 2 (Summer 1999): 234–69; Min Tian, "'Alienation-Effect' for Whom? Brecht's (Mis)interpretation of the Classical Chinese Theatre," *Asian Theatre Journal* 14, no. 2 (Fall 1997): 200–22; and Ronnie Bai, "Dances with Mei Lanfang: Brecht and the Alienation Effect," *Comparative Drama* 32, no. 2 (Fall 1998): 389–433.

3. For a comprehensive analysis of the impact of the Balinese performance on Artaud's writings, see Nicola Savarese, "1931: Antonin Artaud Sees Balinese Theatre at the Paris Colonial Exposition," *TDR* 45, no. 3 (Autumn, 2001): 51–77.

4. Edward Said, *Orientalism* (New York: Pantheon Books, 1978), 3.

5. V. E. Meyerhold, *Meyerhold on Theatre*, trans. and ed. Edward Braun (New York: Hill and Wang, 1969), 100.

6. Artaud, *Theatre and its Double*, 91.

7. Bharucha, *The Politics of Cultural Practice*, 6.

8. Richard Schechner, "Intercultural Themes," in Bonnie Marranca and Gautam Dasgupta (eds.), *Interculturalism & Performance: Writings from PAJ* (New York: PAJ Publications, 1991), 312.

9. Barba and Savarese, *The Secret Art of the Performer*, 187–8.

10. For a full exposition of this theory, see Victor Turner, "Social Dramas and Stories about Them," *Critical Inquiry* 7, no. 1 (Autumn 1980): 141–68.

11. Barba and Savarese, *The Secret Art of the Performer*, 1991, 8.

12. Barba, *The Paper Canoe*, 38.

13. Barba, *The Paper Canoe*, 43.

14. Eugenio Barba, *Theatre: Solitude, Craft, Revolt* (Aberystwyth: Black Mountain Press, 1999), 169–70.

15. Erika Fischer-Lichte, "Theatre Own and Foreign, The Intercultural Trend in Contemporary Theatre," Erika Fischer-Lichte, Josephine Riley, and Michael Gissenwehrer (eds.), in *The Dramatic Touch of Difference: Theatre, Own and Foreign*, (Tübingen: Gunter Narr Verlag, 1990), 12.

16. Schechner and Appel list collaborators as Lita Osmundsen (Wenner-Gren Foundation), Richard Lanier (then director of the Asian Cultural Council), Martha Coigney (then president of the International Theatre Institute), Jack Morrison (then Executive Director of the American Theatre Association), Phillip Zarrilli (then professor of theatre at the University of Wisconsin, Madison), and themselves.

17. Barba, *The Paper Canoe*, 41.

18. Barba, *The Paper Canoe*, 15.

19. Barba, *The Paper Canoe*, 1.

20. Pavis, *Theatre at the Crossroads of Culture*, 2.

21. Lo and Gilbert, "Toward a Topography of Cross-Cultural Theatre Praxis," 31.

22. Chaudhuri, "Beyond a 'Taxonomic Theater'," 34.

23. Holledge and Tompkins, *Women's Intercultural Performance*, 114.

24. Balme, *Decolonizing the Stage*, 1.

25. Bharucha, *Theatre and the World*, 33.

26. Bharucha, *Theatre and the World*, 9.

27. Chakravorti, "From Interculturalism to Historicism," 108.

28. Choudhury, *Interculturalism and Resistance in the London Theatre, 1660–1800*, 18

29. Choudhury, *Interculturalism and Resistance in the London Theatre, 1660–1800*, 20.

30. Holledge and Tompkins, *Women's Intercultural Performance*, 17.

31. Holledge and Tompkins, *Women's Intercultural Performance*, 7.

32. Holledge and Tompkins, *Women's Intercultural Performance*, 3.

33. Chaudhuri, "Beyond a 'Taxonomic Theater'," 35.

34. Lo and Gilbert, "Toward a Topography of Cross-Cultural Theatre Praxis," 34.

35. Lo and Gilbert, "Toward a Topography of Cross-Cultural Theatre Praxis," 35.

36. Lo and Gilbert, "Toward a Topography of Cross-Cultural Theatre Praxis," 36.

37. Lo and Gilbert, "Toward a Topography of Cross-Cultural Theatre Praxis," 36.

38. Lo and Gilbert, "Toward a Topography of Cross-Cultural Theatre Praxis," 37–8.

39. Lo and Gilbert, "Toward a Topography of Cross-Cultural Theatre Praxis," 44.

40. Lo and Gilbert, "Toward a Topography of Cross-Cultural Theatre Praxis," 44.

41. Lo and Gilbert, "Toward a Topography of Cross-Cultural Theatre Praxis," 36.

42. Watson et al., *Negotiating Cultures*, 2.

43. Gilbert and Lo, *Performance and Cosmopolitics*, 5.

44. Gilbert and Lo, *Performance and Cosmopolitics*, 13.

45. Tian, *The Poetics of Difference and Displacement*, 2.

46. Tian, *The Poetics of Difference and Displacement*, 9.

47. Zarrilli, *Psychophysical Acting*, 8.

48. Pavis, "Intercultural Theatre Today," 10.

49. Pavis, "Intercultural Theatre Today," 8.

50. Pavis, "Intercultural Theatre Today," 8.

51. Pavis, "Intercultural Theatre Today," 13.

52. Leo Cabranes-Grant, "Performing the Intercultural in Colonial Mexico," *Theatre Journal* 63, no. 4 (December 2011): 501.

53. See Charlotte McIvor, "Introduction," in Charlotte McIvor and Jason King (eds.), *Interculturalism and Performance Now: New Directions?* (London: Palgrave Macmillan, 2019), 4.

54. Knowles, *Performing the Intercultural City*, 6.

55. Gilles Deleuze and Felix Guattari, *A Thousand Plateaus: Capitalism and Schitzophrenia* (London and New York: Continuum, 1987), 7.

56. Knowles, *Theatre & Interculturalism*, 80.

57. Li and Pitches, "The End of the Hour-Glass," 122.

58. Li and Pitches, "The End of the Hour-Glass," 122.

59. Li and Pitches, "The End of the Hour-Glass," 124.

60. Li and Pitches, "The End of the Hour-Glass," 124.

61. Li and Pitches, "The End of the Hour-Glass," 135.

62. Li and Pitches, "The End of the Hour-Glass," 136.

63. Tan, *Acoustic Interculturalism*, 16.

64. Erika Fischer-Lichte, "Introduction," in Fischer-Lichte, Jost, and Jain, *Interweaving Performance Cultures*, 8.

65. Fischer-Lichte, "Introduction," 11.

66. Fischer-Lichte, "Introduction," 11.

67. Fischer-Lichte, "Introduction," 13.

68. Kwan, "Even as We Keep Trying," 189.

69. Kwan, "Even as We Keep Trying," 191.

70. Mitra, *Akram Khan*, 23.

71. Mitra, *Akram Khan*, 38.

72. Mitra, *Akram Khan*, 23.

73. Mitra, *Akram Khan*, 24.

74. Cabranes-Grant, *From Scenarios to Networks*, 88.

75. Cabranes-Grant, *From Scenarios to Networks*, 85.

76. Tan, "Elephant Head on White Body," 418.

77. Tan, "Elephant Head on White Body," 423.

78. Tan, "Elephant Head on White Body," 426.

79. Tan, "Elephant Head on White Body," 428.

80. Zarrilli, Sasitharan, and Kapur, "Special Issue," 336.

81. Zarrilli, Sasitharan, and Kapur, "Special Issue," 336.

82. Knowles, *Performing the Intercultural City*, 17.

83. Knowles, *Performing the Intercultural City*, 4.

Conclusion

CHARLOTTE MCIVOR

I have spent the last decade of my life studying and writing about interculturalism, this companion the third of a series of publications devoted to this topic.[1] When I began graduate school at the University of California, Berkeley, in 2005, Peter Brook's *Mahabharata* was one of the first things we watched (in full) during my seminar in Postcolonial Theatre with Sudipto Chatterjee, and we even were lucky enough to have Rustom Bharucha visit that same seminar to discuss the history of intercultural performance theory with us in person. Like my co-editor Daphne P. Lei and her three-year-old son at the beginning of this companion, I too had a strong reaction to this performance to the extent that I wasn't sure how much more could be said to add productively to the layers and complexity of the debates which already catalogued this production's controversial reception.

But during my time in graduate school, the discourse on intercultural performance continued to shift rapidly as I consumed landmark publications including Julie Holledge's and Joanne Tompkin's *Women's Intercultural Performance* and Helen Gilbert and Jacqueline Lo's *Performance and Cosmopolitics: Cultural Transactions in Australasia*. I first became conscious of the evolution towards what we have termed here the Third Wave of intercultural performance theory by studying the impact of unprecedented inward-migration on contemporary Irish theatre and performance practices with practice first preceding theory. As part of this work, I studied Irish (and European Union) social and arts policy crafted in response to migration and cultural diversity, noting the ascendance of interculturalism over multiculturalism as a term with charged and utopian meaning that seemed to paraphrase the field of theatre and performance studies, but often without citing our debates and insights. Ric Knowles's *Theatre & Interculturalism* appeared the year before I submitted my dissertation as a theoretical answer to an unsent prayer, providing a language of "interculturalism-from-below" pursued in relationship to and in defiance of state policy that I could map onto the aspirations and complicated trajectories of nascent Irish intercultural projects undertaken by majority and minority ethnic artists in the name of these social and arts policies, or in spite of them.

When we work as scholars, what we sense and find in isolation at first often becomes visible as only one ripple in a much wider circle reverberating across the wider field. I found myself working on intercultural performance theory in this past decade as one ripple among many pushing to understand interculturalism's resurgence, its contemporary possibilities, and why staying with this idea might be worthwhile despite all its discursive baggage. And the more ripples I observed, the more I wanted to reach the other scholars now also working in this area, which was a major impulse behind this companion and previous collaborative projects. While thinking through this water metaphor, I was reminded of Sara Ahmed's recent summary of the impulses which lead to feminist action: "I think of feminist action as like ripples in water, a small wave, possibly created by agitation from weather; here, there, each movement making another possible, another ripple, outward, reaching."[2] The "weather" of late has encompassed the largest forced displacement of people worldwide on record,[3] a global economic crisis, the persistent rise of far-right governments, and the apocalyptic forecast of a climate change clock that cannot be stopped, only desperately kept pace with. I do believe that this immediate weather has influenced many of us, and particularly the contributors to this companion, to return to the choppy waters of interculturalism.

As Ric Knowles offers, interculturalism matters particularly now, because, more than ever, "it seems . . . important to focus on the contested, unsettling and often unequal spaces *between* cultures, space that can function in performance as sites of negotiation,"[4] especially in an era of mass movements of people worldwide under extremely uneven circumstances. I stayed with interculturalism personally because of the term's materialist implications for funding, categorization and legibility for minority ethnic and culturally diverse artists living and working in the creative arts industries not only in Ireland, but in the European Union at large, as my research has recently expanded to address.[5] I have always strongly felt that the use of theory within our field should be directed towards materialist aims that help us understand and map the lived implications of access to and reception of performance forms (and practitioners) within their deep historical, social, political, and cultural contexts. Within my own work, the intersection between government/social policy and arts practices cemented new interculturalism's case for me.

But I have also always had the conviction that our use of theory must be informed by historiographical and genealogical understanding that remains responsible (modeling critical generosity following David Román)[6] to the lines of thought that we develop and take up. It can be easy in working within the subfield of intercultural performance theory to simply malign the aspirations and convictions particularly of First Wave theorists and practitioners (many of whom remain working right up through our present Third Wave). In working on this companion's annotated bibliography chapter with Justine Nakase, I have been personally reminded of the effort expended over time by so many in testing interculturalism as a theoretical concept and, most importantly, as a live mode of encounter between artists through performance. Yes, these efforts have too often resulted in politically naïve and aesthetically confused HIT spectacles and/or uninterrogated workshop or training practices which engender a series of representational and other violences against individuals, groups, and forms. And they have too often been undergirded by privilege earned by colonial legacies and neoliberal bankrolls which mask their provenance with claims of unity, universality, and transcendence. But these limited and/or problematic practices also largely began or are sustained by earnest intentions. In re-engaging with Eugenio Barba and ISTA's work over decades, for example, I was struck by a level of continued critical self-reflexivity and ongoing two-way dialogue with collaborators that I had previously written off but have now benefitted from spending more time with. We cannot ignore what Barba and others have also taught us through their blind spots *and* achievements—how to keep beginning again with the effort of interculturalism, continually nuancing the terms and *ethics* of our engagement with this idea, which is also finally a *practice*, engaged in between individuals or collectives.

After surfing through previous waves, we do now seem to largely acknowledge as a field that interculturalism is best thought through as *process*, rather than as plundered reductivism or elite (theatrical) *product*. Moreover, it is a process that affects most humans living on this planet on a daily basis as our cultural identities remain individually and collectively unstable, subject to constant re-formation chosen or forced upon us through structural inequalities and/or violence. If the stakes of interculturalism are that high, and that widespread (as well as being put to tangible politicized use now through the selected government policies and programs I've personally traced in my work), we do indeed need to continue working within our field through the nuances of interculturalism as a theoretical lens to apply to the world we're living in.

To think with and through the genealogy of intercultural performance theory and practice as we know it within theatre and performance studies over the last fifty years is, I believe, to collectively insist that we cannot look past the ways in which colonial/imperial, racial, and gendered histories are encoded, re-enacted, *and* reworked continuously through performance, that we cannot separate form from politics, or the ethics of the rehearsal room (or training process) from the onstage result. By continuing to resistantly probe interculturalism as theory and practice, scholars and practitioners are able to access, contest, and rework an idea that may constantly reach for the utopian but instead unfailingly (in my experience) reveal its material limits through the experiences of bodies working together in time and space who have come together usually from extremely different circumstances, experiences, and/or aesthetic backgrounds.

In this book, our contributors have engaged with new interculturalism in the archives, contemporary artworks, the classroom, a puppeteering exchange, the internet, the dance studio, and, of course, many theatres and rehearsal rooms. This companion has gone some way towards multiplying the number of case studies undertaken in the name of new interculturalism, or in direct tension with it, as Min Tian's chapter's persuasive critique of the term communicates. We've re-examined familiar figures such as Peter Brook and Ariane Mnouchkine in Marcus Cheng Chye Tan and Emily Sahakian's chapters and explored how the tensions of HIT power dynamics may show up in processes without Western collaborators in Jennifer Goodlander's ethnographic account of the ASEAN exchange. We've engaged the possibilities of a move from the inter- to the polycultural via internet theatre in Roaa Ali's chapter, and considered how Western intercultural genealogies influenced postcolonial metropolitan Bengali theatre contexts through Arnab Banerji's treatment of Badal Sircar. Bi-qi Beatrice Lei rejected the term Asian Shakespeare in order to recenter other formal influences in Asian theatrical experiments that include William Shakespeare only as one influence among many, while Ketu H. Katrak centralized interrogation of sexuality, patriarchy, and colonialism within intercultural performance theory's ongoing evolution. Diana Looser made a powerful argument for mixed methodologies within intercultural performance research (particularly archival and ethnographic approaches) through her examination of Oceanic performances from the historical and contemporary record, while Lisa Jackson-Schebetta turned to contemporary art and installation as a site through which to decolonize intercultural performance theory and re-present it as interculturalidad. SanSan Kwan risked offering love as a model for intercultural engagement in full acknowledgment of the dangers and possibilities for communion this framework provides, while Angeline Young took us into the risky laboratory of the classroom and outlined her own discoveries while also crafting a framework through which we might act as educators. As my criss-crossing summary here demonstrates, this volume's chapters speak across and to each other, ranging wide but not fully encompassing in their coverage of the globe or our field. That is more than we can expect one book to do or even the previous approximately fifty years of debate and practice regarding intercultural performance theory that have led to this publication. But we have, I hope, further opened the conversation.

We still have a lot more work to do, as we continually return to the sites (and scenarios) of performance over time to test and witness interculturalization *not* as an exceptional process controlled by elite networks and practitioners, but as a process continually bubbling up from below, across, and in between in choppy waters that must be navigated in all their complexity. This is a matter of ethical urgency in our current political moment where the multiplicity of culture as an individual and collective lived experience and rights of movement for all and not just the few need more defending than ever—and by means of the kinds of rigorously informed and scholarly perspectives gathered in this volume.

By combing through these waves of intercultural performance theory in this companion, forward and back, and out to sea again, we hope that we have stirred up the sediments of both old and new debates that will inform as yet unforeseen directions, currents, and practices. We ultimately locate our book within the Third Wave of intercultural performance theory. But we do so in the hope that this companion will soon be subsumed by a Fourth Wave that pushes the debates we outline here to new and as yet unforeseen shores, particularly as the discourse continues to be directed by those within the Global North/Western academy (as our institutional affiliations show). It is imperative to increase scholarly traffic between the Global North and South. Because even while the intercultural performance forms/processes and how we study them and from what positionality has proliferated within our field as this companion evidences, the scholars featured are predominantly living and working in Western academia. We must not simply deploy new interculturalism's politicized methodological strategies primarily within Western academic theatre and performance circles, but have these ideas tested, refined, and even rejected by our colleagues from all over the world—a commitment to a more comprehensive inclusion that also needs to be taken up by the field at large, not just the subfield of intercultural performance theory. We look forward to seeing what the next wave brings back and where it takes us.

NOTES

1. See Charlotte McIvor, *Migration and Performance in Contemporary Ireland: Towards a New Interculturalism* (London: Palgrave Macmillan, 2016), and Charlotte McIvor and Jason King (eds.), *Interculturalism and Performance Now: New Directions?* (London: Palgrave Macmillan, 2019).

2. Sara Ahmed, *Living A Feminist Life* (Durham, NC: Duke University Press, 2017), 3.

3. The UN Refugee Agency (UNHCR), "Figures at a Glance," https://www.unhcr.org/en-ie/figures-at-a-glance.html.

4. Ric Knowles, *Theatre & Interculturalism* (Basingstoke, UK: Palgrave Macmillan, 2010), 4.

5. Charlotte McIvor, "When Social Policy Meets Performance Practice: Interculturalism, the European Union and the 'Migratory and Refugee Crisis,'" *Theatre Research International*, 44, no. 3 (October 2019): 230–47.

6. David Román, *Acts of Intervention: Performance, Gay Culture, and AIDS* (Bloomington: Indiana University Press, 1998), xxvi–xxvii.

INDEX